CliffsNotes®
FTCE General Knowledge Test

CliffsNotes®

FTCE General Knowledge Test

3RD EDITION

by
Jeffrey S. Kaplan, Ph.D., and Sandra Luna McCune, Ph.D.

Houghton Mifflin Harcourt
Boston • New York

About the Authors

Jeffrey S. Kaplan, Ph.D., is an Associate Professor and Program Coordinator of English Language Arts Education in the College of Education and Human Performance's School of Teaching, Learning, and Leadership at the University of Central Florida in Orlando, Florida. He received the University of Central Florida Excellence in Professional Service Award in 2014.

Sandra Luna McCune, Ph.D., is professor emeritus and a former Regents professor in the Department of Elementary Education at Stephen F. Austin State University, where she received the Distinguished Professor Award. She now is a full-time author and consultant and resides near Austin, Texas.

Authors' Acknowledgments

The authors would like to thank Grace Freedson for bringing us this project. We also want to thank our families for their love and support.

Editorial

Executive Editor: Greg Tubach

Senior Editor: Christina Stambaugh

Copy Editor: Donna Wright

Technical Editors: Tom Page, Mary Jane Sterling, and Barbara Swovelin

Proofreader: Lynn Northrup

CliffsNotes® FTCE General Knowledge Test, 3rd Edition

Copyright © 2015 by Houghton Mifflin Harcourt Publishing Company

All rights reserved.

Cover image © Shutterstock / Mavrick

Library of Congress Control Number: 2014951477
ISBN: 978-0-544-30988-3 (pbk)

Printed in the United States of America
DOO 10 9 8 7 6 5 4 3

4500550664

For information about permission to reproduce selections from this book, please write Permissions, Houghton Mifflin Harcourt Publishing Company, 215 Park Avenue South, New York, New York 10003.

www.hmhco.com

Note: If you purchased this book without a cover, you should be aware that this book is stolen property. It was reported as "unsold and destroyed" to the publisher, and neither the author nor the publisher has received any payment for this "stripped book."

THE PUBLISHER AND THE AUTHOR MAKE NO REPRESENTATIONS OR WARRANTIES WITH RESPECT TO THE ACCURACY OR COMPLETENESS OF THE CONTENTS OF THIS WORK AND SPECIFICALLY DISCLAIM ALL WARRANTIES, INCLUDING WITHOUT LIMITATION WARRANTIES OF FITNESS FOR A PARTICULAR PURPOSE. NO WARRANTY MAY BE CREATED OR EXTENDED BY SALES OR PROMOTIONAL MATERIALS. THE ADVICE AND STRATEGIES CONTAINED HEREIN MAY NOT BE SUITABLE FOR EVERY SITUATION. THIS WORK IS SOLD WITH THE UNDERSTANDING THAT THE PUBLISHER IS NOT ENGAGED IN RENDERING LEGAL, ACCOUNTING, OR OTHER PROFESSIONAL SERVICES. IF PROFESSIONAL ASSISTANCE IS REQUIRED, THE SERVICES OF A COMPETENT PROFESSIONAL PERSON SHOULD BE SOUGHT. NEITHER THE PUBLISHER NOR THE AUTHOR SHALL BE LIABLE FOR DAMAGES ARISING HEREFROM. THE FACT THAT AN ORGANIZATION OR WEBSITE IS REFERRED TO IN THIS WORK AS A CITATION AND/OR A POTENTIAL SOURCE OF FURTHER INFORMATION DOES NOT MEAN THAT THE AUTHOR OR THE PUBLISHER ENDORSES THE INFORMATION THE ORGANIZATION OR WEBSITE MAY PROVIDE OR RECOMMENDATIONS IT MAY MAKE. FURTHER, READERS SHOULD BE AWARE THAT INTERNET WEBSITES LISTED IN THIS WORK MAY HAVE CHANGED OR DISAPPEARED BETWEEN WHEN THIS WORK WAS WRITTEN AND WHEN IT IS READ.

Trademarks: CliffsNotes, the CliffsNotes logo, Cliffs, CliffsAP, CliffsComplete, CliffsQuickReview, CliffsStudySolver, CliffsTestPrep, CliffsNote-a-Day, cliffsnotes.com, and all related trademarks, logos, and trade dress are trademarks or registered trademarks of Houghton Mifflin Harcourt and/or its affiliates. All other trademarks are the property of their respective owners. Houghton Mifflin Harcourt is not associated with any product or vendor mentioned in this book.

Table of Contents

Introduction 1
   General Description 1
   Format of the General Knowledge Test 1
   The Role of the FTCE General Knowledge Test in Teacher Certification 2
   Questions Commonly Asked About the FTCE General Knowledge Test 2
   How to Use This Book 5
   How to Prepare for the Day of the Test 6
   What to Do During the Test 6

Chapter 1: Review for the General Knowledge Essay Subtest 9
   The Essay Review in This Study Guide 9
   Essay Skills 9
      Determine the Purpose of Writing to Task and Audience 9
      Provide a Section That Effectively Introduces the Topic 11
      Formulate a Relevant Thesis or Claim 11
      Organize Ideas and Details Effectively 12
      Provide Adequate, Relevant Support by Citing Ample Textual Evidence;
        Response May Also Include Anecdotal Experience for Added Support ... 13
      Use a Variety of Transitional Devices Effectively Throughout and Within
        a Written Text 14
      Demonstrate Proficient Use of College-Level, Standard Written English
        (e.g., varied word choice, syntax, language conventions, semantics) .. 15
      Provide a Concluding Statement or Section That Follows From, or Supports,
        the Argument or Information Presented 16
      Use a Variety of Sentence Patterns Effectively 17
      Maintain a Consistent Point of View 18
      Apply the Conventions of Standard English (e.g., avoid inappropriate
        use of slang, jargon, clichés) 19
   Strategies for Writing the Essay for the General Knowledge Test 21
   Scoring Criteria for the General Knowledge Test Essay 21
   Test Yourself 22
      Sample Responses 23

**Chapter 2: Review for the General Knowledge English Language
Skills Subtest** 27
   The English Language Skills Review in This Study Guide 27
   Knowledge of Language Structure 27
      Evaluate Correct Placement of Modifiers 27
      Apply Knowledge of Parallelism, Including Parallel Expressions for Parallel Ideas .. 28
      Apply Knowledge of a Variety of Effective Structures (e.g., recognizing fragments,
        comma splices, run-on sentences, syntax errors) 28
      Determine Patterns of Organization in a Written Passage (i.e., modes
        of rhetoric) 29
      Test Yourself 30
        Answers 32
   Knowledge of Vocabulary Application 33
      Determine the Meaning of Unknown Words, Multiple-Meaning Words,
        and Phrases in Context 33
      Determine and Select the Correct Use of Commonly Confused Words,
        Misused Words, and Phrases 34
      Determine Diction and Tone Appropriate to a Given Audience 39
      Test Yourself 40
        Answers 42

Knowledge of Standard English Conventions 43
　Determine and Select Standard Verb Forms 44
　Determine and Select Inappropriate Shifts in Verb Tense. 44
　Determine and Select Agreement Between Subject and Verb 45
　Determine and Select Agreement Between Pronoun and Antecedent 46
　Determine and Select Inappropriate Pronoun Shifts 46
　Determine and Select Clear Pronoun References 46
　Determine and Select Pronoun Case Forms (e.g., subjective,
　　objective, possessive). 47
　Evaluate the Correct Use of Adjectives and Adverbs 47
　Determine and Select Appropriate Comparative and Superlative
　　Degree Forms. 48
　Demonstrate Command of Standard Spelling Conventions. 49
　Demonstrate Command of Standard Punctuation 51
　Demonstrate Command of Standard Capitalization 52
　Test Yourself 53
　　Answers 54

Chapter 3: Review for the General Knowledge Mathematics Subtest **57**
　The Math Review in This CliffsNotes Guide. 57
　　Mathematics Reference Sheet 58
　　　Area. 58
　　　Surface Area. 58
　　　Volume. 58
　Numeration and Operations 59
　　What Are Operations?. 60
　　　Test Yourself 61
　　　Answers 61
　　What Are Counting Numbers?. 62
　　　Test Yourself 63
　　　Answers 64
　　What Are Rational Numbers? 64
　　　Test Yourself 65
　　　Answers 65
　　What Are Fractions? 65
　　What Are Decimals?. 68
　　How Do You Round a Number? 69
　　What Are Percents? 70
　　　Test Yourself 75
　　　Answers 75
　　What Are Irrational Numbers? 76
　　Are All Square Roots Irrational?. 77
　　What Are Real Numbers? 77
　　　Test Yourself 77
　　　Answers 78
　　What Are Exponents? 78
　　What Is Scientific Notation? 79
　　　Test Yourself 80
　　　Answers 81
　　How Do You Compare and Order Real Numbers? 81
　　What Is Absolute Value?. 82
　　　Test Yourself 83
　　　Answers 84
　　How Do You Add and Subtract Fractions and Decimals? 84
　　　Adding and Subtracting Fractions 84

Adding and Subtracting Decimals 85
Test Yourself 86
Answers 86
How Do You Multiply and Divide Fractions and Decimals? 86
Multiplying and Dividing Fractions 86
Multiplying and Dividing Decimals 87
Test Yourself 88
Answers 88
How Do You Add, Subtract, Multiply, and Divide Signed Numbers? 88
Adding Signed Numbers 88
Subtracting Signed Numbers 90
Multiplying and Dividing Signed Numbers 91
Test Yourself 92
Answers 93
In What Order Do You Perform the Operations? 93
Test Yourself 95
Answers 95
How Do You Solve Real-World Problems Involving Rational Numbers? 95
Ratios and Proportions 97
Percent Problems 100
Contextual Problems Involving Percents 102
Test Yourself 103
Answers 103
Sample Questions 105
Answer Explanations for Sample Questions 106
Geometry and Measurement 107
What Is Congruence? 107
How Do You Classify Angles? 108
How Do You Classify Lines? 110
Test Yourself 111
Answers 112
What Are Two-Dimensional Figures? 112
How Do You Classify Polygons? 112
Test Yourself 114
Answers 115
How Do You Classify Triangles? 115
Test Yourself 117
Answers 117
How Do You Classify Quadrilaterals? 117
Test Yourself 118
Answers 119
What Are the Properties of a Circle? 119
Test Yourself 119
Answers 119
What Are Three-Dimensional Figures? 120
Test Yourself 121
Answers 121
What Is Similarity? 121
What Is Symmetry? 123
Test Yourself 123
Answers 124
How Do You Solve Problems Involving the Pythagorean Theorem? 124
Test Yourself 125
Answers 126
What Are Geometric Transformations? 126
Test Yourself 128

Answers 129
How Do You Convert from One Measurement Unit to Another? 129
How Do You Solve Problems Involving Unit Rates? 132
How Do You Read Measurement Instruments? 133
How Do You Solve Problems Involving Scaled Drawings or Models? 134
   Test Yourself 135
   Answers 135
How Do You Find Perimeter and Circumference? 137
How Do You Find Area? 140
   Finding the Area of a Rectangle 140
   Finding the Area of a Square 141
   Finding the Area of a Triangle 141
   Finding the Area of a Circle 142
How Do You Find Surface Area? 142
How Do You Find Volume? 142
How Do You Solve Real-World Problems Involving Perimeter, Area,
and Volume? 143
   Test Yourself 144
   Answers 144
Sample Questions 145
Answer Explanations for Sample Questions 146
Algebraic Reasoning and the Coordinate Plane 149
How Do You Interpret Algebraic Expressions? 149
   Test Yourself 152
   Answers 152
How Do You Simplify Algebraic Expressions? 153
   Test Yourself 155
   Answers 155
How Do You Solve One-Variable Linear Equations? 155
   Test Yourself 158
   Answers 159
How Do You Solve Inequalities? 160
   Test Yourself 162
   Answers 162
How Do You Use One-Variable Linear Equations and Inequalities to
Solve Contextual Problems? 163
   Test Yourself 166
   Answers 166
How Do You Solve Quadratic Equations? 168
   Solving Quadratic Equations When $b = 0$ 168
   Solving Quadratic Equations When $a = 1, b \neq 0$ by Factoring 170
   Solving Quadratic Equations When $b \neq 0, c = 0$ 171
   Test Yourself 172
   Answers 172
How Do You Use One-Variable Quadratic Equations to Solve
Contextual Problems? 174
   Test Yourself 176
   Answers 176
How Do You Locate and Name Points in a Coordinate Plane? 178
How Do You Find the Slope of the Line Between Two Points? 182
How Do You Find the Distance Between Two Points? 183
How Do You Find the Midpoint Between Two Points? 184
   Test Yourself 185
   Answers 186
What Is a Function? 187
   Test Yourself 190

Answers 191
How Do Recognize Proportional Functions? 191
   Test Yourself 192
   Answers 193
How Do You Graph Linear Equations? 193
   Test Yourself 195
   Answers 195
How Do You Determine the Equation of a Line? 196
   Test Yourself 197
   Answers 198
How Do You Decide Whether an Ordered Pair Satisfies a System
of Equations? 198
   Test Yourself 199
   Answers 199
How Do You Find Patterns in Sequences? 200
   Test Yourself 201
   Answers 201
Sample Questions 201
Answer Explanations for Sample Questions 203
Probability, Statistics, and Data Interpretation 204
How Do You Organize and Present Data? 204
   Charts and Tables 205
   Pictographs 205
   Bar Graphs 206
   Histograms 207
   Circle Graphs and Pie Charts 208
   Line Graphs 209
   Stem-and-Leaf Plots 209
   Scatterplots 210
How Can Presentation of Data Lead to Inappropriate Interpretations? 210
   Test Yourself 212
   Answers 213
What Are Measures of Central Tendency? 213
   Finding the Mean 213
   Finding the Median 214
   Finding the Mode 215
What Are Important Characteristics of the Measures of Central Tendency? 216
What Are Measures of Dispersion? 217
   Test Yourself 218
   Answers 219
What Is Probability? 220
How Do You Count the Number of Ways to Arrange or Combine Things? 222
How Do You Solve Real-World Problems Involving Counting and Probability? . . . 224
   Test Yourself 224
   Answers 225
What Are Differences in Types of Studies? 226
Characteristics of Well-Designed Studies 227
   Test Yourself 227
   Answers 228
Sample Questions 229
Answer Explanations for Sample Questions 230

Chapter 4: Review for the General Knowledge Reading Subtest 233
The Reading Review in This Study Guide 233
Knowledge of Key Ideas and Details Based on Text Selections 233
   Identify Textual Evidence to Support Conclusions Drawn from Text 233

Identify Explicit Meaning and Details Within Text.....................234
Determine Inferences and Conclusions Based on Textual Evidence..........235
Discriminate Among Inferences, Conclusions, and Assumptions Based
  on Textual Evidence....................236
Determine and Analyze the Development of Central Ideas or Themes from
  One or More Texts......................238
Summarize One or More Texts Using Key Supporting Ideas and Details.......239
Determine How and Why Specific Individuals, Events, and Ideas Develop
  Based on Textual Evidence..............239
Determine the Cause and Effect Relationship(s) Among Individuals, Events,
  and Ideas Based on Textual Evidence....241
Knowledge of Craft and Structure Based on Text Selections...............241
Interpret the Meaning of Words and Phrases as Used in Text
  (e.g., figurative language, connotative language, technical meanings).......242
Analyze How Specific Word Choices Shape Meaning or Tone...............243
  Test Yourself........................244
  Answers.............................244
Analyze How the Author Uses Organization and Text Structure(s)
  to Convey Meaning....................245
Contrast the Point of View of Two or More Authors on the Same Topic by
  Analyzing their Claims, Reasoning, and Evidence...................249
  Test Yourself........................250
  Answers.............................251
Analyze How Point of View and Purpose Shape the Content and
  Style of Text.........................253
  Test Yourself........................254
  Answers.............................254
Knowledge of the Integration of Information and Ideas Based on
Text Selections..........................254
  Evaluate and Relate Content Presented in Diverse Formats...............255
  Evaluate Specific Claims in Text Based on Relevancy, Sufficiency, and
    Validity of Reasoning................256
  Test Yourself........................256
  Answers.............................256
Sample Questions......................258
Answer Explanations for Sample Questions.....................261

Chapter 5: General Knowledge Practice Test 1............263
Answer Sheet..........................263
Essay................................265
English Language Skills.................266
Mathematics..........................272
  Mathematics Reference Sheet...........272
    Area.............................272
    Surface Area.....................272
    Volume..........................272
Reading..............................281
Answer Key...........................289
  English Language Skills..............289
  Mathematics........................289
  Reading............................289
Answer Explanations...................290
  Essay..............................290
    Sample Essays....................290
  English Language Skills..............293
  Mathematics........................296
  Reading............................316

Chapter 6: General Knowledge Practice Test 2 321
- Answer Sheet 321
- Essay 323
- English Language Skills 324
- Mathematics 330
  - Mathematics Reference Sheet 330
    - Area 330
    - Surface Area 330
    - Volume 330
- Reading 338
- Answer Key 346
  - English Language Skills 346
  - Mathematics 346
  - Reading 346
- Answer Explanations 347
  - Essay 347
    - Sample Essays 347
  - English Language Skills 349
  - Mathematics 352
  - Reading 367

Introduction

General Description

The Florida Teacher Certification Examination (FTCE) General Knowledge (GK) Test is a computer-based test designed to assess basic skills in reading, writing, and mathematics. The test is composed of four subtests:

- Essay
- English Language Skills
- Mathematics
- Reading

You will have 3 hours and 50 minutes to complete the entire test.

For the Essay Subtest, you choose from two prompts. Each multiple-choice question will contain four response options. You have to click on your choice to record your answer to a question. No penalty is assessed for wrong answers (you score a zero for that test question). For the Mathematics Subtest, the test center provides a calculator and a Mathematics Reference Sheet.

Format of the General Knowledge Test

Subtest Competencies and Skills	Number of Questions	Time Allowed
ESSAY Essay	1 essay	50 minutes
ENGLISH LANGUAGE SKILLS Language structure skills Vocabulary application skills Standard written English convention skills	40 multiple choice	40 minutes
MATHEMATICS Numeration and operations Geometry and measurement Algebraic reasoning and the coordinate plane Probability, statistics, and data interpretation	45 multiple choice	100 minutes
READING Key ideas and details based on text selections Craft and structure based on text selections Integration of information and ideas based on text selections	40 multiple choice	40 minutes

Introduction

The Role of the FTCE General Knowledge Test in Teacher Certification

The FTCE GK Test is one of the state-mandated teacher certification tests in Florida. Most candidates who want to teach in a Florida elementary, middle, or secondary public school have to take and pass at least three tests: the FTCE GK Test, the FTCE Professional Education Test, and a subject area examination (SAE) in the field in which they want to be certified. The tests and the testing program that goes with them are the result of legislation passed by Florida in 1980. For the FTCE GK Test, you have to demonstrate basic skills in reading, writing, and mathematics—which is what this book is designed to help you do. The FTCE Professional Education Test assesses your knowledge about learning, teaching, and professional conduct. The subject area tests cover the content that you are required to teach. Elementary teacher education candidates take the FTCE Elementary Education K-6 Test as their subject area test. The purpose of the certification program in Florida is to ensure that certified teachers possess sufficient professional knowledge and skills to effectively perform their roles as teachers in Florida schools.

Statewide committees of subject area specialists identified and validated the content of the FTCE GK Test. The committee members consisted of public school teachers, district supervisors, and college faculty with expertise in the subject areas—with public school teachers composing the majority of the committees. Selection to committee membership was based on recommendations by professional organizations, subject area experts, and teachers' unions. The test development process involved an extensive literature review, interviews with selected public school teachers, a large-scale survey of teachers, and pilot testing.

Questions Commonly Asked About the FTCE General Knowledge Test

Q. What is the FTCE General Knowledge Test?

A. The FTCE GK Test is the required basic skills test adopted by the Florida Legislature for assessing reading, writing, and mathematics skills of applicants for the Professional Florida Educator's Certificate.

Q. Who administers the FTCE GK Test?

A. The Florida Department of Education (FLDOE) oversees administration of the FTCE GK Test. The Commissioner of Education designates the registration deadlines, administration sites, and examination dates (Rule 6A-4.0021, Florida Administrative Code [FAC]).

Q. When and where is the FTCE GK Test given?

A. Currently, the FTCE GK Test is 100 percent computer-based. It is offered at flexible times throughout the year at locations throughout the state of Florida and in select cities nationwide. Check www.fl.nesinc.com/FL_TestSites.asp for an up-to-date list of test sites. Also check the testing contractor's website for updated information regarding changes in tests and application procedures (www.fl.nesinc.com/index.asp).

Q. Where can I find registration information for the FTCE GK Test?

A. The most recent registration information is available online at www.fldoe.org/asp/ftce/ftceTRI.asp. There are no deadlines for computer-based testing registrations. However, you should register as early as possible before your target test date because test sites accept registrations on a first-come, first-served basis and seating is limited. Be sure to review the testing contractor's testing policies on registration, testing, and score reporting available at www.fl.nesinc.com/FL_policies.asp.

Q. What is the fee for the test?

A. The registration fee in 2014 for first attempt testing is $130. The registration fee for second attempt testing is $150. If you have additional questions about fees or need help calculating the total amount you need to pay to register, call Customer Service at (866) 613-3281 or go to www.fl.nesinc.com/FL_testfees.asp to find information on the testing contractor's website.

Q. What should I bring to the test site?

A. You will receive your admission ticket by e-mail after your registration has been processed. Your admission ticket will include your name, the test(s) you are registered to take, the test date, the test site address, the reporting time, and a reminder of what to bring to the test site. Check the information on your admission ticket to make sure that it is correct. You will not be allowed to make changes at the test site.

The day of the test, you must bring your admission ticket and two valid, unexpired forms of identification that are printed in English, including one that is government issued with a recent, clear photo and signature, such as a driver's license, state-issued ID card, U.S. military ID with signature, or passport. Your valid admission ticket and correct identification are required for entrance into the examination site.

Q. Can I bring my cellphone into the testing room?

A. Absolutely not! If a cellphone or an electronic prohibited aid is found in your possession (regardless of whether it is turned off or on), you will not be allowed to continue testing. The test site will report this information to the Florida Department of Education, and your score will be invalidated. So, to be safe, you should not bring a cellphone to the testing site. You will find a complete list of prohibited items under "Testing Policies" at www.fl.nesinc.com/FL_policies.asp. It is best to not have any such items in your possession when you arrive at the testing site. However, the testing sites do have secure storage in which you may store personal belongings, including prohibited items, during testing.

Q. When will I get my score report?

A. When you finish testing, you will receive an unofficial score report on the screen for the multiple-choice subtests: English Language Skills, Mathematics, and Reading. You will not receive an unofficial subscore for the Essay Subtest at that time, but you will receive proof of testing that documents your completion of that subtest. Official score reports for the English Language Skills, Mathematics, and Reading subtests will be released approximately 3 to 4 weeks after your test date. The Essay Subtest score will be released approximately 6 weeks after your test date.

Q. What is the passing score?

A. The passing score for the FTCE GK Test is a scaled score of 200 or higher. This scaled score was equivalent to the following raw scores on the July 2002 test administration:

- General Knowledge Reading Subtest: 25 correct items.
- General Knowledge English Language Skills Subtest: 29 correct items.
- General Knowledge English Essay Subtest: A total raw score of six (6).
- General Knowledge Mathematics Subtest: 26 correct items. (Rule 6A-4.0021, FAC)

The minimum percentages needed to earn a passing score on any form of the FTCE GK Test currently being administered are as follows (www.fldoe.org/asp/ftce/pdf/percentpass.pdf):

- General Knowledge Reading Subtest: 65 percent of items correct.
- General Knowledge English Language Skills Subtest: 73 percent of items correct.
- General Knowledge Mathematics Subtest: 60 percent of items correct.

Q. What is included in the FTCE GK Test?

A. The sections of the FTCE GK Test include four subtests: Essay, English Language Skills, Mathematics, and Reading.

Q. How much time do I have to complete each subtest?

A. Three hours and 50 minutes are given to complete all four subtests. For the Essay Subtest, you are given 50 minutes to prepare, write, and edit your response. The English Language Skills and Reading subtests are each 40 minutes long. The Mathematics Subtest is 100 minutes.

Introduction

Q. If I pass part, but not all, of the FTCE GK Test, do I have to retake the whole test?

A. You must register for the full FTCE GK Test and pay the second attempt fee of $150. However, you need to retake only the subtests that you did not pass. After you have passed a subtest, you do not have to retake that subtest. Nevertheless, the second attempt fee for the FTCE GK Test is $150, regardless of the number of subtests you are retaking. Also, you will not be given extra testing time when you are retaking subtests. The time allotted for a subtest is the same as that given when you take the entire test.

Q. Do I need to take all the subtests at one time?

A. No. You may take any combination of the subtests at a single appointment on the same day, for a single test fee. However, you must re-register for the full FTCE GK Test and pay a retake fee of $150 every time you retake one or more subtests.

Q. How many times may I retake the test?

A. You may retake the entire test or a subtest as many times as is necessary to pass, but you must wait 31 calendar days before retaking the test. Also, you must re-register for the full FTCE GK Test and pay a retake fee of $150 every time you retake one or more subtests.

Q. What other tests must teacher candidates take?

A. Most candidates seeking a Professional Florida Educator's Certificate must take the FTCE GK Test and the FTCE Professional Education Test. In addition, Professional Certificate candidates and those adding a subject area to a Professional Certificate may need to pass a subject area examination (SAE) in a field in which they are seeking certification.

Q. Can I take all my teacher tests on one day?

A. Not likely. You can register for one test per appointment. Possibly, you might be able to register for multiple appointments on the same day at the same test site; however, there is no guarantee that multiple appointments can be scheduled on the same day.

Q. Should I guess on the test?

A. Yes! Because no penalty is assessed for guessing, guess if you have to. On the multiple-choice sections, first try to eliminate some of the choices to increase your chances of choosing the right answer. But don't leave any questions unanswered. On the Essay Subtest, be sure to write a complete and logically constructed essay.

Q. Will scratch paper be provided?

A. You will be provided with an erasable noteboard and pen for use during the test.

Q. Can I use a calculator for the Mathematics Subtest?

A. Yes, but you cannot bring your own calculator. A calculator is provided at the test site.

Q. What if I've never taken a computer-based test before?

A. After you are seated for your computer-based test, you will complete a tutorial before you take the actual test. The tutorial shows you how to move from question to question, how to mark and change answers, and how to go back and review previously answered or skipped questions. For the Essay Subtest, you will be shown how to record your response during the actual test.

Q. How should I prepare for the FTCE GK Test?

A. Now that you're ready to begin taking your certification exams, using this CliffsNotes guide is your best preparation for the FTCE GK Test. This study guide gives you insights, subject reviews, and strategies for the question types.

Q. How do I get more information about the FTCE GK Test?

A. Check the Florida Department of Education Office of Assessment FTCE website at www.fldoe.org/asp/ftce/ftceTRI.asp. As new information on the testing program becomes available, it is posted on this site.

How to Use This Book

This book is organized around the reading, writing, and mathematics competencies and skills of the FTCE GK Test. It includes a thorough review and study strategies for the test and two full-length practice tests. When you read through the list of competencies and skills covered on the FTCE GK Test, you may feel overwhelmed by the task of preparing for the test. Here are some suggestions for developing an effective study program using this book.

1. To help you organize and budget your time, set up a specific schedule of study sessions. Try to set aside approximately 2 hours for each session. If you complete one session per day (including weekends), it should take you about 5 to 6 weeks to work your way through the review and practice material provided in this book. If your test date is coming up soon, you may need to lengthen your study time per day or skip sections that cover topics that you feel you already know fairly well. Nonetheless, be cautious about deciding to skip sections. You could find yourself struggling through material that would be easier to master if previous sections had been reviewed first. Particularly, be wary of skipping math topics, which are usually highly dependent on previously learned skills.

2. Choose a place for studying that is free of distractions and undue noise so you can concentrate. Make sure you have adequate lighting and a room temperature that is comfortable—not too warm or too cold. Try to have all the necessary study aids (paper, pen, calculator, and so on) within easy reach so you don't have to interrupt your studying to go get something you need. Ask friends not to call you during your study time.

3. Don't make excuses. Studying for the FTCE GK Test must be a priority. It will require a lot of time and a conscientious commitment on your part. Think of it as a job that you must do. In reality, studying for the FTCE GK Test is one of the most important jobs you will ever do. The outcome of the test can determine your future career opportunities. Do not avoid studying for it by making excuses or procrastinating.

4. Take Practice Test 1 (Chapter 5) as a diagnostic test before you begin your study program. For the essay question, try to see where your answer might have failed to adequately address the given prompt. Of course, you have to judge the quality of your response based on the scoring criteria explained in Chapter 1 and in comparison to the sample response given in the answer explanations. For the multiple-choice questions, carefully study the answer explanations for *all* the questions, not just the ones you missed. You might have gotten some of your correct answers by guessing or by using an incorrect method. Plan your study program so that you can concentrate first on topics that your Practice Test 1 results indicate are weak areas for you. If you did fairly well in mathematics and on the essay but poorly in reading, then you should begin your FTCE GK Test preparation with the reading review in Chapter 4.

5. Carefully study the review chapters, being sure to concentrate as you go through the material. Don't let yourself be diverted by extraneous thoughts or outside distractions. Here are some study strategies:

   - Monitor yourself by making a check mark on a separate sheet of paper when your concentration wanders. Work on reducing the number of check marks you record each study session.
   - Take notes as you study, using your own words to express ideas. Leave ample room in the left margin, so that you can revise or make comments when you review your notes. Extract key ideas and write them in the left margin to use as study cues later.
   - Make flashcards to aid you in memorizing key ideas and keep them with you at all times. When you have spare moments, take out the flashcards and go over the information you've recorded on them.
   - Take several brief 2- to 3-minute breaks during your study sessions to give your mind time to absorb the review material you just read. According to brain research, you remember the first part and last part of something you've read more easily than you remember the middle part. Taking several breaks will allow you to create more beginnings and endings to maximize the amount of material you remember. It is best not to leave your study area during a break. Try stretching or simply closing your eyes for a few minutes.
   - Set aside certain days to review material you have already studied. This strategy will allow you to reinforce what you have learned and identify topics you may need to restudy.
   - If possible, set up a regular time to study with one or more classmates or friends. A good way of learning and reinforcing the material is to discuss it with others.

6. When you complete your review, take Practice Test 2 (Chapter 6). Take the test under the same conditions you expect for the actual test, being sure to adhere to the time limits for each subtest. When you finish taking the test, as you did for Practice Test 1, carefully study the answer explanations for *all* the questions.
7. Analyze the results of the practice test, then go back and review any topics in which you performed unsatisfactorily.

After completing your study program, you should find yourself prepared and confident to achieve a passing score on the FTCE GK Test.

How to Prepare for the Day of the Test

There are several things you can do to prepare yourself for the day of the test:

1. Know where the test center is located and how to get there.
2. Make dependable arrangements to get to the test center in plenty of time and know where to park if you plan to go by car.
3. Keep all the materials you will need to bring to the test center—especially your admission ticket and two forms of identification—in a secure place, so that you can easily find them on the day of the test.
4. Go to bed early enough to get a good night's rest. Avoid taking nonprescription drugs or alcohol, as the use of these products may impair your mental faculties on test day.
5. On the day of the test, plan to get to the testing center early.
6. Dress in comfortable clothing and wear comfortable shoes. Even if it is warm outside, wear layers of clothing that can be removed or put on, depending on the temperature in the testing room.
7. Eat a light meal. Select foods that you have found usually give you the most energy and stamina.
8. Drink plenty of water to make sure that your brain remains hydrated during the test for optimal thinking.
9. Make a copy of this list and post it in a strategic location. Check over it before you leave for the testing center.

What to Do During the Test

Here are some general test-taking strategies to help maximize your score on the test. You are given content-specific strategies in the review chapters: Chapters 1, 2, 3, and 4.

1. When you receive the test, take several deep, slow breaths, exhaling slowly while mentally visualizing yourself performing successfully on the test before you begin. Do not get upset if you feel nervous. Most of the people who take the GK Test experience some measure of anxiety.
2. During the test, follow all the directions, including the oral directions of the test administrator and the written directions on the computer screen. If you do not understand something in the directions, ask the test administrator for clarification. The test administrator will indicate how you are to ask for assistance.
3. Move through the test at a steady pace. Work as rapidly as you can without being careless, *but do not rush*.
4. Try to answer the questions in order. However, if a question is taking too much of your time, mark it as one to come back to later and move on.
5. Read each question entirely. Skimming to save time can cause you to misread a question or miss important information.
6. Read all the answer choices before you select an answer. You may find two answer choices that sound good, but one is a better answer to the question.
7. For multiple-choice questions, try to eliminate at least two answer choices. Before you make your final choice, reread the question (don't skip doing this!) and select the response that best answers the question.
8. Change an answer only if you have a good reason to do so.

9. If you are trying to recall information during the test, close your eyes and try to visualize yourself in your study place. This may trigger your memory.
10. Remain calm during the test. If you find yourself getting anxious, stop and take several deep, slow breaths and exhale slowly to help you relax. Keep your mind focused on the task at hand—completing your test. Trust yourself. You should not expect to know the correct response to every question on the test. Think only of doing your personal best.
11. Before submitting your test, be sure you have marked an answer for every test question. You are not penalized for a wrong answer (you score a zero for that test question), so even if you have no clue about the correct answer, make a guess.
12. As you work through the practice tests provided in this book, consciously use the strategies suggested in this section as preparation for the actual FTCE GK Test.

You will benefit greatly from this CliffsNotes book. By using these recommendations as you complete your study program, you will be prepared to walk into the testing room with confidence. Good luck on the test and on your future career as a Florida teacher!

Chapter 1
Review for the General Knowledge Essay Subtest

The Essay Subtest of the FTCE GK Test consists of a choice between two topics; you must select one and write an essay about it in 50 minutes. Within the allotted time you must prepare, write, and edit your essay. Your work will be scored holistically by two graders. "Holistically" means that your essay will receive only one score for both content and mechanics. The personal views you express in your essay are not an issue; you are judged only on the style in which you present your views. Specifically, your essay is evaluated on the logic of your arguments and the degree to which you support your position in a reasonable and coherent manner. The topic may ask you to take a position or develop an argument, but you will be graded on your writing skills, not on your personal beliefs or your knowledge of any particular subject or area. You cannot bring written notes or scratch paper into the testing room.

The Essay Review in This Study Guide

This chapter contains a review of how to write an essay, both in general and for this specific examination. The "Essay Skills" review section presents writing-skills concepts with examples and explanations. At the end of this chapter, you'll find a "Test Yourself" exercise. This exercise gives you an opportunity to practice what you just learned. When doing the "Test Yourself" exercise, choose one of the two essay prompts provided and write an essay response. Then, if possible, have someone proofread your writing for content, style, and grammar. The sample essay topics are similar to those you might receive on the FTCE GK Test. Strong sample responses are provided to aid you in evaluating your essay.

This chapter also includes "Strategies for Writing the Essay for the General Knowledge Test" and the "Scoring Criteria for the General Knowledge Test Essay."

Essay Skills

As listed in the *Competencies and Skills Required for Teacher Certification in Florida,* 20th Edition (www.fldoe.org/asp/ftce/pdf/ftce20edition.pdf), the Essay competencies/skills you should be able to do are the following:

- Determine the purpose of writing to task and audience.
- Provide a section that effectively introduces the topic.
- Formulate a relevant thesis or claim.
- Organize ideas and details effectively.
- Provide adequate, relevant support by citing ample textual evidence; response may also include anecdotal experience for added support.
- Use a variety of transitional devices effectively throughout and within a written text.
- Demonstrate proficient use of college-level, standard written English (e.g., varied word choice, syntax, language conventions, semantics).
- Provide a concluding statement or section that follows from, or supports, the argument or information presented.
- Use a variety of sentence patterns effectively.
- Maintain consistent point of view.
- Apply the conventions of standard English (e.g., avoid inappropriate use of slang, jargon, clichés).

Determine the Purpose of Writing to Task and Audience

Writers write for many reasons. Some write to inform, others to share, and still others to explain. Whatever the reason, you need to determine your purpose for writing before you begin. Knowing your purpose will help clarify your message.

Four common purposes for writing are as follows:

- Self-expression—to express a desire or feeling
- Exposition—to transfer information from writer to reader
- Entertainment—to arouse the interest of the reader
- Persuasion—to convince the reader to embrace a point of view

The more clearly you know what you want to accomplish, the better equipped you will be to write your essay. You will be able to make the proper choices to sharpen your writing and perfect your message.

You also need to know the audience for whom you are writing. Knowing your audience will help you clarify your purpose for writing. If you are writing to a friend, you might write in an open and informal style: "Hey, Steve! What's up? What are ya doin' this summer? Want to have a blast? I know a great summer camp ...." If you are writing to a general audience, you might write in a more formal style: "The following information is intended to help undecided voters select the candidate who most nearly represents their views and interests." Finally, if you are writing to a well-defined audience, you might write in a style that reflects their level of expertise: "The high cost of medical insurance reflects the ever-demanding and volatile relationship between the real and actual cost-ratio factors of doing business in the transactional universe of medical liability."

Look at the examples of the following topics and then ask yourself what might be your purpose for writing in each case and what style of writing you might use:

A. The Debate Over Raising America's Minimum Wage

B. The Decline in Moral Values

C. My Beloved "Talking" Dog

D. Six Easy Ways to Invest Your Money

E. Eat Right! Eat Healthy!

Now that you have had a chance to read these topics, here are some possible reasons or purposes for writing the essays to accompany these titles and also some styles that you might use:

A. The Debate Over Raising America's Minimum Wage

Your purpose for writing could be to explain the growing controversy about raising America's minimum wage. You might use an exposition style to communicate facts to the reader about whether raising the minimum wage for America's hourly employees makes sense in today's current business climate.

B. The Decline in Moral Values

Your purpose for writing may be to draw attention to what you perceive as a decline of civility and decency in today's confusing and conflicting cultural landscape. You might use a self-expressive style to state your feelings.

C. My Beloved "Talking" Dog

Your purpose for writing might be to share the happy and fun-filled misadventures of your beloved "talking" dog, a pet who seems to have a mind of his own. You might use an entertaining style to delight and amuse your readers.

D. Six Easy Ways to Invest Your Money

Your purpose for writing could be to encourage readers to invest their money in profitable ventures that are reasonably guaranteed to provide a safe return on their investment. You might use a persuasive style in writing this essay.

E. Eat Right! Eat Healthy!

Your purpose for writing might be to encourage your readers to eat a healthy, low-fat diet so that they increase their chances of living a long, illness-free life. You might use a persuasive style to motivate your readers to make this change in their lifestyles.

Provide a Section That Effectively Introduces the Topic

In all good writing, the reader should know your topic or main idea by the end of your first paragraph. The reader should have a clear idea of what you are writing about. A well-written essay begins with a paragraph that effectively introduces your topic. This opening paragraph not only helps the reader, but also helps the writer remain focused on what he or she is supposed to be writing.

For example, an opening paragraph might read as follows:

> Have you ever considered taking a cruise? Thousands of vacationers each year, from all walks of life, spend their money on luxurious cruise-liner voyages, where, often, for a low cost relative to a stay at a hotel or joining a tour, these eager travelers find a suitable and pleasant alternative to frequent moving from one tourist destination to the next. Instead, they can stay in one accommodation—enjoying room, board, and entertainment—all at one price. **Clearly, cruises are an alternative to single and multiple destination vacations because they provide vacationers with a safe and practical alternative to seemingly endless packing and unpacking.**

Please note that in the above paragraph, the last sentence provides the focus for this piece. Everything leading to this last sentence represents information to help the reader formulate a more definitive understanding of the writer's point of view.

Similarly, the following paragraph demonstrates the importance of providing an opening paragraph that effectively introduces the topic of your essay:

> Writing is hard work. It is not a skill that comes easily to many people. Often, learning to become a confident and commanding writer is a lifelong journey. It could take years to understand the need to pay attention to every detail of word choice, language convention, and organizational structure. Only individuals with a passion to convey their understandings on paper become proficient and careful writers. **Thus, writing cannot be viewed as a skill that all students will automatically learn, but rather as a habit that all people can acquire when they develop the desire to communicate honestly and efficiently with the written word.**

Please note that in each of the above paragraphs, the writers lead the reader to their central topic. Their writing sets the tone for their piece and provides the necessary detail to establish the writers' premise. Once conveyed, the reader can then proceed to read the rest of the written piece and its attending details.

Formulate a Relevant Thesis or Claim

Formulating a thesis or claim involves two factors: the subject on which you are writing and your attitude or opinion toward that subject. Focusing your attitude or opinion in a single direction gives you a defined purpose for your writing. And since your attitude or opinion may not necessarily be shared by your reader, you need to explain the reasons for your choice.

A good thesis statement not only helps the reader but also helps you, the writer, remain focused on what you are supposed to be writing.

Using the sample topics previously listed, here are five sample thesis statements:

A. The Debate Over Raising America's Minimum Wage

Something needs to be done to help America's working poor whose hourly wages are insufficient to meet their monthly obligations, as the cost for life's necessities—food, fuel, and shelter—keeps rising.

B. The Decline in Moral Values

As I look around my world, I feel disheartened and disappointed at the lack of real civility and decency in today's confusing, conflicting social arena.

C. My Beloved "Talking" Dog

Believe it or not, I have a dog who manages to get everything he wants by talking in a language all his own.

D. Six Easy Ways to Invest Your Money

Money schemes come and go, but after reading this essay, you will walk away with a clear understanding of how to invest your money in safe, reasonable, and risk-free accounts that are guaranteed to yield a modest return.

E. Eat Right! Eat Healthy!

With the variety of foods available to eat, knowing which foods are healthy and which might lead to health problems in years to come is more important than ever.

Notice that each thesis statement names the subject of the essay and provides a clear point of view or opinion about that subject. These factors are the hallmarks of a strong thesis statement.

Organize Ideas and Details Effectively

After constructing a strong thesis statement, you need to begin organizing ideas and details effectively. With a sharply defined and well-written thesis statement, your ideas and details should flow naturally. You should be able to list fairly rapidly the essential reasons for defending and defining your thesis statement.

Before you begin, it is always best to set up a plan of action. Planning ensures a better finished product, as your ideas will flow with greater logic and clarity. There are several different ways to plan an essay, but one of the ways involves the following steps:

1. Write down all the possible ideas you can think of on the essay's topic.
2. Circle the ideas you think are the most important and that you can write about most effectively.
3. Group the ideas that you have circled into possible paragraphs.
4. Organize the groups into possible ways to address the essay's topic.

Most writing projects can be organized into three parts: (1) the introduction, (2) the body, and (3) the conclusion. In the introduction, you briefly state your topic, presenting your reader with a preview of what is to come. The body of the paper—the main and longest portion of your paper—provides the facts and examples that support the main idea expressed in the introduction. The conclusion summarizes your main points and restates the central idea.

The three parts of your essay should work together to make an effective and cohesive whole. Your introduction should be an attention-grabbing device that will "pull" the reader into your essay. In the body of your essay, make sure that every point is relevant to the subject you are discussing. Avoid irrelevant or extraneous information that does not relate to your main topic. Finally, your conclusion should be a strong ending that includes a restatement of your thesis.

A simple technique to remember is tell the reader what you are going to say, say it, and then tell the reader what you said. Keeping this rule in mind will help you considerably as you write your impromptu essay. For example, suppose you were asked to write an essay on the following topic: Choosing a career.

1. Allowing a few minutes to think, you might write something like this:

   Interests, money, location, college, courses, preparation, skills, talents, hobbies, schooling, time, travel, passion, income, standard of living

2. Circle the ideas you think are the most important and that you can write about most effectively. Remember, you cannot write about everything you can imagine; you will only have time to explore a few key points.

3. Group the items you have selected into possible paragraphs. Your grouped ideas might look like this:
   - Personal interests

     Talents, hobbies, passion
   - Preparation for career

     Schooling, time, college, courses
   - Financial considerations

     Money, income, standard of living

4. After you have grouped ideas into similar sections, you can organize your groups into an outline. Outlines are an easy way to organize your thoughts and prepare your essay. For example, an outline for an essay on "choosing a career" might look like this:

   I. Introduction—Many factors impact a career choice.
   II. Personal Interests
      A. Talents
      B. Hobbies
      C. Passion

   III. Preparation for Career
      A. Schooling
      B. Length of study
      C. Practical experience

   IV. Financial Considerations
      A. Potential income
      B. Standard of living
      C. Money to study

   V. Conclusion—Summarize reasons for choosing a career.

When organizing your essay's ideas and details, it is important that you follow a few guidelines:

- **Determine the amount of background information required.** Is your audience familiar with your topic? Do you have to provide background information?
- **Define required terminology.** Does your audience need to know technical terms? If so, which terms?
- **Define the tone of your discussion.** Should you write in a formal or casual style? Which would be most effective?
- **Determine the number of examples required.** You will need to include examples to define your thesis. But how many? Which ones?
- **Determine the organizational pattern to use.** What organizational pattern should you use to explore your thesis? Which style is most effective for your intended purpose?

Organizing your ideas and details to explore your thesis statement requires a deep understanding of your subject matter. Thus, when writing an essay, be sure to select a topic that you know a lot about; otherwise, you will be struggling to add strong details to your writing.

Provide Adequate, Relevant Support by Citing Ample Textual Evidence; Response May Also Include Anecdotal Experience for Added Support

To develop an effective essay, you must provide your reader with adequate and relevant supporting material. The information you select to include in your essay must not only meet your needs as the writer, but should pertain directly to the needs of your reader. Otherwise, your writing serves no real purpose.

To make sure that your writing provides strong and relevant supportive material, always be mindful of your reader. Ask yourself some basic questions:

- Do all your sentences contribute to the development of your thesis?
- Do your sentences follow a logical and clear sequence of ideas?
- Do you include sufficient relevant detail?

- Do you use a consistent style?
- Do you answer readers' potential questions?
- Do you include vivid and specific examples to support your point of view?

The following is an example of a passage in which the writer's thoughts are *not* presented in a coherent, logical, unified, and well-ordered manner:

> Keeping animals happy and healthy is difficult. I like animals, especially, dogs. Sometimes, I like cats. Most dogs are enjoyable to have as pets, yet sometimes, they can be most difficult, especially when you want to take long trips. I once had a dog who loved to bark all night. Taking a dog on a summer road trip is never easy. You must bring along lots of food and water. I remember a trip we once took in the dead of winter, which made traveling with our family pets exceptionally hard. I do not know what I would do without my favorite dog, Millie.

How much better would the above paragraph be if it were written like the following?

> Keeping animals happy and healthy involves five simple rules. The first rule is to keep your pets' food dishes clean. Wash them thoroughly every day. This will help prevent the spread of bacteria and other diseases from infecting your pets. The second rule is to make sure your pets eat right. A balanced diet is necessary if your pets are to be healthy. If you are unsure what your animals should eat, check with a veterinarian. Also, buy food formulated for your pets' needs. By using these foods, you can be sure that your pets receive proper amounts of vitamins, minerals, and protein for their nourishment. The third rule is to never overfeed your pets. Give your animals as much food as they will eat without leaving any food behind. If your pets leave the dish before emptying it, be sure to take the dish away. This will ensure that your pets do not overeat; and next time, you will know to feed them less. The fourth rule is that all pets must have good houses. Whether the house is a cage or a pet bed, make sure that it is dry, warm, and suitable in size for the animal to use comfortably. Finally, the fifth rule is to make sure pets are checked regularly by a veterinarian and given all the required vaccinations. A sick animal can infect other animals—and even people in some cases. By following these five simple rules, you can help your pets to enjoy good health and a long life.

As you can tell, the second paragraph contains relevant and supporting details presented in a logical, coherent, and organized manner.

Use a Variety of Transitional Devices Effectively Throughout and Within a Written Text

Good writers make use of effective transitions. They use transitional words or phrases to connect ideas and thoughts. Transitional words also provide for a logical sequence of ideas.

Look at the following list for a sampling of transitional words and phrases. By incorporating these words and phrases into your own writing, you can begin to develop a writing style that is clear and unified for your readers.

again	conversely	in any case	namely	therefore
also	finally	in any event	nevertheless	thereupon
as a rule	first of all	in brief	of course	thus
as usual	for example	in essence	rather	to sum up
besides	for instance	in short	secondly	
briefly	furthermore	in the long run	similarly	
by and large	generally	instead	that is	
consequently	however	moreover	then indeed	

Many other transitional expressions are available, but you will find that the preceding list will serve you well. Using these words to connect your thoughts will significantly improve your writing style and fluency.

Look at some examples of how these transitional words can be used:

- Learning to laugh at one's mistakes, therefore, can bring a whole new perspective on one's life.
- Briefly, the three main points of this essay are ...
- In short, I intend to run for president of the senior class and win.
- Consequently, the politician had little to say when he was indicted on charges of election fraud.
- The construction crew worked tirelessly; however, they did not manage to finish the Robertsons' new home in time for the start of the Robertsons' summer vacation.
- The President ignored his own good judgment; therefore, the military mission was an abysmal failure.

Demonstrate Proficient Use of College-Level, Standard Written English (e.g., varied word choice, syntax, language conventions, semantics)

Writing a strong and effective essay requires the ability to demonstrate a mature command of language. Writers must be able to articulate their thoughts in a clear, logical fashion so that readers can easily and readily understand what is being said. Any confusion evidenced by a writer's handling of language will result in the reader's misinterpretation of the material. Thus, to avoid such confusion, good writers should do the following:

- Write with a clear and resonant voice. Be sure all your words are chosen to convey the most precise and logical analysis of your argument or thesis statement.
- Use paragraph breaks to divide your thought patterns and make your essay easier to read.
- Use transitions and related word links to connect your thoughts and ideas.
- Provide a sound and logical conclusion to your essay that summarizes your key ideas.
- Avoid spelling and grammatical errors. Proofread your work.
- Avoid wordiness. Using fewer words to express a difficult idea or thought is always better.
- Avoid repetition. State enough ideas to make your point but not so much as to bore the reader.
- Avoid overgeneralization. Rather than make sweeping assertions that overstate reality, qualify your ideas with the words *often, usually,* or *sometimes*.
- Write simply. Often a simpler word is an effective substitute for a more difficult word. By writing simply, you can help clarify your thoughts.

As an example of the need to write simply, examine these two sentences:

1. Joe Smith is the team leader.
2. The undersigned official assumes leadership responsibility for the team.

Which do you prefer? Obviously, the first choice conveys the meaning of the sentence simply and directly. The second choice, however, is obtuse and may imply another agenda other than simply stating the truth.

Now examine these two longer examples:

Passage #1

Bungee jumping was inspired many, many years ago by the celebrated vine jumpers of the world-famous Pentecost Islands in Vanuatu (formerly the New Hebrides) in the vast stretches of the Pacific Ocean, where it is understood by all the inhabitants and natives that bungee jumping is doubly a rite of passage into manhood and a fertility rite performed to ensure a good and plentiful yam harvest. Modern bungee jumping began with four simultaneous jumps off the renowned Clifton Suspension Bridge in Bristol, England, on the very first day of April in 1979. Today, bungee jumping is a sporting event that is practiced all over the world, almost everywhere that people can ever imagine.

Passage #2

Bungee jumping was inspired by the Pentecost Island vine jumpers. There, natives bungee-jumped as a rite of passage into manhood. It was also considered a fertility rite to ensure a strong yam harvest. Modern bungee jumping began with four simultaneous jumps from the Clifton Suspension Bridge in Bristol, England, on April 1, 1979. Today, bungee jumping is practiced worldwide.

As you can see, the second example dispenses with unnecessary wordiness. Following the preceding rules will help you demonstrate a mature command of language and write with proficiency and efficiency.

When writing your essay, observe the conventions of college-level, standard written English. Be careful to pay close attention to word choice, syntax, language conventions, and semantics.

Here are some tips to follow when writing to observe the conventions of standard written English:

1. **Use active voice.** In sentences written in active voice, the subject performs the action expressed in the verb. For example:

   The dog bit the intruder. (active voice) The intruder was bitten by the dog. (passive voice)

   Everyone who attended the housewarming party had a great time. (active voice) A great time was had by everyone who attended the housewarming party. (passive voice)

2. **Be plain-spoken.** Say what you mean simply and plainly.
3. **Write in complete sentences.** Make sure your sentences have a subject and a verb.
4. **Be sure your subject and verb agree.** Make sure your subjects and verbs agree in number.
5. **Be sure your nouns and pronouns agree.** Make sure your pronoun references agree with the nouns to which they refer.
6. **Use clear descriptions.** Be careful that your nouns and descriptors are connected properly.
7. **Use proper grammar symbols.** Be sure you punctuate your sentences correctly.
8. **Check spelling.** Always proofread your writing for common spelling and grammatical errors.

These writing tips will help you adhere to the conventions of standard written English and avoid common grammatical errors. Also, please note that although you will be composing your essay on the computer, you will not have access to spelling and grammar checkers. Thus, avoid words and phrases that are unfamiliar to you to avoid costly errors and mistakes. For a brief grammar review, see "Knowledge of Standard English Conventions" in Chapter 2.

Provide a Concluding Statement or Section That Follows From, or Supports, the Argument or Information Presented

When writing your essay, your concluding statement and/or paragraph brings your central thesis or topic home for your reader. It is a good idea to summarize what you said in your opening paragraph and/or thesis statement in order to suggest to your reader that you have accomplished what you set out to accomplish. It is also important to judge for yourself that you have, in fact, done so.

Writing, like reading, is a process of self-discovery and self-exploration. Having read your essay, the reader should understand your main ideas. Your conclusion should summarize what the reader has learned as he or she read through your reasoning in your essay.

There are some cautions, though, to keep in mind as you write your concluding statement:

- First, your conclusion should contain a definite, positive statement or a call to action, and that statement needs to be based on what you have provided in your essay.

- Second, your conclusion should restate essential points, and not bring up new ideas. If a brilliant new idea appears in your final paragraph, you should either rewrite your essay to include your new thought in one of the previous paragraphs or leave your new idea out altogether.
- Finally, if you promised in the introduction that you were going to cover four points and you covered only two (because you couldn't find enough information or you took too long with the first two or you got tired), don't try to cram those last two points into your final paragraph. The "rush job" will be all too apparent. Instead, revise your introduction or take the time to do justice to these other points.

Below are some suggestions of things that you might accomplish in your concluding paragraph(s). Keep in mind that you definitely do not need to include all these things, and that these are only suggestions:

- Include a brief summary of your main points.
- Ask a question to give your reader something to think about.
- Use a quotation.
- Call for some sort of action.
- End with a word of caution.
- Suggest consequences or results.

Use a Variety of Sentence Patterns Effectively

Using a variety of sentence patterns effectively is essential to good writing. A paper that has all the required information but is uninteresting to read will either bore the readers or leave them more confused than when they started to read. Thus, a good technique to improve your writing is to vary your sentence patterns.

Look at the following example of how sentences may be constructed into interesting patterns:

First, a simple sentence, by definition, is an **independent clause.** An independent clause is a group of words that contains a subject and a verb and expresses a complete thought. An example of an independent clause is

I went to the movies.

Second, a sentence can be enhanced by adding a **dependent clause.** A dependent clause is a group of words that contains a subject and a verb but does not express a complete thought. Thus, it is not a sentence. An example of a dependent clause is

When Lauren was finished with her homework.

Often a dependent clause is marked by a **subordinating conjunction.** The subordinating conjunction is added to the beginning of an independent clause. When this occurs, the independent clause becomes a dependent clause. Some common subordinate conjunctions are

after, although, as, as if, because, before, even if, even though, if, in order that, since, though, unless, until, whatever, when, whenever, whether, and *while*

Third, when successive independent clauses are related to each other, you can connect them with **coordinating conjunctions** or **transitional expressions.** Coordinating conjunctions include

and, but, for, nor, or, so, and *yet*

Transitional expressions include

also, consequently, first, for example, for instance, furthermore, however, moreover, nevertheless, and *therefore*

Also, when the second independent clause in a sentence begins with a transitional expression, a *period* or *semicolon* is needed before the transitional expression. For example:

I went to the movies; however, I went when Lauren was finished with her homework.

Knowing this, here are some examples of how two clauses can be written:

I went to the movies. I went when Lauren was finished with her homework.

I went to the movies; I went when Lauren was finished with her homework.

I went to the movies, but I went when Lauren was finished with her homework.

I went to the movies; however, I did not go until Lauren was finished with her homework.

When Lauren was finished with her homework, I went to the movies.

I went to the movies when Lauren was finished with her homework.

Keep these sentence variations in mind when you write your essays. For more on sentence structure, see "Apply Knowledge of a Variety of Effective Structures (e.g., recognizing fragments, comma splices, run-on sentences, syntax errors)" in Chapter 2.

Maintain a Consistent Point of View

Maintaining a consistent point of view is a quality of strong writing. A good writer maintains consistency in style, content, and theme throughout a piece. To maintain such consistency, it is best for writers to adopt one voice throughout their work.

As a writer, you can choose from three points of view to write your pieces: **first, second,** or **third person.** Each one has specific responsibilities, characteristics, and effects for you and your reader. Here are examples of how each point of view may be used in your essay.

The **first-person point of view** is a narrative written with the word "I," which makes it highly personalized. Use this point of view when you want to cultivate a sense of closeness with your readers or when you want the readers to identify or sympathize with you. An example of a first-person point of view is as follows:

I went home around 2 o'clock yesterday afternoon and checked my refrigerator. Nothing was there to eat. So, hungry, I walked over to my neighbor's apartment and asked whether she would like to go out to grab a snack with me. We knew each other well enough to do those fun things on the spur of the moment, so off we went.

The **second-person point of view** is used when the narrator addresses the reader as "you." Often, second-person point of view is used when the narrator is speaking to a younger or less-experienced reader. Before writing in second person, the narrator should clarify for the reader just who is talking to whom. As you can tell, though, much of the text in this book is written in second person. The reason is that second person is commonly used in technical and reference writing in which a process or technique is being explained. The reader is thought of as a less-experienced version of the writer and someone for whom the writer must carefully explain each step required to learn a new procedure or method.

Here's the earlier example adapted to second-person point of view:

You went home around 2 o'clock yesterday afternoon and checked your refrigerator. You found nothing there to eat. So, being hungry, you walked over to your neighbor's apartment and asked her whether she would like to go out to grab a snack with you. You know each other well enough to do those fun things on the spur of the moment, so off you went.

The **third-person point of view** is used when the narrative is told by a supposedly objective voice (see discussion below) not directly involved in the story. The narrator is the voice of authority and should be telling the story without noticeable prejudice or bias. Third-person point of view is popular in fictional writing and is often present in nonfiction works such as research reports and newspaper articles.

Tip: When writing in the third person, be careful to keep your voice objective. It is very easy to let subjectivity or bias slip into your narrative. See the discussion below of objective and subjective voice.

Here's our earlier example adapted to third-person point of view:

> He went home around 2 o'clock yesterday afternoon and checked his refrigerator. He found nothing there to eat. So, being hungry, he walked over to his neighbor's apartment and asked her whether she would like to go out and grab a snack with him. They knew each other well enough to do those fun things on the spur of the moment, so off they went.

Finally, when writing, there are two kinds of voices in which a narrative may be written. They are objective and subjective voice:

- **Objective voice** is used when the writer takes an impartial approach to the subject. Objective writing focuses on external things and events, without referring to the personal prejudices or emotions of the writer. Newswriting is an example of nonfiction objective writing.
- **Subjective voice** is used when the writer takes a personal approach to the subject. Subjective writing focuses on internal things and events, presenting reality as the writer sees and interprets it, referring continually to the expression of personal thoughts, impulses, and feelings. Editorials, opinion pieces, and personal narratives are examples of nonfiction subjective writing.

When writing, it is imperative that you select a voice and a point of view that is consistent throughout your essay. Knowing what you want to say and how you want to say it are the two key ingredients in any successful writing endeavor. Failure to follow these guidelines will result in poor, unfocused writing.

Apply the Conventions of Standard English (e.g., avoid inappropriate use of slang, jargon, clichés)

When writing an essay, you should apply the conventions of standard written English by avoiding the inappropriate use of slang, jargon, and clichés. The use of common sayings and expressions might be appropriate for creative writing; however, such usage is inappropriate for formal essay writing. Thus, it is wise to keep your writing to standard written English usage and style.

Slang is street language. It is the highly informal language that is acceptable for conversations among friends, but highly inappropriate for formal writing. Slang is sometimes referred to as "colloquial," a word meaning language that is spoken by everyday people.

Some common slang words and their meanings are as follows:

airhead—stupid person
*Dave is a real **airhead**.*
armpit—dirty, unappealing place
*His bedroom is a regular **armpit**.*
cheesy—cheap, outmoded, out of date
*My boyfriend was wearing such **cheesy** clothes.*
chick flick—a movie primarily of interest to females, often a love story or heavy emotional drama
*Last night, my wife went to the movies with her girlfriends to see the latest **chick flick**.*
flick—movie
*Hey, wanna see a **flick**?*
benjamins—one hundred dollar bills
*That watch is worth a lot of **benjamins**.*
hairy—difficult
*Driving super-fast, Arnie took some **hairy** turns.*

lip—fast, cheap talk

The students in fourth period always give their substitute teacher **lip**.

paws—hands

Get your **paws** off my girlfriend!

rug rat—child

My brother has a couple of **rug rats** running around his house.

scarf—to eat fast

Rushing off to school, I **scarfed** down my breakfast as I headed out the door.

threads—clothing

Willie bought a whole new set of **threads**.

turkey—failure

The movie was a real **turkey**.

umpteen—countless

If I have told you once, I have told you **umpteen** times, don't wear your shoes inside the house!

wheels—car, motor vehicle

I took off on the open road in my brand new set of **wheels**.

zero—unimportant person

He is such a **zero**!

Jargon is the specialized language of a discipline or a profession. Individuals involved in a particular discipline, job, or profession use the same words, or jargon, frequently; usually, only the individuals intimately connected to the words know of their meaning. Nothing is wrong with jargon; however, it must be used judiciously so that its meaning is clear to all readers.

Tip: When in doubt, always use a simple word. Simplicity breeds understanding, and understanding means clarity in thought and reason.

Clichés are overused expressions that lack originality. When writing, use clichés when necessary—when they add punch to your writing style—and not when a more apt word or phrase will do. It is always better to use fresh, original expressions to define your writing. Some common examples of clichés are as follows:

A chicken in every pot	In close quarters
A penny for your thoughts	Last but not least
Agree to disagree	No rest for the wicked
As old as dirt	No worse for the wear
Close only counts in horseshoes and hand grenades	On the rocks
	Stay the course
Cut bait and run	The ball's in your court
Don't rock the boat	The worm turns
Easy pickings	Through thick and thin
In any way, shape, or form	Venture a guess

These colorful expressions are fun to say, but avoid them in formal writing.

Strategies for Writing the Essay for the General Knowledge Test

Some strategies for writing the essay for the GK Test are as follows:

1. **Watch your time.**

    Use your time wisely. Take some time at the beginning of the Essay Subtest to plan your essay. Be sure to also allow yourself time to proofread and make some revisions. You do *not* have time to plan, write a rough draft, proofread it, and then completely rewrite it.

2. **Read the instructions carefully.**

    While two topics will be provided, you will select only one on which to write your essay. Read carefully so you are clear on what the topic is asking. Consider how the topic you select relates to your personal knowledge and experience so you can provide strong supporting details in your essay instead of vague generalities.

3. **Prewrite.**

    Brainstorm, jotting down some ideas. Then try sketching a brief outline or using arrows to group your ideas together. Such prewriting steps will help you to "see" your essay taking shape before you start the actual writing.

4. **Write a thesis statement.**

    Develop a thesis statement that states the focus of your essay. Your thesis should state your point of view to guide the purpose and scope of your essay. When writing your thesis statement, consider the point(s) you want to convey to the reader. Avoid a thesis statement that is presented as statement of fact, a question, or an announcement.

5. **Develop the essay to support your thesis statement.**

    Develop paragraphs fully, providing examples that support your thesis. Note that a good essay for the GK Test does not necessarily have to follow the basic five-paragraph format (introduction, three supporting paragraphs, conclusion); your essay might be longer or shorter. The key is to develop the topic with concrete, informative details.

6. **Tie your main ideas together in the last paragraph.**

    The last paragraph of your essay should serve as a conclusion, tying together your essay's points and offering insight(s) about the topic. Do not merely restate your thesis and repeat your supporting details. Again, be aware of how much time you have left. If time is almost up, wrap up quickly, so you have time to proofread and make minor revisions.

7. **Proofread and revise your essay, making sure it conforms to standard written English.**

    Watch for common grammatical or spelling errors. Read each paragraph in order and make corrections.

Scoring Criteria for the General Knowledge Test Essay

Your essay will be scored by two scorers. The score that you receive will be the combined score of the scores you receive from the two scorers. A passing score is 6 out of 12 possible points. The scoring criteria for the GK Test Essay are detailed below:

Scoring for the FTCE General Knowledge Test Essay

Score of 6	The essay contains a fully developed idea, complete with details and examples. The organization of the essay is logical and straightforward. Point of view is consistent. Both word choice and sentence structure are effective and varied. Few, if any, errors in sentence structure, usage, and mechanics occur, and they are insignificant.
Score of 5	The essay has an adequately developed, clear main idea that is supported with details and/or examples. The organization of the essay is logical and easy to follow. Point of view is, for the most part, maintained. Both word choice and sentence structure are mostly varied. There are some errors in sentence structure, usage, and mechanics, but they do not hinder meaning.

(Continued)

Scoring for the FTCE General Knowledge Test Essay (*Continued*)

Score of 4	The essay states a main idea that is supported by some details and examples. Supporting ideas are, for the most part, logical. Point of view is there, but is not always maintained. Word choice and sentence structure have a little variety, but occasional errors in sentence structure, usage, and mechanics may hinder understanding and writer's meaning.
Score of 3	The essay states a main idea, but supports it with generalizations or lists instead of specific details and/or examples. The essay occasionally lacks logic and coherence. Organization is rote, and point of view is inconsistent. Word choice and sentence structure lack variety and are ineffective. Multiple errors in sentence structure, usage, and mechanics hinder understanding.
Score of 2	The essay has an incomplete main idea that is supported with generalizations or lists. Organization is rote, and essay occasionally lacks logic and coherence. Point of view is confusing. Word choice is simplistic, and sentence structure lacks coherence. Errors in sentence structure, usage, and mechanics are frequent and interfere with the writer's ability to effectively communicate.
Score of 1	The essay lacks a main idea and is either underdeveloped or development is irrelevant, Organization is illogical. There is no established point of view. Both word choice and sentence structure are confusing. Significant and numerous errors in sentence structure, usage, and mechanics interfere with the writer's ability to effectively communicate.

Test Yourself

50 Minutes

Directions: This section of the examination involves a written assignment. You are to prepare a written response for *one* of the two topics presented below. Select one of these two topics and prepare a response. Be sure to read both topics very carefully to make sure that you understand the topic for which you are preparing a written response. Use the allotted time to plan, write, review, and edit what you have written for the assignment.

Topic 1

What are qualities you deem important in a good teacher? What do you believe about students? Your answers to these questions form the basis of your teaching philosophy. A teaching philosophy is an articulation of your attitudes and beliefs about teaching and learning. Write an essay in which you describe your teaching philosophy, being sure to support your ideas with specific examples.

Topic 2

The notion that our public schools are becoming increasingly culturally diverse has become self-evident in many of our nation's communities. Evaluate the advantages of a culturally diverse student population and include some of the required precautions that educators should recognize when teaching culturally diverse learners.

Be sure to read the two topics again before attempting to write your response. Remember, you will type your essay on the computer screen. Your essay also must be on only one of the topics presented, and it must address the topic completely.

Your essay will be graded holistically, meaning only one score is assigned for your writing—taking into consideration both mechanics and organization. *You will not be scored on the nature of the content or opinions expressed in your work.* Instead, you will be graded on your ability to write complete sentences, to express and support your opinions, and to organize your work.

At least two evaluators will review your work and assign it a score. Special attention is paid to the following more specific indications in your writing:

- Can the reader determine a strong definitive task and purpose for your writing?
- Can the reader identify a section of your essay that clearly introduces the topic of your paper?
- Can the reader locate a relevant thesis or claim for your essay?
- Can the reader follow your ideas and details in a logical and effective manner?
- Can the reader identify adequate, relevant supporting textual evidence and/or anecdotal experiences to support your central thesis?
- Can the reader identify a variety of transitional devices throughout your written text to enhance and clarify your essay?
- Do you as a writer demonstrate proficient use of college-level, standard written English (e.g., varied word choice, syntax, language conventions, semantics)?
- Can the reader locate a concluding statement or section that follows from, or supports, the argument or information presented?
- Can the reader identify a consistent point of view throughout your essay?
- Do you as a writer apply conventions of standard written English (e.g., avoid inappropriate use of slang, jargon, clichés) throughout your essay?

Sample Responses

Following are sample essay responses to the preceding topics.

Topic 1

What are qualities that you deem important in a good teacher? What do you believe about students? Your answers to these questions form the basis for your teaching philosophy. A teaching philosophy is an articulation of your attitudes and beliefs about teaching and learning. Write an essay in which you describe your teaching philosophy, being sure to support your ideas with specific examples.

Strong Response

Since I was very young, I have wanted to teach. I want to become a teacher because I want to help young people learn and succeed. I believe that developing a caring relationship with my students will stimulate in them the desire, or motivation, to learn. Accordingly, I will value and respect all my students and treat them with dignity and courtesy at all times. Further, I firmly believe that all students can learn and that I as a teacher should have high expectations for all of my students. Thus, the basis of my philosophy of teaching is to nurture others to become the best they can possibly be. Guided by this principle, I will encourage my students to achieve their potential, to develop strong study and work habits, and to make wise and purposeful decisions.

First, I believe that all young people have the potential to become exceptional educated, caring, and responsible adults. Given learning environments that maximize academic success and self-managed behavior, I believe they can develop into intellectually capable and mature individuals. They possess the potential within to blossom into productive and engaged citizens who attack life with a passionate zeal and purpose that defies all expectations. All they need is the adroit expertise and gentle guidance of a respectful and caring teacher who will recognize their capabilities and highlight their strengths. Sometimes, a nudge is often the spark they need to begin their journey. This nudge can come in many shapes and sizes, most notably direct praise for assignments and jobs well done. Teachers who take the time to listen and talk to their students—about their schoolwork and interests—can do much to demonstrate to their students that a caring and compassionate hand can aleviate most any burden. Taking time from a busy schedule to attend to students' immediate concerns can do much to inspire them to achieve any worthy goal they might imagine.

Second, as a teacher, I hope to encourage young people to develop smart study and work habits. By providing them with a recognizable routine in our daily class assignments, I intend to model for my students how they should perceive and organize their own studies. A teacher who demonstrates good work habits and a steady and recognizable routine can do much to improve the learning of often distracted and unfocused youngsters. After all, I know what it is like to be confused and dazed; I was once a student myself, and I appreciate the many teachers that I had who helped me organize my work and learn my school material. Directly and indirectly, they provided me with many useful suggestions and tips for completing my class assignments and arranging my notes into recognizable and coherent patterns. Once done, I was able to streamline my study time and, thus, learn my material quickly and efficiently. When I teach, I hope to model and inspire my students to do the same.

Finally, as a teacher, I hope to encourage young people to make wise and purposeful decisions. I know, of course, that a teacher cannot save the world. A teacher cannot ensure that every child in the teacher's care makes sound choices, but he or she can be a role model for students. By providing young people with lessons in decision-making, I intend to demonstrate simple steps that everyone can take when deciding a course of action. Too often, young people make rash choices without thinking about the consequences of their actions. The results are sometimes near-fatal errors that can cause much pain and harm to all involved. Thus, I believe that lessons in decision-making—how best to decide on a course of action, given a set of circumstances and concerns—is the best approach for helping young people become responsible adults. Whether the decision is as simple as how to behave on the playground or is something more complex like deciding whether to go to college, young people need ways to safely and rationally make the best choice in a given situation. Therefore, I will endeavor to build a positive physical, social, and intellectual classroom environment that is conducive to responsible decision-making.

Overall, I believe that teachers have a unique opportunity to help the young people in their charge to achieve their dreams. Once a teacher, I can strive toward that goal by encouraging young people to develop their potential, to improve their study and work habits, and to hone their decision-making skills. By following this strategy, I intend to become the best teacher that I can possibly be.

Evaluation of Strong Response: This essay is a well-written exposition. The central thesis—the writer's teaching philosophy—is presented clearly and effectively and supported with specific examples. The writer explains the purpose of the writing and introduces the topic effectively. Each paragraph has a clearly identified main idea with carefully selected supporting details. Word choice is generally precise and effective (*Given learning environments that maximize academic success and self-managed behavior…*). The organization is logical and straightforward. Each paragraph transitions smoothly to the next. Point of view is unambiguous and consistent. Word choice and sentence structure vary, and errors in sentence structure, usage, and mechanics are few. Although the writing is not flawless (for instance, in the first and last paragraphs, the phrases *the best they can possibly be* and *the best teacher that I can possibly be* are variations of an overused expression; in the second paragraph, the word *alleviate* is misspelled as *aleviate*; and there are errors in comma usage), this essay is a strong response.

Topic 2

The notion that our public schools are becoming increasingly culturally diverse has become self-evident in many of our nation's communities. Evaluate the advantages of a culturally diverse student population and include some of the required precautions that educators should recognize when teaching culturally diverse learners.

Strong Response

Without a doubt, our country is becoming increasingly diverse. Never before in our nation's history have so many individuals of diverse origin, color, and background gathered together to live together unencumbered and without pre-conditions. Young and old alike, all nationalities and ethnicities, now live in the same neighborhoods, attending to the same needs, functions, and events. More importantly, diverse families and friends send their children to our nation's schools and as a result, schools now reflect the diversity of our neighborhoods. The diverse characteristics of our nation's public school children come with particular strengths and challenges.

As a strength, young people are now befriending young people from all walks of life. No longer, at least in most public schools, do young people meet only others similar to themselves. Indeed, more and more, young people are attending public schools where diversity is a hallmark of their education. They sit in classroom with students who are diverse in background, color, and nationality, and as all learn together, they begin to appreciate the value of their differences and the sameness of their needs.

This is not to say that the situation is without hurdles. Diversity brings not only the celebration of differences but also the struggle to bridge such differences among young people who are naturally hesitant. These youngsters who are faced with others who are different from themselves sometimes wrestle with their own instinctual or learned social prejudices and understandings. Many have a usual tendency to view their own cultural or familial ways of doing things as best and most acceptable. Such inclinations can often exhibit themselves in classroom interactions, where young people may feel threatened by that which is new or different. Knowing this, teachers must accept their professional responsibility to help their students deal with differences, both inside and outside their respective classrooms.

At the same time, teachers must ask themselves what are best practices to optimize learning for all students? How can they reach young people whose values and backgrounds might be different from their own? How can they make their classrooms more inclusive so that diverse learners feel recognized and rewarded for their efforts? To meet this challenge, teachers can begin by developing good teacher-student relationships. Creating an environment that respects and confirms the dignity of students as human beings is essential in meeting the needs of diverse students. Most important, teachers must embrace the attitude that if the materials are suitable and presented on the appropriate level, all students can learn.

The inherent advantages of teaching diverse student populations must be buffeted by the many cautions that educators should recognize when teaching diverse learners. A whole host of questions arise as to how best to deal with learners who come to the equation with differences that might affect their learning and behavior. Teachers need to recognize that the diversity that plays out in their classroom means that for learning to occur, they must meet and embrace the challenge of that diversity.

Evaluation of Strong Response: This essay is a well-written exposition. The writing is focused on the idea that *diverse characteristics of our nation's public school children come with particular strengths and challenges* and presents relevant details (such as *As a strength, young people are now befriending young people from all walks of life* and *Diversity brings not only the celebration of differences but also the struggle to bridge such differences among young people who are naturally hesitant*) that provide insight into the writer's viewpoint on the topic. Each paragraph has a clearly identified topic sentence with carefully selected supporting details. Word choice is precise and effective (*teachers must embrace the attitude that if the materials are suitable and presented on the appropriate level, all students can learn*). The organization of the essay is logical and straightforward. Each paragraph transitions smoothly to the next. Point of view is unambiguous and consistent. Word choice and sentence structure vary, and errors in sentence structure, usage, and mechanics are few. Although the writing is not flawless (for instance, *Never before in our nation's history* and *Young and old alike* in the first paragraph and *from all walks of life* in the second paragraph are overused expressions), this essay is a strong response.

Chapter 2
Review for the General Knowledge English Language Skills Subtest

The English Language Skills Subtest of the FTCE GK Test consists of 40 multiple-choice questions, which you must complete in 40 minutes. Each test question requires that you choose from among four answer choices. You must click on the button corresponding to your answer choice on the computer screen. You cannot bring written notes or scratch paper into the testing room.

The English Language Skills Review in This Study Guide

The English Language Skills review in this CliffsNotes study guide is organized around the three language skill areas tested on the FTCE GK Test:

- Knowledge of Language Structure
- Knowledge of Vocabulary Application
- Knowledge of Standard English Conventions

Each area has a general review and sample questions. The review sections present language skill concepts with examples and explanations for each area. "Test Yourself" exercises are found throughout the review sections. These sample questions are similar to what you might expect to see on the FTCE GK Test; they give you an opportunity to practice what you just learned. The answers to the "Test Yourself" exercises are found immediately following the set of exercises. When doing the "Test Yourself" exercises, you should cover up the answers. Then check your answers when you've finished the exercises.

Knowledge of Language Structure

As listed in the *Competencies and Skills Required for Teacher Certification in Florida,* 20th Edition (www.fldoe.org/asp/ftce/pdf/ftce20edition.pdf), the English language competencies/skills you should have mastered for this area are the following:

- Evaluate correct placement of modifiers.
- Apply knowledge of parallelism, including parallel expressions for parallel ideas.
- Apply knowledge of a variety of effective structures (e.g., recognizing fragments, comma splices, run-on sentences, syntax errors).
- Determine patterns of organization in a written passage (i.e., modes of rhetoric).

Evaluate Correct Placement of Modifiers

A **modifier** is a word or group of words that conveys information about another word or word group. Good writing requires correct placement of modifiers in sentences. To avoid confusion, modifiers should be placed close to the word or words they modify. A modifier is a **misplaced modifier** when it is placed in the sentence in such a way that the intent of the writer is unclear to the reader. Look at this example of a misplaced modifier:

> *The photographer saw several black bears driving through the woods.*

This sentence is confusing because the modifier (*driving through the woods*) is not close to the word it modifies (*photographer*). The way the sentence is written, it sounds like the bears are driving through the woods, a situation that clearly is not the intent of the writer.

You can correct the confusion by revising the sentence like this:

Driving through the woods, the photographer saw several black bears.

Here is another example of a misplaced modifier:

I only have one dollar in my wallet.

In this sentence, the word *only* should be placed immediately before the word *one*, which it modifies:

I have only one dollar in my wallet.

Apply Knowledge of Parallelism, Including Parallel Expressions for Parallel Ideas

The ideas in sentences should be **parallel,** meaning they should be expressed in the same way. For instance, you might write, "I like to sunbathe, but I don't like to swim." Your ideas on sunbathing and swimming are expressed using the same type of grammatical construction. **Faulty parallelism** occurs when the elements in a sentence are not parallel. The result is an awkward construction, the meaning of which is often unclear. Look at this example of faulty parallelism:

Jude's actions were heroic and to be praised.

This sentence sounds awkward because the ideas are not expressed in the same way. The words *heroic* and *to be praised* do not have the same grammatical construction. You can correct the problem by revising the sentence like this:

Jude's actions were heroic and praiseworthy.

Always check for faulty parallelism in the following situations:

- When elements are linked by coordinating conjunctions (*and, but, for, or, nor, so,* or *yet*)

  For example, the phrase *interesting and to be remembered* should be changed to *interesting and memorable.*

- When elements are linked by correlative conjunctions (pairs of connector words such as *both ... and, not only ... but also, either ... or,* and *neither ... nor*)

  For example, the phrase *both kind and a generous person* should be changed to *both a kind and generous person.*

- When making comparisons

  For example, the phrase *Sophia's contribution is more noteworthy than Carla* should be changed to *Sophia's contribution is more noteworthy than Carla's.*

- When creating lists, headings, or outlines

  For example, *Kamal drove to work, turned in the report, and he returned home immediately afterward* should be changed to *Kamal drove to work, turned in the report, and returned home immediately afterward.*

Apply Knowledge of a Variety of Effective Structures (e.g., recognizing fragments, comma splices, run-on sentences, syntax errors)

A **clause** is a group of words that contains a subject and a verb. An **independent** or **main clause** can stand alone as a sentence. A **dependent** or **subordinate clause** begins with a subordinating conjunction (for example, *because, if, when*) or a relative pronoun (for example, *who, whom, that*) and can *never* stand alone.

A **simple sentence** is an example of an independent clause. It has a subject and a verb and expresses a complete thought. Look at this example:

My favorite subject is history.

A **fragment** is a group of words that looks like a sentence, but does not express a complete thought. A fragment is missing something. Sometimes it is missing a subject. Look at this fragment:

Didn't run fast enough.

This fragment needs a subject. Who or what didn't run fast enough? To make this fragment into a sentence, you can add a subject:

Jamie didn't run fast enough.

Sometimes a fragment is missing a verb. Look at this fragment:

Hundreds of screaming fans.

This fragment needs a verb. What did the hundreds of screaming fans do? To make this fragment into a sentence, you can add a verb:

Hundreds of screaming fans rushed through the gates.

Sometimes a fragment has a subject and a verb, but it still does not express a complete thought. This often occurs when the fragment is a subordinate clause. Look at this fragment:

Because I've always liked reading about real events.

To make this fragment into a sentence, you can add a main clause:

My favorite subject is history because I've always liked reading about real events.
Because I've always liked reading about real events, my favorite subject is history.

A **comma splice** is two independent clauses joined (spliced) *only* with a comma. Look at this comma splice:

The test was very hard to finish in the time allotted, it had too many questions on it.

A **run-on sentence** is two independent clauses joined without a proper punctuation mark to separate them or a word to connect them. Look at this run-on sentence:

Your first test in geometry is tomorrow you'd better study.

Correct run-on sentences and comma splices in one of these three ways:

1. Insert a period or a semicolon between the two independent clauses.
   Your first test in geometry is tomorrow. You'd better study.
   The test was very hard to finish in the time allotted; it had too many questions on it.
2. Insert a comma and a connector word (for example, *and, but, or, so*) between the two independent clauses.
   Your first test in geometry is tomorrow, so you'd better study.
3. Make one clause subordinate to the other.
   The test was very hard to finish in the time allotted because it had too many questions on it.

Determine Patterns of Organization in a Written Passage (i.e., modes of rhetoric)

Every written passage should present its information in a logical order. A sentence that is not presented in logical order is a sentence that is out of order or does not relate to its accompanying sentences. Look at this example of a written passage with sentences that are not in logical order:

Starving, Rover ate quickly from his favorite dish. We were relieved to have Rover home. Yet, no matter where we looked, we could not find our beloved pet. Quickly, we notified our neighbors that Rover was missing. Last week, we discovered our dog, Rover, was missing. Soon, everyone was looking for Rover. Finally, after a long, tiring week, Rover came home, hungry but healthy.

The way the passage is written is confusing to the reader because the sentences are not presented in a logical order. You must rearrange the sentences in your mind so that the passage begins to make sense.

You can correct the confusion by revising the passage like this:

Last week, we discovered our dog, Rover, was missing. Quickly, we notified our neighbors. Soon, everyone was looking for Rover. Yet, no matter where we looked, we could not find our beloved pet. Finally, after a long, tiring week, Rover came home, hungry but healthy. Starving, Rover ate quickly from his favorite dish. We were relieved to have Rover home.

Test Yourself

1. Choose the sentence in which the modifiers are placed correctly.
   A. Drifting down the river on a raft, the girls spotted a deer feeding her young fawn.
   B. Feeding her young fawn, the girls spotted a deer drifting down the river on a raft.
   C. The girls spotted a deer feeding her young fawn drifting down the river on a raft.

2. Choose the sentence that BEST represents parallel expressions.
   A. Angelo likes most soft drinks; orange juice is liked by him as well.
   B. Angelo likes most soft drinks; he likes cola and ginger ale especially.
   C. Angelo likes most soft drinks; he rarely drinks soft drinks.

3. Choose the sentence that BEST represents a run-on sentence.
   A. Maria enjoys reading a good book as she rests in her lawn chair beneath her favorite shade tree.
   B. Maria enjoys reading a good book; often, she reads in her lawn chair beneath her favorite shade tree.
   C. Maria enjoys reading a good book in her lawn chair beneath her favorite shade tree it is her preferred pastime on a summer day.

Directions: For questions 4–7, read the entire passage carefully and then answer the questions. (Note: Intentional errors have been included in this passage.)

Questions 4 and 5 are based on the following passage.

(1) Florida's citizens face many serious socioeconomic problems that may leave the state with fewer resources in the twenty-first century. (2) Each day, individuals from across the globe descend upon Florida's large coastal cities—Miami, Tampa, Jacksonville—seeking work and a place to live. (3) First, Florida is the home to many immigrant populations. (4) They come with the promise of finding a new life in America, having been led to believe in their native lands that America is the land of richness and opportunity. (5) And although some find untold riches, many find only minimum-paying jobs and unaffordable housing. (6) Second, with this constant influx, Florida's eligible school population rises exponentially. (7) As more families arrive, the demand for better and improved entertainment venues—from theme parks to restaurants and rodeos—increases. (8) Moreover, Florida, like elsewhere in the country, faces a growing teacher shortage that dramatically impacts the quality of the state's education program. (9) Finally, the gravest socioeconomic problems facing Florida are its serious environmental problems that will threaten proper growth and development. (10) Burgeoning populations mean a greater drain on fewer natural resources and less suitable land upon which to grow. (11) For example, drying up swampland for irrigation of farmland and proper disposal of litter become a constant concern as Florida's population increases uncontrollably. (12) Thus, unless Florida's citizens and leaders come to terms on how best to deal with these serious socioeconomic problems, Florida will soon find itself in a crisis for which there is no immediate solution.

4. Select the arrangement of sentences 1, 2, and 3 that provides the MOST logical sequence of ideas and supporting details in the paragraph. If no change is needed, select Choice A.

   A. (1) Florida's citizens face many serious socioeconomic problems that may leave the state with fewer resources in the twenty-first century. (2) Each day, individuals from across the globe descend upon Florida's large coastal cities—Miami, Tampa, Jacksonville—seeking work and a place to live. (3) First, Florida is the home to many immigrant populations.
   B. (3) First, Florida is the home to many immigrant populations. (1) Florida's citizens face many serious socioeconomic problems that may leave the state with fewer resources in the twenty-first century. (2) Each day, individuals from across the globe descend upon Florida's large coastal cities—Miami, Tampa, Jacksonville—seeking work and a place to live.
   C. (2) Each day, individuals from across the globe descend upon Florida's large coastal cities—Miami, Tampa, Jacksonville—seeking work and a place to live. (3) First, Florida is the home to many immigrant populations. (1) Florida's citizens face many serious socioeconomic problems that may leave the state with fewer resources in the twenty-first century.
   D. (1) Florida's citizens face many serious socioeconomic problems that may leave the state with fewer resources in the twenty-first century. (3) First, Florida is the home to many immigrant populations. (2) Each day, individuals from across the globe descend upon Florida's large coastal cities—Miami, Tampa, Jacksonville—seeking work and a place to live.

5. Which numbered sentence is the LEAST relevant to the passage?

   A. sentence 7
   B. sentence 8
   C. sentence 9
   D. sentence 10

Questions 6 and 7 are based on the following passage.

(1) A zoo is a place where animals—both wild and domesticated—are shown in captivity. (2) In such a special place, animals can be given the kind of care and nurturing that is possible in less protected and more natural preserves. (3) Most zoos show animals of all kinds and types; but in recent years, a few zoos have become more specialized in their approach. (4) Known for its family-oriented theme parks, Walt Disney World is on the cutting edge of animal conservation and research, nurturing and saving many animals throughout the world. (5) For example, at the Animal Kingdom theme park, animals of land, air, and sea are on display for all to see. (6) In Canada, there is African Lion Safari, in which visitors travel in their cars over a 50-acre reserve, where in excess of 1,000 animals from more than 100 species roam freely. (7) From the closeness of their vehicles, visitors see wildlife up close and personal. (8) And in Miami, Florida, one can find Parrot Jungle, a home for 1,100 tropical birds, all flying freely within the confines of the exhibit. (9) There, visitors can enjoy a leisurely lunch and listen to tourists complain about Miami's crowded beaches and roads. (10) Each of these specialized venues demonstrates how the concept of zoo has changed dramatically in the twentieth and twenty-first centuries.

6. Select the arrangement of sentences 4, 5, and 6 that provides the MOST logical sequence of ideas and supporting details in the paragraph. If no change is needed, select Choice A.

   A. (4) Known for its family-oriented theme parks, Walt Disney World is on the cutting edge of animal conservation and research, nurturing and saving many animals throughout the world. (5) For example, at the Animal Kingdom theme park, animals of land, air, and sea are on display for all to see. (6) In Canada, there is African Lion Safari, in which visitors travel in their cars over a 50-acre reserve, where in excess of 1,000 animals from more than 100 species roam freely.

   B. (5) For example, at the Animal Kingdom theme park, animals of land, air, and sea are on display for all to see. (4) Known for its family-oriented theme parks, Walt Disney World is on the cutting edge of animal conservation and research, nurturing and saving many animals throughout the world. (6) In Canada, there is African Lion Safari, in which visitors travel in their cars over a 50-acre reserve, where in excess of 1,000 animals from more than 100 species roam freely.

   C. (6) In Canada, there is African Lion Safari, in which visitors travel in their cars over a 50-acre reserve, where in excess of 1,000 animals from more than 100 species roam freely. (5) For example, at the Animal Kingdom theme park, animals of land, air, and sea are on display for all to see. (4) Known for its family-oriented theme parks, Walt Disney World is on the cutting edge of animal conservation and research, nurturing and saving many animals throughout the world.

   D. (4) Known for its family-oriented theme parks, Walt Disney World is on the cutting edge of animal conservation and research, nurturing and saving many animals throughout the world. (6) In Canada, there is African Lion Safari, in which visitors travel in their cars over a 50-acre reserve, where in excess of 1,000 animals from more than 100 species roam freely. (5) For example, at the Animal Kingdom theme park, animals of land, air, and sea are on display for all to see.

7. Which numbered sentence is the LEAST relevant to the passage?

   A. sentence 1
   B. sentence 8
   C. sentence 9
   D. sentence 10

Answers

1. **A.** The modifiers in Choice **A** are placed correctly. The participial phrase *drifting down the river on a raft* modifies *girls* and should be close to it. In Choices **B** and **C,** *drifting down the river on a raft* is separated from the noun *girls,* resulting in ambiguity. Additionally, the participial phrase *feeding her young fawn* modifies the noun *deer* and should be close to it. In Choice **B,** the participial phrase *feeding her young fawn* is separated from the noun *deer,* resulting in ambiguity.

2. **B.** Choice **B** is the best representation of parallel expressions. The parallel expressions—*Angelo likes most soft drinks* and *he likes cola and ginger ale especially*—are two independent clauses that complement each other and are separated, correctly, with a semicolon. In Choice **A,** the two independent clauses—*Angelo likes most soft* drinks and *orange juice is liked by him as well*— are not parallel to each other as the first is written in active voice and the second in passive voice. In Choice **C,** the two sentences—*Angelo likes most soft* drinks and *he rarely drinks soft* drinks—are not parallel because they contradict each other. Parallel expressions in the same sentence are related to each other in content and form.

3. **C.** Choice **C** is clearly the best representation of a run-on sentence. A run-on sentence is two independent clauses joined without a proper punctuation mark to separate them or a word to connect them. In Choice **A,** the sentence is one defined thought with defined detail that enhances the singular idea of the sentence. Choice **B** is an example of two clauses that complement each other—or parallel structure.

4. **D.** In paragraph, Choice **D** shows the arrangement of sentences 1, 2, and 3 that provides the most logical sequence of ideas and supporting details. Choices **A, B,** and **C** reflect an arrangement of sentences that are disconnected in thought and thus, are not logical choices.

5. **A.** In this paragraph, Choice **A** (sentence 7) is the least relevant to the passage. This sentence about Florida's lack of entertainment venues does not make sense in a paragraph in which the discussion is centered on Florida's ever-increasing socioeconomic needs.

6. **B.** In this paragraph, Choice **B** shows the arrangement of sentences 4, 5, and 6 that provides the most logical sequence of ideas and supporting details. Choices **A, C,** and **D** reflect an arrangement of sentences that are disconnected in thought and thus, are not logical choices.

7. **C.** In this paragraph, Choice **C** (sentence 9) is the least relevant to the passage. This sentence about sitting at Parrot Jungle and eating a leisurely lunch and listening to tourists complain about Miami's crowded beaches and roads does not make sense in a paragraph in which the discussion is centered on innovative venues to preserve wildlife animals.

Knowledge of Vocabulary Application

As listed in the *Competencies and Skills Required for Teacher Certification in Florida,* 20th Edition (www.fldoe.org/asp/ftce/pdf/ftce20edition.pdf), the English language competencies/skills you should master for this area are the following:

- Determine the meaning of unknown words, multiple-meaning words, and phrases in context.
- Determine and select the correct use of commonly confused words, misused words, and phrases.
- Determine diction and tone appropriate to a given audience.

Determine the Meaning of Unknown Words, Multiple-Meaning Words, and Phrases in Context

Choosing the appropriate word or expression in context is essential to good writing. When an inappropriate word or expression is chosen to complete a sentence, then the meaning of the sentence can be obstructed. Look at this example of a sentence with an inappropriate word choice:

Steven has the addiction of eating with his mouth open.

The sentence is poorly written because the word *addiction* is an inappropriate word choice for this sentence. The way the sentence is written, it sounds like eating with your mouth open is a severe and debilitating ailment that requires medical and psychological help, a description that clearly is not the intent of the writer.

You can correct this confusion by revising the sentence like this:

Steven has the habit of eating with his mouth open.

Furthermore, determining the meaning of unknown words, multiple-meaning words, and phrases in context are all required skills to become an effective writer. When selecting what words to use in a given sentence, writers should choose what they know to be true and not what "sounds good" to their ear. Often, fancy words and phrases can be misleading, creating a false understanding and/or impression with the reader.

Look at this example of a sentence with an inappropriate word choice:

Steven is a dilettante when it comes to the sport of baseball.

The sentence is poorly written because the writer has used a fancy word (*dilettante*) and an awkward phrase (*sport of baseball*) to describe his or her impression of Steven's poor playing skills. The sentence would be much better if the writer had simply written it as follows:

Steven acts like he knows how to play baseball.

Examine and Select the Correct Use of Commonly Confused Words, Misused Words, and Phrases

Often, writers incorrectly include **commonly confused or misused words or phrases** in their writing. These are words that may sound appropriate because they are used frequently in everyday language and written text; however, the use of an inappropriate word or expression in a sentence can obstruct the meaning of the sentence. Find the commonly confused or misused word in this example:

The mechanic will access the car's apparent engine trouble.

The sentence is poorly written because the word *access* is an inappropriate choice for this sentence. The writer meant to use the more appropriate word *assess*. The word *access* means "the ability to enter or approach"; the word *assess* means "to evaluate a problem or concern."

You can correct the confusion by revising the sentence like this:

The mechanic will assess the car's apparent engine trouble.

Here is a list of some words or phrases that are commonly confused or misused:

accede—to agree with

*The lawyers will **accede** to the judge's request for more time for the defendant to prepare his case.*

concede—to yield, to compromise, or to grant, but not really agree

*I **concede** that I lack the strength to become an Olympic runner, but I still intend to try.*

exceed—to be more than

*My daily intake of vitamins **exceeds** the minimum daily requirement.*

access—the ability to enter or approach

*The small crowd that assembled at the Vatican was given **access** to see His Holiness, the Pope.*

assess—to evaluate a problem or concern

*Before we proceed, we should **assess** the situation more carefully.*

excess—more than enough

*Our monthly grocery bill is far in **excess** of the money we have allotted to spend.*

accept—to take or to receive

*I will **accept** only a handful of applications.*

except—to exclude (preposition)

*They did not leave the house **except** to buy groceries, get the mail, and walk the dog.*

except—to leave out (verb)

*Everyone was charged admission to the park, but the children were **excepted.***

except—to object (verb)

*The lawyer **excepted** to the judge's ruling that the witness be allowed to testify.*

adapt—to modify or to change

*Most of my colleagues can **adapt** to the sudden mood changes of our boss.*

adopt—to take on or to assume

*The young couple decided to **adopt** a baby from China.*

adept—to be skillful or to have aptitude

*The star athlete was **adept** at playing many sports, most notably football, hockey, and baseball.*

affect—to influence (verb)

*The cold wind and rain will **affect** your health.*

effect—the outcome or consequence (noun)

*The **effect** of the last hurricane is still felt among the residents of the badly damaged village.*

effect—to cause change or accomplish (verb)

*The unexpected blizzard **effected** a dramatic lack of activity at the ski resort; patrons wanted to ski, but were stuck inside for several days until it became safe to go out on the slopes.*

all ready—to have everyone or everything together and prepared

*The students were **all ready** to take the examination when the teacher arrived.*

already—to have come before or to have happened previously

*The dancers had **already** been practicing their routines when their director entered the room.*

all right—to be acceptable or to be agreeable

*As long as you practice for an hour, going to the movies is **all right** with me.*
(**alright** is not a word; it is always spelled as two words: **all right**.)

all together—to include everybody or everything

*At the end of the campfire, the two competing camp tribes sang the closing songs **all together**.*

altogether—to be totally inclusive

*Without a doubt, I was **altogether** confused by his sudden change of mood.*

all ways—to include every possible way

*To our chagrin, the laziest student was in **all ways** amenable to doing the least amount of schoolwork.*

always—to happen at all times

*His sense of humor was **always** present when he was around a crowd of people.*

a lot—to include a large number

*There were **a lot** of people at tonight's ice-hockey game.*
(**alot** is not a word; it is always spelled as two words: **a lot**.)

among—refers to three or more people or things

*At the end of the day, the grandfather made sure that his hugs and kisses were evenly distributed **among** his four grandchildren.*

between—refers to only two people or things

*I had to decide **between** going to the movies or staying home; I stayed home.*

amount—refers to uncountable quantities that are measured in bulk

*We had a large **amount** of grain stored in a bin to be used during the long winter months.*

number—refers to quantities that can be counted

*I counted the **number** of bags of candy; and there were approximately 36, one for each child present.*

as—refers to a similarity or to the same extent

*The film wasn't nearly **as** bad as you made it out to be.*

like—to resemble something or to be similar to

*That cat is **like** a small tiger.*

both—refers to two things considered together

***Both** of them were being considered for the high school honor award.*

each—refers to only one of two or more things

*The wrestling coach made sure that **each** member of the team wrestled in the competition.*

can—to be physically able to complete a task

*The little boy **can** tie his shoes without his mother's help.*

may—to ask (or be given) permission to complete a task

*"**May** I leave my dessert and go out and play?" the young girl asked her grandmother.*
*"You **may** be seated," said the pastor to the congregation.*

capital—refers to the city; the town wherein the seat of government resides

*This vacation, we are visiting the old and beautiful town of Albany, the **capital** of New York.*

Capitol—refers to the building; the building that houses the United States Congress

*All eyes were on the Washington **Capitol** as the nation waited to hear the vote on the impending legislation.*

cease—to end or to bring to a conclusion

*Soon, the army will **cease** its fire and set up camp for the night.*

seize—to take hold of or to capture

*In short order, the detectives will **seize** the unsuspecting thief.*

cite—to summon to court; to quote; to mention in a citation

*The officer **cited** the suspect for breaking and entering.*
*Responsible writers **cite** the sources of their material.*

sight—to glimpse or view with the eyes or mind (or something glimpsed or viewed)

*The balloon rose higher and higher until it disappeared from **sight**.*
*Listening to Paul's defense of his actions caused Sheila to lose **sight** of her original complaint.*

site—the place where something is, was, or will be

*Gettysburg National Military Park in southeastern Pennsylvania is the **site** of the Battle of Gettysburg.*

coarse—vulgar or unduly rude

***Coarse** mannerisms are repulsive to most people.*

course—a path

*Looking straight ahead, the captain told the first mate to steer the ship on a **course** heading due north.*

course—prescribed studies

*After looking at the schedule, I have decided to take another geometry **course**.*

complement—to complete a part or to bring to perfection

*Your brand new black-and-white checked shirt **complements** your black Bermuda shorts.*

compliment—to praise or to show admiration for

*I paid my sister a **compliment** for the wonderful love and care she gives my new baby boy.*

desert—a dry arid piece of land (noun)

*The army heads to the **desert**, equipped with plenty of water, sunscreen, and dark glasses.*

desert—to abandon or to leave behind (verb)

*When we go to the mall, my mother always **deserts** us and heads right for the latest sales.*

dessert—the final course of a meal

*My favorite **dessert** is a strawberry ice cream sundae, complete with real whipped cream and a cherry.*

disinterested—to be impartial or without judgment

*The bystander served as a **disinterested** witness to the accident.*

uninterested—to show no interest or fondness for

*Jack and Barbara are **uninterested** in anything Mary and Bill do or say.*

either ... or—to be used when referring to choices

*"**Either** we go to the Grand Canyon **or** we explore the Rocky Mountains this summer," my father said emphatically. "We cannot do both."*

neither ... nor—to be used when referring to two unacceptable or unlikely choices

***Neither** you **nor** I have any real chance of winning the position of Student Council President.*

eligible—to be acceptable or chosen

*Lauren's winning ticket number makes her **eligible** to become the next recipient of an all-expense paid vacation to Hawaii.*

ineligible—to be unacceptable or not chosen

*Because she was under twelve, Marie was **ineligible** to ride on the high-speed roller coaster by herself.*

illegible—to be difficult or nearly impossible to read or understand

*The doctor's handwriting was **illegible**, making it difficult for the pharmacist to read the prescription.*

emigrate—to leave one's native country for a new country

*Most of America's Jewish people **emigrated** from Eastern Europe prior to the start of World War II.*

immigrate—to enter and live in a new country

*In June, I will **immigrate** to South Africa to live with my aunt and uncle.*

elicit—to call forth or draw out

*My shocking red hair always **elicits** the strangest looks.*

illicit—to be not sanctioned by custom or law; to be unlawful

*Underage drinking is **illicit** behavior.*

fewer—refers to people and things that can be counted by hand; used for plural nouns

*There are **fewer** people on hand for the store's grand opening than were anticipated.*

less—refers to people and things that are usually considered in mass numbers; used for singular nouns

*I have **less** gas than I imagined.*

formally—to be considered in an official and dignified manner

*When we went to see the Justice of the Peace, my boyfriend was dressed **formally**.*

formerly—refers to an earlier time or position

***Formerly** a member of the United States Congress, my uncle now teaches at Harvard.*

if—introduces a conditional statement

If I exercise regularly, I will certainly lose weight.

whether—refers to introducing a decision or choice

Whether you win or lose depends not on how hard you practice, but on how lucky you prove to be.

weather—refers to the general climate

When we were in Arizona, the weather was hot but dry; there was little humidity.

imply—to suggest, to hint, or to indicate indirectly

By asking you about your hair color, I did not mean to imply that I thought you dyed it.

infer—to deduce, to conclude, or to conclude from evidence

"Are we to infer that you simply do not care about your schoolwork?" the desperate mother asked her tenth-grade son when he showed his parents his poor report card.

incite—to provoke and to urge on

"The politician's inflammatory language is sure to incite the crowd to riot," thought the police officer standing watch.

insight—the ability to discern the true nature of something

The news commentator had much insight into why the President was so reluctant to tell the nation the truth.

peak—the highest part of anything

Climbing to the peak of Mount Everest is considered to be a great feat of courage and determination.

peek—to glance or look quickly, to look furtively from behind or through something

Toto gave Dorothy, the Scarecrow, the Tin Man, and the Lion more than just a peek at the so-called wizard.

persecute—to torture or to make life horrible for someone

We should not persecute people whose beliefs are different from ours.

prosecute—to conduct a criminal investigation or to take legal action against someone

After much deliberation, the district attorney decided to prosecute the accused for manslaughter.

precede—to come before

We will precede the marching bands and floats as we lead the Christmas parade down Main Street.

proceed—to move on ahead

After being given the proper verification, we will proceed with the experimentation of the new cancer drug.

supersede—to replace or to take the place of

It is more than likely that our initial discovery will supersede in knowledge and importance all our latest discoveries.

principal—the head or main leader of an organization; the building supervisor of a school (noun)

After school, the new principal was introduced to the anticipating faculty.

principal—main or chief (adjective)

The principal reason for the meeting is to elect a new president.

principle—a basic and fundamental truth, value, or belief (noun)

Conan believes in the principle of treating every individual with kindness and respect.

respectably—acting in a decent and moral manner

*"When attending a formal function, you should dress **respectably**," admonished my socially conscious mother.*

respectfully—marked by a proper manner

*Despite sitting in the cramped and crowded gym bleachers for over an hour, the students listened **respectfully** to the school assembly's guest speaker.*

respectively—refers to the order mentioned or designated

*The first contestant and the second contestant were Jan and Jill, **respectively**.*

their—is the possessive form; refers to belonging to a group of people

***Their** plane arrived late because of inclement weather.*

there—is the directional word; refers to a specific place

*I saw my many friends from school walk over **there** to the ice cream store.*

they're—is the contraction for *they are*

*After the movies, **they're** coming with us to the diner for dinner.*

then—is used to refer to time or consequence

*After holding up the convenience mart, the perpetrator was **then** tried, found guilty, and incarcerated.*
*If this is true, **then** the butler must be the murderer.*

than—is used to compare or contrast things

*He is smarter **than** his younger brother.*

two—is the number 2

*The teacher had only **two** tickets left for the field trip to the ballet.*

to—is the directional word

*I went **to** the grocery store to buy my mother's favorite cookies.*

too—means more than or also

*The young campers wanted to go hiking in the mountains, **too**.*

your—is the possessive form; refers to belonging to one person

*"I am sure **your** mother will not want you to sleep in the backyard without a sleeping bag," my best friend's dad said to me just before our sleepover.*

you're—is the contraction for *you are*

*When **you're** ready, we will leave for the train station.*

Determine Diction and Tone Appropriate to a Given Audience

The vocabulary and manner of presentation in a passage must be appropriate for the intended audience and purpose. Would you talk to police officers and attorneys the same way you would to a group of 4-year-olds in a preschool? Recognizing diction and tone appropriate to a given audience is essential to good writing. **Diction** refers to the choice of words and their arrangement. **Tone** is the attitude adopted by the speaker or writer to be communicated or transferred to the listener or reader. When diction or tone for a given sentence is inappropriate, the intent of the author's meaning can be unclear to the reader.

Look at this example of a sentence that is inappropriate in its diction or tone:

As the new student body president, Michael addressed his high school teachers during the faculty meeting by shouting, "Hey, teachers! What's up?"

Clearly, Michael should not have addressed his high school teachers in such a loose and cavalier fashion. Michael's teachers are not his friends or relatives. You can correct this inappropriate diction and tone by revising the sentence like this:

As the new student body president, Michael addressed his high school teachers during the faculty meeting by saying, "Good afternoon, ladies and gentlemen. As the new student body president, I would like to tell you ...."

Test Yourself

Directions: For questions 1–3, choose the *most* appropriate word to complete the sentence.

1. After the football game, the players on the losing team _____ their mistakes and discussed how they could improve their game.

   A. reviewed
   B. reminded
   C. received
   D. relished

2. With seconds left, the frightened family _____ quickly into the shelter, hoping to escape the path of the oncoming storm.

   A. ambled
   B. sauntered
   C. scurried
   D. meandered

3. Filled with trepidation, the little child stepped _____ onto the roller coaster.

   A. eagerly
   B. hurriedly
   C. gingerly
   D. willingly

Directions: For questions 4–13, choose the option that corrects an error in an underlined portion. If no error exists, choose D indicating "No change is necessary."

4. The principle talked to everyone, except the misbehaving boys' parents.
       A   B   C

   A. principal
   B. every one
   C. accept
   D. No change is necessary.

5. "Either you go to school nor stay home," said the child's father.
           A B   C

   A. you're
   B. goes
   C. or
   D. No change is necessary.

6. After their school day, the talented young boys took an extra coarse in math.
　　　　　A　　　　　　　　　　　　　　　　　　　B　　　　　　C

　　A. they're
　　B. have taken
　　C. course
　　D. No change is necessary.

7. Upon finishing their dessert, the two lovers preceded to walk home, enjoying the cool weather.
　　　　　　　　　　　　　　A　　　　　　　　　　　　　B　　　　　　　　　　　　　　　　　　　C

　　A. desert
　　B. proceeded
　　C. whether
　　D. No change is necessary.

8. Their insights about the upcoming elections were most appreciated by the graduate students in political science.
　　　A　　B　　　　　　　　　　　　　　　　　　C

　　A. They're
　　B. incites
　　C. was
　　D. No change is necessary.

9. Your brother is more helpful then everyone else all together.
　　　A　　　　　　　　　　　　　B　　　　　　　　　　C

　　A. You're
　　B. than
　　C. altogether
　　D. No change is necessary.

10. Only 13 years old, he is ineligible to play varsity baseball.
　　　　　　　　　　　　　　　A　　B　　　C

　　A. are
　　B. uneligible
　　C. too
　　D. No change is necessary.

11. Despite the great weather, we were disinterested in sitting among the team players and watching the game.
　　　　　　　　　　　A　　　　　　　　　　　B　　　　　　　　　　C

　　A. whether
　　B. uninterested
　　C. between
　　D. No change is necessary.

12. All afternoon, everyone except Mother complemented me on my new dress.
　　　　　　　　　　　　　　　　A　　　B　　　　　C

　　A. accept
　　B. mother
　　C. complimented
　　D. No change is necessary.

13. We'll need to decide among two places to visit.
　　　A　　　　　　　　　　B　　　　　　　　C

　　A. Will
　　B. between
　　C. too
　　D. No change is necessary.

Directions: For questions 14 and 15, choose the most appropriate option to answer the question.

14. Angelo, president of the student debate team, is speaking to his community's civic club about the need for the debate team to raise money for their trip to participate in the national debate championship.

    Choose the most appropriate opening statement.

    A. "My friends and fellow citizens, please attend to the following observations as I proceed to enumerate the many substantial reasons that you should choose to sponsor the illustrious debate team's winning journey."
    B. "As you are well aware, the high school debate team plays a vital role in helping students understand today's social issues."
    C. "Hey, have you noticed? The debate team has no money."
    D. "The debate team is lots of fun. Would you be willing to give us some money so we can go to the championship game?"

15. Luisa is a student of unexpected fortitude, tenacity, perseverance, and intelligence with an extraordinary capacity to make her most minimal movement a startling and revealing portrait of who she is in a realistic and demonstrable light of understanding.

    Choose the most appropriate rewording of this sentence

    A. Luisa knows how to speak well before her peers.
    B. Luisa is an individual with great poise and intellect.
    C. Luisa knows her stuff.
    D. Luisa reads, writes, and speaks well.

Answers

1. **A.** In this sentence, the missing word is *reviewed* (Choice **A**), meaning "to evaluate or assess," as in *the losing team reviewed their mistakes.* Choices **B, C,** and **D** are not logical selections, given the context of this sentence. Choice **B** is the word *reminded,* and you would not write "the losing team reminded their mistakes." Choice **C** is the word *received,* and although you might write "the losing team received their mistakes," it is not the most logical choice. Choice **D** is the word *relished,* meaning "to enjoy." Clearly, a losing team would not relish their mistakes.

2. **C.** In this sentence, the missing word is *scurried* (Choice **C**), meaning "to dash or rush," as in *the frightened family scurried into the shelter.* Choices **A, B,** and **D** are not logical selections, given the context of this sentence. Choice **A,** *ambled,* means "to stroll or wander," and you would not write *the frightened family ambled into the shelter.* Choice **B,** *sauntered,* means "to amble or walk," and you would not write *the frightened family sauntered into the shelter.* Choice **D,** *meandered,* means "to ramble or roam," and you would not write *the frightened family meandered into the shelter.* Clearly, a frightened family would *scurry* in the face of an impending storm.

3. **C.** In this sentence, the missing word is *gingerly* (Choice **C**), meaning "cautiously or tentatively," as in *the little girl stepped gingerly onto the roller coaster.* Choices **A, B,** and **D** are not logical selections, given the context of this sentence. Choice **A,** *eagerly,* implies enthusiastically, and you would not write *Filled with trepidation (or fear), the little girl stepped enthusiastically onto the roller coaster.* Choice **B,** *hurriedly,* implies quickly, and you would not write *Filled with trepidation, the little girl stepped hurriedly onto the roller coaster.* Choice **D,** *willingly,* implies without hesitation, and you would not write *Filled with trepidation, the little girl stepped willingly onto the roller coaster.* Clearly, the word *gingerly* is the most logical choice to demonstrate the little girl's fear.

4. **A.** In this sentence, the word *principle* should be replaced with the word *principal* (Choice **A**). The word *principle* means "a standard or a belief," whereas the word *principal* means "a school administrator." In Choice **B**, the word *everyone* is used as a pronoun, and thus is spelled correctly. In Choice **C**, the word *except,* meaning "to leave out," is used correctly.

5. **C.** In this sentence, the word *nor* should be replaced with the word *or* (Choice **C**). *Either ... or* is used when referring to choices; *Neither ... nor* is used when referring to negative choices. In Choice **A,** the pronoun *you* is used correctly. In Choice **B,** the correct form of the verb *to go* is used correctly.

6. **C.** In this sentence, the word *coarse* should be replaced with the word *course* (Choice **C**). The word *coarse* is an adjective meaning "rough or abrasive." The word *course,* though, is a noun of which one of its meanings is "a lesson or a class." In Choice **A,** the word *their,* indicating possession, is used correctly. In Choice **B,** the word *took,* the correct verb form of the word *taken,* is used correctly.

7. **B.** In this sentence, the word *preceded* should be replaced with the word *proceeded* (Choice **B**). The word *preceded* means "to come before," whereas the word *proceeded* means "to go ahead." In Choice **A,** the word *dessert,* meaning "a sweet dish served after a meal," is used correctly. In Choice **C,** the word *weather* is used correctly.

8. **D.** In this sentence, no changes are necessary. Choices **A, B,** and **C** are used correctly.

9. **B.** In this sentence, the word *then* should be replaced with the word *than* (Choice **B**). The word *then* refers to time or consequences; the word *than* refers to comparing and/or contrasting things. In Choice **A,** the word *your,* the possessive form of *you,* is used correctly. In Choice **C,** the phrase *all together,* meaning "everybody or everything," is used correctly.

10. **D.** In this sentence, no changes are necessary. Choices **A, B,** and **C** are used correctly.

11. **B.** In this sentence, the word *disinterested* should be replaced with *uninterested* (Choice **B**). The word *disinterested* means "impartial"; the word *uninterested* means "not interested." In Choice **A,** the word *weather* is used correctly. In Choice **C,** the word *among,* used when referring to more than two people or things, is used correctly.

12. **C.** In this sentence, the word *complemented* should be replaced with the word *complimented* (Choice **C**). The word *complemented* means "a completing or finishing part." The word *compliment* means "an expression of admiration." In Choice **A,** the word *except,* meaning "excluding," is used correctly. In Choice **B,** the word *Mother* is capitalized correctly because the name refers to a specific person in the family.

13. **B.** In this sentence, the word *among* should be replaced with the word *between* (Choice **B**). The word *among* is used when referring to more than two people or things; the word *between* is used when referring to only two people or things. In Choice **A,** the word *We'll,* the contraction of *we will,* is used correctly. In Choice **C,** the word *to,* meaning "in the direction of," is used correctly.

14. **B.** In this question, the most appropriate opening statement is Choice **B**. The high school student speaks in a reasonable tone. Choice **A** reflects a ponderous and obsequious tone. Choice **C** is much too casual for a high school student speaking to a civic club. Choice **D** is not as casual as Choice **C,** but still seems to lack the dignity and respect that a student should demonstrate when speaking to a civic club.

15. **B.** In this question, the most appropriate response is Choice **B**. Luisa is an individual with great poise and intellect. Choice **A** reflects an idea that is not mentioned in the sentence (that she *knows how to speak well before her peers*). Choice **C** is much too casual and vague to convey the real meaning of the overly wordy, yet well-intentioned sentence. Choice **D** is probably correct, but does not fully convey the intention of the initial statement as Choice **B** does.

Knowledge of Standard English Conventions

As listed in the *Competencies and Skills Required for Teacher Certification in Florida,* 20th Edition (www.fldoe.org/asp/ftce/pdf/ftce20edition.pdf), the English language competencies/skills you should have mastered for this area are the following:

- Determine and select standard verb forms.
- Determine and select inappropriate shifts in verb tense.

- Determine and select agreement between subject and verb.
- Determine and select agreement between pronoun and antecedent.
- Determine and select inappropriate pronoun shifts.
- Determine and select clear pronoun references.
- Determine and select pronoun case forms (e.g., subjective, objective, possessive).
- Evaluate the correct use of adjectives and adverbs.
- Determine and select appropriate comparative and superlative degree forms.
- Demonstrate command of standard spelling conventions.
- Demonstrate command of standard punctuation.
- Demonstrate command of standard capitalization.

Determine and Select Standard Verb Forms

Verbs—action words—have different forms called **tenses.**

The **tense** of a verb in a sentence tells you when the action of the verb takes place. For the FTCE GK Test, you will need to know the **simple tenses** and the **perfect tenses**. The simple tenses are the **present tense** (*I work, he writes*), the **past tense** (*I worked, he wrote*), and the **future tense** (*I will work, he will write*).

The perfect tenses use a form of the helping verb *have* in their construction. The perfect tenses are the **present perfect** (*I have worked, he has written*), which indicates a past action that is ongoing; the **past perfect** (*I had worked, he had written*), which indicates a past action that occurred before a previous past action; and the **future perfect** (*I will have worked, he will have written*), which indicates a past action that will occur before a future action.

The tenses of a verb are formed using three **principal parts (or forms):** present (*work*), past (*worked*), and past participle (*worked*). For **regular verbs,** the past and past participle are formed by adding *–ed*. Some verbs do not form their past and past participle this way. These verbs are **irregular verbs.** Table 2.1 lists the principal parts of 27 frequently used irregular verbs that you should memorize in preparation for the FTCE GK Test.

Table 2.1 Principal Parts of 27 Frequently Used Irregular Verbs

Present	begin	break	bring	catch	choose	come	do	drink	drive
Past	began	broke	brought	caught	chose	came	did	drank	drove
Past participle	begun	broken	brought	caught	chosen	come	done	drunk	driven

Present	eat	fall	get	give	go	grow	know	lose	ride
Past	ate	fell	got	gave	went	grew	knew	lost	rode
Past participle	eaten	fallen	gotten	given	gone	grown	known	lost	ridden

Present	rise	run	see	sing	speak	swim	take	throw	write
Past	rose	ran	saw	sang	spoke	swam	took	threw	wrote
Past participle	risen	run	seen	sung	spoken	swum	taken	thrown	written

Determine and Select Inappropriate Shifts in Verb Tense

Sometimes a writer will start a sentence with one tense and shift to another tense for no logical reason. This error is an **inappropriate tense shift.** Look at this example of an inappropriate tense shift:

My fearless sister walks up to the tiger and quickly took a picture.

This sentence starts off in the present tense, but then shifts to the past tense for no reason. This shifting of tenses is distracting and confusing to the reader. Revise the sentence by using the same tense for both verbs:

My fearless sister walked up to the tiger and quickly took a picture.

Determine and Select Agreement Between Subject and Verb

Subject-verb agreement means a singular subject must have a singular verb and a plural subject must have a plural verb. In other words, a subject and its verb must agree *in number*. To make sure the subject and verb agree, you need to be able to identify the subject of the sentence, decide whether it is singular or plural, and then match the verb accordingly. If the subject is singular, the verb will end in *–s* or *–es* (*the dog barks, the bird flies*). If the subject is plural, the verb will *not* have an *–s* or *–es* ending (*the dogs bark, the birds fly*).

Errors in subject-verb agreement may occur when other words in the sentence separate the subject and verb. Look at this example of an error in subject-verb agreement:

A chorus of cheers were heard from the crowd.

The verb must agree with its singular noun subject *chorus,* not the plural word *cheers*. Change *were* to *was* to make the sentence grammatically correct:

A chorus of cheers was heard from the crowd.

To help with recognizing errors in subject-verb agreement, read the sentence without the intervening words. Try this example:

The president of the club, as well as the other officers, feel that the membership dues need to be raised.

The subject of the verb is *president*. Does *The president… feel* sound correct to you? Change *feel* to *feels* to make the sentence grammatically correct:

The president of the club, as well as the other officers, feels that the membership dues need to be raised.

It should be noted that if the sentence began with *The president and the other officers of the club …* , the verb would be *feel*:

The president and the other officers of the club feel that the membership dues need to be raised.

The reason for using the word *feel* in this example is that *the president and the other officers of the club* is regarded as a plural subject and thus requires a plural verb to complete the sentence.

The contractions *doesn't* and *don't* can also cause errors in subject-verb agreement.

Doesn't is a contraction of *does not,* so it is used when you have a singular subject. *Don't* is a contraction of *do not,* so it is used when you have a plural subject.

For example, change *He don't like me* to *He doesn't like me.*

> **Tip:** When in doubt, mentally substitute *does not* for *doesn't* and *do not* for *don't* to see which sounds correct.

When two or more subjects are joined by the word *or* or *nor,* the verb agrees with the noun that is closest to the verb. Look at these examples:

The woman's children or her husband has the videotape of the event.

Neither the teacher nor the students care that the bell has rung.

Most indefinite pronouns (for example, *each, everyone, everybody*) take singular verbs. Look at this example:

Everybody needs to bring a sack lunch to the picnic.

The words *there* and *here* are never subjects, so look for the subject to come after the verb.

For example, change *There is many reasons to be upset* to *There are many reasons to be upset*.

For further clarification, see the section on pronoun-antecedent agreement that follows.

Determine and Select Agreement Between Pronoun and Antecedent

A **pronoun** stands for or refers to a person, place, or thing whose identity is made clear earlier in the text. The noun to which a pronoun refers is the pronoun's **antecedent.** Look at the following example:

Dentists are concerned with oral health. They say that flossing is good for your gums.

In this example, *They* is a pronoun referring to the antecedent *Dentists.*

A pronoun must agree with its **antecedent,** the noun it replaces. Therefore, if the antecedent is singular, the pronoun must be singular; if the antecedent is plural, the pronoun must be plural; if the antecedent is feminine, the pronoun must be a feminine pronoun; and so on.

Errors in pronoun-antecedent agreement make it difficult for the reader to understand what the writer means. Look at this example:

A woman who works hard to achieve success may find they are not accepted as equals in certain situations.

The pronoun *they* does not agree with its singular antecedent, *woman.* Change *they are* to *she is* to make the sentence grammatically correct. Also change *equals* to *an equal:*

A woman who works hard to achieve success may find she is not accepted as an equal in certain situations.

Most indefinite pronoun antecedents (for example, *each, everyone, everybody*) take singular pronouns. Look at this example:

Each of the girls needs to obtain her parents' permission to go on the trip.

The pronoun *her* agrees with its singular antecedent, *each.*

For further clarification on pronoun-antecedent agreement, see the section on subject-verb agreement earlier in this chapter.

Determine and Select Inappropriate Pronoun Shifts

The **form** of a personal pronoun tells you whether the pronoun is the speaker (**first person**—*I talk; we talk*), the person spoken to (**second person**—*you talk*), or the person spoken about (**third person**—*he, she, it talks; they talk*).

Pronouns should have the same person form as their antecedents. When a writer fails to do this, the resulting faulty construction is an **inappropriate pronoun shift.** Look at this example of an inappropriate pronoun shift:

If one studies hard for the test, you will make a good grade.

The sentence goes from third person (*one*) to the second person (*you*). To fix, you can revise the sentence like this:

If you study hard for the test, you will make a good grade.

Determine and Select Clear Pronoun References

When a writer uses a pronoun, it should be clear to the reader what the antecedent for the pronoun is. When it is unclear, the reader may find the sentence ambiguous. Look at this example of an unclear pronoun reference:

My mother removed the roses from the two vases and threw them in the trash.

What did the mother throw in the trash? The *roses* or the *vases*? The pronoun *they* does not have a clear reference. You can revise the sentence (so that it has a clear pronoun reference) like this:

My mother removed the roses from the two vases and threw the flowers in the trash.

Determine and Select Pronoun Case Forms (e.g., subjective, objective, possessive)

Case shows the function of a pronoun in a sentence. The form of the pronoun tells you whether the pronoun is a subject (**subjective case**—*I, you, he, she, it, we, they, who, whoever*), an object (**objective case**—*me, you, him, her, it, us, them, whom, whomever*), or shows ownership (**possessive case**—*my, mine, her, hers, his, its, our, ours, your, yours, their, theirs, whose*).

Use the subjective case when the pronoun is the subject of a verb or has an antecedent that is the subject of a verb. Look at these examples:

My spouse and I often travel abroad.

The pronoun *I* is in the subjective case because it is part of the subject of the verb *travel*.

The coach gave tickets to whoever arrived first.

The relative pronoun *whoever* is in the subjective case because it is the subject of the verb *arrived*.

Use the objective case when the pronoun is the object of a verb or a verbal (a verb form used as a noun, adjective, or adverb), the object of a preposition, or the subject of an infinitive. Look at these examples:

Ask whomever you want.

The relative pronoun *whomever* is in the objective case because it is the object of the verb *want*.

I hope there will be no secrets between you and me.

The pronoun *me* is in the objective case because it is the object of the preposition *between*.

I could not believe that the committee invited her to serve as master of ceremonies at the banquet.

The pronoun *her* is in the objective case because it is the subject of the infinitive *to serve*.

Use the possessive case when the pronoun shows ownership or if it precedes a gerund (the *–ing* form of a verb used as noun). Look at these examples:

Her jewelry is exquisite.

The pronoun *her* is in the possessive case because it shows ownership of the noun *jewelry*.

His interrupting every few minutes is becoming annoying.

The pronoun *his* is in the possessive case because it precedes the gerund *interrupting*.

Evaluate the Correct Use of Adjectives and Adverbs

Adjectives and **adverbs** are modifiers that describe things or actions in a sentence. **Adjectives** modify nouns or pronouns. **Adverbs** modify verbs, adjectives, or other adverbs.

To decide whether a word used as a modifier is an adjective or an adverb, ask yourself what word does the modifier describe? If it describes a noun or pronoun, it is an adjective. If it describes a verb, adjective, or other adverb, it is an adverb. Look at these examples:

The <u>rotten</u> fruit smells <u>bad</u>.

In this sentence the word *rotten* describes the noun *fruit*, so *rotten* is an adjective. The word *bad* following the verb *smells* also tells you something about the noun *fruit*—that it has a bad odor. Therefore, the word *bad* is an adjective describing the noun *fruit*.

> The racer drove <u>slowly</u> as he passed the accident on the track.

In this sentence the word *slowly* following the verb *drove* tells how the racer drove, so *slowly* is an adverb describing the verb *drove*.

On the FTCE GK Test, you will need to recognize incorrect use of adjectives or adverbs. Be wary when the verb in the sentence is based on one of your senses (*feel, taste, smell, look, sound*) or is a form of the verb *to be*. Usually, adjectives should follow such verbs. Here is an example of incorrect construction:

> I feel <u>badly</u> that I missed your college graduation.

The modifier after the verb *feel* describes the pronoun *I*, so it should be an adjective, not an adverb. Replace *badly* with *bad* to make the sentence grammatically correct:

> I feel <u>bad</u> that I missed your college graduation.

Here is another example:

> He ran <u>quick</u> and turned off the alarm.

The modifier *quick* describes the verb *ran*, so it should be an adverb, not an adjective. Replace *quick* with *quickly* to make the sentence grammatically correct:

> He ran <u>quickly</u> and turned off the alarm.

Determine and Select Appropriate Comparative and Superlative Degree Forms

When you compare two things, you either add *–er* to the modifier or precede the modifier with the word *more* or *less*. The resulting grammatical construction is the **comparative** form of the adjective or adverb. When you compare more than two things, you either add *–est* to the modifier or precede the modifier with the word *most* or *least*. The resulting grammatical construction is the **superlative** form of the adjective or adverb.

Use *–er* to form the comparative and *–est* to form the superlative of most one-syllable adjectives and adverbs. For most two-syllable adjectives and adverbs, you can use *–er* and *–est*, *more* and *most*, or *less* and *least*. With all adjectives and adverbs of three or more syllables, use *more* and *most* or *less* and *least*. Look at these examples:

> The boy on the left is taller than the boy on the right, but the boy in the middle is the tallest of all three.

> The lab assistant poured the liquid more (or less) carefully the second time than he did the first time.

> **Tip: You'll often find the word *than* used with an adjective or adverb to form the comparative. *The cheetah ran faster than the antelope. Peggy's book bag is larger than Alicia's.***

If an adverb ends in *–ly*, change the *–y* to *–i* when using the *–er* or *–est* ending. Look at this example:

> Sam is lucky, but Kendra is luckier than he.

When making a comparison, do not include the person or thing being compared. Look at this example:

> That movie is more entertaining than any movie currently in theaters.

This sentence says that the movie is more entertaining than itself! To correct this misunderstanding, revise the sentence as follows:

That movie is more entertaining than any other movie currently in theaters.

The word *other* is needed to make the sentence logical.

Some common adjectives and adverbs have irregular forms (*good/well, better, the best; bad/badly, worse, the worst*). Look at these examples:

Kim submitted a good essay, but Juan's was better because it was more interesting. When your essay is due, you should try to write the best one of all.

My favorite driver drove badly in the race last week. This week he drove worse than before. Frankly, I think he drove the worst of all the drivers in the race.

Avoid redundant constructions like *more better, most easiest,* and so on:

*The room temperature is better (not **more better**) after you lowered the thermostat.*

*That was the easiest (not **most easiest**) exam I have ever taken.*

> **Tip: For some adjectives and adverbs, such as *unique, universal,* and *perfect,* it is illogical to form comparative and superlative forms. These words are absolute in their meaning, so constructions like *more unique* or *most unique,* for example, should be avoided.**

Demonstrate Command of Standard Spelling Conventions

Standard written English has many rules for spelling. This section describes the basic rules that should prove most helpful on the FTCE GK Test.

Memorize the following guidelines for correct spelling:

- When you know a word contains *ie* or *ei,* recall the following rhyme:

  i before *e,* except after *c,*

  Or when sounding like "*ay*" as in *neighbor* and *weigh.*

  Look at these examples:

i before e	*Comes after c*	*Sounds like "ay"*
believe	receive	eight

  Exceptions: heifer, height, seize, surfeit, weird

- When a word ends in silent *–e,* drop the *–e* before you add an ending that begins with a vowel. Keep the final *–e* if the ending begins with a consonant or to prevent mispronunciation. Look at these examples:

Ending begins with a vowel	*Ending begins with a consonant*	*Mispronunciation may occur*
care + –ing = caring	care + –ful = careful	notice + –able = noticeable

  Exceptions: Sometimes the final *–e* is dropped when it comes after another vowel, as in *truly* (true + –ly) and *argument* (argue + –ment).

- When a word ends in *–y* preceded by a consonant, change *–y* to *–i* before you add an ending. Keep the *–y* if it is preceded by a vowel, the ending is *–ing,* or the word is a proper name. Look at these examples:

–y preceded by a consonant	–y preceded by a vowel	Ending is –ing	Proper noun
happy + –ly = happily	day + –s = days	study + –ing = studying	Murphy + –s = Murphys

- In one-syllable words that have a consonant-vowel-consonant (CVC) pattern, double a final consonant that is preceded by a single vowel when you add a suffix beginning with a vowel (for example, –ed, –ing). For multisyllabic words ending in –CVC, where the stress is on the CVC syllable after the suffix is added, double the final consonant when you add a suffix beginning with a vowel. *Note:* This rule does not apply to words ending in –v, –w, –x, or –y because these consonants should never be doubled when adding suffixes.

Look at these examples:

One-syllable CVC word	Multisyllabic word ending in –CVC, where stress is on CVC syllable	Word ending in –v, –w, –x, or –y
pat + –ed = patted	begin + –ing = beginning	tow + –ing = towing

- When you add a prefix (for example, *mis–, dis–*), do not add to or drop a letter from the original word. For instance, *mis–* + *spell* = *misspell*.
- When you are deciding whether a word should end in *–ible* or *–able,* a general rule is that if the root is not a complete word, the ending is *–ible;* otherwise, the ending is *–able.* Here are examples:

    terrible, dependable, permissible, acceptable

    If the root is a complete word ending in *–e,* drop the final *–e* and add *–able.* For instance, *love + –able = lovable.*

    Exceptions: *contemptible, digestible, flexible, inevitable, irritable, changeable, responsible*

- Use *–sede* to spell *supersede*. Use *–ceed* to spell *exceed, proceed,* and *succeed.* For all other words, the "seed" sound is spelled *–cede.* For example, *intercede, precede,* and *concede.*
- When a word has a **homophone** (word that sounds like it, but is spelled differently), check how the word is used in the sentence. Look at this example of a spelling error caused by homophone confusion:

    The students displayed there projects at the science fair.

    In this sentence the word preceding the noun *project* should be a possessive pronoun referring to the antecedent *students.* Change *there* to *their* to make the sentence grammatically correct:

    The students displayed their projects at the science fair.

- Avoid faulty pronunciation that can lead to misspelling. For instance, *mathematics* has an *e* that you might omit in the spelling if you say, "math • mat • ics" instead of "math • e • mat • ics."
- When you form the plural of a singular noun, you add *–s* or *–es*. If the noun ends in *–s, –sh, –ch,* or *–x,* or if the noun ends in *–o* preceded by a consonant, add *–es;* otherwise, just add *–s*. These rules apply to proper names as well. *Note:* If the singular noun ends in *–y,* follow the rules given earlier for adding suffixes to nouns ending in *–y*. Look at these examples:

    girl, girls; face, faces; video, videos; kiss, kisses; church, churches; box, boxes; tomato, tomatoes; Hutto; Huttoes

- Some nouns have irregular plurals. Look at these examples:

    child, children; woman/man, women/men; person, people; goose, geese; tooth, teeth; mouse, mice; deer, deer; sheep, sheep; knife, knives; life, lives; half, halves; criterion, criteria; analysis, analyses; crisis, crises; focus, foci; die, dice

- To form the plural of words, letters, and numbers used as words, italicize the character or word, and then add *s*. For example, "How many *4*s are in that number?
- Do not insert apostrophes anywhere to form plurals. For example, write "ands," not "and's" to mean more than one instance of the word *and.*

Demonstrate Command of Standard Punctuation

Standard written English has many rules for punctuation. This section describes the basic rules that should prove most helpful on the FTCE GK Test.

Memorize the following guidelines for correct punctuation.

You use end punctuation to show when a sentence ends. Depending on the type of sentence, end punctuation might be a period, a question mark, or an exclamation point:

- Use a period at the end of a statement. Example: *I love to read.*
- Use a question mark at the end of a question. Example: *Is this your book?*
- Use an exclamation point after an emphatic statement. Example: *That is an exciting idea!*

You use commas to indicate pauses and to prevent confusion:

- Use commas to separate three or more words or phrases in a series. Example: *I will need scissors, paper, and glue.*
- Use a comma to separate a date from its year. Example: *He was born on August 7, 1976.*
- Use a comma to separate a date and year from the rest of the sentence. Example: *Our family reunion on July 4, 2014, was a memorable one.*
- Use a comma to separate a city and its state from the rest of the sentence. Example: *We were living in Austin, Texas, before we moved to Florida.*
- Use a comma to set off most introductory elements. Example: *Fortunately, I was allowed to use a calculator when I took the mathematics portion of the test.*
- Use a comma to separate two main clauses joined by a connector word (*and, or, but, so, for, nor, yet*). Example: *I broke my watch, so I couldn't tell what time it was.*
- Use a comma to set off an introductory subordinate clause. Example: *When I'm working on a project, I find it hard to stop to eat.*
- Use a comma to set off an introductory participial phrase. Example: *Driving through the park, I saw several squirrels gathering nuts.*
- Use commas to separate nonrestrictive elements from the rest of the sentence. Nonrestrictive elements are elements that are not essential to the meaning of the sentence. Example: *My neighbor, who is a mathematics professor, often chats with me in the front yard.*
- Use a comma to set off a direct quotation. Example: *"I wish you wouldn't do that," she pleaded.*

Semicolons are used in three main ways:

- Use a semicolon between two independent clauses when no connector word is used. Example: *I broke my watch; I couldn't tell what time it was.*
- Use a semicolon between two independent clauses linked by a transitional word or phrase. Example: *I broke my watch; therefore, I couldn't tell what time it was.*
- Use semicolons to separate three or more items in a series that already contains commas. Example: *We have lived in Chicago, Illinois; Austin, Texas; and Tampa, Florida.*

Colons are used in four main ways:

- Use a colon to alert the reader to pay attention to something that follows. Example: *The number 13 has only two factors: 1 and 13.*
- Use a colon to punctuate time. Example: *We will leave at 12:15 p.m.*
- Use a colon in the salutation of a business letter. Example: *Dear Committee Members:*
- Use a colon to separate titles and subtitles. Example: *Study Skills: A Guide for Students*

> **Tip:** Do not use a colon between a verb and its object, a preposition and its object, or directly after a form of the verb *to be*. Do not use a colon after *such as* or directly after *include, includes,* or *including*.

Apostrophes are used in three main ways:

- Use an apostrophe to stand in for a missing letter or letters in a contraction. Example: *You shouldn't worry.*
- Use an apostrophe to show possession. Add –'s to singular nouns or indefinite pronouns and to plural nouns that do not end in –s. Add –'s to singular nouns ending in –s. Add only an apostrophe to plural nouns ending in –s. Look at these examples:

Singular noun or indefinite pronoun	*Plural noun not ending in –s*	*Plural noun ending in –s*
the car's motor, everyone's name, James's father	*the children's mother*	*the dogs' collars*

Quotation marks are used to show the exact words of a speaker and to set off certain titles (for example, song titles). Place commas and periods within quotation marks. Place other punctuation within the quotation marks only when the punctuation is part of the quotation. Look at these examples:

Commas and periods go inside	Other punctuation that's not part of the quotation goes outside	Punctuation that's part of the quotation goes inside
"I dislike washing my car," she complained.	*I am excited about singing "The Star-Spangled Banner"!*	*"Stop that!" the teacher demanded.*

Demonstrate Command of Standard Capitalization

Standard written English has many rules for capitalization. This section describes the basic rules that should prove most helpful on the FTCE GK Test.

Memorize the following guidelines for correct capitalization.

Capitalization tells the reader when a sentence begins and when specific persons, places, or things are being named:

- Capitalize the first word of a sentence. Example: *This sentence begins with a capital letter.*
- Capitalize proper nouns. Example: *I live in Florida.*
- Capitalize adjectives derived from proper nouns. Example: *My English teacher has a good sense of humor.*
- Capitalize titles when they precede a proper name. Example: *The memo came from Dean Jacobson.*

In modern writing, the trend is toward *less* capitalization. Therefore, as a general rule, do not capitalize the following words (unless a specific convention given in the previous capitalization guidelines requires it):

- Common names or adjectives used in place of proper nouns or adjectives
- Compass directions: north, south, east, west, southeast, and so on that do not refer to specific geographic locations
- The names of the seasons: spring, summer, fall/autumn, winter
- Titles (president, major, dean) that do not directly precede a proper name
  Exception: The title *President of the United States*
- Relationships (mom, dad, aunt, uncle, cousin) preceded by a possessive and not used in place of or as part of a proper name

Test Yourself

Directions: For questions 1 and 2, choose the *most* appropriate word or phrase to complete the sentence.

1. Last night my daughter's homework assignment in English was to write her spelling words, memorize her vocabulary word definitions, and _____ her favorite things to do.

    A. list
    B. to list
    C. listing

2. Amazingly, my children like to help out at home by both washing clothes and occasionally _____ dinner.

    A. cook
    B. cooking
    C. to cook

3. Choose the option that is punctuated correctly.

    A. Of course, you should take your allergy medicine, your doctor told you that it would relieve your symptoms.
    B. Of course, you should take your allergy medicine your doctor told you that it would relieve your symptoms.
    C. Of course, you should take your allergy medicine. Your doctor told you that it would relieve your symptoms.
    D. Of course you should take your allergy medicine your doctor told you that it would relieve your symptoms.

Directions: For questions 4–6, select the answer choice that corrects an error in the underlined portion. If there is no error, choose D indicating "No change is necessary."

4. The <u>Dean</u> of the College of Education <u>occasionally</u> visits one or two <u>professors'</u> classes.
        A   B   C

    A. dean
    B. ocassionally
    C. professor's
    D. No change is necessary.

5. When the guest of honor <u>arrived, everyone</u> in the room <u>cheered</u> <u>loud</u> and with gusto.
                                             A   B   C

    A. arrived everyone
    B. cheared
    C. loudly
    D. No change is necessary.

6. As the curtain <u>closes</u>, the audience rose and gave the performance a standing ovation.

    A. is closing
    B. closed
    C. is closed
    D. No change is necessary.

53

7. Choose the option that is punctuated correctly.

    A. The bridesmaids' dresses for the bride's three sisters were the boldest blue color that I have ever seen.
    B. The bridesmaid's dresses for the bride's three sisters were the boldest blue color that I have ever seen.
    C. The bridesmaids' dresses, for the bride's three sisters' were the boldest blue color that I have ever seen.
    D. The bridesmaids' dresses for the brides three sisters were the boldest blue color, that I have ever seen.

8. Choose the option that is expressed correctly.

    A. Each of the young boys enjoys the love of his parents and grandparents.
    B. Each of the young boys enjoy the love of his parents and grandparents.
    C. Each of the young boy enjoys the love of his parents and grandparents.
    D. Both of the young boys enjoys the love of his parents and grandparents.

9. Choose the option that is expressed correctly.

    A. There house is the most expensive in their neighborhood.
    B. They're house is the most expensive in there neighborhood.
    C. Their house is the most expensive in their neighborhood.
    D. Their house is the most expensive in there neighborhood.

10. Choose the option that is expressed correctly.

    A. They are the most weirdest people I know.
    B. They are the very weirdest people I know.
    C. They are the more weirdest people I know.
    D. They are the weirdest people I know.

Answers

1. **A.** In this sentence, the missing word is parallel with the words *write* and *memorize,* so it needs to have the same grammatical construction. The correct form is *list* (Choice **A**). Choices **B** and **C** result in faulty parallelism. *Note:* The word *to* does not have to be repeated before each verb.

2. **B.** In this sentence, the missing word is parallel with the word *washing,* so it needs to have the same grammatical construction. The correct form is *cooking* (Choice **B**). Choices **A** and **C** result in faulty parallelism.

3. **C.** All punctuation in sentence C is correct. Choice **A** is incorrect because it is a comma splice. It consists of two independent clauses connected by only a comma. Choices **B** and **D** are run-on sentences. Each consists of two independent clauses joined without a proper punctuation mark to separate them or a word to connect them. Further, in Choice **D** a comma is needed to set off the introductory element *Of course*.

4. **A.** In this sentence, the title *dean* should not be capitalized (Choice **A**). Titles are capitalized when they precede proper names, but as a rule are not capitalized when used alone. The word *occasionally* (Choice **B**) is spelled correctly. The possessive word *professors'* (Choice **C**) is punctuated correctly. Add only an apostrophe to plural nouns ending in *–s*.

5. **C.** In this sentence, the word *loud* (Choice **C**) tells how everyone cheered, so it should be an adverb. Change *loud* to *loudly* to make the sentence grammatically correct. The comma (Choice **A**) to separate the introductory subordinate clause from the rest of the sentence is correct. The word *cheered* (Choice **B**) is spelled correctly.

6. **B.** The tense of the verb *closed* in Choice **B** relates logically to the verb in the main clause. The verb tenses in Choices **A** and **C** do not. These choices result in an inappropriate tense shift in the sentence.

7. **A.** All punctuation in Choice **A** is correct. In Choice **B**, the word *bridesmaid's* should be *bridesmaids'*. To form the possessive of a plural noun ending in *–s*, add an apostrophe after the *–s*. In Choice **C**, the word *sisters'* should not have an apostrophe because no ownership is indicated for this word in the sentence. Also, in Choice **C**, no comma is needed after the word *dresses*. In Choice **D**, the word *brides* should be *bride's* because ownership is indicated for this word in the sentence. Also, in Choice **D**, no comma is needed after the word *color*.

8. **A.** In Choice **A,** the pronoun *each* and its verb *enjoys* demonstrate pronoun-verb agreement. *Each* is a singular pronoun and *enjoys* is the singular form of the verb *enjoy*. In Choice **B,** the word *Each* needs to be followed by the verb *enjoys,* as *each* is a singular pronoun and thus, should be followed by a verb in the singular form. In Choice **C,** the word *boy* should be written *boys* because it refers to two or more boys in the context of the sentence. In Choice **D,** the word *Both* should be *Each* for the sentence to be logically correct and for the pronoun to agree with the verb.

9. **C.** In Choice **C,** the possessive plural pronoun *their* is used correctly to modify both *house* and *neighborhood*. In Choice **A,** the word *house* needs to be followed by *their,* as the word *their* is the correct possessive plural pronoun and the word *there* indicates a direction (e.g., *over there*). In Choice **B,** the word *they're is* a contraction for *they are,* and thus the sentence reads incorrectly: *They are house is the most expensive*. Also, in Choice **B,** *there neighborhood* should be written *their neighborhood*. In Choice **D,** again the correct phrase is *their neighborhood* as *their* is a plural possessive pronoun.

10. **D.** In Choice **D,** the simpler sentence is the best sentence. In Choices **A, B,** and **C,** the modifiers *most, very,* and *more,* respectively, are used incorrectly to modify the word *weirdest*. In Choice **D,** the word *weirdest* needs to be preceded only by *the,* as the word *the* emphasizes the singularity of their weirdness.

Chapter 3
Review for the General Knowledge Mathematics Subtest

The Mathematics Subtest of the FTCE GK Test consists of 45 multiple-choice questions, which you must complete in 100 minutes. Each test question requires you to choose from among four answer choices. You must click on the button corresponding to your answer choice on the computer screen. The test center provides a four-function calculator and a Mathematics Reference Sheet for you to use during the test. You cannot bring written notes or scratch paper into the testing room.

The Math Review in This CliffsNotes Guide

The mathematics review in this CliffsNotes study guide is organized around the four broad areas of mathematics knowledge tested on the FTCE GK Test:

1. Numeration and operations
2. Geometry and measurement
3. Algebraic reasoning and the coordinate plane
4. Probability, statistics, and data interpretation

Each area has a general review and sample questions. The review sections present math concepts with examples and explanations for each area. "Test Yourself" exercises are found throughout the review sections. These exercises give you an opportunity to practice what you just learned. The answers to the "Test Yourself" exercises are found immediately following the set of exercises. When doing the "Test Yourself" exercises, you should cover up the answers. Then check your answers after you've finished the exercises. The sample questions are multiple-choice questions that are similar to what you might expect to see on the FTCE GK Test. The answer explanations for the sample questions are provided immediately after the questions. A Mathematics Reference Sheet is included on the next two pages.

Mathematics Reference Sheet

Area

Triangle		$A = \frac{1}{2}bh$
Rectangle		$A = lw$
Trapezoid		$A = \frac{1}{2}h(b_1 + b_2)$
Parallelogram		$A = bh$
Circle		$A = \pi r^2 \quad C = \pi d = 2\pi r$

Key	
b = base	d = diameter
h = height	r = radius
l = length	A = area
w = width	C = circumference
$S.A.$ = surface area	V = volume
	B = area of base
Use $\pi = 3.14$ or $\frac{22}{7}$.	

Surface Area

1. Surface area of a prism or pyramid = the sum of the areas of all faces of the figure
2. Surface area of a cylinder = the sum of the areas of the two bases + the area of its rectangular wrap

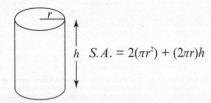

$S.A. = 2(\pi r^2) + (2\pi r)h$

3. Surface area of a sphere: $S.A. = 4\pi r^2$

Volume

1. Volume of a prism or cylinder equals (area of base) times (height): $V = Bh$
2. Volume of a pyramid or cone equals $\frac{1}{3}$ times (area of base) times (height): $V = \frac{1}{3}Bh$
3. Volume of a sphere: $V = \frac{4}{3}\pi r^3$

Mathematics Reference Sheet, continued

Pythagorean Theorem: $a^2 + b^2 = c^2$

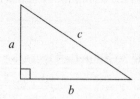

Simple Interest Formula: $I = prt$

I = simple interest, p = principal, r = rate, t = time

Distance Formula: $d = rt$

d = distance, r = rate, t = time

Given a line containing points (x_1, y_1) and (x_2, y_2),

- Slope of line $= \dfrac{y_2 - y_1}{x_2 - x_1}$

- Distance between two points $= \sqrt{(x_2 - x_1)^2 + (y_2 - y_1)^2}$

- Midpoint between two points $= \left(\dfrac{x_2 + x_1}{2}, \dfrac{y_2 + y_1}{2}\right)$

Conversions	
1 yard = 3 feet = 36 inches	1 cup = 8 fluid ounces
1 mile = 1,760 yards = 5,280 feet	1 pint = 2 cups
1 acre = 43,560 square feet	1 quart = 2 pints
1 hour = 60 minutes	1 gallon = 4 quarts
1 minute = 60 seconds	
	1 pound = 16 ounces
1 liter = 1000 milliliters = 1000 cubic centimeters	1 ton = 2,000 pounds
1 meter = 100 centimeters = 1000 millimeters	
1 kilometer = 1000 meters	
1 gram = 1000 milligrams	
1 kilogram = 1000 grams	

Note: Metric numbers with four digits are written without a comma (e.g., 2543 grams). For metric numbers with more than four digits, a space is used instead of a comma (e.g., 24 300 liters).

Numeration and Operations

According to the *Competencies and Skills Required for Teacher Certification in Florida*, 20th Edition (available at www.fldoe.org/asp/ftce/pdf/ftce20edition.pdf), the competencies/skills you should be able to do for this area of mathematics are the following:

- Compare real numbers and identify their location on a number line.
- Solve real-world problems involving the four operations with rational numbers.
- Evaluate expressions involving order of operations.

What Are Operations?

Addition, **subtraction**, **multiplication**, and **division** are the four basic arithmetic operations. Each of the operations has special symbolism and terminology associated with it. Make it a point to learn this symbolism and terminology, so that you can better understand mathematical "talk." Table 3.1 shows the terminology and symbolism you need to know.

Table 3.1 Terminology and Symbolism for the Four Basic Arithmetic Operations

Operation	Symbol(s) Used	Name of Parts	Example
Addition	+ (plus sign)	addend + addend = sum	$4 + 9 = 13$
Subtraction	− (minus sign)	minuend − subtrahend = difference	$13 − 4 = 9$
Multiplication	× (times sign)	factor × factor = product	$10 \times 5 = 50$
	· (raised dot)	factor · factor = product	$10 \cdot 5 = 50$
	( )( ) parentheses	(factor)(factor) = product	$(10)(5) = 50$
Division	÷ (division sign)	dividend ÷ divisor = quotient	$50 \div 10 = 5$
	$\overline{)}$ (long division symbol)	$\text{divisor}\overline{)\text{dividend}}^{\text{quotient}}$	$10\overline{)50}^{\;5}$
	/ (fraction bar or slash)	$\dfrac{\text{dividend}}{\text{divisor}} = \text{quotient}$	$\dfrac{50}{10} = 5$
		dividend/divisor = quotient	$50/10 = 5$

As you can see from the examples in Table 3.1, addition and subtraction "undo" each other. Mathematicians express this relationship by saying addition and subtraction are **inverses** of each other. Similarly, multiplication and division are **inverses** of each other; they "undo" each other, *as long as division by 0 is not involved*.

You must be *very* careful when division involves zero. Zero can be a dividend; that is, you can divide a nonzero number into zero—the quotient will be zero. However, 0 *cannot* be a divisor, which means you *cannot* divide by 0. The quotient of any number divided by zero has no meaning; that is, **division by zero is undefined—you can't do it!** Table 3.2 provides a summary of division involving zero.

Table 3.2 Division Involving Zero

Rule	Meaning	Example
You <u>cannot</u> divide by zero.	any number ÷ 0 = can't do it!	$6 \div 0$ = can't do it! $0 \div 0$ = can't do it!
	$\dfrac{\text{any number}}{0}$ = can't do it!	$\dfrac{25}{0}$ = can't do it! $\dfrac{0}{0}$ = can't do it!
	$0\overline{)\text{any number}}$ = can't do it!	$0\overline{)14}$ = can't do it! $0\overline{)0}$ = can't do it!

Table 3.2 Division Involving Zero (*Continued*)

Rule	Meaning	Example
You can divide zero by a nonzero number. The quotient is always zero.	0 ÷ any nonzero number = 0	0 ÷ 8 = 0
	$\frac{0}{\text{any number}} = 0$	$\frac{0}{15} = 0$
	any nonzero number $\overline{)0}$	$3\overline{)0}$

Test Yourself

1. The parts of an addition problem are _____ + _____ = _____.

2. The answer to a subtraction problem is the _____.

3. The numbers that are multiplied together in a multiplication problem are _____.

4. The answer to a multiplication problem is the _____.

5. Zero _____ (can, cannot) be a divisor in a division problem.

6. 30 ÷ 0 = _____.

7. 0 ÷ 30 = _____.

8. $\frac{0}{17}$ = _____.

9. $\frac{17}{0}$ = _____.

10. $\frac{0}{0}$ = _____.

Answers

1. addend, addend, sum
2. difference
3. factors
4. product
5. cannot
6. can't do it!
7. 0
8. 0
9. can't do it!
10. can't do it!

What Are Counting Numbers?

The **counting numbers** (also called the **natural numbers**) are 1, 2, 3, and so on. Counting numbers that are greater than 1 are either *prime* or *composite*. A **prime number** is a whole number greater than 1 that has exactly two distinct factors: itself and 1. Thus, the primes are 2, 3, 5, 7, 11, 13, and so on.

The counting numbers greater than 1 that are *not* prime are the **composite numbers**. They are 4, 6, 8, 9, 10, 12, and so on.

The counting number 1 is neither prime nor composite.

Besides classifying a counting number as prime or composite, a counting number can be classified as either *even* or *odd*. Counting numbers that divide evenly by 2 are **even**. The **even counting numbers** are 2, 4, 6, 8, 10, and so on.

Counting numbers that do *not* divide evenly by 2 are **odd**. The **odd counting numbers** are 1, 3, 5, 7, 9, and so on.

The **Fundamental Theorem of Arithmetic** states every counting number ≥2 is either a prime or can be factored into a product of primes in one and only one way, except for the order in which the factors appear. To find the prime factors of a number, you can use a **factor "tree."** Here is an example of using a factor tree to find the prime factors of the number 36.

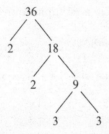

The numbers at the bottom of each branch of the tree are the prime factors of 36—you cannot factor them any further. So the prime factors of 36 are 2 and 3. You can write 36 as the product of its prime factors like this: $36 = 2 \cdot 2 \cdot 3 \cdot 3$.

Divisibility rules can help with factoring numbers. A counting number is **divisible by** another counting number if, after dividing by that number, the remainder is zero. You write $a|b$ to mean a divides b evenly or, equivalently, b "is divisible by" a. For example $3|36$ means 36 is divisible by 3. Therefore, 3 is a factor of 36. Table 3.3 shows some common divisibility rules you will find helpful.

Table 3.3 Some Common Divisibility Rules

Divisibility by	Rule	Example
2	A number is divisible by 2 if and only if the last digit of the number is even.	$2|2,347,854$ since 4 (the last digit) is even.
3	A number is divisible by 3 if and only if the sum of its digits is divisible by 3.	$3|151,515$ since 3 divides $1 + 5 + 1 + 5 + 1 + 5 = 18$ (the sum of the digits).
4	A number is divisible by 4 if and only if the last two digits form a number that is divisible by 4.	$4|47,816$ since 4 divides 16 (the number formed by the last two digits).
5	A number is divisible by 5 if and only if the last digit of the number is 0 or 5.	$5|42,115$ since the last digit is 5.
6	A number is divisible by 6 if and only if it is divisible by both 2 and 3.	$6|18,122,124$ since $2|18,122,124$ (the last digit is even) and $3|18,122,124$ (21, the sum of the digits, is divisible by 3).

Table 3.3 Some Common Divisibility Rules (*Continued*)

Divisibility by	Rule	Example
7	To test for divisibility by 7, double the last digit and subtract the product from the number formed by the remaining digits. If the result is a number divisible by 7, the original number is also divisible by 7.	7|875 since 87 – 10 = 77, which is divisible by 7.
8	A number is divisible by 8 if and only if the last three digits form a number that is divisible by 8.	8|55,864 since 8 divides 864 (the number formed by the last three digits).
9	A number is divisible by 9 if and only if the sum of its digits is divisible by 9.	9|151,515 since 9 divides 1 + 5 + 1 + 5 + 1 + 5 = 18 (the sum of the digits).
10	A number is divisible by 10 if and only if the last digit of the number is 0.	10|66,660 since the last digit is 0.

The **greatest common factor** of two or more counting numbers is the largest number that will divide evenly into each of the counting numbers. It can be obtained by listing the factors of each number, and then selecting the greatest factor that appears on both lists. The greatest common factor of two counting numbers m and n is denoted **GCF (m, n)**. For example, the greatest common factor of 24 and 36 is denoted GCF (24, 36). To find GCF (24, 36), first, list the factors of each of these numbers. The factors of 24 are 1, 2, 3, 4, 6, 8, 12, and 24; the factors of 36 are 1, 2, 3, 4, 6, 9, 12, 18, and 36. Next, select the greatest common factor that appears on both lists, namely, 12; therefore, GCF (24, 36) is 12.

The **least common multiple** of a set of counting numbers is the smallest number that is divisible by each of the numbers in the set. It is the smallest product that is a multiple of each of the counting numbers. It can be obtained by factoring each counting number and building a product consisting of each factor the *most* number of times it appears as a factor in any *one* of the counting numbers in the set. The least common multiple of two counting numbers m and n is denoted **LCM (m, n)**. For example, $24 = 2 \cdot 2 \cdot 2 \cdot 3$ and $36 = 2 \cdot 2 \cdot 3 \cdot 3$, so LCM (24, 36) = $\underbrace{2 \cdot 2 \cdot 2}_{\text{3 factors of 2}} \cdot \underbrace{3 \cdot 3}_{\text{2 factors of 3}}$ = 72. A quick way to get the LCM of two numbers is to divide their product by their GCF. For example, LCM (24, 36) = $\frac{(24)(36)}{\text{GCF}(24, 36)} = \frac{(24)(36)}{12} = \frac{(^2 24)(36)}{\cancel{12}_1} = (2)(36) = 72$. With the calculator, you key in 24 × 36 ÷ 12 =. The display will show 72, the LCM.

Test Yourself

1. A prime number has exactly _____ distinct factors.

2. The number 1 is prime. True or False?

3. The number 2 is prime. True or False?

4. The number 15 is composite. True or False?

5. The number zero is even. True or False?

6. The number 414 is divisible by 4. True or False?

7. The number 414 is divisible by 3. True or False?

8. The prime factorization of 96 = _____.

9. GCF (18, 24) = _____.

10. LCM (18, 24) = _____.

Answers

1. two
2. False. The counting number 1 is neither prime nor composite.
3. True, because it has only two factors: 2 and 1.
4. True, because it has more than two factors: 15, 5, 3, and 1.
5. True, because $\frac{0}{2} = 0$ meaning 0 is divisible by 2.
6. False, because 14 (the number formed by the last two digits of 414) is not divisible by 4.
7. True, because 3 divides $4 + 1 + 4 = 9$ (the sum of the digits of the number 414).
8. The prime factorization of $96 = 2 \cdot 2 \cdot 2 \cdot 2 \cdot 2 \cdot 3$.
9. GCF (18, 24) = 6
10. LCM (18, 24) = 72

What Are Rational Numbers?

The **rational numbers** are the numbers you are familiar with from school and from your everyday experiences with numbers. The rational numbers include the whole numbers, integers, positive and negative fractions, decimals, and percents.

The **whole numbers** are the counting numbers and zero: 0, 1, 2, 3, ... (The three dots to the right of the number 3 mean you are to keep going in the same manner.)

The **integers** are the numbers ..., –3, –2, –1, 0, 1, 2, 3, ...

Integers are either **positive** (1, 2, 3, ...), **negative** (..., –3, –2, –1), or **zero**. Negative numbers have a small horizontal line (–) to the left of the number. Notice you do not have to write the + sign on positive numbers (although it's not wrong to do so). If no sign is written with a number, then you know it is a positive number. The number zero is neither positive nor negative.

Integers that are divisible by 2 are **even integers**. The **even integers** are ... , –8, –6, –4, –2, 0, 2, 4, 6, 8, ... (Notice zero is an even integer because 0 divided by 2 is 0 with no remainder.)

Integers that are *not* divisible by 2 are **odd integers**. The **odd integers** are ... , –7, –5, –3, –1, 1, 3, 5, 7, ...

The **rational numbers** are all the numbers that can be written in the form $\frac{a}{b}$ where a and b are integers and b is not zero. In other words, the rational numbers include zero and all the numbers that can be written as positive or negative fractions. Here are examples.

$\frac{3}{4}, -\frac{2}{5}$, and $\frac{9}{2}$ are rational numbers

All the counting numbers, whole numbers, and integers are rational numbers because you can write each in the form $\frac{a}{b}$ with 1 as the bottom number. For instance, ..., $-3 = \frac{-3}{1}, -2 = \frac{-2}{1}, -1 = \frac{-1}{1}, 0 = \frac{0}{1}, 1 = \frac{1}{1}, 2 = \frac{2}{1}, 3 = \frac{3}{1}, ...$
Rational numbers can be expressed as **fractions, decimals**, or **percents**.

Test Yourself

1. A rational number is a number that can be written in the form $\frac{a}{b}$, where a and b are _____ and b is *not* _____.

2. Which of the numbers in the following set are rational numbers? $\frac{2}{3}$, 0, $\frac{-1}{1}$, 100, $-\frac{4}{5}$

3. Is $\frac{0}{4}$ a rational number?

4. Is $\frac{12}{0}$ a rational number?

5. Which of the following sets of numbers are rational numbers? whole numbers, integers, positive and negative fractions, decimals, and percents.

Answers

1. integers; zero

2. All of them

3. Yes, $\frac{0}{4} = 0$, which is a rational number.

4. No, $\frac{12}{0}$ has no meaning because you can't divide by zero.

5. All of them

What Are Fractions?

Fractions are used to express parts of a whole; for example, $\frac{3}{4}$ is a fraction. The **denominator**, the number below the **fraction bar (division line)**, tells you the number of equal parts into which the whole has been divided. The **numerator**, the number above the fraction bar, tells how many equal parts you have.

The whole can be a single quantity or entity or the whole can be a set of objects or quantities. Here is an example when the whole is a single entity, a circle.

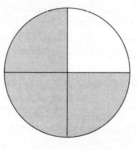

$\frac{3}{4}$ of a circle

Here is an example when the whole is a set of 8 smiley faces.

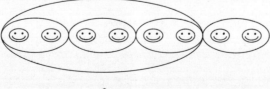

$\frac{3}{4}$ of a set of 8

When you work with a fraction, you need to make sure you know what is the whole for the fraction. This isn't always easy because in some problems the whole shifts from one quantity to another quantity. Here is an example.

> What is $\frac{3}{4}$ of $\frac{1}{2}$?

To illustrate this problem, you must first show $\frac{1}{2}$ of a whole. Let's use rectangle *A* for the whole.

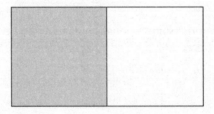

$\frac{1}{2}$ of rectangle *A*

Next, you must find $\frac{3}{4}$ of this $\frac{1}{2}$. This means you must treat the $\frac{1}{2}$ of rectangle *A* as a whole and divide it into four equal parts. Three of these four equal parts is $\frac{3}{4}$ of $\frac{1}{2}$.

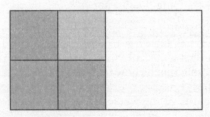

$\frac{3}{4}$ of $\frac{1}{2}$ of rectangle *A*

Finally, you shift back to rectangle *A* as the whole, to determine the part shaded is $\frac{3}{8}$ of rectangle *A*.

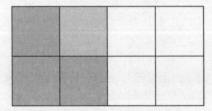

$\frac{3}{8}$ of rectangle *A*

Thus, $\frac{3}{4}$ of $\frac{1}{2} = \frac{3}{8}$.

Equivalent fractions are fractions that have the same value. For example, $\frac{1}{2}$ and $\frac{4}{8}$ are equivalent fractions. You can illustrate the equivalency as shown in the following.

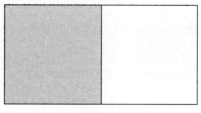

$\frac{1}{2}$ of a whole

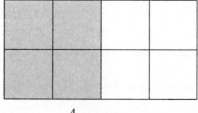

$\frac{4}{8}$ of a whole

The shaded portion is the same size in the two figures, which shows $\frac{1}{2} = \frac{4}{8}$.

If the numerator and denominator of a fraction can be divided by the same number, you can **simplify** the fraction to an equivalent fraction in **lowest terms** by doing the division, as in $\frac{4}{8} = \frac{4 \div 4}{8 \div 4} = \frac{1}{2}$. The number you divide by is the greatest common factor (GCF) of the numerator and denominator. In this case, GCF (4, 8) = 4, the largest number that will divide evenly into both the numerator and denominator.

Other times when you are working with fractions, you may need to write a fraction as an equivalent fraction with a larger denominator. You can accomplish this by multiplying the numerator and denominator by the same whole number (greater than 1). For example, $\frac{3}{4} = \frac{3 \times 25}{4 \times 25} = \frac{75}{100}$.

It is important for you to recognize that even though it takes two numerical components—a numerator and a denominator—to make a fraction, the fraction itself is just one number. Specifically, it is a rational number. For instance, $\frac{3}{4}$ is a rational number that lies between 0 and 1 on a number line as shown here.

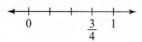

Fractions like $\frac{1}{2}$, $\frac{3}{8}$, and $\frac{75}{100}$, in which the numerator is smaller than the denominator, are **proper fractions**.

Fractions like $\frac{7}{4}$, $\frac{29}{8}$, and $\frac{6}{6}$, in which the numerator is greater than or equal to the denominator, are **improper fractions**. An improper fraction has a value greater than or equal to 1. A **mixed number** is the sum of a whole number and a fraction, written together like these examples: $1\frac{3}{4}$, $2\frac{1}{3}$, and $3\frac{5}{8}$. Although a mixed number is a sum, you don't put a plus sign in it; but you do say the word "and" in between the whole number and the fraction when you read it. For instance, $2\frac{1}{3}$ is read as "two and one-third."

You can change an improper fraction to a mixed number or a whole number by dividing the numerator by the denominator and writing the remainder like this: $\frac{\text{remainder}}{\text{denominator}}$. For example, $\frac{7}{4} = 4\overline{)7}^{1R3} = 1\frac{3}{4}$.

You can change a mixed number to an improper fraction by multiplying the whole number part by the denominator of the fractional part, adding the numerator of the fractional part to the resulting product, and then placing the resulting sum over the denominator of the fractional part. For example, $2\frac{1}{3} = \frac{2 \times 3 + 1}{3} = \frac{6+1}{3} = \frac{7}{3}$.

What Are Decimals?

Decimals are rational numbers that are written using a **base-10 place-value system**. The value of a decimal number is based on the placement of the decimal point in the number as shown below.

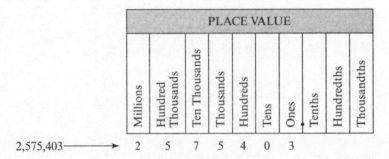

To interpret the value of a decimal number, look at each digit and determine the value it represents according to its place in the number. For example, the value of the number 2,575,403 is

2 millions + 5 hundred thousands + 7 ten thousands + 5 thousands + 4 hundreds + 0 tens + 3 ones

or

2,000,000 + 500,000 + 70,000 + 5,000 + 400 + 0 + 3

Each digit has a **face value** and a **place value**. For example, in the number 2,575,403, starting at the decimal point (which is understood to be at the far right of a whole number) and counting left, the 4th digit and the 6th digit both have the same face value, namely 5. However, they represent different amounts because their place values are different. The 5 that is the 4th digit from the decimal point represents 5,000, while the 5 that is the 6th digit from the decimal point represents 500,000. Place value makes a big difference!

> **Tip:** If no decimal point is shown in a number, the decimal point is understood to be to the immediate right of the rightmost digit.

To write numbers that are less than 1, you must recognize numbers to the right of the decimal point represent fractions whose denominators are powers of 10: 10, 100, 1,000, and so on. Here are examples.

	Millions	Hundred Thousands	Ten Thousands	Thousands	Hundreds	Tens	Ones	Tenths	Hundredths	Thousandths
				PLACE VALUE						
0.7 →							0	7		
0.07 →							0	0	7	
0.007 →							0	0	0	7

Chapter 3: Review for the General Knowledge Mathematics Subtest

The value of 0.7 is 7 tenths or $\frac{7}{10}$.

The value of 0.07 is 7 hundredths or $\frac{7}{100}$.

The value of 0.007 is 7 thousandths or $\frac{7}{1,000}$.

> **Tip:** Notice the place values after the decimal point start with tenths.

In a decimal number, the number of digits to the right of the decimal point up to and including the final digit is the number of decimal places in the number. For instance, 0.7 has one decimal place, 0.07 has two decimal places, and 0.007 has three decimal places. Other examples are 35.62, which has two decimal places, and 4.250, which has three decimal places.

You can obtain the decimal representation of a fractional number by dividing the numerator by the denominator.

> **Tip:** To remember the denominator is the divisor, notice both of these words begin with the letter *d*. A visual way to remember is to think of the fraction as a cowhand riding a horse: $\frac{\text{cowhand (numerator)}}{\text{horse (denominator)}}$. The horse stays outside when the cowhand goes into the bunkhouse, represented by the long division symbol $\overline{)}$: horse (denominator)$\overline{)}$cowhand (numerator).

Here are examples.

$$\frac{1}{2} = 0.5 \text{ because } \frac{1}{2} = 2\overline{)1.0}^{0.5}; \quad \frac{3}{5} = 0.6 \text{ because } \frac{3}{5} = 5\overline{)3.0}^{0.6}; \quad \frac{7}{4} = 1.75 \text{ because } \frac{7}{4} = 4\overline{)7.00}^{1.75}$$

In these cases, the decimal **terminates** (eventually has a zero remainder). For some rational numbers, the decimal keeps going, but in a block of one or more digits that repeats over and over again. These decimals are **repeating**.

Here is an example of a repeating decimal.

$$\frac{2}{3} = 3\overline{)2.000...}^{0.666...}$$

No matter how long you continue to add zeroes and divide, the 6s in the quotient continue without end. Put a bar over the repeating digit (or digits when more than one digit repeats) to indicate the repetition. Thus, $\frac{2}{3} = 0.\overline{6}$. All terminating and repeating decimals are rational numbers.

How Do You Round a Number?

To **round a number** to a specified place value, find the digit in the place value to which you want to round and look at the digit to the immediate right of it. If that digit is *less than* 5, do not change the digit in the specified place value but change each digit to the right of the specified place value digit to zero. If the digit to the immediate right of the specified place value digit is 5 or *greater*, replace the digit in the specified place value with the digit that is one greater and change each digit to the right of the specified place value digit to zero. Here are examples.

- Round 253,410 to the nearest thousand.

    The digit in the thousands place is 3; 4 is the digit to the immediate right of it, and 4 is less than 5. Keep 3 and change each digit to its right to zero. Thus, 253,410 rounded to the nearest thousand is 253,000.

- Round 0.8729 to the nearest thousandth.

  The digit in the thousandths place is 2; 9 is the digit to the immediate right of it, and 9 is greater than 5. Change 2 to 3 and change each digit to its right to zero. Thus, 0.8729 rounded to the nearest thousandth is 0.8730 = 0.873.

- Round 3.652171 to the nearest tenth.

  The digit in the tenths place is 6; 5 is the digit to the immediate right of it. Change 6 to 7 and change each digit to its right to zero. Thus, 3.652171 rounded to the nearest tenth is 3.700000 = 3.7.

Exception: When the digit in the specified place value is 9 and the digit to its immediate right is 5 or greater, treat 9 and all digits to its left as a whole number. Replace this whole number with the number that is 1 greater and change each digit to its right to zero. If the number being rounded has decimal places, ignore the decimal point and treat the 9 and all digits to its left as a "whole number." Replace this number with the number that is 1 greater and change each digit to its right to zero. Put a decimal point in this new number so that it has the same number of decimal places as the original number. Here are examples.

- Round 27,963 to the nearest hundred.

  The digit in the hundreds place is 9; 6 is the digit to the immediate right of it, and 6 is greater than 5. Change 279 to 280 and change each digit to its right to zero. Thus, 27,963 rounded to the nearest hundred is 28,000.

- Round 35.697 to the nearest hundredth.

  The digit in the hundredths place is 9; 7 is the digit to the immediate right of it, and 7 is greater than 5. Change 3569 to 3570 and change each digit to its right to zero to obtain 35700. Put in a decimal point between 5 and 7 to obtain 35.700. Thus, 35.697 to the nearest hundredth is 35.700 = 35.70.

Note: When decimals repeat, they are usually rounded to a specified degree of accuracy; for example, 0.666... is 0.67 when rounded to two decimal places.

What Are Percents?

You can write rational numbers as **percents**. Percent means "per hundred." The percent sign is a short way of writing $\frac{1}{100}$ or 0.01. When you see a percent sign, you can substitute $\frac{1}{100}$ or 0.01 for the percent sign.

A percent is a way of writing a fraction as an equivalent fraction in which the denominator is 100. Thus, $25\% = 25 \cdot \frac{1}{100} = \frac{25}{100}$. Think of percents as special ways to write ordinary decimals or fractions. For instance, 100% is just a special way to write the number 1, because $100\% = 100 \cdot \frac{1}{100} = \frac{100}{100} = 1$. If you have 100% of something, you have all of it. Here are examples.

100% of a circle

100% of a set of 8

100% of a rectangle

A percent that is less than 100% is less than 1. When you have less than 100% of something, you have less than the whole thing. Here are examples.

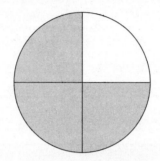

75% of a circle

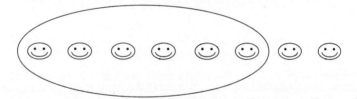

75% of a set of 8

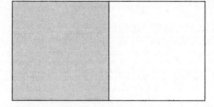

50% of a rectangle

A percent that is greater than 100% is greater than 1. When you have more than 100% of something, you have more than the whole thing. Here are examples.

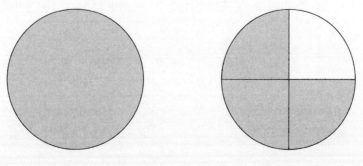

175% of a circle

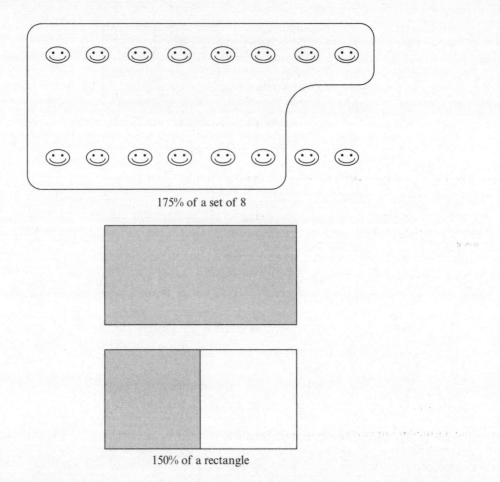

175% of a set of 8

150% of a rectangle

Any percent can be written as an equivalent fraction by writing the number in front of the percent sign as the numerator of a fraction in which the denominator is 100. The resulting fraction may then be simplified to lowest terms, if possible. Here are examples.

$$5\% = \frac{5}{100} = \frac{5 \div 5}{100 \div 5} = \frac{1}{20}$$

$$25\% = \frac{25}{100} = \frac{25 \div 25}{100 \div 25} = \frac{1}{4}$$

$$50\% = \frac{50}{100} = \frac{50 \div 50}{100 \div 50} = \frac{1}{2}$$

$$125\% = \frac{125}{100} = \frac{125 \div 25}{100 \div 25} = \frac{5}{4} = 1\frac{1}{4}$$

When percents contain decimal fractions, multiply the numerator and denominator by 10, 100, or 1,000, and so on, to remove the decimal in the numerator and then simplify the resulting fraction, if possible. You determine what to use as the multiplier based on the number of decimal places in the numerator. If the numerator has one decimal place, multiply by 10. If the numerator has two decimal places, multiply by 100, and so on. Here are examples.

$$12.5\% = \frac{12.5}{100} = \frac{12.5 \times 10}{100 \times 10} = \frac{125}{1,000} = \frac{125 \div 125}{1,000 \div 125} = \frac{1}{8}$$

$$0.25\% = \frac{0.25}{100} = \frac{0.25 \times 100}{100 \times 100} = \frac{25}{10,000} = \frac{25 \div 25}{10,000 \div 25} = \frac{1}{400}$$

> **Tip: 0.25% is less than 1%. It is NOT the same as 25%, which is $\frac{1}{4}$.**

If a percent contains a simple common fraction, multiply the fraction by $\frac{1}{100}$ and then simplify, if possible. Here is an example.

$$\frac{1}{4}\% = \frac{1}{4} \times \frac{1}{100} = \frac{1}{400}$$

> **Tip: Notice both $\frac{1}{4}\%$ and 0.25% equal $\frac{1}{400}$. In other words, $\frac{1}{4}\% = 0.25\% = \frac{1}{400}$.**

When percents contain mixed fractions, change the mixed fraction to an improper fraction, use $\frac{1}{100}$ for the percent sign, and then multiply and simplify, if possible. Here are examples.

$$12\frac{1}{2}\% = \frac{25}{2}\% = \frac{25}{2} \times \frac{1}{100} = \frac{25}{200} = \frac{25 \div 25}{200 \div 25} = \frac{1}{8}$$

$$33\frac{1}{3}\% = \frac{100}{3}\% = \frac{100}{3} \times \frac{1}{100} = \frac{\cancel{100}^{1}}{3} \times \frac{1}{\cancel{100}_{1}} = \frac{1}{3}$$

A percent can be written as an equivalent decimal number by changing it to an equivalent fraction in which the denominator is 100, and then dividing by 100. For example, $75\% = \frac{75}{100} = 100\overline{)75.00}^{\,0.75}$. A shortcut for this process is **to move the decimal point two places to the left** (which is the same as dividing by 100) and drop the percent sign. Here are examples.

$$25\% = 0.25$$
$$32\% = 0.32$$
$$45.5\% = 0.455$$
$$8\% = 0.08$$
$$200\% = 2.00 = 2$$

To write a decimal number in percent form, move the decimal point two places to the right and insert the percent sign (%) at the end. Why does this make sense? Recall the percent sign is a short way to write $\frac{1}{100}$ which means 1 divided by 100. When you move the decimal place in your number two places to the right, you are multiplying by 100. Since the percent sign has division by 100 built into it, when you put the percent sign at the end of the number, you undo the multiplication by 100 you did earlier. Thus, the value of the number does not change. Here are examples.

$$0.45 = 45\%$$
$$0.01 = 1\%$$
$$0.125 = 12.5\%$$
$$2 = 2.00 = 200\%$$
$$0.0025 = 0.25\%$$

> **Tip: Notice the % sign is equivalent to two decimal places. When your number "gives up" two decimal places, you replace the two decimal places with a % sign.**

To write a fraction in percent form, first convert the fraction to a decimal number by performing the indicated division and then change the resulting decimal number to a percent. When the quotient is a repeating decimal number, carry the division to two places, and then write the remainder as a fraction like this: $\frac{\text{remainder}}{\text{divisor}}$. Here are examples.

$$\frac{1}{2} = 2\overline{)1.00}^{0.50} = 0.50 = 50\%$$

Tip: You can convert simple fractions to percents "in your head" by thinking of dividing 100% into equal parts. For instance, when you divide 100% into two equal parts, you get 50%, so $\frac{1}{2}$ = 50%.

$$\frac{1}{3} = 3\overline{)1.00}^{0.33R1} = 0.33\frac{1}{3} = 33\frac{1}{3}\%$$

Tip: When you divide 100% into three equal parts, you get $33\frac{1}{3}\%$, so $\frac{1}{3} = 33\frac{1}{3}\%$. Note $\frac{1}{3} \neq 33\%$.

$$\frac{1}{4} = 4\overline{)1.00}^{0.25} = 0.25 = 25\%$$

Tip: When you divide 100% into four equal parts, you get 25%, so $\frac{1}{4}$ = 25%.

$$\frac{3}{5} = 5\overline{)3.00}^{0.60} = 0.60 = 60\%$$

Tip: When you divide 100% into five equal parts, you get 20%, so $\frac{1}{5}$ = 20%. Thus, $\frac{3}{5}$ is 3 times $\frac{1}{5}$, which equals 3 times 20% = 60%.

$$\frac{5}{8} = 8\overline{)5.000}^{0.625} = 0.625 = 62.5\%$$

Tip: When you divide 100% into eight equal parts, you get 12.5%, so $\frac{1}{8}$ = 12.5%. Thus, $\frac{5}{8}$ is 5 times $\frac{1}{8}$, which equals 5 times 12.5% = 62.5%.

Before you take the FTCE GK Test, you should memorize the following list of common percents with their fraction and decimal equivalents. Make a set of flashcards to carry with you, and drill on these when you have spare time. To help you gain ownership of the list, practice figuring out the percents mentally (as illustrated in the tips above) so that the equivalencies make sense to you.

$100\% = 1.00 = 1$, $75\% = 0.75 = \frac{3}{4}$, $50\% = 0.50 = 0.5 = \frac{1}{2}$, $25\% = 0.25 = \frac{1}{4}$

$90\% = 0.90 = 0.9 = \frac{9}{10}$, $80\% = 0.80 = 0.8 = \frac{4}{5}$, $70\% = 0.70 = 0.7 = \frac{7}{10}$, $60\% = 0.60 = 0.6 = \frac{3}{5}$

$40\% = 0.40 = 0.4 = \frac{2}{5}$, $30\% = 0.30 = 0.3 = \frac{3}{10}$, $20\% = 0.20 = 0.2 = \frac{1}{5}$, $10\% = 0.10 = 0.1 = \frac{1}{10}$

$87\frac{1}{2}\% = 87.5\% = 0.875 = \frac{7}{8}$, $62\frac{1}{2}\% = 62.5\% = 0.625 = \frac{5}{8}$, $37\frac{1}{2}\% = 37.5\% = 0.375 = \frac{3}{8}$, $12\frac{1}{2}\% = 12.5\% = 0.125 = \frac{1}{8}$

$66\frac{2}{3}\% = 0.66\frac{2}{3} = 0.\overline{6} = \frac{2}{3}$, $33\frac{1}{3}\% = 0.33\frac{1}{3} = 0.\overline{3} = \frac{1}{3}$

$5\% = 0.05 = \frac{1}{20}$, $4\% = 0.04 = \frac{1}{25}$, $1\% = 0.01 = \frac{1}{100}$

Test Yourself

1. In the fraction $\frac{3}{10}$, the whole is divided into _____ equal parts, and you have _____ of the equal parts.

2. Which of the following fractions, $\frac{30}{100}, \frac{6}{10}, \frac{12}{20}$, are equivalent to $\frac{3}{5}$?

3. What is the greatest common factor of 16 and 24? Simplify the fraction $\frac{16}{24}$ to lowest terms by dividing the numerator and denominator by the GCF (16, 24).

4. Which of the following fractions, $\frac{20}{17}, 1\frac{3}{5}, \frac{12}{24}, \frac{4}{4}$, are improper fractions?

5. Change $\frac{8}{5}$ to a mixed number.

6. In the number 564.27, the 6 represents what value?

7. Write the fraction $\frac{4}{5}$ as a decimal and as a percent.

8. Write 0.34 as a percent.

9. Write 73.5% as a decimal number.

10. Which of the following are rational numbers?

    $\frac{3}{8}, 0, 9.3, \frac{-7}{0}, 225\%, -5, 100, -\frac{20}{17}, \frac{9}{0}, -0.4, 0.\bar{3}, 100\%, 1\frac{3}{5}, \frac{12}{24}, \frac{4}{4}, 0.85$

Answers

1. 10, 3

2. $\frac{6}{10}$, because $\frac{3}{5} = \frac{3 \times 2}{5 \times 2} = \frac{6}{10}$; and $\frac{12}{20}$, because $\frac{3}{5} = \frac{3 \times 4}{5 \times 4} = \frac{12}{20}$.

3. The greatest common factor of 16 and 24 is the greatest number that will divide into both 16 and 24 evenly. The factors of 16 are 1, 2, 4, 8, and 16. The factors of 24 are 1, 2, 3, 4, 6, 8, 12, and 24. Looking at the two lists of factors, you can see 8 is the greatest factor that appears in both lists. Thus, GCF (16, 24) = 8;

    $\frac{16}{24} = \frac{16 \div 8}{24 \div 8} = \frac{2}{3}$

4. $\frac{20}{17}$ and $\frac{4}{4}$

5. $\frac{8}{5} = 5\overline{)8}^{1R3} = 1\frac{3}{5}$

6. 6 tens or 60

7. $\frac{4}{5} = 5\overline{)4.00}^{0.80} = 0.80 = 80\%$ (Another way: Think $\frac{1}{5} = 20\%$ (100% divided by 5), so $\frac{4}{5}$ is 4 times 20% = 80%.)

8. 0.34 = 34%

9. 73.5% = 0.735

10. All of them, except $\frac{-7}{0}$ and $\frac{9}{0}$ (which have no meaning because you can't divide by zero).

What Are Irrational Numbers?

Irrational numbers are numbers that cannot be written in the form $\frac{a}{b}$, where a and b are integers and b is not zero. They have nonterminating, nonrepeating decimal representations. An example of an irrational number is the positive number that multiplies by itself to give 2. This number is the principal square root of 2. The square root symbol $(\sqrt{\ })$ is used to show a principal square root. Thus, the principal square root of 2 is written like this: $\sqrt{2}$. Every number, except zero, has two square roots: a positive square root (designated the *principal* square root) and a negative square root. The other square root of 2 is $-\sqrt{2}$. It also is an irrational number. *Note:* Zero has only one square root, namely, zero (which is a rational number).

You cannot express $\sqrt{2}$ as $\frac{a}{b}$, where a and b are integers (b, not zero), and neither can you express it precisely in decimal form. No matter how many decimal places you use, you can only approximate $\sqrt{2}$. If you use the calculator to take the square root of the number 2, the display will show a decimal approximation of $\sqrt{2}$. An approximation of $\sqrt{2}$ to nine decimal places is 1.414213562. You can check to see whether this is $\sqrt{2}$ by multiplying it by itself to see whether you get 2.

$1.414213562 \cdot 1.414213562 = 1.999999999$

The number 1.999999999 is very close to 2, but it is not equal to 2. For most purposes, you can use 1.41 as an approximation for $\sqrt{2}$.

Even though an exact value for $\sqrt{2}$ cannot be determined, $\sqrt{2}$ is a number that occurs frequently in the real world. For instance, architects, carpenters, and other builders encounter $\sqrt{2}$ when they measure the length of the diagonal of a square that has sides with lengths of one unit as shown here.

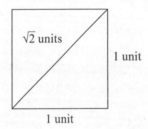

The diagonal of such a square measures $\sqrt{2}$ units.

There are an infinite number of square roots that are irrational. Here are a few examples.

$$\sqrt{3},\ \sqrt{10},\ -\sqrt{24},\ \sqrt{41},\ \sqrt{89}$$

On the FTCE GK Test, you might have to estimate the value of an irrational square root by finding a pair of consecutive whole numbers that the square root lies between. Here is an example.

> Estimate $\sqrt{41}$.

To do this problem, you need to find two consecutive integers such that the square of the first integer is less than 41 and the square of the second integer is greater than 41. Since $6 \times 6 = 36$, which is less than 41, and $7 \times 7 = 49$, which is greater than 41, the approximate value of $\sqrt{41}$ is between 6 and 7.

Another important irrational number is the number represented by the symbol π (pi). The number π also occurs frequently in the real world. For instance, π is the number you get when you divide the circumference of a circle by its diameter. The number π cannot be expressed as a fraction, nor can it be written as a terminating or repeating decimal. Here is an approximation of π to nine decimal places: 3.141592654.

Tip: There is no pattern to the digits of π. For the FTCE GK Test, use the rational number 3.14 as an approximation for the irrational number π in problems involving π.

Are All Square Roots Irrational?

Not all square roots are irrational. For example, the principal square root of 25, denoted $\sqrt{25}$, is not irrational because $\sqrt{25} = 5$, which is a rational number. The number 25 is a **perfect square** because its square root is rational. When you want to find the principal square root of a number, try to find a nonnegative number that multiplies by itself to give the number. To be well-prepared for the FTCE GK Test, you should memorize the following principal square roots.

$$\sqrt{1} = 1 \quad \sqrt{25} = 5 \quad \sqrt{81} = 9 \quad \sqrt{169} = 13 \quad \sqrt{289} = 17$$
$$\sqrt{4} = 2 \quad \sqrt{36} = 6 \quad \sqrt{100} = 10 \quad \sqrt{196} = 14 \quad \sqrt{400} = 20$$
$$\sqrt{9} = 3 \quad \sqrt{49} = 7 \quad \sqrt{121} = 11 \quad \sqrt{225} = 15 \quad \sqrt{625} = 25$$
$$\sqrt{16} = 4 \quad \sqrt{64} = 8 \quad \sqrt{144} = 12 \quad \sqrt{256} = 16$$

Make yourself a set of flashcards or make matching cards for a game of "Memory." For the Memory game, turn all the cards face down. Turn up two cards at a time. If they match (for instance $\sqrt{144}$ and 12 are a match), remove the two cards; otherwise, turn them face down again. Repeat until you have matched all the cards.

Keep in mind, though, every positive number has <u>two</u> square roots. The two square roots are equal in absolute value, but opposite in sign. For instance, the two square roots of 25 are 5 and –5 (read "negative 5"), with 5 being the principal square root. The square root symbol *always* gives just <u>one</u> number as the answer and that number is either positive or zero! Thus, $\sqrt{25} = 5$, not –5 or ±5 (read "plus or minus 5"). If you want ±5, then do this: $\pm\sqrt{25} = \pm 5$. (See the next section for a discussion of positive and negative numbers.)

Tip: When you're working with only real numbers, don't try to find square roots of negative numbers because not one real number will multiply by itself to give a negative number (see "Multiplying and Dividing Signed Numbers" on page 91 to see why this is the case). So, for instance, $\sqrt{-25} \neq -5$. No real number multiplies by itself to give –25. Questions on the FTCE GK Test involve only real numbers, which are discussed in the next section.

What Are Real Numbers?

Real numbers are the numbers that describe the world in which we live. They are made up of all the rational numbers and all the irrational numbers. You can show real numbers on a number line. Every point on the real number line corresponds to a real number and every real number corresponds to a point on the real number line. Positive numbers are located to the right of zero, and negative numbers are to the left of zero. Here are examples.

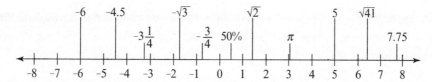

Test Yourself

1. A real number is any _____ or _____ number.

2. Which of the following numbers are rational? –15, 0, $\sqrt{36}$, –3.45, 130%, $\sqrt{12}$, $\dfrac{6}{10}$, $-\dfrac{1}{20}$, 0.0005, π, 3.14.

3. Which of the following numbers are irrational? –25, 0, $\sqrt{36}$, –125.4, 50%, $\sqrt{6}$, $-\frac{1}{200}$, 0.0005, π, 3.14, $0.\overline{3}$.

4. Which of the following numbers are real numbers? –16, 0, $\sqrt{37}$, –13.25, 30%, $\sqrt{49}$, $\frac{3}{5}$, $-\frac{12}{24}$, 0.03, π.

5. A decimal number that terminates is a(n) _____ (rational, irrational) number.

6. A decimal number that repeats is a(n) _____ (rational, irrational) number.

7. Nonterminating or nonrepeating decimal numbers are _____ (rational, irrational).

8. Estimate the value of $\sqrt{37}$.

9. The number $\sqrt{400}$ is _____ (rational, irrational).

10. Is $\frac{1}{0}$ a real number?

Answers

1. rational, irrational
2. All except $\sqrt{12}$ and π
3. $\sqrt{6}$ and π
4. All of them
5. rational
6. rational
7. irrational
8. between 6 and 7
9. rational, because $\sqrt{400} = 20$.
10. No, $\frac{1}{0}$ has no meaning because you can't divide by zero.

What Are Exponents?

An **exponent** is a small raised number written to the upper right of a quantity, which is called the **base** for the exponent. For the product $2 \times 2 \times 2 \times 2 \times 2$, write 2^5. The expression 2^5 means "use 2 as a factor 5 times." The number 2 is the base, and the small ^{5} to the upper right of 2 is the exponent.

$$2^5 \;\substack{\leftarrow \text{Exponent} \\ \leftarrow \text{Base}}$$

Tip: Exponents are superscripts, so they are smaller than the other numbers in a problem. Write an exponent slightly raised and immediately to the right of the number that is its base. Do this carefully so that, for example, 2^5 is not mistaken for 25.

An exponent, n, that is a nonzero whole number tells how many times the base, b, is used as a factor. That is, $b^n = \underbrace{b \times b \times \cdots b}_{n \text{ times}}$. The resulting **exponential expression** is a **power** of the base. For instance, 2^5 is "2 to the fifth power."

Here are other examples.

$3 \times 3 \times 3 \times 3 = 3^4$, "3 to the fourth power"

$(2)(2)(2)(2)(2)(2) = 2^6$, "2 to the sixth power"

$15 \cdot 15 = 15^2$, "15 to the second power," but more commonly—"15 squared"
$6 \cdot 6 \cdot 6 = 6^3$, "6 to the third power," but more commonly—"6 cubed"
$2 \cdot 2 \cdot 2 \cdot 5 \cdot 5 = 2^3 \cdot 5^2$, "2 cubed times 5 squared"

To **evaluate** an exponential expressions, do to the base what the exponent tells you to do. Here are examples when the exponent is a whole number.

$3^4 = 3 \times 3 \times 3 \times 3 = 81$, "the fourth power of 3"
$2^6 = (2)(2)(2)(2)(2)(2) = 64$, "the sixth power of 2"
$15^2 = 15 \cdot 15 = 225$, "the square of 15"
$6^3 = 6 \cdot 6 \cdot 6 = 216$, "the cube of 6"
$2^3 \cdot 5^2 = 2 \cdot 2 \cdot 2 \cdot 5 \cdot 5 = 8 \cdot 25 = 200$

Tip: Don't multiply the base by the exponent! That mistake is a common one. $3^4 = 3 \times 3 \times 3 \times 3 = 81$, not $3 \times 4 = 12$.

Negative exponents are used to show reciprocals. Here are examples.

$$2^{-3} = \frac{1}{2^3}$$
$$10^{-4} = \frac{1}{10^4}$$

You evaluate exponential expressions that use negative (integer) exponents by writing the reciprocal (in which you use a positive version of the original exponent), performing the indicated multiplication, and converting to a decimal (if desired). Here are examples.

$$2^{-3} = \frac{1}{2^3} = \frac{1}{8} = 0.125$$
$$10^{-4} = \frac{1}{10^4} = \frac{1}{10,000} = 0.0001$$

Caution: Do not make the mistake of putting a negative sign in front of your answer. The negative part of the exponent means for you to write a reciprocal; it does not mean you should make your answer negative.

You can use **zero as an exponent**. When zero is the exponent on a *nonzero* number, the value of the exponential expression is 1. Here are examples.

$$3^0 = 1$$
$$(-3)^0 = 1$$
$$\left(\frac{3}{4}\right)^0 = 1$$
$$(5.12)^0 = 1$$

What Is Scientific Notation?

Scientific notation is a way to write real numbers in a shortened form. When the numbers are very large or very small, scientific notation helps keep track of the decimal places and makes performing computations with these numbers easier.

A number written in scientific notation is written as a product of two factors. The first factor is a number that is greater than or equal to 1, but less than 10. The second factor is a power of 10. The idea is to make a product that will equal the given number. Any decimal number can be written in scientific notation. Here are examples of numbers written in scientific notation.

- Written in scientific notation, $34{,}000 = 3.4 \times 10^4$
- Written in scientific notation, $6.5 = 6.5 \times 10^0$
- Written in scientific notation, $1{,}235{,}000 = 1.235 \times 10^6$
- Written in scientific notation, $0.00047 = 4.7 \times 10^{-4}$
- Written in scientific notation, $0.00000001662 = 1.662 \times 10^{-8}$

Follow these steps to write a number in scientific notation:

1. Move the decimal point to the immediate right of the first *nonzero* digit of the number.
2. Indicate multiplication by the proper power of 10. The exponent for the power of 10 is the number of places you moved the decimal point in Step 1.

If you moved the decimal point to the left, make the exponent positive. For example,

$$34{,}000 = 3.4000 \times 10^? = 3.4 \times 10^4$$

4 places left

If you moved the decimal point to the right, make the exponent negative. For example,

$$0.00047 = 0\,0004.7 \times 10^? = 4.7 \times 10^{-4}$$

4 places right

As long as you make sure your first factor is greater than or equal to 1 and less than 10, you can always check to see whether you did it right by multiplying out your answer to see whether you get your original number back. Look at these examples.

$$3.4 \times 10^4 = 3.4 \times 10 \times 10 \times 10 \times 10 = 34{,}000$$

$$4.7 \times 10^{-4} = 4.7 \times \frac{1}{10^4} = 4.7 \times \frac{1}{10 \times 10 \times 10 \times 10} = 4.7 \times \frac{1}{10{,}000} = \frac{4.7}{10{,}000} = 0.00047$$

Test Yourself

1. In the exponential expression 4^3, _____ is the base and _____ is the exponent.

2. Write 144 as a product of its prime factors using exponents on the factors.

3. Evaluate 4^3.

4. Evaluate 5^{-4}.

5. Evaluate $\left(\dfrac{4}{5}\right)^0$.

6. Write 456,000,000 in scientific notation.

7. Write 0.000000975 in scientific notation.

8. Write 2.68×10^9 in standard form.

9. Write 1.572×10^{-3} in standard form.

10. Exponential expressions such as 10^{-2}, 10^{-8}, 10^3, and 10^7 are _____ of 10.

Answers

1. 4, 3
2. $144 = 2 \cdot 2 \cdot 2 \cdot 2 \cdot 3 \cdot 3 = 2^4 \cdot 3^2$
3. $4^3 = 4 \cdot 4 \cdot 4 = 64$
4. $5^{-4} = \dfrac{1}{5^4} = \dfrac{1}{5 \cdot 5 \cdot 5 \cdot 5} = \dfrac{1}{625} = 0.0016$
5. $\left(\dfrac{4}{5}\right)^0 = 1$
6. $456{,}000{,}000 = 4.\underbrace{56000000}_{\substack{\text{8 places} \\ \text{left}}} \times 10^? = 4.56 \times 10^8$
7. $0.000000975 = \underbrace{00000009}_{\substack{\text{7 places} \\ \text{right}}}.75 \times 10^? = 9.75 \times 10^{-7}$
8. $2.68 \times 10^9 = 2.68 \times 10 \times 10 \times 10 \times 10 \times 10 \times 10 \times 10 \times 10 \times 10 = 2.68 \times 1{,}000{,}000{,}000 = 2{,}680{,}000{,}000$
9. $1.572 \times 10^{-3} = 1.572 \times \dfrac{1}{10^3} = 1.572 \times \dfrac{1}{10 \times 10 \times 10} = 1.572 \times \dfrac{1}{1{,}000} = \dfrac{1.572}{1{,}000} = 0.001572$
10. powers

How Do You Compare and Order Real Numbers?

For the FTCE GK Test, you will need to know how to compare two or more real numbers to determine which is greater and which is less. For these questions, you will need to understand inequality symbols. Table 3.4 summarizes commonly used inequality symbols.

Table 3.4 Common Inequality Symbols

Inequality Symbol	Read As	Example
<	"is less than"	0.5 < 1
>	"is greater than"	7.2 > 3.1
≤	"is less than or equal to"	9 ≤ 9
≥	"is greater than or equal to"	$3\dfrac{4}{5} \geq 2$
≠	"is not equal to"	0 ≠ −10

When comparing two real numbers, think of their relative location on the number line. If the numbers have the same location, they are equal. If they don't, they are unequal. Then, the number that is farther to the *right* is the greater number. For example, −7 < −2 because −2 lies to the right of −7 on the number line.

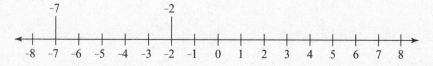

When you compare decimal numbers, compare the digits in each place value from left to right. If the decimal numbers do not have the same number of decimal places, annex or delete zeroes after the last digit to the right of the decimal point to make the number of decimal places the same. Remember, annexing or deleting zeroes after the last digit to the right of the decimal point does not change the value of a decimal number.

For example, 2.5 = 2.50 = 2.500 = 2.5000, and so on. Thus, 2.28 < 2.5 because 2.28 < 2.50.

When comparing fractions that have the same denominator, compare the numerators. For example, $\frac{7}{8} > \frac{5}{8}$ because 7 > 5.

If the denominators of the fractions are not the same, write the fractions as equivalent fractions using a common denominator. For example, $\frac{3}{4} < \frac{7}{8}$ because $\frac{6}{8} < \frac{7}{8}$.

To compare a mixture of decimals and fractions, use the calculator to change the fractions to decimals. Round them off if they repeat. When you are instructed to order a list of numbers, you put them in order from **least to greatest** or from **greatest to least**, depending on how the question is stated. Here is an example.

Order the numbers $\frac{7}{8}$, 0.35, 4.8, and $\frac{2}{3}$ from least to greatest.

Before proceeding, write $\frac{7}{8}$ as a decimal by performing the division on the calculator like this: 7 ÷ 8 = 0.875. Similarly, write $\frac{2}{3}$ as 0.667 (rounding to 3 places). Write 0.35 as 0.350 and 4.8 as 4.800. Next, compare the transformed numbers and put them in order as follows: 0.350, 0.667, 0.875, 4.800. Lastly, substitute the original numbers for their stand-ins to obtain the final answer: 0.35, $\frac{2}{3}$, $\frac{7}{8}$, 4.8.

Here are some tips on handling other situations that may occur in problems that involve comparing and ordering real numbers.

- If negative numbers are involved, they will be less than all the positive numbers and 0.
- If percents are involved, change the percents to decimals.
- If the problem contains exponential expressions, evaluate them before making comparisons.
- If you have square roots that are rational numbers, find the square roots before making comparisons.
- If you have irrational square roots, estimate the square roots before comparing them to other numbers.

For example, order the following list of numbers from least to greatest: $\sqrt{37}$, 3^2, 4.39, –4, $\frac{9}{2}$

You do not have to proceed in the order the numbers are listed. Clearly, –4 is less than all the other numbers. Evaluate 3^2 to obtain 9, and write $\frac{9}{2}$ as 4.50. The order from least to greatest for these four numbers is as follows: –4, 4.39, 4.50, 9.

Lastly, estimate $\sqrt{37}$ to be between 6 and 7, which puts it between 4.50 and 9 in the list. Thus, your final answer is –4, 4.39, $\frac{9}{2}$, $\sqrt{37}$, 3^2.

What Is Absolute Value?

The **absolute value** of a real number is its distance from zero on the number line. The absolute value is indicated by two vertical bars, one on either side of the number. For example, as shown |–6| = |6| = 6 because each is 6 units from zero on the number line.

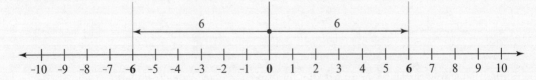

Here are additional examples.

$$|-17| = 17, \quad \left|\frac{2}{3}\right| = \frac{2}{3}, \quad |0| = 0, \quad |-2.5| = 2.5, \quad |245| = 245$$

Because distance always has a *nonnegative* (*positive* or *zero*) value, absolute value is always nonnegative. Furthermore, the absolute value of any *nonzero* number is positive. That is, |nonzero number| > 0.

Tip: As you likely observed, the absolute values of the numbers in the examples are the values of the numbers with no signs attached. This strategy works for a number with a value you know, but do not use it when you don't know the value of the number. The absolute value of an unknown number *x* could be *x* (as in |245| = 245 or |0| = 0) or it could be *x*'s opposite (as in |–17| = 17). A good rule of thumb is you can determine the numerical value of the absolute value of a number *only* if you can mark the number's exact location on a number line.

If a negative sign immediately precedes an absolute value expression, always *first* determine the absolute value before applying the negative sign. Here are examples.

$$-|-17| = -17, \quad -\left|\frac{2}{3}\right| = -\frac{2}{3}, \quad -|-2.5| = -2.5, \quad -|245| = -245$$

Tip: Don't try to "cancel out" the two negative signs when you have expressions like $-|-17| = -17$. The absolute value bars keep you from doing that.

Test Yourself

For questions 1–13, insert <, >, or = in the blank to make a true statement.

1. –100 ____ –2

2. –25 ____ 0

3. –3.25 ____ –3.5

4. $3\frac{3}{4}$ ____ 3.34

5. $\frac{7}{15}$ ____ $\frac{4}{15}$

6. $\frac{1}{3}$ ____ 0.35

7. $\sqrt{37}$ ____ 5.4

8. 0.625 ____ $\frac{5}{8}$

9. 100% ____ 99

10. 3 ____ 200%

11. |–64| ____ |64|

12. $-\left|-\frac{9}{10}\right|$ ____ $\left|-\frac{9}{10}\right|$

13. |–5| ____ 0

14. Order the following list of numbers from least to greatest: –25, 0, $\sqrt{36}$, 50%, $\sqrt{6}$

15. Order the following list of numbers from least to greatest: 3.265, $\frac{3}{5}$, $-\frac{6}{7}$, 3.9, 2^2

Answers

1. <
2. <
3. >
4. >
5. >
6. <
7. >
8. =
9. <
10. >
11. =
12. <
13. >
14. $-25, 0, 50\%, \sqrt{6}, \sqrt{36}$
15. $-\dfrac{6}{7}, \dfrac{3}{5}, 3.265, 3.9, 2^2$

How Do You Add and Subtract Fractions and Decimals?

Even though you are allowed to use a four-function calculator on the FTCE GK Test, you still need to know and understand how to add and subtract fractions and decimals. Understanding the process will make it less likely you will make an error when performing a calculation and will also help you evaluate the reasonableness of the result of your computation.

Adding and Subtracting Fractions

Table 3.5 summarizes the rules for addition and subtraction of fractions.

Table 3.5 Rules for Addition and Subtraction of Fractions

Operation	Rule	Example
Addition	1. **To add two fractions that have the same denominator:**	$\dfrac{5}{8} + \dfrac{1}{8} =$
	Add the numerators of the fractions to find the numerator of the answer, which is placed over the common denominator.	$\dfrac{5+1}{8} = \dfrac{6}{8}$
	Simplify to lowest terms, if possible.	$= \dfrac{6 \div 2}{8 \div 2} = \dfrac{3}{4}$
	2. **To add two fractions that have different denominators:**	$\dfrac{1}{4} + \dfrac{2}{3} =$
	Find a common denominator. The best choice for a common denominator is the least common multiple (LCM) of the denominators.	LCM (3, 4) = 12

Table 3.5 Rules for Addition and Subtraction of Fractions (*Continued*)

Operation	Rule	Example
	Write each fraction as an equivalent fraction having the common denominator as a denominator.	$\frac{1}{4} = \frac{1 \times 3}{4 \times 3} = \frac{3}{12}$ $\frac{2}{3} = \frac{2 \times 4}{3 \times 4} = \frac{8}{12}$
	Add the numerators of the transformed fractions to find the numerator of the answer, which is placed over the common denominator.	$\frac{1}{4} + \frac{2}{3} = \frac{3}{12} + \frac{8}{12} = \frac{3+8}{12} = \frac{11}{12}$
	Simplify to lowest terms, if possible.	Not needed in this problem.
Subtraction	**1. To subtract two fractions that have the same denominator:**	$\frac{5}{8} - \frac{1}{8} =$
	Subtract the numerators of the fractions to find the numerator of the answer, which is placed over the common denominator.	$\frac{5-1}{8} = \frac{4}{8}$
	Simplify to lowest terms, if needed.	$= \frac{4 \div 4}{8 \div 4} = \frac{1}{2}$
	2. To subtract two fractions that have different denominators:	$\frac{3}{4} - \frac{2}{3} =$
	Find a common denominator.	LCM (4, 3) = 12
	Write each fraction as an equivalent fraction having the common denominator as a denominator.	$\frac{3}{4} = \frac{3 \times 3}{4 \times 3} = \frac{9}{12}$ $\frac{2}{3} = \frac{2 \times 4}{3 \times 4} = \frac{8}{12}$
	Subtract the numerators of the transformed fractions to find the numerator of the answer, which is placed over the common denominator.	$\frac{3}{4} - \frac{2}{3} = \frac{9}{12} - \frac{8}{12} = \frac{9-8}{12} = \frac{1}{12}$
	Simplify to lowest terms, if possible.	Not needed in this problem.

Adding and Subtracting Decimals

Given you are allowed to use a calculator on the FTCE GK Test, you should do your decimal computations with the calculator when you take the test. Just to refresh your memory, Table 3.6 summarizes rules for addition and subtraction with decimals.

Table 3.6 Rules for Addition and Subtraction of Decimals

Operation	Rule	Example
Addition	**To add decimals:** Line up the decimal points vertically. *Tip:* Fill in empty decimal places with zeroes to avoid adding incorrectly. Add as you would with whole numbers. Place the decimal point in the answer directly under the decimal points in the problem.	$65.3 + 0.34 + 7.008 =$ $\begin{array}{r} 65.300 \\ 0.340 \\ +\ 7.008 \\ \hline 72.648 \end{array}$
Subtraction	**To subtract decimals:** Line up the decimal points vertically, filling in empty decimal places with zeroes when needed. Subtract as you would with whole numbers. Place the decimal point in the answer directly under the decimal points in the problem.	$9.4 - 3.65 =$ $\begin{array}{r} 9.40 \\ -\ 3.65 \\ \hline 5.75 \end{array}$

Test Yourself

1. Find the greatest common factor of 16 and 20.
2. Find the sum: $\dfrac{3}{10} + \dfrac{1}{2} =$
3. Find the difference: $\dfrac{1}{2} - \dfrac{3}{10} =$
4. Find the sum: 0.125 + 7.2 + 320 + 4.23 =
5. Find the difference: 75.2 − 35.046 =

Answers

1. The largest number that will divide evenly into both 16 and 20 is 4, so GCF (16, 20) = 4.
2. $\dfrac{3}{10} + \dfrac{1}{2} = \dfrac{3}{10} + \dfrac{5}{10} = \dfrac{3+5}{10} = \dfrac{8}{10} = \dfrac{8 \div 2}{10 \div 2} = \dfrac{4}{5}$
3. $\dfrac{1}{2} - \dfrac{3}{10} = \dfrac{5}{10} - \dfrac{3}{10} = \dfrac{5-3}{10} = \dfrac{2}{10} = \dfrac{2 \div 2}{10 \div 2} = \dfrac{1}{5}$
4. 331.555
5. 40.154

How Do You Multiply and Divide Fractions and Decimals?

As with adding and subtracting, if you know and understand how to multiply and divide fractions and decimals, you will be less likely to make an error when doing these calculations. You will also be able to evaluate the reasonableness of the results of your computations.

Multiplying and Dividing Fractions

Table 3.7 summarizes the rules for multiplication and division of fractions.

Table 3.7 Rules for Multiplication and Division of Fractions

Operation	Rule	Example
Multiplication	1. **To multiply two proper fractions, two improper fractions, or a proper fraction and an improper fraction:**	$\dfrac{1}{3} \times \dfrac{3}{4} =$
	Multiply the numerators to obtain the numerator of the product and multiply the denominators to find the denominator of the product.	$\dfrac{1}{3} \times \dfrac{3}{4} = \dfrac{3}{12}$
	Simplify to lowest terms, if possible.	$= \dfrac{3 \div 3}{12 \div 3} = \dfrac{1}{4}$
	2. **To multiply a fraction and a whole number:**	$\dfrac{3}{4} \times 12 =$
	Write the whole number as an equivalent fraction with denominator 1, and then follow Multiplication Rule 1.	$\dfrac{3}{4} \times \dfrac{12}{1} = \dfrac{3 \times 12}{4 \times 1} = \dfrac{36}{4} = \dfrac{36 \div 4}{4 \div 4} = \dfrac{9}{1} = 9$

Table 3.7 Rules for Multiplication and Division of Fractions (*Continued*)

Operation	Rule	Example
	3. To multiply fractions when mixed numbers are involved: Change the mixed numbers to improper fractions and then follow Multiplication Rule 1.	$2\frac{3}{4} \times 1\frac{1}{3} =$ $\frac{11}{4} \times \frac{4}{3} = \frac{11 \times 4}{4 \times 3} = \frac{44}{12}$ $\frac{44 \div 4}{12 \div 4} = \frac{11}{3}$ or $3\frac{2}{3}$
Division	1. To divide two proper fractions, two improper fractions, or a proper fraction and an improper fraction: Multiply the first fraction by the reciprocal of the second fraction using Multiplication Rule 1.	$\frac{4}{3} \div \frac{1}{2} =$ $\frac{4}{3} \times \frac{2}{1} = \frac{8}{3}$ or $2\frac{2}{3}$
	2. To divide a fraction by a whole number: Write the whole number as an equivalent fraction with denominator 1, and then follow Division Rule 1.	$\frac{4}{5} \div 3 =$ $\frac{4}{5} \div \frac{3}{1} = \frac{4}{5} \times \frac{1}{3} = \frac{4 \times 1}{5 \times 3} = \frac{4}{15}$
	3. To divide fractions when mixed numbers are involved: Change the mixed numbers to improper fractions, and then follow Division Rule 1.	$2\frac{1}{3} \div 1\frac{1}{2} =$ $\frac{7}{3} \div \frac{3}{2} = \frac{7}{3} \times \frac{2}{3} = \frac{7 \times 2}{3 \times 3} = \frac{14}{9}$ or $1\frac{5}{9}$

> **Tip:** Here is a mnemonic to help you remember division of fractions: "Keep, change, flip," meaning <u>Keep</u> the first fraction, <u>change</u> division to multiplication, and then <u>flip</u> the second fraction to its reciprocal.

The process of multiplying or dividing fractions can be simplified by dividing out common factors, if any, before any multiplication is performed. For example, $\frac{1}{3} \times \frac{3}{4} = \frac{1}{\cancel{3}_1} \times \frac{\cancel{3}^1}{4} = \frac{1}{4}$. Also, remember you do *not* have to find a common denominator when multiplying or dividing fractions.

Multiplying and Dividing Decimals

As mentioned before, you should do your decimal computations with the calculator when you take the FTCE GK Test. Just for review, Table 3.8 summarizes the rules for multiplication and division with decimals.

Table 3.8 Rules for Multiplication and Division of Decimals

Operation	Rule	Example
Multiplication	To multiply decimals: Multiply the numbers as whole numbers. Place the decimal point in the proper place in the product. The number of decimal places in the product is the sum of the number of decimal places in the numbers being multiplied. If there are not enough places, insert one or more zeroes as needed to the left of the leftmost nonzero digit.	$55.7 \times 0.25 =$ 55.7 (1 place) $\underline{\times 0.25}$ (+ 2 places) 13.925 (3 places)

(*Continued*)

Table 3.8 Rules for Multiplication and Division of Decimals (*Continued*)

Operation	Rule	Example
Division	To divide two decimals:	$2.04 \div 0.002 =$
	Rewrite the problem as an equivalent fractional problem with a whole number divisor. Do this by multiplying the numerator and denominator by the power of 10 that makes the divisor/denominator a whole number.	$\dfrac{2.04}{0.002} = \dfrac{2.04 \times 1000}{0.002 \times 1000} = \dfrac{2040}{2}$
	Divide as with whole numbers. Place the decimal point in the quotient directly above the decimal point in the dividend.	$2\overline{)2040}^{\,1020}$; thus, $2.04 \div 0.002 = 1020$

Don't be concerned about having to do computations on the FTCE GK Test. Because you are allowed to use a four-function calculator, you should be able to do the calculations with little or no difficulty. Most of the required computations on the test will be simple calculations, some of which you probably could do mentally.

Test Yourself

1. Find the product: $\dfrac{3}{10} \times \dfrac{1}{2} =$

2. Find the product: $1\dfrac{1}{2} \times \dfrac{2}{5} =$

3. Find the quotient: $\dfrac{3}{10} \div \dfrac{1}{2} =$

4. Find the product: $(0.0125)(7.2) =$

5. Find the quotient: $345.75 \div 0.0005 =$

Answers

1. $\dfrac{3}{10} \times \dfrac{1}{2} = \dfrac{3 \times 1}{10 \times 2} = \dfrac{3}{20}$

2. $1\dfrac{1}{2} \times \dfrac{2}{5} = \dfrac{3}{2} \times \dfrac{2}{5} = \dfrac{3}{_1\cancel{2}} \times \dfrac{\cancel{2}^1}{5} = \dfrac{3 \times 1}{1 \times 5} = \dfrac{3}{5}$

3. $\dfrac{3}{10} \div \dfrac{1}{2} = \dfrac{3}{10} \times \dfrac{2}{1} = \dfrac{3}{_5\cancel{10}} \times \dfrac{\cancel{2}^1}{1} = \dfrac{3}{5}$

4. 0.09

5. 691,500

How Do You Add, Subtract, Multiply, and Divide Signed Numbers?

The real numbers are often called **signed numbers** because they may be positive (+), negative (−), or zero (no sign). On the FTCE GK Test you will need to know how to perform addition, subtraction, multiplication, and division with signed numbers.

Adding Signed Numbers

When you add two signed numbers, note whether the two numbers have the same sign (both positive or both negative) or have different signs (one positive and one negative). How you do the addition depends on which of these situations is the case. This type of addition is **algebraic addition**. Table 3.9 summarizes the rules for algebraic addition of two signed numbers.

Table 3.9 Rules for Adding Two Signed Numbers

If the signs are:	The rule is:	Examples:
1. the same—both positive or both negative	Add the absolute values and attach the common sign to the sum.	$4 + 6 = 10$ $-4 + -6 = -10$
2. different—one positive and one negative	Subtract the lesser absolute value from the greater absolute value, and indicate the result has the same sign as the number with the greater absolute value; if both numbers have the same absolute value, the sum is zero.	$-4 + 6 = 2$ $4 + -6 = -2$ $5 + -5 = 0$

As you can see, algebraic addition is different from arithmetic addition; particularly, given you don't always "add" to get the sum. In fact, if the signs are different, you subtract to find the sum. How does this make sense? What you must keep in mind is the numbers you worked with in arithmetic were amounts only—they had no signs. Real numbers have an amount *and* a sign. The sign adds a direction to the number. Every real number has an amount and a direction. The number +5 is 5 units in the positive direction. The number –5 is 5 units in the negative direction.

When you add signed numbers, you have to take into account both the amount and the direction of the number. You can illustrate addition on a number line to help you understand the process. Here are examples.

$2 + 5 = ?$

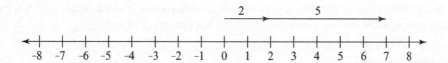

Start at 0 and go 2 units in the positive direction. Then from that point go 5 additional units in the positive direction. You end up at 7. The number line shows $2 + 5 = 7$.

$-2 + -5 = ?$

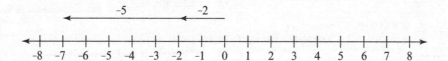

Start at 0 and go 2 units in the negative direction. Then from that point go 5 additional units in the negative direction. You end up at –7. The number line shows $-2 + -5 = -7$.

$2 + -5 = ?$

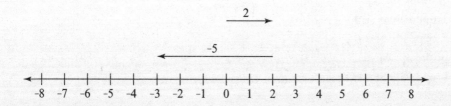

Start at 0 and go 2 units in the positive direction. Then from that point go 5 units in the negative direction. You end up at –3. The number line shows 2 + –5 = –3.

–2 + 5 = ?

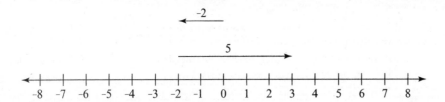

Start at 0 and go 2 units in the negative direction. Then from that point go 5 units in the positive direction. You end up at +3. The number line shows –2 + 5 = 3.

If you have three or more signed numbers to add together, you may find it convenient to, first, add up all the positive numbers; second, add up all the negative numbers; and then add the resulting two answers. Here is an example.

14 + –35 + 6 + –25 =

Add the positives together: 14 + 6 = 20

Add the negatives together: –35 + –25 = –60

Add the two results: 20 + –60 = –40

When two numbers have the same absolute value, but different signs, they are **opposites** of each other. The number zero is its own opposite. The algebraic sum of two numbers that are opposites is zero. For example, –5 + 5 = 0.

Subtracting Signed Numbers

You may be happily surprised to learn you do not have to memorize a set of new rules for subtraction of signed numbers. The reason is subtraction of signed numbers is accomplished by changing the subtraction problem in a special way to an algebraic addition problem, so that the rules listed in Table 3.9 will apply. Here's how you do it (see Table 3.10).

Table 3.10 Algebraic Subtraction of Signed Numbers

Operation	Steps	Example
Subtraction	To subtract two signed numbers: (1) Keep the first number. (2) Change the minus (–) sign to a plus sign (+). (3) Change the sign of the second number. (4) Perform algebraic addition according to the rules of Table 3.9.	–10 – 4 = –10 + –10 + –4 = (Change 4 to –4) –10 + –4 = –14

Think of the minus sign as "+ opposite of." Incorrectly interpreting subtraction is a common mistake. Here are examples of correctly rewriting subtraction problems.

     9 – 16 = 9 + –16 (9 + opposite of 16)

     24 – 15 = 24 + –15 (24 + opposite of 15)

     –8 – 20 = –8 + –20 (–8 + opposite of 20)

     3 – –6 = 3 + 6 (3 + opposite of –6)

   –18 – –4 = –18 + 4 (–18 + opposite of –4)

Here are the solutions to the above examples of algebraic subtraction.

$$9 - 16 = 9 + -16 = -7$$
$$24 - 15 = 24 + -15 = 9$$
$$-8 - 20 = -8 + -20 = -28$$
$$3 - -6 = 3 + 6 = 9$$
$$-18 - -4 = -18 + 4 = -14$$

> **Tip:** Here is a mnemonic to help you remember subtraction of signed numbers: "Keep, change, change," meaning <u>Keep</u> the first number, <u>change</u> subtraction to addition, and then <u>change</u> the second number to its opposite.

Multiplying and Dividing Signed Numbers

Algebraic multiplication and division of signed numbers share the same pattern. Table 3.11 summarizes the rules for multiplying or dividing two signed numbers.

Table 3.11 Rules for Multiplying or Dividing Two Signed Numbers

If the signs are:	The rule is:	Examples:
1. the same—both positive or both negative	Multiply or divide the absolute values as indicated, and label the product as positive (no sign is necessary).	$2 \cdot 5 = 10$ $-2 \cdot -5 = 10$ $\dfrac{12}{4} = 3$ $\dfrac{-12}{-4} = 3$
2. different—one positive and one negative	Multiply or divide the absolute values as indicated, and label the product as negative.	$-2 \cdot 5 = -10$ $2 \cdot -5 = -10$ $\dfrac{-12}{4} = -3$ $\dfrac{12}{-4} = -3$

Notice, unlike algebraic addition, for algebraic multiplication and division when the signs are the same, it doesn't matter what the common sign is, the product/quotient is positive no matter what.

Similarly, unlike algebraic addition, for algebraic multiplication and division when the signs are different, it doesn't matter which number has the greater absolute value—the product and quotient is negative no matter what.

The rules for algebraic addition, subtraction, multiplication, and division apply to all real numbers. Here are examples.

$$-\frac{5}{8} + -\frac{1}{8} = -\frac{6}{8} = -\frac{3}{4}$$

$$\frac{2}{3} - \frac{3}{4} = \frac{8}{12} - \frac{9}{12} = \frac{8}{12} \underset{\substack{\uparrow \\ \text{Apply} \\ \text{to} \\ \text{numerator}}}{-} \frac{9}{12} = \frac{8 + -9}{12} = \frac{-1}{12} = -\frac{1}{12}$$

$$24.5 + 134.28 = 158.78$$

$$-18.5 + 7.25 = -11.25$$

$$\frac{3}{4} \cdot -12 = \frac{3}{{}_1\cancel{4}} \cdot \frac{-\cancel{12}^{-3}}{1} = -\frac{9}{1} = -9$$

$$\left(-2\frac{3}{4}\right)\left(-1\frac{1}{3}\right) = -\frac{11}{{}_1\cancel{4}} \cdot -\frac{\cancel{4}^1}{3} = \frac{11}{3} \text{ or } 3\frac{2}{3}$$

$$(-0.75)(400) = -300$$

$$(-125.43)(-0.005) = 0.62715$$

The two rules for multiplication tell you how to multiply two numbers, but often you will want to find the product of more than two numbers. To do this, **multiply in pairs. You can keep track of the appropriate sign as you** proceed, or you can use the following:

When *zero* is one of the factors, the product is *always* zero; otherwise, products involving an *even* number of *negative* factors are *positive*, whereas, those involving an *odd* number of *negative* factors are *negative*.

Here are examples.

$$\underbrace{(-10)(2)(0)(-5)}_{\text{zero is a factor}} = 0$$

$$\underbrace{(-10)(2)(3)(-5)(-1)(-2)}_{\text{even number of negative factors}} = 600$$

$$\underbrace{(-10)(2)(3)(-5)(-1)}_{\text{odd number of negative factors}} = -300$$

$$(-2)^5 = -32$$

$$(-3)^4 = 81$$

> **Tip:** When you use a negative number as the base in an exponential expression, enclose the negative number in parentheses as shown in $(-3)^4 = 81$. Putting -3 in parentheses means -3 is the number that is used as a factor 4 times. If you write -3^4, Only the 3 will be raised to the 4th power. Thus, $-3^4 = -81$, not 81.

Test Yourself

1. The sum of two positive numbers is always _____ (positive, negative).

2. The sum of two negative numbers is always _____ (positive, negative).

3. The sum of a positive number and a negative number can be either positive or negative, depending on which of the two numbers has the _____ (lesser, greater) absolute value.

4. The product of two positive numbers is always _____ (positive, negative).

5. The product of two negative numbers is always _____ (positive, negative).

6. The product of a positive number and a negative number is always _____ (positive, negative).

7. $-5 + 20 =$ _____.

8. $2.45 + -8 =$ _____.

9. $-\frac{2}{5} + -\frac{4}{5} =$ _____.

10. $45 - -15 = 45 +$ _____ $=$ _____.

11. $-\frac{1}{2} - -\frac{1}{2} = -\frac{1}{2} +$ _____ $=$ _____.

12. $-304.75 - 20.015 = -304.75 +$ _____ $=$ _____.

13. $\left(\frac{1}{2}\right)\left(-\frac{2}{5}\right) =$ _____.

14. $-\frac{3}{10} \div 2 =$ _____.

15. $(-0.0125)(-7.2) =$ _____.

Answers

1. positive
2. negative
3. greater
4. positive
5. positive
6. negative
7. 15
8. −5.55
9. $-\frac{2}{5} + -\frac{4}{5} = \frac{-2 + -4}{5} = \frac{-6}{5} = -\frac{6}{5}$ or $-1\frac{1}{5}$
10. 15, 60
11. $\frac{1}{2}$, 0
12. −20.015, −324.765
13. $\left(\frac{1}{2}\right)\left(-\frac{2}{5}\right) = \frac{1}{{}_1\cancel{2}} \cdot -\frac{\cancel{2}^1}{5} = -\frac{1}{5}$
14. $-\frac{3}{10} \div 2 = -\frac{3}{10} \cdot \frac{1}{2} = -\frac{3}{20}$
15. 0.09

In What Order Do You Perform the Operations?

When more than one operation is involved in a numerical expression, you must follow the **order of operations** to **simplify** the expression:

1. Do computations inside **Parentheses** (or other grouping symbols). If there is more than one operation inside the parentheses, follow the order of operations given here as you do the computations inside the parentheses. If there are grouping symbols within grouping symbols, start with the innermost grouping symbols.

2. Evaluate any terms with **Exponents**.

3. **Multiply** and **Divide** in the order in which they occur from left to right.
4. **Add** and **Subtract** in the order in which they occur from left to right.

Grouping symbols such as parentheses ( ), brackets [ ], and braces { } keep things together that belong together. Fraction bars, absolute value bars, and square root symbols also are grouping symbols. Always do the operations inside grouping symbols FIRST—especially when you have addition and/or subtraction inside the grouping symbol. Otherwise, you might get an incorrect result. When you no longer need the grouping symbol, omit it. Look at this example.

Do this: $(1 + 1)^3 = 2^3 = 8$ (correct answer); NOT this: $(1 + 1)^3 = 1^3 + 1^3 = 1 + 1 = 2$ (wrong answer)

Here is a sentence to help you remember the order of operations: **P**lease **E**xcuse **M**y **D**ear **A**unt **S**ally—abbreviated as **PE(MD)(AS)**. The first letter of each word gives the order of operations:

1. **P**arentheses
2. **E**xponents
3. **M**ultiply and **D**ivide from left to right, whichever comes first.
4. **A**dd and **S**ubtract from left to right, whichever comes first.

Note multiplication does not always have to be done before division, or addition before subtraction. You multiply and divide in the order from left to right they occur in the problem. Similarly, you add and subtract in the order they occur in the problem. That's why there are parentheses around **MD** and **AS** in **PE(MD)(AS)**.

Here are examples of using the order of operations to evaluate numerical expressions.

Evaluate: $90 - 5 \cdot 3^2 + 42 \div (5 + 2)$

$$
\begin{aligned}
90 - 5 \cdot 3^2 + 42 \div (5 + 2) &= 90 - 5 \cdot 3^2 + 42 \div (7) && \text{First, do computations inside parentheses.} \\
&= 90 - 5 \cdot 9 + 42 \div 7 && \text{Next, evaluate exponents.} \\
&= 90 - 45 + 6 && \text{Then, multiply and divide from left to right.} \\
&= 51 && \text{Finally, add and subtract from left to right.}
\end{aligned}
$$

Thus, the numerical expression $90 - 5 \cdot 3^2 + 42 \div (5 + 2) = 51$

Evaluate: $-50 + 40 \div 2^3 - 5(4 + 6)$

$$
\begin{aligned}
-50 + 40 \div 2^3 - 5(4 + 6) &= -50 + 40 \div 2^3 - 5(10) && \text{First, do computations inside parentheses.} \\
&= -50 + 40 \div 8 - 5(10) && \text{Next, evaluate exponents.} \\
&= -50 + 5 - 50 && \text{Then, multiply and divide from left to right.} \\
&= -95 && \text{Finally, add and subtract from left to right.}
\end{aligned}
$$

Thus, the numerical expression $-50 + 40 \div 2^3 - 5(4 + 6) = -95$

Evaluate: $8 - 4 \div (7 - 5) - (7 + 3) \div 2$

$$
\begin{aligned}
8 - 4 \div (7 - 5) - (7 + 3) \div 2 &= 8 - 4 \div (2) - (10) \div 2 && \text{First, do computations inside parentheses.} \\
&= 8 - 4 \div 2 - 10 \div 2 && \text{Next, evaluate exponents — none, so skip this step.} \\
&= 8 - 2 - 5 && \text{Then, divide from left to right.} \\
&= 1 && \text{Finally, subtract from left to right.}
\end{aligned}
$$

Thus, the numerical expression $8 - 4 \div (7 - 5) - (7 + 3) \div 2 = 1$.

> **Caution:** Don't count on the calculator from the testing center to follow the order of operations. Some four-function calculators are not programmed to follow the order of operations. They perform operations in the order they are keyed into the calculator. If you start at the left and key in the problem from left to right and then press the equal sign, most likely the answer displayed will not be the correct answer. Instead, key in the computations according to the order of operations, starting with the computations inside parentheses and ending with addition and subtraction from left to right. As shown in the examples, rewrite the problem as you work through the computations to avoid making careless errors.

Test Yourself

1. When simplifying numerical expressions, follow the _____ _____ _____ (three words).

2. Simplify: $(3 + 2)(14 + 4) \div 9 - 2^4 \cdot 10 + 148$

3. Simplify: $24 \div 6 - 2 \cdot 10 + 34$

4. Simplify: $-2(3 - 8) + 9^2 \div 3$

5. Simplify: $20 + 5 \cdot 7 - 4$

Answers

1. order of operations

2. $(3+2)(14+4) \div 9 - 2^4 \cdot 10 + 148 = (5)(18) \div 9 - 2^4 \cdot 10 + 148$
$= (5)(18) \div 9 - 16 \cdot 10 + 148$
$= 90 \div 9 - 160 + 148$
$= 10 - 160 + 148$
$= -2$

3. $24 \div 6 - 2 \cdot 10 + 34 = 4 - 20 + 34$
$= 18$

4. $-2(3-8) + 9^2 \div 3 = -2(-5) + 9^2 \div 3$
$= -2(-5) + 81 \div 3$
$= 10 + 27$
$= 37$

5. $20 + 5 \cdot 7 - 4 = 20 + 35 - 4$
$= 51$

How Do You Solve Real-World Problems Involving Rational Numbers?

On the FTCE GK Test, you will have to solve real-world contextual problems (commonly known as "word" or "story" problems) involving rational numbers. Use the following steps when solving contextual problems.

1. **Understand the problem.**
   Read the problem and identify what you need to find. Look for a sentence that has words like *find, determine, what is, how many, how far,* or *how much*. Often (but not always) this is the last sentence in the problem.

Organize the information you are given. Ask yourself, "What information is given in the problem that will help me answer the question? Is there a formula I need that is not provided? Are any facts missing? Is there information given I don't need? Are measurement units involved and, if so, what units should my answer have? Can I draw a sketch to help me better understand the problem? Would it help to make a chart or table?

2. **Make a plan.**

   Decide how you can use the information you are given to solve the problem. Ask yourself, "What math concepts apply to this situation?" Decide which operation or operations to use. Table 3.12 has some guidelines to help you decide.

Table 3.12 Guidelines for Selecting Operations

When You Need To:	Use:
Find a sum. Find a total. Combine quantities. Increase a quantity.	Addition
Find a difference. Take away. Find how many or how much is left. Find out how many more or how many less. Decrease a quantity.	Subtraction
Find a product. Perform repeated addition to find a total. Determine how much or how many is a portion of a whole. Find the cost of a given number of units when you know the unit price. Find a percent of a quantity. Determine how many different ways something can occur. Determine how many different combinations are possible.	Multiplication
Find a quotient. Find a ratio or fractional part. Determine how many equal parts are in a whole. Determine the size of equal parts of a whole. Separate an amount into groups of equal size. Find the probability of a simple event.	Division

After you have decided on what operation or operations to use, roughly outline how you will proceed. If measurement units are involved, make sure they work out to give the proper units. This is a powerful tool that is used extensively in the sciences.

3. **Carry out your plan.**

   Solve the problem, using the information and the operation or operations you decided upon.

   Double-check to make sure you copied all of the information accurately. Check the order of the numbers if subtraction or division is involved. Check the signs if you are using positive and negative numbers.

   Key the numbers into the calculator carefully. Look at the display after every entry to make sure you entered what you intended to enter. Be especially careful when decimals or fractions are involved.

4. **Look back.**

   Ask yourself:

   Did I answer the question? Check whether you answered the question asked.

   Does my answer make sense? Note: Explanations will vary in response to this question. Sample explanations are given in this chapter.

   Is the answer stated in the correct units? Make sure the units are the proper units for the answer.

Here is an example of using the problem-solving steps.

> A motor home rents for $250 per week plus $0.20 per mile. Find the rental cost for a 3-week trip of 600 miles for a family of four.

1. **Understand the problem.**
   What do you need to find?
   The rental cost for a 3-week trip of 600 miles.
   What information are you given?
   cost per week: $250
   cost per mile: $0.20
   number of weeks: 3
   number of miles: 600
   number of family members: four
   Is there information given you don't need?
   number of family members: four
2. **Make a plan.**
   The total rental cost includes the cost for 3 weeks of rental and the cost for mileage. To solve the problem use three steps. First, find the cost for the 3 weeks of rental. Next, find the cost for mileage. Then, find the total rental cost.
3. **Carry out the plan.**
   Step 1. Find the cost for 3 weeks of rental. You know the cost per week is $250. Multiply to get the cost for 3 weeks.

   $$\frac{3 \text{ wk}}{1} \cdot \frac{\$250}{\text{wk}} = \frac{3 \,\cancel{\text{wk}}}{1} \cdot \frac{\$250}{\cancel{\text{wk}}} = \$750 \quad \text{Notice that weeks divide out, leaving \$ as the units.}$$

   Step 2. Find the cost for mileage. You know the cost per mile is $0.20. Multiply to get the cost for 600 miles.

   $$\frac{600 \text{ mi}}{1} \cdot \frac{\$0.20}{\text{mi}} = \frac{600 \,\cancel{\text{mi}}}{1} \cdot \frac{\$0.20}{\cancel{\text{mi}}} = \$120 \quad \text{Notice that miles divide out, leaving \$ as the units.}$$

   Step 3. Find the total rental cost for the motor home. Add the results from steps 1 and 2 to find the total.
   cost for 3 weeks of rental + cost for mileage = $750 + $120 = $870
   The total rental cost for the motor home is $870.
4. **Look back.**
   Did I answer the question? Yes, I found the total rental cost for the motor home. ✓
   Does my answer make sense? Yes, the answer seems like a reasonable cost. ✓
   Is the answer stated in the correct units? Yes, the units are dollars, which is correct. ✓

Ratios and Proportions

A ratio is a multiplicative comparison of two quantities. In a paint mixture that uses 2 parts white paint to 5 parts blue paint, the ratio of white paint to blue paint is 2 to 5. You can express this ratio in three different forms: 2 to 5, 2:5, or $\frac{2}{5}$. The numbers 2 and 5 are the **terms** of the ratio. A ratio is a pure number—it does not have any units.

When you find the ratio of two quantities, you must make sure they have the same units so that when you write the ratio, the units will divide out. For example, the ratio of 2 pints to 5 quarts is *not* $\frac{2}{5}$ because these quantities are not expressed in the same units. Since 2 pints = 1 quart, the relationship is 1 quart to 5 quarts, which gives a ratio of $\frac{1}{5}$. If the two quantities cannot be converted to like units, then you must keep the units and write the quotient as a **rate**. For instance, $\frac{140 \text{ miles}}{2 \text{ hours}} = 70 \frac{\text{miles}}{\text{hour}}$ (mph) is a rate of speed.

A **proportion** is a mathematical statement two ratios are equal. The **terms** of the proportion are the four numbers that make up the two ratios. For example, take the proportion $\frac{3}{4} = \frac{9}{12}$. This proportion has terms 3, 4, 9, and 12. The fundamental property of proportions is $\frac{a}{b} = \frac{c}{d}$ if and only if $ad = bc$. In other words, cross products of a proportion are equal. **Cross products** are the product of the numerator of the first ratio times the denominator of the second ratio and the product of the denominator of the first ratio times the numerator of the second ratio.

Here is an example showing the equal cross products for the proportion, $\frac{3}{4} = \frac{9}{12}$.

$$\frac{3}{4} \times \frac{9}{12}$$
$$3 \cdot 12 = 4 \cdot 9$$
$$36 = 36$$

When you are given a proportion that has a missing term, you can use cross products to find the missing term. Look at this example.

> Find the value of x that makes the following proportion true.
> $$\frac{x}{40} = \frac{3}{4}$$

$x \cdot 4 = 40 \cdot 3$ Find the cross products.
$x \cdot 4 = 120$

You can see from the cross products x is the number that multiplies times 4 to give 120. Logical reasoning should tell you

$$x = \frac{120}{4}$$
$$x = 30$$

Note: In the "Algebraic Reasoning and the Coordinate Plane" section of this chapter (page 149), you will learn to solve the equation $x \cdot 4 = 120$ by dividing both sides of the equation by 4, which also gives $x = 30$.

You can shorten the preceding process for solving a proportion by doing the following: Find a cross product you can calculate, and then divide by the numerical term in the proportion you did not use. Given you are allowed to use a calculator on the FTCE GK Test, this is the quickest and most reliable way to solve a proportion on the test. Here's how it would work for the previous example.

> Find the value of x that makes the following proportion true.
> $$\frac{x}{40} = \frac{3}{4}$$

Here's how you key the computations into the calculator: $40 \times 3 \div 4 =$. The display will show 30, the correct answer. *Note:* This keying is one of the instances you can count on the provided calculator to give you a correct answer.

Contextual problems involving proportional relationships are one type of contextual problem you will encounter on the FTCE GK Test. These are problems that deal with ratios, map scales, and scale factors. Here is an example.

> On a map, the distance between two cities is 10.5 inches. If 0.5 inch represents 20 miles, how far, in miles, is it between the two cities (to the nearest mile)?

1. **Understand the problem.**

   What do you need to find?

   the actual distance in miles between the two cities

   What information are you given?

   distance between the cities on the map is 10.5 inches

   scale for map: 0.5 inch represents 20 miles

   Is there information given you don't need?

   No

2. **Make a plan.**

   This problem is a proportion problem involving a map scale. To solve the problem, first, determine the ratios being compared, being sure to compare corresponding quantities in the same order. Next, write a proportion using the two ratios. Then, use cross products to solve the proportion.

3. **Carry out the plan.**

   Step 1. Determine the ratios being compared.

   Let d be the actual distance in miles between the two cities. The first sentence ("the distance between two cities is 10.5 inches") gives the first ratio: $\frac{d(\text{in miles})}{10.5 \text{ in}}$. The second sentence ("0.5 inch represents 20 miles") gives the second ratio: $\frac{20 \text{ miles}}{0.5 \text{ in}}$. (Notice, you put miles in the numerator in the second ratio because you have miles in the numerator in the first ratio.)

   Step 2. Write a proportion using the two ratios.

   $$\frac{d(\text{in miles})}{10.5 \text{ in}} = \frac{20 \text{ miles}}{0.5 \text{ in}}$$

   Step 3. Use cross products to solve the proportion (omitting the units for convenience).

   $\frac{d}{10.5} = \frac{20}{0.5}$

   $(10.5)(20)$ Find a cross product you can calculate. You don't know the value of d, so the only cross product you can calculate is 10.5 times 20.

   $d = \frac{(10.5)(20)}{0.5}$ Divide by 0.5, the numerical term you didn't use.

   $d = \frac{210}{0.5}$ (You can skip this step)

   $d = 420$ miles

   You can skip $d = \frac{210}{0.5}$ (and save time) by doing the computation above it with your calculator like this: $10.5 \times 20 \div 0.5 =$. The display will show 420, the correct answer.

   The actual distance in miles between the two cities is 420 miles.

4. **Look back.**

   Did I answer the question? Yes, I found the actual distance in miles between the two cities. ✓

   Does my answer make sense? Yes, if 0.5 inch corresponds to 20 miles, then 1 inch corresponds to 40 miles, so 10.5 inches should represent at least 400 miles. ✓

   Is the answer stated in the correct units? Yes, the units are miles, which is correct. ✓

Percent Problems

Percent problems can be solved in several ways. Most of the percent problems on the FTCE GK Test can be solved using a "percent proportion" that has the following form:

$$\frac{r}{100} = \frac{part}{whole}$$

r = the number in front of the % sign
part = the quantity that is near the word "is"
whole = the quantity that immediately follows the word "of"

Tip: Think *"is over of"* to help you get $\frac{part\ ("is")}{whole\ ("of")}$ correct.

The relationship between the three elements r, **part**, and **whole** can be explained in a percent statement like this:

The part is r% of the whole.

The secret to solving percent problems is being able to identify the three elements correctly. Start with r and the whole because they are usually easier to find. The part will be the other amount in the problem. The value of two of the elements will be given in the problem, and you will be solving for the third element. After you identify the three elements, plug the two you know into the percent proportion and solve for the one you don't know.

Here is an example of what to do when the part is missing.

> What is 20% of 560?

Identify the elements.

$$r = 20$$
$$part = ? = x$$
$$whole = 560$$

Plug into the percent proportion.

$$\frac{r}{100} = \frac{part}{whole}$$
$$\frac{20}{100} = \frac{x}{560}$$

Solve the proportion.

$20 \cdot 560$ — Find a cross product you can calculate. You don't know the value of x, so the only cross product you can calculate is 20 times 560.

$x = \dfrac{20 \cdot 560}{100}$ — Divide by 100, the numerical term you didn't use.

$x = 112$

Here's how you key the computations into the calculator: $20 \times 560 \div 100 =$. The display will show 112, the correct answer.

Here is an example of what to do when the whole is missing.

> 30 is 25% of what amount?

Identify the elements.

$$r = 25$$
$$\text{part} = 30$$
$$\text{whole} = ? = x$$

Plug into the percent proportion.

$$\frac{r}{100} = \frac{\text{part}}{\text{whole}}$$
$$\frac{25}{100} = \frac{30}{x}$$

Solve the proportion.

$100 \cdot 30$ — Find a cross product you can calculate. You don't know the value of x, so the only cross product you can calculate is 100 times 30.

$x = \dfrac{100 \cdot 30}{25}$ — Divide by 25, the numerical term you didn't use.

$x = 120$

Here's how you key the computations into the calculator: $100 \times 30 \div 25 =$. The display will show 120, the correct answer.

Here is an example when r is missing.

> 400 is what percent of 500?

Identify the elements.

$$r = ?$$
$$\text{part} = 400$$
$$\text{whole} = 500$$

Plug into the percent proportion.

$$\frac{r}{100} = \frac{\text{part}}{\text{whole}}$$
$$\frac{r}{100} = \frac{400}{500}$$

Solve the proportion.

$100 \cdot 400$ — Find a cross product you can calculate. You don't know the value of r, so the only cross product you can calculate is 100 times 400.

$r = \dfrac{100 \cdot 400}{500}$ — Divide by 500, the numerical term you didn't use.

$r = 80$

$r\% = 80\%$

Notice because r is the number attached to the percent sign in the percent statement, you have to put a % sign after your calculated value of r to answer the question.

Just so you know, there are other ways to work percent problems. For instance, to answer "What is 20% of 560?", change 20% to a fraction or a decimal fraction and then multiply 560 by the converted number.

$$20\% \text{ of } 560 = (0.20)(560) = 112 \quad \text{or} \quad 20\% \text{ of } 560 = \frac{1}{5} \cdot \frac{560}{1} = \frac{1}{1\cancel{5}} \cdot \frac{\cancel{560}^{112}}{1} = 112$$

You get the same answer as was obtained earlier. The proportion method is emphasized in this CliffsNotes guide because when you are allowed to use a calculator, it is a reliable and efficient way to solve simple percent problems.

Contextual Problems Involving Percents

You can expect to encounter contextual problems involving percents on the FTCE GK Test. These are problems that deal with finding percentages, percents, and wholes in various everyday situations. Here is an example.

> A stereo system that regularly sells for $650 is marked 20% off for a 1-day sale. What is the amount saved if the stereo is purchased at the sale price?

1. **Understand the problem.**

   What do you need to find?

   the amount saved at the sale price

   What information are you given?

   regular price: $650

   amount saved: 20% off regular price

   It's a 1-day sale.

   Is there information given you don't need?

   that it's a 1-day sale

2. **Make a plan.**

   To find the amount saved, you will need to answer the question: What is 20% of $650? To solve the problem: Identify the elements of the percent problem, plug the values into the percent proportion, and then solve the proportion.

3. **Carry out the plan.**

   Step 1. Identify the elements.

   $$r = 20$$
   $$\text{part} = ? = x$$
   $$\text{whole} = \$650$$

   Step 2. Plug into the percent proportion (omitting the units for convenience).

   $$\frac{r}{100} = \frac{\text{part}}{\text{whole}}$$
   $$\frac{20}{100} = \frac{x}{650}$$

   Step 3. Solve the proportion.

   $20 \cdot 650$ Find a cross product you can calculate. You don't know the value of x, so the only cross product you can calculate is 20 times 650.

   $x = \dfrac{20 \cdot 650}{100}$ Divide by 100, the numerical term you didn't use.

   $x = 130$

   Here's how you key the computations into the calculator: $20 \times 650 \div 100 =$. The display will show 130, the correct answer.

   The amount saved is $130.

4. **Look back.**

   Did I answer the question? Yes, I found the amount saved. ✓

   Does my answer make sense? Yes, 20% is $\frac{1}{5}$. For a $500 item, the savings would be $100. For a $650 item, the savings would be a little over $100. ✓

   Is the answer stated in the correct units? Yes, the units are dollars, which is correct. ✓

Test Yourself

1. The four problem-solving steps are _____, _____, _____, and _____.

2. A _____ is the comparison of two quantities. It is a pure number. It does not have any _____.

3. A _____ is a statement that two _____ are equal.

4. If 12 ounces of salt are mixed with 5 ounces of ground pepper, what is the ratio of salt to pepper?

5. What are the terms of the proportion $\frac{x}{50} = \frac{7}{25}$?

6. In a proportion, the _____ (two words) are equal.

7. Solve the proportion $\frac{x}{50} = \frac{7}{25}$ for x.

8. What is 40% of $1,200?

9. In a paint mixture that uses 2 parts white paint to 5 parts blue paint, how many quarts of white paint are needed to mix with 20 quarts of blue paint?

10. At an art exhibit at a local gallery, 15 of the 25 paintings displayed were purchased by a well-known art connoisseur. What percent of the paintings were purchased by the art connoisseur?

Answers

1. understand the problem, make a plan, carry out the plan, look back

2. ratio, units

3. proportion, ratios

4. 12 to 5

5. x, 50, 7, 25

6. cross products

7. $\frac{x}{50} = \frac{7}{25}$

   $50 \cdot 7$ Find a cross product you can calculate. You don't know the value of x, so the only cross product you can calculate is 50 times 7.

   $x = \frac{50 \cdot 7}{25}$ Divide by 25, the numerical term you didn't use.

   $x = 14$

8. What is 40% of $1,200?

   Identify the elements.

   $$r = 40$$
   $$\text{part} = ? = x$$
   $$\text{whole} = \$1,200$$

   Plug into the percent proportion.

   $$\frac{r}{100} = \frac{\text{part}}{\text{whole}}$$
   $$\frac{40}{100} = \frac{x}{\$1,200}$$

   Solve the proportion (omitting the units for convenience).

   $40 \cdot 1,200$ Find a cross product you can calculate. You don't know the value of x, so the only cross product you can calculate is 40 times 1,200.

   $x = \dfrac{40 \cdot 1,200}{100}$ Divide by 100, the numerical term you didn't use.

   $x = 480$

   40% of $1,200 is $480.

9. This problem is a proportion problem involving ratios in a mixture. To solve the problem, determine the ratios being compared, being sure to compare corresponding quantities in the same order; write a proportion using the two ratios; and then use cross products to solve the proportion.

   Step 1. Determine the ratios being compared.

   Let x be the amount (in quarts) of white paint needed. The first part of the sentence ("2 parts white paint to 5 parts blue paint") gives the first ratio: $\dfrac{2 \text{ parts white paint}}{5 \text{ parts blue paint}}$. The second part of the sentence ("how many quarts of white paint are needed to mix with 20 quarts of blue paint") gives the second ratio: $\dfrac{x \text{ (quarts) white paint}}{20 \text{ quarts blue paint}}$

   Step 2. Write a proportion using the two ratios.

   $$\frac{2 \text{ parts white paint}}{5 \text{ parts blue paint}} = \frac{x \text{ (quarts) white paint}}{20 \text{ quarts blue paint}}$$

   Step 3. Use cross products to solve the proportion (omitting the units for convenience).

   $$\frac{2}{5} = \frac{x}{20}$$

   $2 \cdot 20$ Find a cross product you can calculate. You don't know the value of x, so the only cross product you can calculate is 2 times 20.

   $x = \dfrac{2 \cdot 20}{5}$ Divide by 5, the numerical term you didn't use.

   $x = 8$

   The number of quarts of white paint needed is 8 quarts.

   Did I answer the question? Yes, I found the number of quarts of white paint needed. ✓

Does my answer make sense? Yes, the paint is mixed in a ratio of 2 parts white paint to 5 parts blue paint, so you need 2 quarts of white paint for every 5 quarts of blue paint. Thus, 8 quarts of white paint for 20 quarts of blue paint makes sense. ✓

Is the answer stated in the correct units? Yes, the units are quarts, which is correct. ✓

10. To find the percent purchased, you will need to answer the question: 15 is $r\%$ of 25? To solve the problem: Identify the elements of the percent problem, plug the values into the percent proportion, and solve the proportion.

    Step 1. Identify the elements.

    $$r = ?$$
    $$\text{part} = 15$$
    $$\text{whole} = 25$$

    Step 2. Plug into the percent proportion.

    $$\frac{r}{100} = \frac{\text{part}}{\text{whole}}$$
    $$\frac{r}{100} = \frac{15}{25}$$

    Step 3. Solve the proportion.

    $100 \cdot 15$ Find a cross product you can calculate. You don't know the value of r, so the only cross product you can calculate is 100 times 15.

    $r = \dfrac{100 \cdot 15}{25}$ Divide by 25, the numerical term you didn't use.

    $r = 60$

    $r\% = 60\%$

    The percent of the paintings purchased by the art connoisseur is 60%.

    Did I answer the question? Yes, I found the percent of the paintings purchased by the art connoisseur. ✓

    Does my answer make sense? Yes, since $\frac{15}{25}$ is a little over one-half (50%), 60% is a reasonable answer. ✓

    Is the answer stated in the correct units? The answer is a percent, so it should not have any units. ✓

Sample Questions

Directions: Read each question and select the best answer choice.

1. Find the greatest common factor of 18 and 30.

    A. 2
    B. 3
    C. 6
    D. 90

2. Express the product $5 \cdot 5 \cdot 7 \cdot 7 \cdot 7$ using exponents.

    A. $2^5 \cdot 3^7$
    B. 57^5
    C. $5^2 \cdot 7^3$
    D. $5^3 \cdot 7^2$

3. Which calculation should be performed first to simplify this expression?

$$-8 + 45 \cdot 18 \div 3^2$$

   A. $-8 + 45$
   B. $45 \cdot 18$
   C. $18 \div 3^2$
   D. 3^2

4. If 25% of a monthly salary of $2,800 is budgeted for food, how much money is budgeted for food?

   A. $70
   B. $210
   C. $700
   D. $2,100

Answer Explanations for Sample Questions

1. **C.** The greatest common factor of 18 and 30 is the largest number that will divide into both 18 and 30 evenly. The factors of 18 are 1, 2, 3, 6, 9, and 18. The factors of 30 are 1, 2, 3, 5, 6, 10, 15, and 30. Looking at the two lists of factors, you can see 6 is the largest factor that is common to both lists, so it is the largest number that will divide into both 18 and 30 evenly. Thus, GCF (18, 30) = 6.

2. **C.** The product $5 \cdot 5 \cdot 7 \cdot 7 \cdot 7 = 5^2 \cdot 7^3$, which indicates 2 factors of 5 and 3 factors of 7. The other answer choices do not indicate 2 factors of 5 and 3 factors of 7.

3. **D.** To simplify the expression $-8 + 45 \cdot 18 \div 3^2$, follow the order of operations. Operations in parentheses, if present, should be performed first. There are no parentheses in the given expression, so simplify exponents, if present. Because 3^2 is an exponential expression, it should be performed first. It would be incorrect to perform $-8 + 45$ first (Choice **A**) because addition and subtraction, from left to right, are performed last when there are no parentheses indicating to do otherwise. It would be incorrect to perform $45 \cdot 18$ (Choice **B**) or $18 \div 3$ (Choice **C**) first because multiplication and division, from left to right, are performed after exponentiation, unless there are parentheses indicating to do otherwise.

4. **C.** To find the amount budgeted for food, answer the following question: What is 25% of 2,800?

   Method 1: To solve the problem, identify the elements of the percent problem, plug the values into the percent proportion, and solve the proportion.

   Step 1. Identify the elements.

   $$r = 25$$
   $$\text{part} = ? = x$$
   $$\text{whole} = \$2,800$$

   Step 2. Plug into the percent proportion.

   $$\frac{r}{100} = \frac{\text{part}}{\text{whole}}$$
   $$\frac{25}{100} = \frac{x}{\$2,800}$$

   Step 3. Solve the proportion (omitting the units for convenience).

   $25 \cdot 2,800$ Find a cross product you can calculate. You don't know the value of x, so the only cross product you can calculate is 25 times 2,800.

   $x = \dfrac{25 \cdot 2,800}{100}$ Divide by 100, the numerical term you didn't use.

   $x = \$700$

The amount budgeted for food is $700, Choice **C**.

Did I answer the question? Yes, I found the amount budgeted for food. ✓

Does my answer make sense? Yes, 25% is one-fourth, so $700 is a reasonable answer. ✓

Is the answer stated in the correct units? Yes, the units are dollars, which is correct. ✓

Method 2: Change 25% to a decimal fraction or common fraction and multiply:

25% of $2,800 = (0.25)($2,800) = $700

Or 25% of $\$2{,}800 = \dfrac{1}{4} \cdot \dfrac{\$2{,}800}{1} = \dfrac{1}{\cancel{4}_1} \cdot \dfrac{\cancel{\$2{,}800}^{700}}{1} = \$700$

Choice **A** results if you make a decimal point error. Choice **B** results if you solve the problem incorrectly by finding 75% of $2,800 and you make a decimal point error. Choice **D** results if you solve the problem incorrectly by finding 75% of $2,800.

Geometry and Measurement

According to the *Competencies and Skills Required for Teacher Certification in Florida*, 20th Edition (see page 59 for the Web address), the competencies/skills you should be able to do for this area of mathematics are the following:

- Identify and classify simple two- and three-dimensional figures according to their mathematical properties.
- Solve problems involving ratio and proportion (e.g., scaled drawings, models, real-world scenarios).
- Determine an appropriate measurement unit and form (e.g., scientific notation) for real-world problems involving length, area, volume, or mass.
- Solve real-world measurement problems including fundamental units (e.g., length, mass, time), derived units (e.g., miles per hour, dollars per gallon), and unit conversions.

What Is Congruence?

Congruent (denoted as ≅) geometric figures have exactly the same size and same shape. They are superimposable, meaning they will fit exactly on top of each other. Corresponding parts of congruent figures are congruent.

Here are examples of congruent figures (same size and shape).

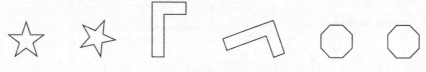

Congruent Figures

Hash marks (as shown in the figure below) can be used to draw attention to corresponding congruent parts.

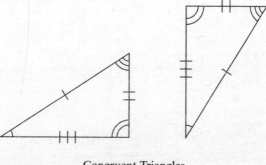

Congruent Triangles

107

The figures below are not congruent. They have the same shape, but not the same size.

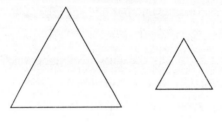

Not Congruent

These figures are not congruent. They are about the same size, but they do not have the same shape. One is a right triangle and the other is an equilateral triangle.

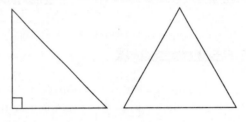

Not Congruent

How Do You Classify Angles?

In geometry, the terms **point**, **line**, and **plane** are undefined. You can think of a point as a location in space. You can think of a line as a set of points that extends infinitely far in both directions. You can think of a plane as a set of points that form a flat infinite surface. *Note:* For discussions in this CliffsNotes guide, unless specifically stated otherwise, all plane figures and objects are considered to lie in the same plane.

See the section "What Are Two-Dimensional Figures?" later in this chapter (page 112) for a discussion of plane (two-dimensional) figures.

A **ray** is a portion of a line extending from a point in one direction. When two rays meet at a common point, they form an **angle**. The point where the rays meet is the **vertex** of the angle.

Tip: The plural of *vertex* is *vertices*.

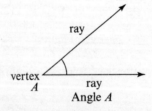

Angle A

You can measure angles in **degrees**. The symbol ° stands for degrees. The measure of angle A is written $m\angle A$. Congruent angles have equal measures.

An **acute angle** measures between 0° and 90°.

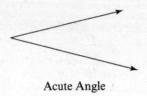

Acute Angle

A **right angle** measures exactly 90°. A small box in the angle indicates a right angle.

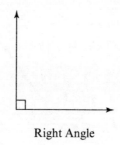

Right Angle

An **obtuse angle** measures between 90° and 180°.

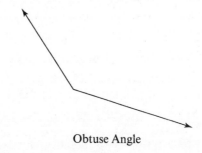

Obtuse Angle

A **straight angle** measures exactly 180°.

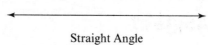

Straight Angle

Two angles whose sum is 90° are **complementary angles.**

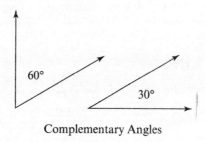

Complementary Angles

Two angles whose sum is 180° are **supplementary angles.**

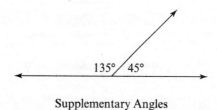

Supplementary Angles

Adjacent angles are two angles that have a common vertex, a common side, and do not overlap.

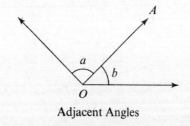

Adjacent Angles

109

Two nonadjacent angles formed by intersecting lines are **vertical angles.** Vertical angles formed by two intersecting lines are congruent as shown in the following figure.

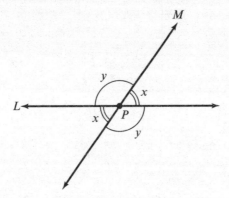

Two Pairs of Congruent Vertical Angles

A **bisector of an angle** is a line or ray that passes through the vertex of the angle and divides it into two congruent angles.

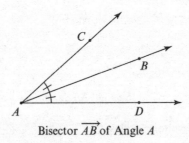

Bisector $\overrightarrow{AB}$ of Angle A

How Do You Classify Lines?

Lines in a plane can be parallel or intersecting.

Intersecting lines cross at a point in the plane.

Intersecting Lines

Parallel lines (in a plane) never meet. The distance between them is always the same.

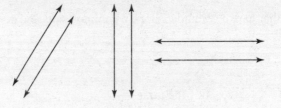

Pairs of Parallel Lines

A shorthand way to indicate that $\overleftrightarrow{AB}$ is parallel to $\overleftrightarrow{CD}$ is to write $\overleftrightarrow{AB} \parallel \overleftrightarrow{CD}$.

Note: $\overleftrightarrow{AB}$ means the line that contains the points A and B and extends infinitely far in both directions.

Perpendicular lines intersect at right angles.

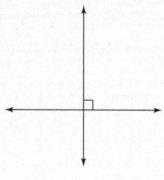

Perpendicular Lines

A shorthand way to indicate $\overleftrightarrow{AB}$ is perpendicular to $\overleftrightarrow{EF}$ is to write $\overleftrightarrow{AB} \perp \overleftrightarrow{EF}$.

The **line segment** $\overline{AB}$ is a part of a line connecting the points A and B and includes A and B. A and B are its **endpoints**. Its length is AB. Congruent segments have equal lengths.

A **tangent line** to a circle intersects the circle in exactly one point.

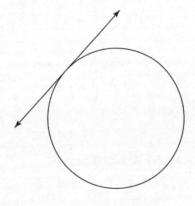

Tangent Line

Following are theorems about lines that are useful to know.

- The shortest distance from a point to a line is the measure of the perpendicular line segment from the point to the line.
- Two distinct lines (in a plane) that are perpendicular to the same line are parallel.
- If a line in a plane is perpendicular to one of two parallel lines, it is perpendicular to the other parallel line.
- A radius drawn to the point of contact of a tangent to a circle is perpendicular to the tangent at that exact point.

Test Yourself

1. Congruent geometric figures have exactly the same _____ and _____.

2. A right angle measures exactly _____.

3. An angle that measures 40° is a(n) _____ angle.

4. An angle that measures 165° is a(n) _____ angle.

5. An angle that measures exactly 180° is a(n) _____ angle.

6. If one of two complementary angles measures 25°, what is the measure of the other angle?

7. If two angles measure 120° and 60°, the two angles are _____ angles.

8. Two lines in a plane that never meet are _____ lines.

9. Two lines that intersect at right angles are _____ lines.

10. A line that meets a circle in exactly one point is a _____ line to the circle.

Answers

1. size, shape
2. 90°
3. acute
4. obtuse
5. straight
6. 90° − 25° = 65°
7. supplementary
8. parallel
9. perpendicular
10. tangent

What Are Two-Dimensional Figures?

Two-dimensional (plane) figures are flat shapes that lie in a plane. The plane figures that are most important for you to know for the FTCE GK Test are the circle and polygons, including triangles, quadrilaterals, pentagons, hexagons, and octagons.

How Do You Classify Polygons?

A **polygon** is a closed plane figure composed of **sides** that are straight line segments. The point at which the two sides of a polygon intersect is a **vertex**. A **regular polygon** has all sides and angles congruent. Polygons are classified by the number of sides they have. Following are examples of regular polygons.

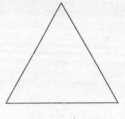

Triangle (3 sides)

Quadrilateral (4 sides)

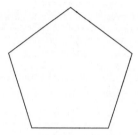

Pentagon (5 sides)

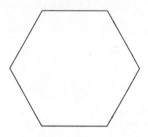

Hexagon (6 sides)

A line segment that connects two nonconsecutive vertices of a polygon is a **diagonal.** The number of diagonals of an *n*-sided polygon is given by the formula $\frac{n(n-3)}{2}$. Here are examples of regular polygons with the number of diagonals indicated below the figure.

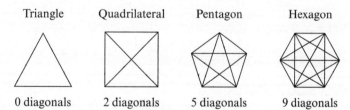

If all the diagonals of a polygon lie within the interior of the polygon, the polygon is **convex;** otherwise, the polygon is **concave.** Here are examples.

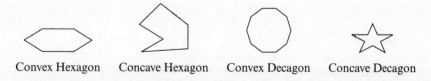

The sum of the measures of the interior angles of an *n*-sided polygon equals $(n-2)180°$. Thus, the sum of the measures of the interior angles of a triangle is $(3-2)180° = 1 \cdot 180° = 180°$, of a quadrilateral is

(4 − 2)180° = 2 · 180° = 360°, of a pentagon is (5 − 2)180° = 3 · 180° = 540°, and so on. The figure below shows the five interior angles of a regular pentagon.

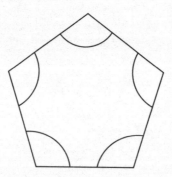

An exterior angle of a polygon is the angle between one side of the polygon and the extension of the side adjacent to it. The sum of the measures of the exterior angles of a polygon is 360°, no matter how many sides the polygon has.

The figure below shows an exterior angle of a regular pentagon.

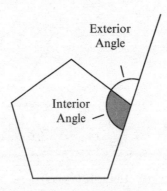

Test Yourself

1. A _____ polygon has all sides and angles congruent.

2. A four-sided polygon is a _____.

3. A pentagon has exactly _____ sides.

4. A hexagon has exactly _____ sides.

5. An octagon has exactly _____ sides.

6. The sum of the measures of the interior angles of a pentagon equals _____.

7. The sum of the measures of the exterior angles of a pentagon equals _____.

8. A line segment that connects two nonconsecutive vertices of a polygon is a _____.

9. A triangle has _____ diagonals.

Answers

1. regular
2. quadrilateral
3. five
4. six
5. eight
6. $(5 - 2)180° = (3)180° = 540°$
7. $360°$
8. diagonal
9. zero

How Do You Classify Triangles?

A **triangle** is a three-sided polygon. The sum of the interior angles of a triangle is 180°. Triangles can be classified by sides or by angles.

By sides, triangles are equilateral, isosceles, or scalene. An **equilateral triangle** has three congruent sides. An **isosceles** triangle has at least two congruent sides. A **scalene** triangle has no congruent sides.

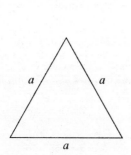
Equilateral Triangle

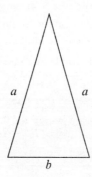
Isosceles Triangle

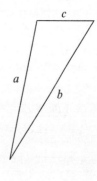
Scalene Triangle

Another way to classify triangles is by their interior angles. An **acute** triangle has three acute interior angles. A **right** triangle has exactly one interior right angle. An **obtuse** triangle has exactly one obtuse interior angle.

Acute Triangle

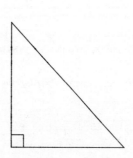
Right Triangle

Obtuse Triangle

Congruent triangles are triangles for which corresponding sides and corresponding angles are congruent. In the figure shown, triangle *ABC* is congruent to triangle *DEF*, denoted as $\triangle ABC \cong \triangle DEF$.

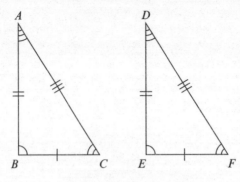

Congruent Triangles

> **Tip: Corresponding parts of congruent triangles have equal measures.**

You can use the following theorems to prove two triangles are congruent.

- If three sides of one triangle are congruent, correspondingly, to three sides of another triangle, then the two triangles are congruent: **SSS** (side-side-side).
- If two sides and the included angle of one triangle are congruent, correspondingly, to two sides and the included angle of another triangle, then the two triangles are congruent: **SAS** (side-angle-side).
- If two angles and the included side of one triangle are congruent, correspondingly, to two angles and the included side of another triangle, then the two triangles are congruent: **ASA** (angle-side-angle).
- If two angles and the nonincluded side of one triangle are congruent, correspondingly, to two angles and the nonincluded side of another triangle, then the two triangles are congruent: **AAS** (angle-angle-side).

> **Tip: Two methods that do NOT work for proving congruence are AAA (three corresponding angles congruent) and SSA (two corresponding sides and the <u>nonincluded</u> angle congruent).**

Here are useful theorems to know about triangles.

- **Triangle inequality:** The sum of the measures of any two sides of a triangle must be greater than the measure of the third side. Look at these examples.

    Can 4, 5, and 7 be the lengths of the sides of a triangle?

    Yes, because $4 + 5 = 9 > 7$, $4 + 7 = 11 > 9$, and $5 + 7 = 12 > 4$.

    Can 3, 5, and 10 be the lengths of the sides of a triangle?

    No, because $3 + 5 = 8 < 10$.

- If two sides of a triangle are congruent, then the angles opposite those sides are congruent; and, conversely, if two angles of a triangle are congruent, then the sides opposite those angles are congruent. Look at these examples.

    In triangle *ABC* shown below, $\overline{AC} \cong \overline{AB}$. Therefore, $\angle B \cong \angle C$.

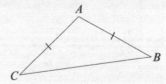

In triangle RST shown below, $\angle S \cong \angle T$. Therefore, $\overline{RT} \cong \overline{RS}$.

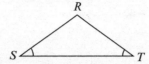

Test Yourself

1. The sum of the interior angles of a triangle is _____.

2. A(n) _____ triangle has three congruent sides.

3. A scalene triangle has _____ congruent sides.

4. An acute triangle has _____ acute angles.

5. Can 8, 5, and 15 be the lengths of the sides of a triangle? _____ (Yes, No)

Answers

1. 180°
2. equilateral
3. No
4. three
5. No, because 8 + 5 = 13 < 15.

How Do You Classify Quadrilaterals?

Quadrilaterals can be classified as either trapezoids or parallelograms.

A **trapezoid** has two definitions, both of which are widely accepted. One definition is a trapezoid is a quadrilateral that has *exactly* one pair of opposite sides that are parallel. This definition would exclude parallelograms as a special case. The other definition is a trapezoid is a quadrilateral that has *at least* one pair of parallel sides. This definition would allow any parallelogram to be considered a special kind of trapezoid. This conflicting situation is one of the few times mathematicians do not agree on the definition of a term. You can expect that answers to problems involving trapezoids on the FTCE GK Test will not hinge on which of these definitions for trapezoid you choose to use during the test. This CliffsNotes guide uses the following definition for trapezoid:

A **trapezoid** is a quadrilateral that has exactly one pair of parallel sides.

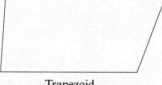

Trapezoid

In a **parallelogram**, opposite sides are parallel and congruent.

Parallelogram

Some parallelograms have special names because of their special properties.

A **rhombus** is a parallelogram that has four congruent sides.

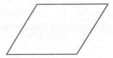

Rhombus

A **rectangle** is a parallelogram that has four right angles.

Rectangle

A **square** is a parallelogram that has four right angles and four congruent sides.

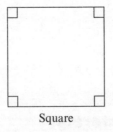

Square

Tip: A square is a rhombus that has four right angles, and a square is a rectangle that has four congruent sides.

Following are useful theorems about quadrilaterals to know.

- The sum of the angles of a quadrilateral is 360°.
- If the diagonals of a quadrilateral bisect each other, the quadrilateral is a parallelogram.
- If two sides of a quadrilateral are parallel and congruent, the quadrilateral is a parallelogram.
- The lengths of the diagonals of a rectangle, square, or rhombus are equal.
- In a rhombus or square, the diagonals are perpendicular to each other.
- If the diagonals of a quadrilateral are perpendicular bisectors of each other, the quadrilateral is a rhombus.
- If a parallelogram has one right angle, it has four right angles and is a rectangle.

Test Yourself

1. A _____ is a quadrilateral that has exactly one pair of parallel sides.

2. In a parallelogram, opposite sides are _____ and _____.

3. Rhombuses, rectangles, and squares are _____.

4. Rectangles and squares have four _____ angles.

5. Rhombuses and squares have four _____ sides.

Answers

1. trapezoid
2. congruent, parallel
3. parallelograms
4. right
5. congruent

What Are the Properties of a Circle?

A **circle** is a closed plane figure for which all points are the same distance from a point within, called the **center**. A **radius** of a circle is a line segment joining the center of the circle to any point on the circle. A **diameter** is a line segment through the center of the circle with endpoints on the circle. The diameter of a circle is twice the radius. Conversely, the radius of a circle is half the diameter. A **chord** of a circle is a segment whose endpoints lie on the circle.

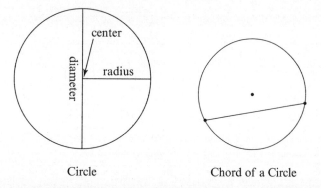

Circle   Chord of a Circle

Tip: The plural of *radius* is *radii*.

Test Yourself

1. A circle is a closed plane figure for which all points are the same distance from a point within, called the _____.

2. The diameter of a circle is _____ the radius.

3. A _____ is a segment whose endpoints lie on the circle.

Indicate whether the statement is true or false.

4. All radii of a circle are congruent.

5. A chord of a circle that passes through its center is a diameter.

Answers

1. center
2. twice

3. chord
4. true
5. true

What Are Three-Dimensional Figures?

Three-dimensional figures are solid figures that occupy space. The solid figures you should be able to recognize for the FTCE GK Test are prisms, pyramids, cylinders, cones, and spheres.

A **prism** is a solid figure with two congruent and parallel bases. The sides of a prism are rectangles. The bases of a prism can have the shape of any polygon. Prisms are named according to the shape of their bases.

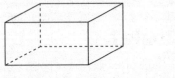
Rectangular Prism

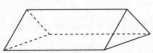
Triangular Prism

A **cube** is a special rectangular prism that has six congruent faces, all of which are squares.

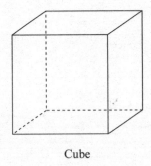
Cube

A **pyramid** is a solid figure with exactly one base. The sides of a pyramid are triangles. The base can have the shape of any polygon. Pyramids are named according to the shape of their bases.

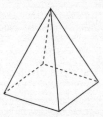
Square Pyramid

Triangular Pyramid

A **cylinder** has two parallel congruent bases, which are circles. It has one rectangular side that wraps around.

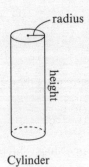
Cylinder

120

A **cone** has one circular base and a curved side that wraps around.

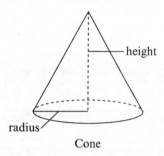
Cone

A **sphere** is shaped like a ball. Every point on the sphere is the same distance from a point within, called the **center** of the sphere. The **radius** of the sphere is a line segment from the center of the sphere to any point on the sphere. The **diameter** of the sphere is a line segment joining two points of the sphere and passing through its center. The radius of the sphere is half the diameter. Conversely, the diameter is twice the radius.

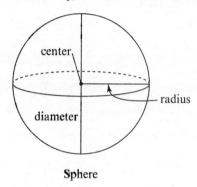
Sphere

Test Yourself

1. The sides of a prism are _____, and its bases can have the shape of any _____.

2. Prisms and cylinders have _____ congruent and parallel bases.

3. _____ and _____ have exactly one base.

4. A _____ is a rectangular prism that has six congruent faces.

5. The points on a _____ are the same distance from a point within, called its center.

Answers

1. rectangles, polygon
2. two
3. Pyramids, cones
4. cube
5. sphere

What Is Similarity?

Similar (denoted as ~) geometric figures have the same shape, but not necessarily the same size. Corresponding angles of similar figures are congruent.

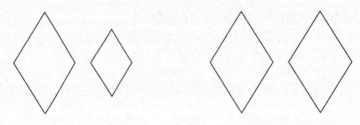

Similar, but <u>not</u> congruent   Similar <u>and</u> congruent

Corresponding sides of similar shapes are proportional. That is, the ratios of the lengths of corresponding sides are equal. Here is an example.

> In the figure shown, rectangle *A* is similar to rectangle *B*. What is the ratio of the lengths of the sides of rectangle *A* compared to the lengths of the corresponding sides of rectangle *B*?
>
>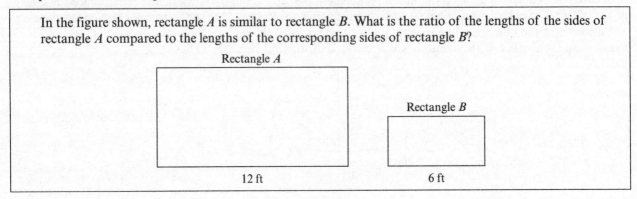

The ratio of the lengths of corresponding sides is $\dfrac{12\text{ ft}}{6\text{ ft}} = \dfrac{12}{6} = \dfrac{2}{1}$ or 2 to 1.

The ratio of the areas of two similar figures is the square of the ratio of the lengths of any two corresponding sides. Here is an example.

The ratio of the lengths of corresponding sides of two similar pentagons is 3 to 2. Therefore, the ratio of the areas of the two pentagons is 3^2 to 2^2, or 9 to 4.

Similar triangles are triangles for which corresponding sides are proportional and corresponding angles are congruent. In the figure shown, triangle *CAB* is similar to triangle *EAD*, denoted as $\triangle CAB \sim \triangle EAD$.

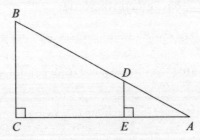

You can use the following theorems to prove two triangles are similar.

- If corresponding angles of two triangles are congruent, the two triangles are similar.
- If corresponding sides of two triangles are proportional, the two triangles are similar.
- If two angles of one triangle are congruent to two corresponding angles of another triangle, then the two triangles are similar.
- If two sides of one triangle are proportional to two corresponding sides of another triangle, and the included angles are congruent, then the two triangles are similar.

What Is Symmetry?

Symmetry describes a relationship between the parts of a figure or object. A figure or object has symmetry if it can be folded exactly in half and the two parts are congruent. The line along the fold is the **line of symmetry.**

Here are three examples of symmetric shapes. A line of symmetry is shown in each figure.

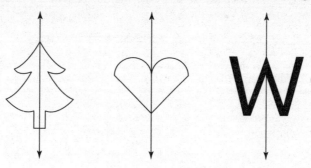

Symmetric Figures

Some shapes have more than one line of symmetry. The following figures can be folded along any of the lines of symmetry, and the two halves will be congruent.

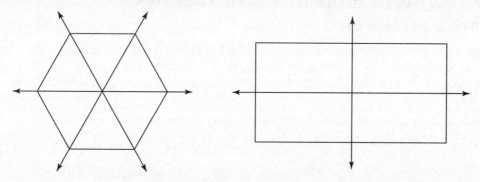

Symmetric Figures with More Than One Line of Symmetry

Test Yourself

1. Similar geometric figures have the same _____, but not necessarily the same _____.

2. In the figure shown, hexagon A is similar to hexagon B. What is the ratio of the lengths of the sides of hexagon A compared to the lengths of corresponding sides of hexagon B?

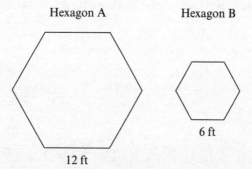

123

3. If corresponding angles of two triangles are congruent, the two triangles are _____.

4. The ratio of the lengths of corresponding sides of two similar triangles is 4 to 1. Therefore, the ratio of the areas of the two triangles is _____ to 1.

5. A figure is _____ if it can be folded exactly into congruent halves.

Answers

1. shape, size
2. $\dfrac{12 \text{ ft}}{6 \text{ ft}} = \dfrac{12}{6} = \dfrac{2}{1}$ or 2 to 1.
3. similar
4. 16
5. symmetric

How Do You Solve Problems Involving the Pythagorean Theorem?

A **right triangle** is a triangle that has exactly one right angle. The side opposite the right angle is the **hypotenuse** of the triangle. The hypotenuse is *always* the longest side of the right triangle. The other two sides are the **legs** of the triangle. Commonly, the letter c is used to represent the hypotenuse of a right triangle, and the letters a and b to represent the legs.

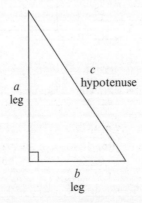

A special relationship, named after the famous Greek mathematician Pythagoras, exists between the sides of a right triangle. This special relationship is the Pythagorean theorem: $a^2 + b^2 = c^2$; or, equivalently, $c^2 = a^2 + b^2$.

The Pythagorean theorem applies only to right triangles. If you know any two sides of a right triangle, you can find the third side by using the formula $c^2 = a^2 + b^2$. Here is an example.

Using the diagram, find the length of the diagonal of a rectangular flower garden that has dimensions of 16 feet by 12 feet.

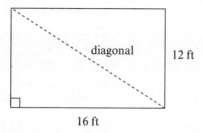

From the diagram, you can see the diagonal is the hypotenuse of a right triangle that has legs of 12 ft and 16 ft. Plug into the formula, omitting the units:

c = hypotenuse = ?, $a = 12$, and $b = 16$
$c^2 = a^2 + b^2 = (12)^2 + (16)^2 = 144 + 256 = 400$

Given $c = 400$, to obtain c, you find the square root of 400.
Thus, $c = 20$.

Note: If you memorized the list of square roots given in "Are All Square Roots Irrational?" (see page 77), you know $\sqrt{400} = 20$.

The length of the diagonal of the flower garden is 20 feet.

Did I answer the question? Yes, I found the length of the diagonal of the flower garden. ✓

Does my answer make sense? Yes, given that the legs are 12 feet and 16 feet in length, 20 feet for the length of the hypotenuse, which is the longest side, seems reasonable. ✓

Is the answer stated in the correct units? Yes, the units are feet, which is correct. ✓

If the measurements of the three sides of a triangle satisfy the Pythagorean relationship, the triangle is a right triangle. Numbers, such as 3, 4, and 5, that satisfy the Pythagorean relationship are **Pythagorean triples.**

Tip: Once you identify a Pythagorean triple, any multiple of the three numbers is also a Pythagorean triple. For example, since 3, 4, and 5 is a Pythagorean triple, then so is 30, 40, and 50.

Test Yourself

1. In a right triangle, the side opposite the right angle is the _____.

2. If you know any two sides of a right triangle, you can find the third side by using the formula _____.

3. What is the length of the hypotenuse of a right triangle that has legs $a = 7$ and $b = 24$?

4. What is the length of the hypotenuse of a right triangle that has legs $a = 300$ and $b = 400$?

5. Which of the following sets of numbers can be the lengths of the sides of a right triangle?

   (a) 5, 13, 12
   (b) 1, $\sqrt{3}$, 2
   (c) 2, 2, 4

Answers

1. hypotenuse
2. $c^2 = a^2 + b^2$
3. Sketch a diagram and label it.

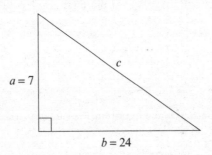

Plug into the formula:

c = hypotenuse = ?, $a = 7$, and $b = 24$

$c^2 = a^2 + b^2 = (7)^2 + (24)^2 = 49 + 576 = 625$

Given $c^2 = 625$, to obtain c, you find the square root of 625.

Thus, $c = 25$.

Note: From the list of square roots given on page 77, you know $\sqrt{625} = 25$.

4. 500 (Because 3, 4, 5 is a Pythagorean triple, then so is 300, 400, and 500.)
5. **(a)** because

$$13^2 = 5^2 + 12^2$$
$$169 = 25 + 144$$
$$169 = 169$$

(b) because

$$2^2 = \sqrt{3}^2 + 1^2$$
$$4 = 3 + 1$$
$$4 = 4$$

What Are Geometric Transformations?

Geometric transformations are ways to change geometric figures without changing their basic properties. The four geometric transformations are translations, reflections, rotations, and dilations. A transformation produces an **image** of the original figure (the **preimage**).

A **translation** is a sliding movement—horizontally, vertically, or both. Here is an example of a translation consisting of four units down.

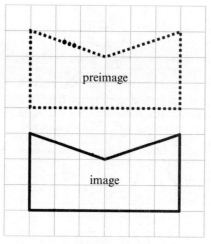

Translation

A **reflection** is a flip across a line. Here is an example of a reflection.

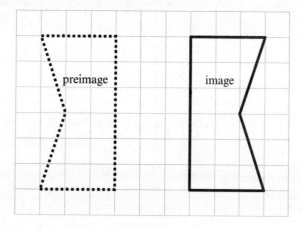

Reflection

A **rotation** is a turn around a point. Here is an example of a rotation.

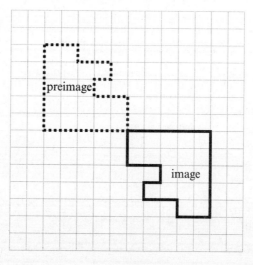

Rotation

A **dilation** is an expanding or shrinking of a geometric shape. Here is an example of a dilation: Triangle *X'Y'Z'* is a dilation of triangle *XYZ*.

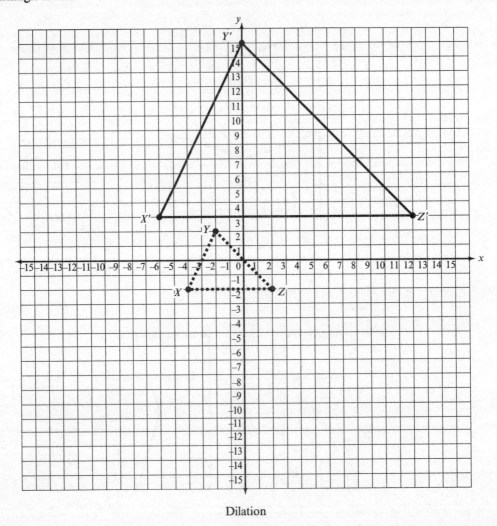

Dilation

Translations, reflections, and rotations produce images that are the same sizes and shapes as their respective preimages. Dilations produce images that have the same shapes, but are different sizes from their respective preimages.

Test Yourself

1. A translation is a _____ movement—horizontally, vertically, or both.

2. A reflection is a _____ across a line.

3. A rotation is a _____ around a point.

4. The following diagram shows an example of a _____.

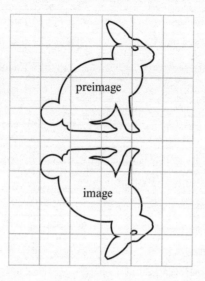

5. The following diagram shows an example of a _____.

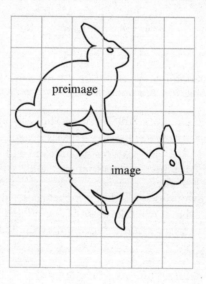

Answers

1. sliding
2. flip
3. turn
4. reflection
5. rotation

How Do You Convert from One Measurement Unit to Another?

On the FTCE GK Test, you will have to demonstrate your knowledge of measurement using the U.S. customary system and the metric system. Your Mathematics Reference Sheet contains the conversions, as shown here, that you should know for the test.

129

Chapter 3: Review for the General Knowledge Mathematics Subtest

Conversions	
1 yard = 3 feet = 36 inches	1 cup = 8 fluid ounces
1 mile = 1,760 yards = 5,280 feet	1 pint = 2 cups
1 acre = 43,560 square feet	1 quart = 2 pints
1 hour = 60 minutes	1 gallon = 4 quarts
1 minute = 60 seconds	
	1 pound = 16 ounces
1 liter = 1000 milliliters = 1000 cubic centimeters	1 ton = 2,000 pounds
1 meter = 100 centimeters = 1000 millimeters	
1 kilometer = 1000 meters	
1 gram = 1000 milligrams	
1 kilogram = 1000 grams	

Note: Metric numbers with four digits are written without a comma (e.g., 2543 grams).
For metric numbers with more than four digits, a space is used instead of a comma (e.g., 24 300 liters).

You can convert from one measurement unit to another by using an appropriate "conversion fraction." You make conversion fractions by using the conversion facts given in the Mathematics Reference Sheet. For each conversion fact in the table, you can write *two* conversion fractions. For example, for the conversion fact 1 yard = 3 feet, you have $\frac{1 \text{ yd}}{3 \text{ ft}}$ and $\frac{3 \text{ ft}}{1 \text{ yd}}$ as your two conversion fractions. Each of these conversion fractions is equivalent to the number 1 because the numerator and denominator are different names for the same length. Therefore, if you multiply a quantity by either of these fractions, you will not change the value of the quantity.

When you need to change one measurement unit to another unit, multiply by the conversion fraction whose *denominator is the same as the units of the quantity to be converted*. This strategy is called **unit analysis.** When you do the multiplication, the units you started out with will "divide out," and you will be left with the new units. If this doesn't happen, then you used the wrong conversion fraction, so do it over again with the other conversion fraction.

It is a good idea to assess your final answer to see whether it makes sense. When you are converting from *a larger unit to a smaller unit*, you should expect that it will take *more* of the smaller units to equal the same amount. When you are converting from *a smaller unit to a larger unit*, you should expect that it will take *less* of the larger units to equal the same amount.

Here is an example of converting from a larger unit to a smaller unit:

> Convert 5 yards to feet.

The conversion fractions are $\frac{1 \text{ yd}}{3 \text{ ft}}$ and $\frac{3 \text{ ft}}{1 \text{ yd}}$. Write 5 yards as a fraction with denominator 1, and let unit analysis tell you whether to multiply by $\frac{1 \text{ yd}}{3 \text{ ft}}$ or $\frac{3 \text{ ft}}{1 \text{ yd}}$. Multiply by $\frac{3 \text{ ft}}{1 \text{ yd}}$ because the denominator has the same units as the quantity to be converted:

$$\frac{5 \text{ yd}}{1} \times \frac{3 \text{ ft}}{1 \text{ yd}} = \frac{5 \text{ yd}}{1} \times \frac{3 \text{ ft}}{1 \text{ yd}} = 15 \text{ ft}.$$ The yards (yd) units divide out, leaving feet (ft) as the units for the answer.

Does this answer make sense? Yes. Feet are smaller than yards, so it should take more of them to equal the same length as 5 yards.

Here is an example of converting from a smaller unit to a larger unit:

> Convert 250 centimeters to meters.

The conversion fractions are $\frac{1 \text{ m}}{100 \text{ cm}}$ and $\frac{100 \text{ cm}}{1 \text{ m}}$. Write 250 centimeters as a fraction with denominator 1, and let unit analysis tell you whether to multiply by $\frac{1 \text{ m}}{100 \text{ cm}}$ or $\frac{100 \text{ cm}}{1 \text{ m}}$. Multiply 250 centimeters by $\frac{1 \text{ m}}{100 \text{ cm}}$ because the denominator has the same units as the quantity to be converted:

$$\frac{250 \text{ cm}}{1} \times \frac{1 \text{ m}}{100 \text{ cm}} = \frac{250 \text{ cm}}{1} \times \frac{1 \text{ m}}{100 \text{ cm}} = \frac{250 \text{ m}}{100} = 2.5 \text{ m}$$

The centimeters (cm) units divide out, leaving meters (m) as the units for the answer. Notice that since 100 is in the denominator, you divide 250 by 100 to obtain 2.5 in the answer.

Does this answer make sense? Yes. Meters are larger than centimeters, so it should take fewer of them to equal the same distance as 250 centimeters.

Another way to work this problem is to use "**K**ing **H**enry **D**oesn't **U**sually **D**rink **C**hocolate **M**ilk," which is a mnemonic for remembering the following metric prefixes:

> kilo-, hecto-, deca-, unit measurement (no prefix), deci-, centi-, milli-
> (1000) (100)   (10)   (.1) (.01) (.001)

Because the metric system is a decimal-based system, the prefixes are based on powers of 10. You can convert from one unit to another by either multiplying or dividing by a power of 10. If you move from left to right on the list, then you multiply by the power of 10 that corresponds to the number of times you moved. If you move from right to left on the list, then you divide by the power of 10 that corresponds to the number of times you moved.

In this problem, the unit measurement is meters. You are going from centimeters to meters. To go from centi- to your unit measurement (meters), you move left two times on the list above. Therefore, divide by $10^2 = 100$ to convert centimeters to meters. Thus,

$$250 \text{ cm} = 250 \div 10^2 \text{ (2 moves left)} = 250 \div 100 = 2.5 \text{ m}$$

For some conversions, you may need to make a "chain" of conversion fractions to obtain your desired units. Here is an example:

> Convert 3 gallons to cups.

The conversion table does not have a fact that shows the equivalency between gallons and cups. You have 1 pint = 2 cups, 1 quart = 2 pints, and 1 gallon = 4 quarts. These facts yield 3 conversion fraction pairs, respectively: $\frac{1 \text{ pt}}{2 \text{ c}}$ and $\frac{2 \text{ c}}{1 \text{ pt}}$, $\frac{1 \text{ qt}}{2 \text{ pt}}$ and $\frac{2 \text{ pt}}{1 \text{ qt}}$, and $\frac{1 \text{ gal}}{4 \text{ qt}}$ and $\frac{4 \text{ qt}}{1 \text{ gal}}$. Start with your quantity to be converted and keep multiplying by conversion fractions until you obtain your desired units.

$$\frac{3 \text{ gal}}{1} \times \frac{4 \text{ qt}}{1 \text{ gal}} \times \frac{2 \text{ pt}}{1 \text{ qt}} \times \frac{2 \text{ c}}{1 \text{ pt}} = \frac{3 \text{ gal}}{1} \times \frac{4 \text{ qt}}{1 \text{ gal}} \times \frac{2 \text{ pt}}{1 \text{ qt}} \times \frac{2 \text{ c}}{1 \text{ pt}} = 48 \text{ c}$$

Does this answer make sense? Yes. Cups are smaller than gallons, so it should take more of them to equal the same amount as 3 gallons.

For the FTCE GK Test, you will not have to convert between the customary system and the metric system. You will convert only within a given system. If you are not very familiar with the metric system, here are some "rough" equivalencies of the more common units for your general knowledge.

Equivalencies Chart	
Meter	about 3 inches longer than a yard
Centimeter	about the width of a large paper clip
Millimeter	about the thickness of a dime
Kilometer	about five city blocks or a little farther than half a mile
Liter	a little more than a quart
Milliliter	takes about five to make a teaspoon
Gram	about the weight of a small paper clip
Milligram	about the weight of a grain of salt
Kilogram	the weight of a liter of water or a little more than 2 pounds

How Do You Solve Problems Involving Unit Rates?

A **unit rate** is an amount per unit. It is a rated measure such as miles per hour, cost per item, cost per unit, words per page, and so on. Unit rates are used in many real-life situations.

Here is an example of using unit rates for comparison shopping.

> Which is a better buy: three $10\frac{3}{4}$ oz cans of soup for $2.00 or four $10\frac{3}{4}$ oz cans for $3.50?

The unit price for three cans for $2.00 = $\dfrac{\$2.00}{3 \text{ cans}}$ = $0.67 per can (rounded to the nearest cent).

The unit price for four cans for $3.50 = $\dfrac{\$3.50}{4 \text{ cans}}$ = $0.88 per can (rounded to the nearest cent).

Assuming there's no difference in quality, the better buy is three cans for $2.00.

> **Tip: The fraction bar indicates division. Use your calculator to divide the numerator number by the denominator number.** For example, $\dfrac{2.00}{3} = 2.00 \div 3 \approx 0.67$ and $\dfrac{3.50}{4} = 3.50 \div 4 \approx 0.88$.

Here is an example of using unit rates to compare the speeds of two vehicles.

> Car A traveled 156 miles in 2.4 hours. Car B traveled 245 miles in 3.5 hours. Which car had the faster average speed?

The average speed (unit rate) for car A is $\dfrac{156 \text{ miles}}{2.4 \text{ hours}}$ = 65 miles per hour (mph).

The average speed (unit rate) for car B is $\dfrac{245 \text{ miles}}{3.5 \text{ hours}}$ = 70 miles per hour (mph).

Car B had a faster average speed.

You can use unit rates to find the total miles, total cost, total words, and so on by multiplying by the unit rate. Here are examples.

> A train travels 3 hours at a rate of 55 miles per hour. How many miles did the train travel?

From the Mathematics Reference Sheet, you have $d = rt$; that is, distance = rate × time. To find the total miles traveled, multiply 55 mph (the unit rate) times 3 hours:

$$d = \frac{55 \text{ miles}}{h} \times 3 \text{ h} = \frac{55 \text{ miles}}{\cancel{h}} \times \frac{3 \cancel{h}}{1} = 165 \text{ miles}$$ The hours (h) units divide out, leaving miles as the units for the answer.

> If it costs $220 to rent a motor home for 1 week, how much will it cost to rent the motor home for 2 weeks?

To find the total cost, multiply 2 weeks by $220 per week (the unit rate).

$$\text{total cost} = 2 \text{ wk} \times \frac{\$220}{\text{wk}} = \frac{2 \cancel{\text{wk}}}{1} \times \frac{\$220}{\cancel{\text{wk}}} = \$440$$ The weeks (wk) units divide out, leaving dollars ($) as the units for the answer.

Tip: Put quantities that follow the word "per" in the denominator of a fraction.

How Do You Read Measurement Instruments?

The gauge or scale of a measuring instrument has markings that divide the gauge or scale into equal intervals. Usually, not every mark is labeled with a number.

To read a measuring instrument, determine what each mark on the measuring instrument represents. To do this, find the two consecutive labeled points immediately below and above the reading on the scale. Find the difference between the two points. Count the number of markings it takes to get from the lower point to the higher point. Divide the difference between the two points by the number of marks you counted. After you determine what each mark represents, take the reading. Here is an example.

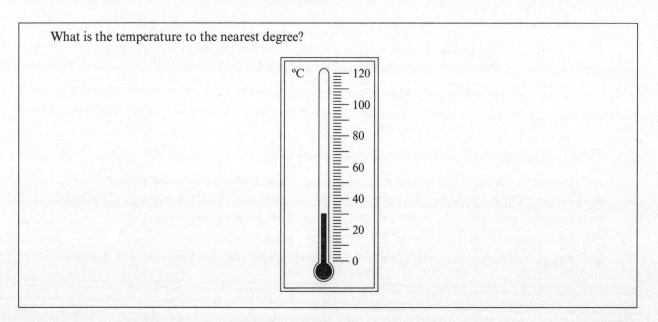

133

The thermometer is reading between 20° and 40°. The difference between these two points is 40° − 20° = 20°. It takes ten marks to go from 20° up to 40°. Divide the difference between the two points by 10: 20° ÷ 10 = 2°. Therefore, each mark on the thermometer represents 2°. The thermometer is reading five marks above 20°. Since each mark represents 2°, the thermometer is reading 10° above 20°, which is 30°C.

How Do You Solve Problems Involving Scaled Drawings or Models?

The scale for a drawing or model is a ratio that compares the measurement on the drawing (or model) to the actual measurement in real life. For example, if a drawing has a scale of 1 centimeter = 10 meters, for every centimeter measured on the drawing, the actual length is 10 meters. To solve problems involving scaled drawings or models, set up a proportion and solve the problem. Here is an example.

> On a map, the distance between two cities is 18 inches. If 0.75 inch represents 20 miles, how far, in miles, is it between the two cities (to the nearest mile)?

This problem is a proportion problem involving a map scale. To solve the problem, determine the ratios being compared, being sure to compare corresponding quantities in the same order; write a proportion using the two ratios; and then use cross products to solve the proportion.

Step 1. Determine the ratios being compared.

Let d be the actual distance in miles between the two cities. The first sentence gives the first ratio: $\frac{d \text{ (in miles)}}{18 \text{ in}}$. The second sentence gives the second ratio: $\frac{20 \text{ miles}}{0.75 \text{ in}}$. (Notice, you put miles in the numerator in the second ratio because you have miles in the numerator in the first ratio.)

Step 2. Write a proportion using the two ratios.

$$\frac{d \text{ (in miles)}}{18 \text{ in}} = \frac{20 \text{ miles}}{0.75 \text{ in}}$$

Step 3. Use cross products to solve the proportion (omitting the units for convenience).

$\frac{d}{18} = \frac{20}{0.75}$

$18 \cdot 20$ Find a cross product you can calculate. You don't know the value of d, so the only cross product you can calculate is 18 times 20.

$d = \frac{18 \cdot 20}{0.75}$ Divide by 0.75, the numerical term you didn't use.

$d = 480$

The actual distance in miles between the two cities is 480 miles.

Did I answer the question? Yes, I found the actual distance in miles between the two cities. ✓

Does my answer make sense? Yes, since 0.75 inch represents 20 miles, a rough estimate of the answer is 20 inches times 20 miles per inch, which is 400 miles. Thus, 480 miles is a reasonable answer. ✓

Is the answer stated in the correct units? Yes, the units are miles, which is correct. ✓

See "Ratios and Proportions" earlier in this chapter (page 97) for additional discussion of this topic.

Test Yourself

1. The conversion fractions for the conversion fact 1 yard = 36 inches are _____ and _____.

2. To change 2.5 yards to inches, multiply by _____.

3. To change 720 inches to yards, multiply by _____.

4. 720 inches = _____ yards.

5. 4.35 kilometers = _____ meters.

6. 2 hours = _____ seconds.

7. Which is a better buy for an item: five for $4.25 or six for $5.00?

8. A motor home rents for a weekly rate plus $0.25 per mile. What is the total cost for mileage for a trip of 500 miles?

9. The scale for a model airplane is 1:10. If the actual airplane has a wingspan of 42 feet, what is the wingspan of the model airplane?

10. What is the temperature to the nearest degree?

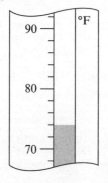

Answers

1. $\dfrac{1 \text{ yd}}{36 \text{ in}}, \dfrac{36 \text{ in}}{1 \text{ yd}}$

2. $\dfrac{36 \text{ in}}{1 \text{ yd}}$

3. $\dfrac{1 \text{ yd}}{36 \text{ in}}$

4. $\dfrac{720 \text{ in}}{1} \cdot \dfrac{1 \text{ yd}}{36 \text{ in}} = \dfrac{720 \not{\text{in}}}{1} \cdot \dfrac{1 \text{ yd}}{36 \not{\text{in}}} = \dfrac{720 \text{ yd}}{36} = 20 \text{ yd}$

5. **Method 1:** $\dfrac{4.35 \text{ km}}{1} \cdot \dfrac{1000 \text{ m}}{1 \text{ km}} = \dfrac{4.35 \not{\text{km}}}{1} \cdot \dfrac{1000 \text{ m}}{1 \not{\text{km}}} = 4350 \text{ m}$

   Method 2: $4.35 \text{ km} = 4.35 \cdot 10^3$ (3 moves right) $= 4.35 \cdot 1000 = 4350 \text{ m}$

6. $\dfrac{2 \text{ h}}{1} \times \dfrac{60 \text{ min}}{1 \text{ h}} \times \dfrac{60 \text{ sec}}{1 \text{ min}} = \dfrac{2 \not{\text{h}}}{1} \times \dfrac{60 \not{\text{min}}}{1 \not{\text{h}}} \times \dfrac{60 \text{ sec}}{1 \not{\text{min}}} = 7{,}200 \text{ sec}$

7. The unit price for five items for $4.25 is $\frac{\$4.25}{5 \text{ items}} = \$0.85$ per item.

   The unit price for six items for $5.00 is $\frac{\$5.00}{6 \text{ items}} = \$0.83$ per item (rounded to the nearest cent).

   The better buy is six items for $5.00.

   Did I answer the question? Yes, I found the better buy. ✓

   Does my answer make sense? Yes. ✓

   Is the answer stated in the correct units? No units are required. ✓

8. To find the total cost for mileage, multiply 500 miles by $0.25 per mile (the unit rate).

   $$500 \text{ miles} \times \frac{\$0.25}{1 \text{ mile}} = \frac{500 \text{ miles}}{1} \times \frac{\$0.25}{1 \text{ mile}} = \$125$$

   The miles units divide out, leaving dollars ($) as the units for the answer.

   The total cost for mileage is $125.

   Did I answer the question? Yes, I found the total cost for the mileage. ✓

   Does my answer make sense? Yes, $0.25 is one-fourth of a dollar. A 400-mile trip would cost $100, so $125 for a 500-mile trip is a reasonable answer. ✓

   Is the answer stated in the correct units? Yes, the units are dollars, which is correct. ✓

9. This problem is a proportion problem involving a scale model. To solve the problem, determine the ratios being compared, being sure to compare corresponding quantities in the same order; write a proportion using the two ratios; and then use cross products to solve the proportion.

   Step 1. Determine the ratios being compared.

   The scale of the model as 1:10. This means: $\frac{\text{wingspan of model}}{\text{wingspan of actual plane}} = \frac{1}{10}$.

   Step 2. Let w = the wingspan of the model. Write a proportion using the two ratios.

   $$\frac{w \text{ (in feet)}}{42 \text{ ft}} = \frac{1}{10}$$

   Step 3. Use cross products to solve the proportion (omitting the units for convenience).

   $$\frac{w}{42} = \frac{1}{10}$$

   $42 \cdot 1$ Find a cross product you can calculate. You don't know the value of w, so the only cross product you can calculate is 42 times 1.

   $w = \frac{42 \cdot 1}{10}$ Divide by 10, the numerical term you didn't use.

   $w = 4.2$

   The wingspan of the model is 4.2 feet.

   Did I answer the question? Yes, I found the wingspan of the model. ✓

   Does my answer make sense? Yes, the model is smaller than the actual plane, so the wingspan of the model should be less than the wingspan of the actual plane. ✓

   Is the answer stated in the correct units? Yes, the units are feet, which is correct. ✓

10.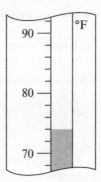

The thermometer is reading between 70° and 80°. The difference between these two points is 80° − 70° = 10°. It takes five marks to go from 70° up to 80°. Divide the difference between the two points by 5: 10° ÷ 5 = 2°. Therefore, each mark on the thermometer represents 2°. The thermometer is reading two marks above 70°. Since each mark represents 2°, the thermometer is reading 4° above 70°, which is 74°F.

How Do You Find Perimeter and Circumference?

The perimeter of a figure is the distance around it. You measure perimeter in units of length, such as inches, feet, yards, miles, kilometers, meters, centimeters, and millimeters. To find the perimeter of a closed figure that is made up of line segments, add up the lengths of the line segments. Here is an example.

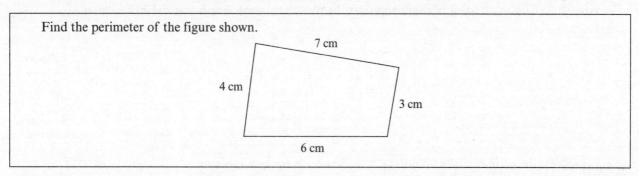

Find the perimeter of the figure shown.

To find the perimeter, add the lengths of the four sides:

Perimeter = 6 cm + 3 cm + 7 cm + 4 cm = 20 cm

Sometimes, the lengths for every side are not labeled. This occurs when the figure is a special geometric shape. On the FTCE GK Test, the four figures that you most likely will encounter when this happens are a rectangle, a square, an equilateral triangle, or an isosceles triangle. The Mathematics Reference Sheet does not give formulas for the perimeters of these figures. If you are finding the perimeter of such a figure, you can simply add up the lengths of the sides—so you really don't need a formula as such. In the discussion that follows, formulas are given because they often simplify the process of finding the perimeter, but more important, the formulas are very useful when you are given a perimeter and asked to determine one or more dimensions of these special geometric shapes.

Tip: When you work problems involving geometric figures, sketch a diagram if no diagram is given.

A **rectangle** is a closed, four-sided plane figure that has four right angles. It has two dimensions: **length** and **width**. Both pairs of opposite sides are congruent (the same size).

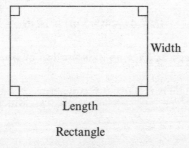

Rectangle

137

The formula for the perimeter of a rectangle is $P = 2l + 2w$, where l is the length and w is the width.

Here is an example of finding the perimeter of a rectangle.

> How many feet of fencing are needed to enclose a rectangular garden that is 25 feet by 35 feet?

Sketch a diagram and label it.

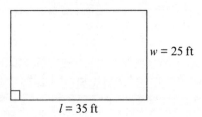

Plug into the formula:

$$P = 2l + 2w = 2(35 \text{ ft}) + 2(25 \text{ ft}) = 70 \text{ ft} + 50 \text{ ft} = 120 \text{ ft}$$

Thus, 120 feet of fencing is needed.

A **square** is a rectangle that has four congruent **sides.** Its two dimensions, length and width, are equal.

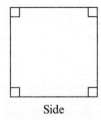
Side

The formula for the perimeter of a square is $P = 4s$, where s is the length of one of its congruent sides.

Here is an example of finding the perimeter of a square.

> What is the perimeter of a square that is 3.5 meters on a side?

Sketch a diagram and label it.

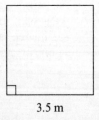
3.5 m

Plug into the formula:

$$P = 4s = 4(3.5 \text{ m}) = 14 \text{ m}$$

Tip: See "What Is Congruence?" on page 107 for an explanation of what "congruent" means.

The formula for the perimeter of a triangle is $P = a + b + c$, where a, b, and c are the lengths of the sides of the triangle.

Here is an example of finding the perimeter of an equilateral triangle.

> What is the perimeter of an equilateral triangle that is 20 centimeters on a side?

Sketch a diagram and label it.

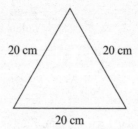

Plug into the formula:

$$P = a + b + c = 20 \text{ cm} + 20 \text{ cm} + 20 \text{ cm} = 60 \text{ cm}$$

Here is an example of finding the perimeter of an isosceles triangle.

> Find the perimeter of an isosceles triangle with congruent sides of 10 feet and a third side of 6 feet.

Sketch a diagram and label it.

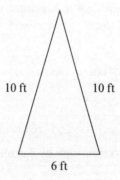

Plug into the formula:

$$P = a + b + c = 10 \text{ ft} + 10 \text{ ft} + 6 \text{ ft} = 26 \text{ ft}$$

The **circumference** of a circle is the distance around the circle. In other words, the circumference of a circle is its perimeter. The formula for the circumference of a circle is $C = \pi d = 2\pi r$, where d and r are the diameter and radius of the circle, respectively. The Mathematics Reference Sheet states that you are to use 3.14 or $\frac{22}{7}$ for the number π. Because you are allowed to use a calculator, you should use 3.14 for π for ease of calculation. **Reminder:** π is the ratio of the circumference of a circle to its diameter.

Here is an example of finding the circumference of a circle.

> Find the circumference of the circle in the diagram. Use $\pi = 3.14$.
>
> 20 in radius

From the diagram, you can see the radius of the circle is 20 in. Plug into the formula:

$$C = 2\pi r = 2\pi(20 \text{ in}) = 2 \cdot 3.14 \cdot 20 \text{ in} = 125.6 \text{ in}$$

How Do You Find Area?

The **area** of a plane figure is the amount of surface enclosed by the boundary of the figure. You measure area in square units, such as square inches (in^2), square feet (ft^2), square miles (mi^2), square meters (m^2), square kilometers (km^2), square centimeters (cm^2), and square millimeters (mm^2). The area is always described in terms of square units, regardless of the shape of the figure.

The boundary measurements of a figure are measured in two dimensions (that is, length and width, base and height). The units for the boundary measurements are linear units (for example, inches, feet, miles, meters, and so on). You obtain the square units needed to describe area when you multiply the unit by itself. For example, $(1 \text{ in})(1 \text{ in}) = 1 \text{ in}^2 = 1$ square inch.

Finding the Area of a Rectangle

Here is an example of finding the area of a rectangle.

> The formula for the area of a rectangle is $A = lw$, where l is the length and w is the width.
>
> **What is the area of a rectangle that is 4 centimeters by 3 centimeters?**

Sketch a diagram and label it.

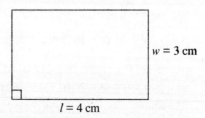

Plug into the formula:

$$A = lw = (4 \text{ cm})(3 \text{ cm}) = 12 \text{ cm}^2$$

You can verify that the formula works by dividing the rectangle into 1-cm squares and counting how many square centimeters are inside the boundary.

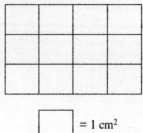

Multiplying 4 cm by 3 cm gives you the same number of square centimeters as counting the squares inside the rectangle. The rectangle has an area of 12 cm².

Finding the Area of a Square

The formula for the area of a square is $A = s^2$, where s is the length of a side.

This formula is not given on the Mathematics Reference Sheet. To find the area of a square, you can also use the formula for the area of a rectangle, $A = lw$. You will get the same answer either way.

Here is an example of finding the area of a square.

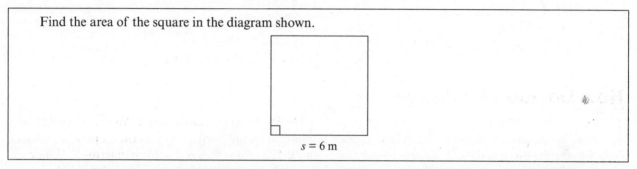

From the diagram, you can see s, the length of a side of the square, is 6 m. Because all sides are congruent, the width is also 6 m. Plug into either formula:

$$A = lw = (6\text{ m})(6\text{ m}) = 36\text{ m}^2 \text{ or } A = s^2 = (6\text{ m})^2 = 36\text{ m}^2$$

Finding the Area of a Triangle

To find the area of a triangle, you must know the measure of the triangle's **base** and **height.** The base can be any of the three sides of the triangle. The height for the base is a line drawn from the opposite vertex that meets that base (or an extension of it) at a right angle. *Reminder:* A **vertex** of a triangle is the point where two sides meet.

The formula for the area of a triangle is $A = \frac{1}{2}bh$, where b is the length of a base of the triangle, and h is the height for that base. When you are finding the area of a triangle, you can pick any convenient side of the triangle to serve as the base in the formula.

Here is an example of finding the area of a triangle.

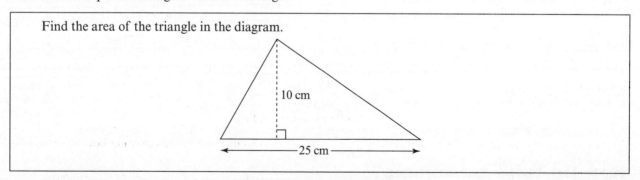

The diagram shows $b = 25$ cm and $h = 10$ cm. Plug into the formula:

$$A = \frac{1}{2}bh = \frac{1}{2}(25\text{ cm})(10\text{ cm}) = \frac{(25\text{ cm})(10\text{ cm})}{2} = 125\text{ cm}^2$$

Here is how to key in the calculation: 25 × 10 ÷ 2 = . The display will show 125, the correct value.

Finding the Area of a Circle

The formula for the area of a circle is $A = \pi r^2$, where r is the radius of the circle.

Here is an example of finding the area of a circle.

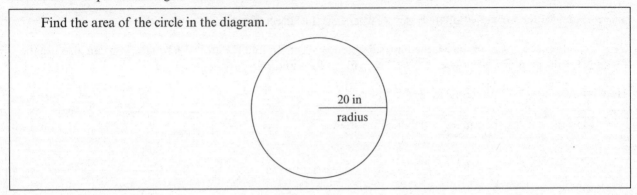

From the diagram, the radius is 20 in. Plug into the formula:

$$A = \pi r^2 = \pi(20 \text{ in})^2 = 3.14 \cdot 400 \text{ in}^2 = 1{,}256 \text{ in}^2$$

Notice that you must perform the exponentiation before multiplying by 3.14. Don't forget to follow the order of operations when performing calculations. You cannot rely on the calculator to do the operations in the correct order.

How Do You Find Surface Area?

When you have a solid figure such as a rectangular prism (a box), a cylinder, or a pyramid, you can find the area of every face (surface) and add the areas together. The sum is the **surface area** of the solid figure.

Here is an example of finding the surface area of a rectangular box.

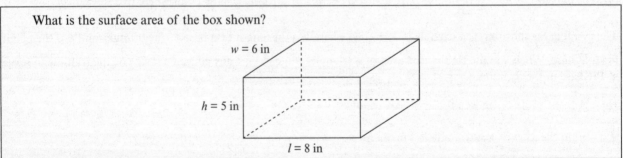

The box is composed of six **faces**, all of which are rectangles. Use the length and height to find the areas of the congruent front and back faces. Use the length and width to find the areas of the congruent top and bottom faces. Use the width and height to find the areas of the two congruent side faces.

$$\text{Surface Area} = 2(8 \text{ in})(5 \text{ in}) + 2(8 \text{ in})(6 \text{ in}) + 2(6 \text{ in})(5 \text{ in}) = 80 \text{ in}^2 + 96 \text{ in}^2 + 60 \text{ in}^2 = 236 \text{ in}^2$$

How Do You Find Volume?

The **volume** of a solid figure is the amount of space inside the figure. Solid figures have three dimensions (for example, length, width, and height of a box). When you use the dimensions of a figure to find its volume, the units for the volume are cubic units such as cubic inches (in^3), cubic feet (ft^3), cubic miles (mi^3), cubic meters (m^3), cubic kilometers (km^3), cubic centimeters (cm^3), and cubic millimeters (mm^3).

The Mathematics Reference Sheet gives the formula for the volume of a prism as $V = Bh$, where $B =$ the area of the base of the figure. For a rectangular prism, $B = lw$. Thus, the formula for the volume of a rectangular prism is $V = lwh$, where l is the **length**, w is the **width**, and h is the **height**.

Here is an example of finding the volume of a rectangular prism.

What is the volume of the box shown?

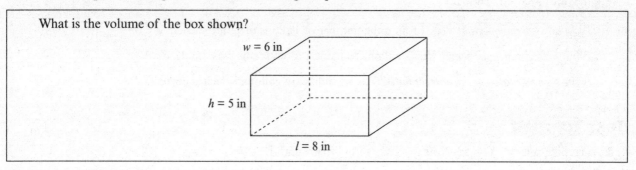

Plug into the formula:

$$V = Bh = lwh = (8 \text{ in})(6 \text{ in})(5 \text{ in}) = 240 \text{ in}^3$$

Notice that the units for the volume of the box are in³ = cubic inches. Cubic units are obtained when a unit is used as a factor in a product three times, as in the following: (in)(in)(in) = in³.

How Do You Solve Real-World Problems Involving Perimeter, Area, and Volume?

When you have real-world contextual problems involving perimeter, area, or volume on the FTCE GK Test, make a sketch (if none is provided) to help you understand the problem. Otherwise, you solve these problems the same way you solve other contextual problems on the test. Here is an example.

A homeowner wants to apply one coat of paint to the walls in a large playroom that is 20 feet by 14 feet with an 8-foot-high ceiling. One gallon of paint will cover 350 square feet (ft²). The paint is sold in gallon containers only. How many gallons of paint will the homeowner need to buy?

Make a sketch to illustrate the problem.

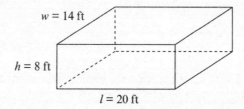

Solve the problem using two steps. First, find the surface area of the walls to be painted. Second, find the number of gallons needed to cover the walls by using the unit rate: 350 ft² per gallon.

Step 1. Find the surface area of the walls to be painted. Use the length and the height to find the areas of the two congruent longer walls. Use the width and the height to find the area of the other two congruent walls.

Surface area to be painted = 2(20 ft)(8 ft) + 2(14 ft)(8 ft) = 320 ft² + 224 ft² = 544 ft²

Step 2. Find the number of gallons of paint needed.

$$350 \text{ ft}^2 \text{ per gallon} = \frac{350 \text{ ft}^2}{1 \text{ gal}}$$

number of gallons needed = 544 ft² ÷ $\frac{350 \text{ ft}^2}{1 \text{ gal}}$ = $\frac{544 \text{ ft}^2}{1}$ × $\frac{1 \text{ gal}}{350 \text{ ft}^2}$ = $\frac{544 \cancel{\text{ft}^2}}{1}$ × $\frac{1 \text{ gal}}{350 \cancel{\text{ft}^2}}$ = $\frac{544 \text{ gal}}{350}$ ≈ 1.55 gal

Because the paint is sold in gallon containers only, the homeowner will need to buy 2 gallons of paint to have enough paint to paint the walls.

Did I answer the question? Yes, I found the number of gallons of paint needed. ✓

Does my answer make sense? Yes, 2 gallons to paint a room seems reasonable. ✓

Is the answer stated in the correct units? Yes, the units are gallons, which is correct. ✓

Test Yourself

1. The perimeter of a figure is the _____ around it.

2. Perimeter is measured in units of _____.

3. To find the perimeter of a closed figure whose sides are line segments, add up the _____ of the _____.

4. The formula for the circumference of a circle is _____ or _____.

5. The area of a plane figure is the amount of _____ enclosed by the boundary of the figure.

6. Area is measured in _____ units.

7. The formula for the area of a rectangle is _____.

8. The formula for the area of a circle is _____.

9. The formula for the volume of a rectangular prism is _____.

10. How many square yards (yd²) of carpet are needed to carpet a room that measures 15 feet by 18 feet?

Answers

1. distance

2. length

3. lengths, sides

4. πd, $2\pi r$

5. surface

6. square

7. $A = lw$

8. $A = \pi r^2$

9. $V = Bh$ or $V = lwh$

10. Sketch a diagram to illustrate the problem.

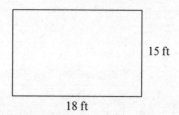

Square yards are units of area, so find the area of the carpet in square yards. To find how many square yards of carpet are needed, use two steps. First, convert the dimensions of the room from feet to yards. Next, find the area of the rectangular room in square yards.

Step 1. Convert the dimensions of the floor to yards.

The conversion fractions are $\frac{1 \text{ yd}}{3 \text{ ft}}$ and $\frac{3 \text{ ft}}{1 \text{ yd}}$. Write your measurement as a fraction with denominator 1 and let unit analysis tell you whether to multiply by $\frac{1 \text{ yd}}{3 \text{ ft}}$ or $\frac{3 \text{ ft}}{1 \text{ yd}}$. Because you want the feet to divide out, multiply by $\frac{1 \text{ yd}}{3 \text{ ft}}$.

$$\frac{18 \text{ ft}}{1} \times \frac{1 \text{ yd}}{3 \text{ ft}} = \frac{18 \text{ ft}}{1} \times \frac{1 \text{ yd}}{3 \text{ ft}} = \frac{18 \text{ yd}}{3} = 6 \text{ yd}$$

$$\frac{15 \text{ ft}}{1} \times \frac{1 \text{ yd}}{3 \text{ ft}} = \frac{15 \text{ ft}}{1} \times \frac{1 \text{ yd}}{3 \text{ ft}} = \frac{15 \text{ yd}}{3} = 5 \text{ yd}$$

Step 2. Find the area of the carpet:

The area of a rectangle is $A = lw$.

$A = lw = (6 \text{ yd})(5 \text{ yd}) = 30 \text{ yd}^2$

At least 30 yd² of carpet are needed to carpet the room.

Did I answer the question? Yes, I found how many square yards of carpet are needed. ✓

Does my answer make sense? Yes, it is consistent with my knowledge of the real world. ✓

Is the answer stated in the correct units? Yes, the units are square yards (yd²), which is correct. ✓

Sample Questions

Directions: Read each question and select the best answer choice.

1. Which of the following is the most specific name for the figure below?

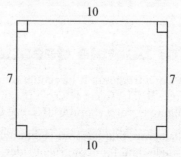

    A. parallelogram
    B. rectangle
    C. rhombus
    D. square

2. Every parallelogram is also a

   A. square.
   B. rhombus.
   C. rectangle.
   D. polygon.

3. A length of cable is attached to the top of a 12-foot building. The cable is anchored 5 feet from the base of the building. What is the length of the cable?

   A. 7 ft
   B. 13 ft
   C. 17 ft
   D. 169 ft

4. A runner ran a cross-country race of 14 500 meters. How many kilometers did the runner run in the race?

   A. 1.45 km
   B. 14.5 km
   C. 145 km
   D. 14 500 000 km

5. A biology textbook has scale drawings of grasshoppers. The scale shows that 1 centimeter in the drawing represents 2.5 centimeters of actual length. What is the length, in centimeters, of the scale drawing of a grasshopper if the grasshopper is actually 9.0 centimeters long?

   A. 3.6
   B. 4.0
   C. 4.5
   D. 18.0

6. What is the perimeter of a rectangle that measures 6 yards by 5 yards?

   A. 11 yd
   B. 22 yd
   C. 30 yd
   D. 60 yd

7. How many cubic feet (ft^3) of cement are in a rectangular cement slab that is 3 inches thick and measures 10 feet long and 5 feet wide?

   A. 12.5 ft^3
   B. 15.25 ft^3
   C. 40 ft^3
   D. 150 ft^3

Answer Explanations for Sample Questions

1. **B.** The figure has four sides, so it is a quadrilateral. It has congruent opposite sides and four right angles. It is best described as a rectangle, Choice **B**. The figure is also a parallelogram (Choice **A**), but this description is not as specific as rectangle. The figure is not a rhombus (Choice **C**) or a square (Choice **D**).

2. **D.** Eliminate **A**. A square is a parallelogram that has four right angles and four congruent sides, but not every parallelogram has four right angles and four congruent sides. Eliminate **B**. A rhombus is a parallelogram that has four congruent sides, but not every parallelogram has four congruent sides. Eliminate **C**. A rectangle is a parallelogram that has four right angles, but not every parallelogram has four right angles. Choice **D** is correct because a polygon is a closed plane figure composed of sides that are straight line segments. Every parallelogram satisfies this definition.

3. **B.** Sketch a diagram to illustrate the problem.

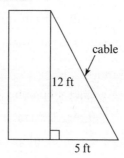

The building and the cable form a right triangle. From the diagram, you can see the length of the cable is the hypotenuse of the right triangle that has legs of 12 ft and 5 ft. Plug into the formula omitting the units:

c = hypotenuse = ?, a = 12, and b = 5

$c^2 = a^2 + b^2 = (12)^2 + (5)^2 = 144 + 25 = 169$

Given $c^2 = 169$, to obtain c, you find the square root of 169.

Thus, $c = 13$.

Note: From the list of square roots given in "Are All Square Roots Irrational?" (page 77), you know $\sqrt{169} = 13$.

The length of the cable is 13 ft, Choice **B**.

Did I answer the question? Yes, I found the length of the cable. ✓

Does my answer make sense? Yes, given that the legs are 12 feet and 5 feet in length, 13 feet for the length of the hypotenuse, the longest side, seems reasonable. ✓

Is the answer stated in the correct units? Yes, the units are feet, which is correct. ✓

Choice **A** results if you mistakenly decide to solve the problem by finding the difference between the lengths of the two legs to find the length of the hypotenuse. Choice **C** results if you mistakenly decide to solve the problem by adding the lengths of the two legs to find the length of the hypotenuse. Choice **D** results if you neglect to find the square root of 169.

4. **B.** Two ways to solve this problem are shown here.

Method 1: The conversion fractions are $\dfrac{1 \text{ km}}{1000 \text{ m}}$ and $\dfrac{1000 \text{ m}}{1 \text{ km}}$. Write your measurement as a fraction with denominator 1, and let unit analysis tell you whether to multiply by $\dfrac{1 \text{ km}}{1000 \text{ m}}$ or $\dfrac{1000 \text{ m}}{1 \text{ km}}$. Since you want the meters to divide out, multiply by $\dfrac{1 \text{ km}}{1000 \text{ m}}$.

$$\dfrac{14\,500 \text{ m}}{1} \times \dfrac{1 \text{ km}}{1000 \text{ m}} = \dfrac{14\,500 \cancel{\text{ m}}}{1} \times \dfrac{1 \text{ km}}{1000 \cancel{\text{ m}}} = \dfrac{14\,500}{1} \times \dfrac{1 \text{ km}}{1000} = \dfrac{14\,500 \text{ km}}{1000} = 14.5 \text{ km}$$

The runner ran 14.5 km in the race, Choice **B**.

Method 2: 14 500 m = 14 500 ÷ 10^3 (3 moves left) = 14 500 ÷ 1000 = 14.5 km, Choice **B**.

The other choices occur if you make a mistake in placing the decimal point in your answer.

5. **A.** This problem is a proportion problem involving a scale drawing. To solve the problem, determine the ratios being compared, being sure to compare corresponding quantities in the same order; write a proportion using the two ratios; and then use cross products to solve the proportion.

Step 1. Determine the ratios being compared.

Let x be the length (in centimeters) of the scale drawing of the grasshopper. The second sentence gives the first ratio: $\dfrac{1 \text{ cm}}{2.5 \text{ cm}}$. The third sentence gives the second ratio: $\dfrac{x \text{ (cm)}}{9.0 \text{ cm}}$.

Step 2. Write a proportion using the two ratios.

$$\frac{x \text{ (cm)}}{9.0 \text{ cm}} = \frac{1 \text{ cm}}{2.5 \text{ cm}}$$

Step 3. Use cross products to solve the proportion (omitting the units for convenience).

$\dfrac{x}{9.0} = \dfrac{1}{2.5}$

$(9.0)(1)$ Find a cross product you can calculate. You don't know the value of x, so the only cross product you can calculate is 9.0 times 1.

$x = \dfrac{(9.0)(1)}{2.5}$ Divide by 2.5, the numerical term you didn't use.

$x = 3.6$

The length of the scale drawing (in centimeters) is 3.6.

Did I answer the question? Yes, I found the length of the scale drawing. ✓

Does my answer make sense? Yes, the scale drawing is smaller than the actual grasshopper, so the length of the scale drawing should be less than the length of the actual grasshopper. ✓

Is the answer stated in the correct units? Yes, the units are centimeters, which is correct. ✓

The other answer choices occur if you solve the proportion incorrectly or set it up incorrectly.

6. **B.** Sketch a diagram to illustrate the problem.

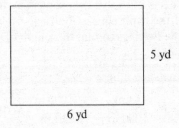

Plug into the formula.

$P = 2l + 2w = 2(6 \text{ yd}) + 2(5 \text{ yd}) = 12 \text{ yd} + 10 \text{ yd} = 22 \text{ yd}$. The perimeter is 22 yards, Choice **B**.

Choice **A** results if you fail to multiply each dimension by 2. Choice **C** results if you incorrectly confuse perimeter with area. Choice **D** results if you use an incorrect formula.

7. **A.** Sketch a diagram to illustrate the problem.

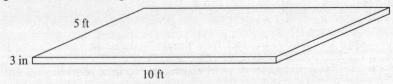

Cubic feet (ft³) are units of volume. The amount of cement in the slab is equal to the volume of the slab, which is a rectangular prism. To find the volume of the slab in ft³, use two steps. First, convert 3 inches to feet. Next, find the volume of the cement in ft³.

Step 1. Convert 3 inches to feet.

The conversion fractions are $\frac{1\text{ ft}}{12\text{ in}}$ and $\frac{12\text{ in}}{1\text{ ft}}$. Write 3 inches as a fraction with denominator 1, and let unit analysis tell you whether to multiply by $\frac{1\text{ ft}}{12\text{ in}}$ or $\frac{12\text{ in}}{1\text{ ft}}$. Because you want the inches to divide out, multiply by $\frac{1\text{ ft}}{12\text{ in}}$.

$$\frac{3\text{ in}}{1} \times \frac{1\text{ ft}}{12\text{ in}} = \frac{3\text{ in}}{1} \times \frac{1\text{ ft}}{12\text{ in}} = \frac{3\text{ ft}}{12} = 0.25\text{ ft}$$

Step 2. Find the volume of the cement in cubic feet.

$$V = Bh = lwh = (10\text{ ft})(5\text{ ft})(0.25\text{ ft}) = 12.5\text{ ft}^3$$

There are 12.5 ft³ of cement in the slab, Choice **A**.

Did I answer the question? Yes, I found how many cubic feet of cement are in the slab. ✓

Does my answer make sense? Yes, for a slab 1 foot thick, the volume is (10 ft)(5 ft)(1 ft) = 50 ft³, so 12.5 ft³ is a reasonable volume for a slab that is 0.25 feet thick. ✓

Is the answer stated in the correct units? Yes, the units are cubic feet (ft³), which is correct. ✓

Choices **B** and **C** result if you use an incorrect formula for the volume of a rectangular prism. Choice **D** results if you neglect to convert 3 inches to 0.25 feet.

Algebraic Reasoning and the Coordinate Plane

According to the *Competencies and Skills Required for Teacher Certification in Florida*, 20th Edition (see page 59 for Web address), the competencies/skills you should be able to do for this area of mathematics are the following:

- Determine whether two algebraic expressions are equivalent by applying properties of operations or equality.
- Identify an algebraic expression, equation, or inequality that models a real-world situation.
- Solve equations and inequalities (e.g., linear, quadratic) graphically or algebraically.
- Determine and solve equations or inequalities, graphically or algebraically, in real-world problems.
- Graph and interpret a linear equation in real-world problems (e.g., use data to plot points, explain slope and *y*-intercept, determine additional solutions).
- Identify relations that satisfy the definition of a function.
- Compare the slopes of two linear functions represented algebraically and graphically.

How Do You Interpret Algebraic Expressions?

An **algebraic expression** uses symbols to represent a number. The symbols can be arithmetic numbers, letters, and operation symbols. The arithmetic numbers are **constants.** You know their values. The letters, such as *x* or *n*, for example, are **variables.** They stand for numbers. Without further information, you do not know the value of *x* or *n*. The **operation symbols** indicate calculations to be performed on the variables and/or numbers in the expression.

Look at these examples of algebraic expressions.

$$2x$$
$$5(a+b)$$
$$p^2n$$
$$9x^2 - 6x + 1$$
$$3(x+4)$$

$$\frac{1}{2}mv^2$$
$$x + 2y$$
$$abc$$
$$\frac{3x^4 y^6}{5x^3}$$

$$\frac{1}{2}h(b_1 + b_2)$$
$$2(\pi r^2) + (2\pi r)h$$
$$\frac{4}{3}\pi r^3$$

You likely recognized the three expressions in the third column as formulas from the Mathematics Reference Sheet. Formulas are examples of algebraic expressions.

Variables play a major role in algebra. A variable represents some unknown quantity. It holds a place open for a specific number or, in some cases, a set of numbers. Often, your task is to figure out what number (or numbers) the variable is standing in for. Variables are usually represented by upper- or lowercase letters (for example, x, y, z, A, B, or C). The letter is the variable's "name." So you refer to variable x simply as "x," its letter representation.

If there is a number immediately next to the variable (usually preceding it), that number is the variable's **numerical coefficient.** For instance, in the expression $2x$, 2 is the numerical coefficient of x. If no number is written immediately next to a variable, it is understood the numerical coefficient is 1. Writing a variable with a coefficient or writing two or more variables in juxtaposition (side by side) is a way to show multiplication. In other words, $2x$ means 2 times x and $3abc$ means 3 times a times b times c. No multiplication symbol is necessary.

A **constant** is a quantity whose value remains fixed throughout a discussion. For example, all the real numbers are constants. Each has a fixed, definite value. Thus, when a letter is used to name a constant, the letter has one fixed value. For instance, the Greek letter π (pi) stands for the number (approximately 3.14159) that equals the ratio of the circumference of a circle to its diameter.

A **numerical expression** is any constant or combination of two or more constants joined by operational symbols. For example, 100, 3.5, $\frac{3 \cdot 25}{4 \cdot 5}$, 0.75(2,000) + 2,500, and $\pi(6)^2$ are numerical expressions.

A **term** is a number, a variable, or an indicated product or quotient of numbers and variables. In an algebraic expression, terms are separated by plus or minus signs. For example, the algebraic expression $9x^2 - 6x + 1$ has three terms. A **monomial** is a term that when it has one or more variables, contains no division by variables and has only whole number exponents on its variables. For instance, 1, $6x$, and $9x^2$ are monomials, but $\frac{5}{2x^2}$ and $7\sqrt{x}$ are not.

> **Tip:** Roots can be written as fractional exponents. That is, $7\sqrt{x} = 7x^{\frac{1}{2}}$, in which the exponent is not a whole number.

A **polynomial** consists of a single monomial or it is composed of two or more unlike monomials joined together by plus or minus signs. A polynomial having exactly two terms is a **binomial.** A polynomial having exactly three terms is a **trinomial.**

The first step in learning to interpret the language of algebra is to understand how addition, subtraction, multiplication, and division are expressed algebraically. Table 3.13 summarizes the most commonly used algebraic symbolism for the operations. The letter x is used in the table to represent an unknown number.

Table 3.13 Algebraic Symbolism for the Operations

Operation	Symbol(s) Used	Example	Sample Word Phrases
Addition	+	$x + 10$	x plus 10, the sum of x and 10, x increased by 10, 10 added to x, 10 more than x, the number that exceeds x by 10
Subtraction	−	$x - 2$	x minus 2, 2 subtracted from x, the difference between x and 2, 2 less than x, x decreased by 2, x reduced by 2
Multiplication	juxtaposition, ·, or ( )	$2x$ $2 \cdot x$ $2(x)$	2 times x, x multiplied by 2, the product of 2 and x, twice x, 2 of x, double x
Division	fraction bar	$\frac{x}{5}$	x divided by 5, the quotient of x and 5, the ratio of x to 5, one-fifth of x, x for each 5, x for every 5

A **power** is the product of equal factors. For example, $5 \cdot 5 = 5^2$, $x \cdot x \cdot x = x^3$, and $2 \cdot 2 \cdot 2 \cdot 2 = 2^4 = 16$ are powers.

An exponent is applied only to the number, variable, or grouped quantity immediately to its left. For example, $3x^4$ means $3 \cdot x \cdot x \cdot x \cdot x$; but $(3x)^4$ means $3x \cdot 3x \cdot 3x \cdot 3x$.

Besides indicating multiplication, parentheses are used as grouping symbols. Similarly, a fraction bar can be a grouping symbol as well as indicating division. When interpreting an algebraic expression, use the words "sum," "difference," "product," "quotient," or "quantity" to indicate terms are enclosed in a grouping symbol and to avoid ambiguity.

Here are examples.

$3(x + 10)$ is "3 times the sum of x and 10."

$\dfrac{x-2}{5}$ is "the difference, x minus 2, divided by 5."

$(ab)^3$ is "the cube of the product, ab."

$(x + 5)^2$ is "the square of the sum, x plus 5."

When you have more than one operation involved in an algebraic expression, keep in mind the variables are standing in for numbers, so the indicated calculations must follow the order of operations.

Also, as mentioned earlier, it is important to avoid ambiguity. That is, you want your interpretation to have only one meaning.

Here is an example of an ambiguous interpretation.

"the product of 3 and x squared"   Does this mean $(3x)^2$ or $3x^2$?

Here are examples of interpreting algebraic expressions.

Interpret the formula $\dfrac{4}{3}\pi r^3$.

This expression is a product of three terms: $\dfrac{4}{3}$, π, and r^3. Notice the exponent ^{3} on r applies only to r. A correct interpretation of the expression is "$\dfrac{4}{3}$ times π times the quantity r cubed." Another correct interpretation is "the product of $\dfrac{4}{3}$, π, and the quantity r cubed."

Interpret the expression $\dfrac{1}{2}h(b_1 + b_2)$.

This expression is the product of three terms: $\dfrac{1}{2}$, h, and the sum, $b_1 + b_2$. A correct interpretation of the expression is "half the product of h and the sum, $b_1 + b_2$." Another correct interpretation is "$\dfrac{1}{2}$ times h times the sum, $b_1 + b_2$."

To model a real-world expression algebraically, represent the real-world expression using algebraic symbols. Here are examples.

A car traveled x kilometers. If a bus traveled 50 kilometers farther than the car, the number of kilometers traveled by the bus is represented by $x + 50$.

A chair costs $125. The cost of n chairs is $125n$.

To help with representing real-world expressions using algebraic symbols, try this: First, write a similar expression using a specific value for the unknown quantity. Next, replace the specific value with a letter representing the variable. Here is **an example**.

> A printing shop charges $0.10 per copy for the first hundred copies. Additional copies are $0.08 per copy. What is the cost of x copies, where x is greater than 100?

First, write a similar expression using a specific value for x. Pick a number greater than 100, say 120. The cost of 120 copies is $0.10(100) + $0.08(120 − 100)$. Next, replace 120 with the letter x. The cost of x copies is $0.10(100) + $0.08(x − 100)$.

Test Yourself

1. An algebraic expression uses symbols to represent a _____ .
2. The numerical coefficient of x is _____ .
3. Interpret $2x$.
4. Interpret $\frac{m}{3}$.
5. Interpret mv^2.
6. Express 10 less than y in symbols.
7. Interpret the expression $\frac{1}{2}(x+10)$.
8. Interpret the expression $4(x + 5)^3$.
9. The width of a rectangle is w. Represent the rectangle's length if it exceeds twice the width by 3.
10. A car travels for 2 hours at r miles per hour. Represent the distance (in miles) traveled by the car.

Answers

1. number
2. 1
3. "2 times x"
4. "m divided by 3"
5. "m times the quantity v squared"
6. $y - 10$
7. "half the sum, $x + 10$" or "$\frac{1}{2}$ times the sum, $x + 10$"
8. "4 times the cube of the sum, $x + 5$"
9. length = $2w + 3$
10. distance = $2r$

How Do You Simplify Algebraic Expressions?

You simplify algebraic expressions by using the commutative, associative, and distributive properties of operations with real numbers. These properties are summarized in Table 3.14.

Table 3.14 Useful Properties of Operations with Real Numbers

Property	Explanation	Numerical Example
Commutative Property of Addition	When you add two real numbers, you can change the order of the numbers being added and still obtain the correct sum.	$10 + 25 = 25 + 10$ $35 \checkmark = 35 \checkmark$
Commutative Property of Multiplication	When you multiply two real numbers, you can change the order of the numbers being multiplied and still obtain the correct product.	$(10)25 = (25)10$ $250 \checkmark = 250 \checkmark$
Associative Property of Addition	When you add more than two real numbers, you can group the way you add the numbers in different ways and still obtain the correct sum.	$(4 + 6) + 5 = 4 + (6 + 5)$ $10 + 5 = 4 + 11$ $15 \checkmark = 15 \checkmark$
Associative Property of Multiplication	When you multiply more than two real numbers, you can group the way you multiply the numbers in different ways and still obtain the correct product.	$(4)(6) \cdot 5 = 4 \cdot (6)(5)$ $24 \cdot 5 = 4 \cdot 30$ $120 \checkmark = 120 \checkmark$
Distributive Property	When a sum (or difference) of two real numbers is multiplied by a real number, you can add (or subtract) first and then multiply, or you can multiply first and then add (or subtract) the products. Either way, you still obtain the correct result.	$5(10 + 8) = 5 \cdot 10 + 5 \cdot 8$ $5 \cdot 18 = 50 + 40$ $90 \checkmark = 90 \checkmark$

You may use one or a combination of these properties to simplify algebraic expressions. Here is an example.

> Simplify: $5(2x + 3)$

$5(2x + 3) = 5 \cdot 2x + 5 \cdot 3$ Using the distributive property, multiply each term in the parentheses by 5.
$\quad\quad\quad\quad = (5 \cdot 2)x + 5 \cdot 3$ Using the associative property, regroup $5 \cdot 2x$ as $(5 \cdot 2)x$, then multiply.
$\quad\quad\quad\quad = 10x + 15$

This process shows $5(2x + 3)$ is **equivalent** to $10x + 15$.

Of course, in practice you can do the intermediate steps mentally as shown in this example.

> Simplify: $3(5x + 4)$

$3(5x + 4) = 15x + 12$ Using the distributive property, multiply each term in the parentheses by 3.

Tip: Be sure to multiply each term in the parentheses by the multiplier immediately next to the parentheses.

Notice the distributive property means if you have the sum of two products that have a common factor, you can rewrite the expression as the common factor times the sum of the other two factors. Here is an example.

$6 \cdot 30 + 6 \cdot 70 =$ 6 is a common factor in the two products.
$6(30 + 70) =$ Use the distributive property to rewrite the expression as 6 times the sum of the other two factors.
$\quad 6(100) = 600$

This use of the distributive property allows you to combine variable expressions that are the same except for their numerical coefficients into a single term. Variable expressions that are the same except for their numerical coefficients are **like terms**.

> **Tip:** Like terms have exactly the same variables with the same respective exponents. For instance, $2xy^2$ and $5xy^2$ are like terms, but $2xy^2$ and $5x^2y$ are not.

Here are examples of simplifying like terms.

Simplify: $2x + 3x$

$2x + 3x = x \cdot 2 + x \cdot 3$	Apply the commutative property of multiplication and observe that the variable x is a common factor in the two products.
$= x(2 + 3)$	Use the distributive property to rewrite the expression as x times the sum of the other two factors.
$= x(5)$	Simplify.
$= 5x$	Apply the commutative property of multiplication.

Simplify: $15y - 8y$

$15y - 8y = y \cdot 15 - y \cdot 8$	Apply the commutative property of multiplication and observe that the variable y is a common factor in the two products.
$= y(15 - 8)$	Use the distributive property to rewrite the expression as y times the difference of the other two factors.
$= y(7)$	Simplify.
$= 7y$	Apply the commutative property of multiplication.

When you understand the mathematical basis for combining like terms, you can abbreviate the process to the following rule:

To add like terms, you add (algebraically) their numerical coefficients and use the result as the numerical coefficient for the common variable. Here are examples.

$20x + 30x = 50x$
$15z - 40z = -25z$

> **Tip:** Using the rules for combining signed numbers (see "Numeration and Operations" on page 59), $20 + 30 = 50$ and $15 - 40 = 15 + -40 = -25$.

The addition or subtraction of terms that are *not* like terms can only be indicated. You cannot put them together into a single term. For instance, you would have to leave $2a + 3b$ as it is—you can't make it into a single term.

One further note: When you simplify expressions containing subtraction, as a practical matter, you might find it more convenient not to rewrite subtraction in terms of algebraic addition. Just mentally insert a + sign to the immediate right of the first number. Apply the – sign to the second number. Then combine the results. For $15 - 40$, think "15 plus negative 40 is negative 25." For the remainder of this CliffsNotes guide, we will adopt the practice of not rewriting subtraction unless it is necessary to do so to avoid making a sign error in the problem.

Test Yourself

Simplify.

1. $\frac{1}{2}x + 1\frac{1}{2}x$
2. $-8x + 3x$
3. $3x - 8x$
4. $25y - 45y$
5. $-2x + x + 5x - 11x - 3x + 4x$
6. $15x - 8y - 9x + 10y$
7. $3(x + 4) + 2x$
8. $5 + 2(x - 4)$
9. $5x - 2(x + 4)$
10. $x(x + 2) + 3(x + 2)$

Answers

1. $2x$
2. $-5x$
3. $-5x$
4. $-20y$
5. $-6x$
6. $6x + 2y$ (This expression cannot be simplified further.)
7. $3(x + 4) + 2x = 3x + 12 + 2x = 3x + 2x + 12 = 5x + 12$
8. $5 + 2(x - 4) = 5 + 2(x + -4) = 5 + 2x + -8 = 2x + 5 + -8 = 2x + -3 = 2x - 3$
9. $5x - 2(x + 4) = 5x + -2(x + 4) = 5x + (-2)(x) + (-2)(4) = 5x + -2x + -8 = 3x + -8 = 3x - 8$
10. $x(x + 2) + 3(x + 2) = x \cdot x + 2x + 3x + 6 = x^2 + 5x + 6$

How Do You Solve One-Variable Linear Equations?

An **equation** is a statement that two mathematical expressions are equal. An equation has two sides. Whatever is on the left side of the equal sign is the *left side* of the equation, and whatever is on the right side of the equal sign is the *right side* of the equation.

Equations that contain only numbers are either true or false. For instance, the equation $8 + 5 = 13$ is true, but the equation $0 = 2$ is false. When a variable or variables hold the place for numbers in an equation, the equation is **open.** The equation $x + 8 = 18$ is an open equation that has only one variable, x. Without knowing what number x is standing for, you cannot say whether $x + 8 = 18$ is true or false. Replace x with 5. Then $x + 8 = 18$ is false because $5 + 8 = 13$, not 18. Replace x with 10. Then $x + 8 = 18$ is true because $10 + 8 = 18$. In fact, 10 is the only replacement for x that makes $x + 8 = 18$ a true statement.

To **solve** an equation means to find a numerical replacement for the variable that makes the equation true. An equation is true when the left side has the same value as the right side. A number that makes an equation true is a **solution** of the equation. For example, the number 10 is a solution of the equation $x + 8 = 18$. The set of all solutions of an equation is its **solution set.**

Chapter 3: Review for the General Knowledge Mathematics Subtest

A **one-variable linear equation** can be written in the form $ax + b = c$, where a, b, and c are constants and x is a variable. For example, $2x + 50 = 650$, $125n = 1{,}000$, $0.10(100) + 0.08(x - 100) = 16.40$, $0.25q + 0.10(30 - q) = 4.50$, $p + 8\% \, p = 91.80$, $\dfrac{y}{200} = \dfrac{5}{8}$, and $5x + 8 = 2x - 46$ are linear equations in one variable. Observe that in a one-variable linear equation, you have only constants and a single variable (x, n, q, and so on).

To solve a one-variable linear equation, you work backward (so to speak) to find the value of the variable. You "undo" what has been done to the variable until you get an expression like this: variable = number. In other words, the equation is solved when you succeed in getting the variable by itself on one side of the equation only and the variable's coefficient is an understood 1, and on the equation's other side there is a single number or an expression that does not contain the variable of interest.

The equal sign in an equation is like a balance point. To keep the equation in balance, whatever you do to one side of the equation you must do to the other side of the equation. The main tools you use in solving equations are

- Adding the same number to both sides.
- Subtracting the same number from both sides.
- Multiplying both sides by the same *nonzero* number.
- Dividing both sides by the same *nonzero* number.

What has been done to the variable determines the operation you choose to do. You do it to both sides to keep the equation balanced. You "undo" an operation by using the inverse of the operation. Addition and subtraction undo each other, as do multiplication and division.

With that said, how do you proceed? To solve an equation, follow these five steps.

1. If parentheses are involved, use the distributive property to remove parentheses.
2. Combine like terms, if any, on each side of the equation.
3. If the variable appears on both sides of the equation, add or subtract a variable expression to both sides of the equation so that the variable appears on only one side of the equation, and then simplify.
4. Undo addition or subtraction and then simplify. If a number is added to the variable term, subtract that number from both sides of the equation. If a number is subtracted from the variable term, add that number to both sides of the equation.
5. Divide both sides of the equation by the variable's coefficient or multiply both sides by its reciprocal.

Here are examples of solving linear equations.

Solve: $5x + 8 = 2x - 46$

$5x + 8 = 2x - 46$	No parentheses are involved, and there are no like terms to combine, so skip steps 1 and 2.
$5x + 8 - 2x = 2x - 46 - 2x$	The variable appears on both sides of the equation, so subtract $2x$ from the right side to remove it from that side. To keep the equation balanced, subtract $2x$ from the left side, too.
$3x + 8 = -46$	Simplify.
$3x + 8 - 8 = -46 - 8$	8 is added to the variable term, so subtract 8 from both sides of the equation.
$3x = -54$	Simplify.
$\dfrac{3x}{3} = \dfrac{-54}{3}$	You want the coefficient of x to be 1, so divide both sides by 3. On the left side, the 3s cancel out. On the right side, you have $-54 \div 3$, which is -18.
$x = -18$	

Tip: To obtain $-54 \div 3 = -18$ using the calculator, divide 54 by 3 ($54 \div 3 = 18$). Make the answer negative because -54 and 3 have opposite signs.

Chapter 3: Review for the General Knowledge Mathematics Subtest

You can check your solution by plugging it back into the original equation: $5x + 8 = 2x - 46$.

Put in –18 for x on the left side of the equation: $5x + 8 = 5(-18) + 8 = -90 + 8 = -82$.
Put in –18 for x on the right side of the equation: $2x - 46 = 2(-18) - 46 = -36 - 46 = -82$.
Both sides equal –82, so –18 is the correct solution.

Tip: When you replace the variable with a negative number, enclose the number in parentheses.

Solve: $5(x + 7) = 78$

$5(x + 7) = 78$	
$5x + 35 = 78$	Use the distributive property to remove parentheses.
$5x + 35 - 35 = 78 - 35$	35 is added to the variable term, so subtract 35 from both sides of the equation.
$5x = 43$	Simplify.
$\dfrac{\cancel{5}x}{\cancel{5}} = \dfrac{43}{5}$	You want the coefficient of x to be 1, so divide both sides by 5. On the left side, the 5s cancel out. On the right side, you have $43 \div 5$, which is 8.6.
$x = 8.6$	

Check by plugging your solution back into the original equation: $5(x + 7) = 78$.
Put in 8.6 for x on the left side of the equation: $5(x + 7) = 5(8.6 + 7) = 5(15.6) = 78$.
The right side of the equation is also 78. Both sides equal 78, so 8.6 is the correct solution.

Solve: $\dfrac{2x - 3}{3} = x + 1$

Tip: To eliminate fractions, multiply each term on both sides of the equation by the least common multiple (LCM) of the denominators when you have fractional terms. The fraction bar is a grouping symbol, so enclose numerators of two or more terms in parentheses before you multiply.

$\dfrac{2x - 3}{3} = x + 1$	
$\cancel{3} \cdot \dfrac{(2x - 3)}{\cancel{3}} = 3x + 3 \cdot 1$	Eliminate fractions by multiplying each term on both sides of the equation by 3.
$2x - 3 = 3x + 3$	Simplify.
$2x - 3 - 3x = 3x + 3 - 3x$	The variable appears on both sides of the equation, so subtract $3x$ from the right side to remove it from that side. To keep the equation balanced, subtract $3x$ from the left side, too.
$-x - 3 = 3$	Simplify.
$-x - 3 + 3 = 3 + 3$	3 is subtracted from the variable term, so add 3 to both sides of the equation.
$-x = 6$	Simplify.
$\dfrac{\cancel{-1}x}{\cancel{-1}} = \dfrac{6}{-1}$	You want the coefficient of x to be 1, so divide both sides of the equation by -1.
$x = -6$	Simplify.

Check by plugging your solution back into the original equation: $\frac{2x-3}{3} = x+1$.

Put in –6 for x on the left side of the equation: $\frac{2(-6)-3}{3} = \frac{-12-3}{3} = \frac{-15}{3} = -5$.

Put in –6 for x on the right side of the equation: $x + 1 = -6 + 1 = -5$.

Both sides equal –5, so –6 is the correct solution.

Sometimes you can find a replacement for the variable that makes the equation true simply by "guessing and checking." This is a good test-taking strategy for multiple-choice math tests.

Here is an example of using guessing and checking to solve an equation.

Solve: $5x + 8 = 2x - 1$

A. –1
B. –3
C. 1
D. 3

Check the answer choices by plugging the values into the equation, being careful to enclose in parentheses the values that you put in and to follow the order of operations when you do your calculations.

Check Choice **A**: Put in –1 for x on the left side of the equation: $5x + 8 = 5(-1) + 8 = -5 + 8 = 3$. Put in –1 for x on the right side of the equation: $2x - 1 = 2(-1) - 1 = -2 - 1 = -3$. Choice **A** is incorrect because $3 \neq -3$.

Check Choice **B**: Put in –3 for x on the left side of the equation: $5x + 8 = 5(-3) + 8 = -15 + 8 = -7$. Put in –3 for x on the right side of the equation: $2x - 1 = 2(-3) - 1 = -6 - 1 = -7$. Choice **B** is the correct response because $x = -3$ made the equation true—both sides equal –7.

When you're taking the FTCE GK Test, you would not have to check the other answer choices because the correct answer is **B**. Since the test is timed, it would be best to move on to the next question.

Test Yourself

1. An equation is true when the left side has the _____ value as the right side.

2. When solving an equation, which should you "undo" first: addition or multiplication? _____

Solve for the given variable.

3. $3x + 50 = 35$

4. $25 - 3y = 3y + 1$

5. $6x - 36 = 6(2 - 3x)$

6. $\frac{3x - 10}{5} - 6 = \frac{x}{3}$

Answers

1. same

2. addition

3. $x = -5$

    Solution:

    $$3x + 50 = 35$$
    $$3x + 50 - 50 = 35 - 50 \quad \text{Subtract 50 from both sides of the equation.}$$
    $$3x = -15 \quad \text{Simplify.}$$
    $$\frac{\cancel{3}x}{\cancel{3}} = \frac{-15}{3} \quad \text{Divide both sides of the equation by 3.}$$
    $$x = -5 \quad \text{Simplify.}$$

4. $y = 4$

    Solution:

    $$25 - 3y = 3y + 1$$
    $$25 - 3y - 3y = 3y + 1 - 3y \quad \text{Subtract } 3y \text{ from both sides of the equation.}$$
    $$25 - 6y = 1 \quad \text{Simplify.}$$
    $$25 - 6y - 25 = 1 - 25 \quad \text{Subtract 25 from both sides of the equation.}$$
    $$-6y = -24 \quad \text{Simplify.}$$
    $$\frac{\cancel{-6}y}{\cancel{-6}} = \frac{-24}{-6} \quad \text{Divide both sides of the equation by } -6.$$
    $$y = 4 \quad \text{Simplify.}$$

5. $x = 2$

    Solution:

    $$6x - 36 = 6(2 - 3x)$$
    $$6x - 36 = 12 - 18x \quad \text{Use the distributive property to remove parentheses.}$$
    $$6x - 36 + 18x = 12 - 18x + 18x \quad \text{Add } 18x \text{ to both sides of the equation.}$$
    $$24x - 36 = 12 \quad \text{Simplify.}$$
    $$24x - 36 + 36 = 12 + 36 \quad \text{Add 36 to both sides of the equation.}$$
    $$24x = 48 \quad \text{Simplify.}$$
    $$\frac{\cancel{24}x}{\cancel{24}} = \frac{48}{24} \quad \text{Divide both sides of the equation by 24.}$$
    $$x = 2$$

6. $x = 30$

Solution:

$$\frac{3x-10}{5} - 6 = \frac{x}{3}$$

$$\overset{3}{\cancel{15}} \cdot \frac{(3x-10)}{\cancel{5}_1} - 15 \cdot 6 = \overset{5}{\cancel{15}} \cdot \frac{x}{\cancel{3}_1}$$ Eliminate fractions by multiplying each term on both sides of the equation by 15, the LCM (3, 5).

$3(3x-10) - 15 \cdot 6 = 5 \cdot x$ Simplify.

$9x - 30 - 90 = 5x$ Use the distributive property to remove parentheses.

$9x - 120 = 5x$ Simplify.

$9x - 120 - 5x = 5x - 5x$ Subtract $5x$ from both sides of the equation.

$4x - 120 = 0$ Simplify.

$4x - 120 + 120 = 0 + 120$ Add 120 to both sides of the equation.

$4x = 120$ Simplify.

$\dfrac{\cancel{4}x}{\cancel{4}} = \dfrac{120}{4}$ Divide both sides of the equation by 4.

$x = 30$ Simplify.

How Do You Solve Inequalities?

An **inequality** is a mathematical statement that contains one of the following inequality symbols: $\neq, <, >, \leq,$ or $\geq$. Like equations, inequalities may be true, false, or open. For instance, the inequalities $7 + 5 < 20$ and $\dfrac{-20}{-4} \neq -5$ are true, but the inequality $0 \geq 5$ is false. The inequality $2x > 20$ is open.

Inequalities may contain variables. For example, the inequality $x \leq 6$ is *true* if x is 2 and is *false* if x is 10. In fact, this inequality is true if x is any number that is less than or equal to 6 and is false if x is any number greater than 6. You can show the set of numbers that make the inequality true on a number line. You draw a dark arrow on the number line to the left of 6. The tip of the arrow should point left. To indicate the number 6 also belongs in the solution set, shade in a small circle at the point 6.

For the inequality $x < 6$, indicate the number 6 does not belong in the solution set by drawing an open circle at the point 6.

You solve inequalities containing $<, >, \leq,$ or $\geq$ basically the same way you solve equations. However, there is one important difference. When you multiply or divide both sides of the inequality by a *negative* number, you must *reverse* the direction of the inequality. To understand why you must do this, consider the following.

You know $8 > 2$ is a true inequality because 8 is to the right of 2 on the number line, as shown in the following figure.

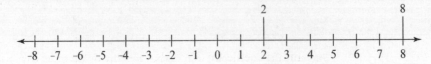

If both sides of the inequality 8 > 2 are multiplied by a negative number, say –1, the direction of the inequality must be reversed, yielding the inequality –8 < –2. This is a true inequality because –2 is to the right of –8 on the number line, as shown in the following figure.

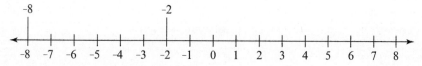

If you do not reverse the inequality symbol after multiplying both sides of 8 > 2 by –1, you obtain –8 > –2, which is clearly false.

Tip: The above example illustrates if $a < b$, it must be true $-a > -b$, and if $a > b$, it must be true $-a < -b$.

Here are examples of solving inequalities.

Solve: $6x - 5 < 37$

$6x - 5 < 37$
$6x - 5 + 5 < 37 + 5$ 5 is subtracted from the variable term, so add 5 to both sides of the inequality.
$6x < 42$ Simplify.
$\dfrac{\cancel{6}x}{\cancel{6}} < \dfrac{42}{6}$ You want the coefficient of x to be 1, so divide both sides by 6.
  On the left side, the 6s cancel out. On the right side, you have $42 \div 6$, which is 7.
$x < 7$

Solve: $-5(x - 2) \leq 15$

$-5(x - 2) \leq 15$
$-5x + 10 \leq 15$ Use the distributive property to remove parentheses.
$-5x + 10 - 10 \leq 15 - 10$ 10 is added to the variable term, so subtract 10 from both sides of the inequality.
$-5x \leq 5$ Simplify.
$\dfrac{\cancel{-5}x}{\cancel{-5}} \geq \dfrac{5}{-5}$ You want the coefficient of x to be 1, so divide both sides by -5 and reverse the inequality because you divided both sides by a negative number.
$x \geq -1$ On the left side the -5s cancel out. On the right side, you have $5 \div -5$, which is -1.

Caution: Reverse the direction of the inequality only when you are multiplying or dividing both sides by a negative number. It does not apply if the number is positive or if the operation is addition or subtraction.

You can write the two inequalities, $-5 < 2x + 3$ and $2x + 3 < 7$, as the **double inequality**, $-5 < 2x + 3 < 7$. To solve double inequalities, undo what has been done to the variable in the expression between the two inequality symbols. Apply the "undoing" operations to all three expressions that make up the double inequality. Here is an example.

Solve: $-5 < 2x + 3 < 7$

$-5 < 2x + 3 < 7$
$-5 - 3 < 2x + 3 - 3 < 7 - 3$ 3 is added to the variable term, so subtract 3 from all three expressions.
$-8 < 2x < 4$ Simplify.
$\dfrac{-8}{2} < \dfrac{\cancel{2}x}{\cancel{2}} < \dfrac{4}{2}$ You want the coefficient of x to be 1, so divide all three expressions by 2.
$-4 < x < 2$ Simplify.

Test Yourself

1. When you _____ or _____ an inequality by a _____ number, you must reverse the direction of the inequality.

2. Does $x = -5$ make the inequality $x \geq -9$ true? Justify your answer.

3. Solve: $2x + 5 > 21$

4. Solve: $3x - 4(x + 2) \leq -6$

5. Solve: $-7 < 2x + 1 < 7$

6. Graph the solution of $-13x + 50 > 24$.

Answers

1. multiply, divide, negative

2. Yes, -5 is located to the right of -9 on the number line, so $-5 \geq -9$ is true.

3. $x > 8$

    Solution:
    $$2x + 5 > 21$$
    $$2x + 5 - 5 > 21 - 5 \quad \text{Subtract 5 from both sides of the inequality.}$$
    $$2x > 16 \quad \text{Simplify.}$$
    $$\frac{2x}{2} > \frac{16}{2} \quad \text{Divide both sides by 2.}$$
    $$x > 8 \quad \text{Simplify.}$$

4. $x \geq -2$

    $$3x - 4(x + 2) \leq -6$$
    $$3x - 4x - 8 \leq -6 \quad \text{Use the distributive property to remove parentheses.}$$
    $$-x - 8 \leq -6 \quad \text{Simplify.}$$
    $$-x - 8 + 8 \leq -6 + 8 \quad \text{Add 8 to both sides of the inequality.}$$
    $$-x \leq 2 \quad \text{Simplify.}$$
    $$\frac{-x}{-1} \geq \frac{2}{-1} \quad \text{Divide both sides of the inequality by } -1 \text{ and reverse the inequality because you divided both sides by a negative number.}$$
    $$x \geq -2$$

5. $-4 < x < 3$

    Solution:
    $$-7 < 2x + 1 < 7$$
    $$-7 - 1 < 2x + 1 - 1 < 7 - 1 \quad \text{Subtract 1 from all three expressions.}$$
    $$-8 < 2x < 6 \quad \text{Simplify.}$$
    $$\frac{-8}{2} < \frac{2x}{2} < \frac{6}{2} \quad \text{You want the coefficient of } x \text{ to be 1, so divide all three expressions by 2.}$$
    $$-4 < x < 3 \quad \text{Simplify.}$$

6.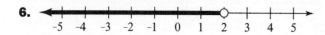

Solution:

$$-13x + 50 > 24$$
$$-13x + 50 - 50 > 24 - 50 \quad \text{Subtract 50 from both sides of the equation.}$$
$$-13x > -26 \quad \text{Simplify.}$$
$$\frac{-13x}{-13} < \frac{-26}{-13} \quad \text{Divide both sides of the inequality by } -13 \text{ and reverse the inequality because you divided both sides by a negative number.}$$
$$x < 2 \quad \text{Simplify.}$$

To show this solution on a number line, draw a dark arrow going to the left from the number 2. Draw an open circle at 2 to show 2 is not included in the solution.

How Do You Use One-Variable Linear Equations and Inequalities to Solve Contextual Problems?

Many real-world contextual problems can be modeled and solved using one-variable linear equations. To solve such contextual problems, write and solve an equation or inequality that represents the facts given in the problem. Here are examples.

> A car and a bus leave a location at exactly the same time, but travel in opposite directions. The car travels due north and the bus travels due south. After 3 hours, the two vehicles are 650 kilometers apart. The car has traveled x kilometers and the bus has traveled 50 kilometers farther in the opposite direction. How far has the car traveled at this time?
>
> Write an equation to represent the facts.

$$x \text{ kilometers} + (x + 50) \text{ kilometers} = 650 \text{ kilometers}$$

Solve the equation (omitting the units for convenience).

$$x + (x + 50) = 650$$
$$x + x + 50 = 650$$

Tip: When a + sign immediately precedes a parentheses, remove the parentheses without changing anything inside.

$$2x + 50 = 650$$
$$2x + 50 - 50 = 650 - 50$$
$$2x = 600$$
$$\frac{2x}{2} = \frac{600}{2}$$
$$x = 300$$

The car has traveled 300 kilometers.

Did I answer the question? Yes, I found the distance traveled by the car. ✓

Does my answer make sense? Yes, the bus traveled 50 kilometers farther than the car, so the car's distance, 300 kilometers, is reasonable because it is a little less than half of the total distance, 650 kilometers. ✓

Is the answer stated in the correct units? Yes, the units are kilometers, which is correct. ✓

> A printing shop charges $0.10 per copy for the first hundred copies. Additional copies are $0.08 per copy. A customer spent $16.40 for copies of an advertising flyer. How many copies of the flyer did the customer receive?

Let x = the number of copies. The first 100 copies at $0.10 each cost $10 (because 100 × $0.10 = $10). The customer spent $16.40, which is more than $10, so you know x is greater than 100. Write an equation to represent the facts.

$$\$0.10(100) + \$0.08(x - 100) = \$16.40$$

Solve the equation (omitting the units for convenience).

$$0.10(100) + 0.08(x - 100) = 16.40$$
$$10 + 0.08x - 8 = 16.40$$
$$2 + 0.08x = 16.40$$
$$2 + 0.08x - 2 = 16.40 - 2$$
$$0.08x = 14.40$$
$$\frac{0.08x}{0.08} = \frac{14.40}{0.08}$$
$$x = 180$$

The customer received 180 copies of the flyer.

Did I answer the question? Yes, I found the number of copies. ✓

Does my answer make sense? Yes, the number of copies is greater than 100, which is consistent with the facts. ✓

Is the answer stated in the correct units? No units are necessary. ✓

> Angle A is twice the size of $\angle B$. If the two angles are supplementary, what is the measure of $\angle A$?

Tip: When you have two or more unknowns and one of them is described in terms of the second one, designate the variable as the second unknown. For instance, $\angle A$ is described as "twice the size of $\angle B$," so designate the variable as the measure of $\angle B$.

Let x = the measure of $\angle B$ (in degrees) and $2x$ = the measure of $\angle A$ (in degrees). A fact from geometry is the sum of the measures of two supplementary angles is 180°. Write an equation to represent the facts.

$$x + 2x = 180°$$

Solve the equation.

$$x + 2x = 180°$$
$$3x = 180°$$
$$\frac{3x}{3} = \frac{180°}{3}$$
$$x = 60° = \text{the measure of } \angle B$$
$$2x = 2(60°) = 120° = \text{the measure of } \angle A$$

Tip: Make sure you answer the question asked. The question asks for the measure of $\angle A$, so after you find the measure of $\angle B$, calculate the measure of $\angle A$.

Did I answer the question? Yes, I found the measure of $\angle A$. ✓

Does my answer make sense? Yes, $\angle A$ is twice the size of $\angle B$ and their sum is 180°, so its measure of 120° seems reasonable. ✓

Is the answer stated in the correct units? Yes, the units are degrees, which is correct. ✓

> Alyssia is twice as old as Ivan. In 5 years, the sum of their ages will be 52. How old will Alyssia be 5 years from now?

Let x = Ivan's age now. Then $2x$ = Alyssia's age now. Make a chart to organize the information in the question.

When?	Ivan's Age	Alyssia's Age	Sum
Now	x	$2x$	?
5 years from now	$x + 5$	$2x + 5$	52

Using the information in the chart, set up an equation and solve for x.

$$(x+5)+(2x+5)=52$$
$$x+5+2x+5=52$$
$$3x+10=52$$
$$3x+10-10=52-10$$
$$3x=42$$
$$\frac{3x}{3}=\frac{42}{3}$$
$$x=14, \text{ Ivan's age now}$$
$$2x=2(14)=28, \text{ Alyssia's age now}$$
$$28+5=33, \text{ Alyssia's age 5 years from now}$$

Tip: Make sure you answer the question asked. In this question, after you obtain Ivan's age now, calculate Alyssia's age 5 years from now.

Did I answer the question? Yes, I found Alyssia's age 5 years from now. ✓

Does my answer make sense? Yes, Alyssia is older than Ivan, and the sum of her and Ivan's age in 5 years is 52, so 33 seems reasonable for her age in 5 years. ✓

Is the answer stated in the correct units? Yes, the units are understood to be years, which is correct. ✓

> Armi is paid $300 per week plus $1.25 per sale. This week Armi wants her pay to be at least $500. What is the minimum number of sales Armi will have to make to achieve her goal?

Let x = the minimum number of sales Armi will have to make. Write an inequality to represent the facts.

$$\$300 + \$1.25x \geq \$500$$

Solve the inequality (omitting the units for convenience).

$$300+1.25x \geq 500$$
$$300+1.25x-300 \geq 500-300$$
$$1.25x \geq 200$$
$$\frac{1.25x}{1.25} \geq \frac{200}{1.25}$$
$$x \geq 160$$

165

Armi will need to make at least 160 sales.

Did I answer the question? Yes, I determined the minimum number of sales Armi will have to make. ✓

Does my answer make sense? Yes, Armi wants $200 above her $300 regular pay. She would need at least 200 sales if she got $1.00 per sale. She's getting $1.25 so she needs less than 200 sales, so 160 sales is reasonable. ✓

Is the answer stated in the correct units? No units are necessary. ✓

Test Yourself

Solve using a variable and a linear equation or inequality.

1. At a resale shop, a pair of shoes cost $15 less than a pair of boots. Cameron purchased four pairs of shoes and two pairs of boots for $90. What is the cost of one pair of boots?

2. The sum of three consecutive integers is 255. What is the greatest of the three integers?

3. The cost of a jacket including sales tax is $91.80. If the sales tax rate is 8%, what is the price of the jacket before sales tax is added?

4. Seth and Carlos will divide $480 in the ratio 3:5, respectively. What amount will Seth receive?

5. Anya has $750, which she saved over the summer. She wants to have at least $200 of this money left by December. How many weeks can she spend $55 of her $750 savings and still have $200 left?

Answers

1. $25

   Let x = the cost of one pair of boots and $x - \$15$ = the cost of one pair of shoes. Write an equation to represent the facts.

   $$4(x - \$15) + 2x = \$90$$

   Solve the equation (omitting the units for convenience).

   $$4(x-15)+2x = 90$$
   $$4x - 60 + 2x = 90$$
   $$6x - 60 = 90$$
   $$6x - 60 + 60 = 90 + 60$$
   $$6x = 150$$
   $$\frac{6x}{6} = \frac{150}{6}$$
   $$x = 25$$

   The cost of one pair of boots is $25.

   Did I answer the question? Yes, I found the cost of one pair of boots. ✓

   Does my answer make sense? Yes, $25 for a pair of boots and $10 ($25 − $15) for a pair of shoes sound reasonable for prices at a resale shop. ✓

   Is the answer stated in the correct units? Yes, the units are dollars, which is correct. ✓

2. 86

   Consecutive integers differ by 1. Let x = the first integer, $x + 1$ = the second integer, and $x + 2$ = the third integer (greatest). Write an equation to represent the facts.

   $$x + (x + 1) + (x + 2) = 255$$

Solve the equation.

$$x+(x+1)+(x+2)=255$$
$$x+x+1+x+2=255$$
$$3x+3=255$$
$$3x+3-3=255-3$$
$$3x=252$$
$$\frac{\cancel{3}x}{\cancel{3}}=\frac{252}{3}$$
$$x=84$$
$$x+1=84+1=85$$
$$x+2=84+2=86=\text{the greatest of the three integers}$$

Did I answer the question? Yes, I found the greatest of the three integers. ✓

Does my answer make sense? Yes, the sum of the three integers is 255, so it's reasonable the greatest of the three is 86. ✓

Is the answer stated in the correct units? No units are necessary. ✓

3. $85

Let p = the price of the jacket. Write an equation to represent the facts.

$$p + 8\%p = \$91.80$$

Tip: When sales tax is added to an item, multiply the price of the item times the sales tax rate.

Solve the equation (omitting the units for convenience).

$$p+8\%p=91.80$$
$$p+0.08p=91.80$$
$$1.08p=91.80$$
$$\frac{\cancel{1.08}p}{\cancel{1.08}}=\frac{91.80}{1.08}$$
$$p=85$$

The price of the jacket before sales tax is added is $85.

Did I answer the question? Yes, I found the price of the jacket before sales tax. ✓

Does my answer make sense? Yes, $85 seems reasonable given the jacket plus tax is $91.80. ✓

Is the answer stated in the correct units? Yes, the units are dollars, which is correct. ✓

4. $180

Let $3x$ = the amount Seth receives and $5x$ = the amount Carlos receives.

Tip: You don't have to specify what *x* represents. The two unknowns are 3*x* and 5*x* and these two amounts are in the required ratio of 3:5.

Write an equation to represent the facts.

$$3x + 5x = \$480$$

Solve the equation (omitting the units for convenience).

$$3x + 5x = 480$$
$$8x = 480$$
$$\frac{\cancel{8}x}{\cancel{8}} = \frac{480}{8}$$
$$x = 60$$
$$3x = 3(60) = 180$$

Seth receives $180.

Did I answer the question? Yes, I found the amount Seth receives. ✓

Does my answer make sense? Yes, because the ratio is 3 to 5, Seth should receive less than one-half of $480. ✓

Is the answer stated in the correct units? Yes, the units are dollars, which is correct. ✓

5. 10 weeks

Let n = the maximum number of weeks. Write an inequality to represent the facts.

$$\$750 - \$55n \geq \$200$$

Solve the inequality (omitting the units for convenience).

$$750 - 55n \geq 200$$
$$750 - 55n - 750 \geq 200 - 750$$
$$-55n \geq -550$$
$$\frac{\cancel{-55}n}{\cancel{-55}} \leq \frac{-550}{-55}$$
$$n \leq 10$$

Tip: Remember to reverse the inequality when dividing by a negative number.

The maximum number of weeks Anya can spend $55 of her $750 and still have $200 left is 10.

Did I answer the question? Yes, I determined Anya can spend $55 a week for at most 10 weeks. ✓

Does my answer make sense? Yes, Anya can spend no more than $550 ($750 − $200), so $55 for at most 10 weeks is a reasonable answer. ✓

Is the answer stated in the correct units? No units are necessary. ✓

How Do You Solve Quadratic Equations?

A **quadratic equation** in one variable is an equation that can be written in **standard form** as $ax^2 + bx + c = 0$, where a, b, and c are real numbers and $a \neq 0$. The **roots** of a quadratic equation are the values for the variable that make the equation true. When you work only with real numbers, quadratic equations have two distinct real roots, one real root, or no real roots. The roots are the values in the solution set.

Solving Quadratic Equations When $b = 0$

On the FTCE GK Test, you might be asked to solve quadratic equations in which the middle term, bx, is "missing"—that is, when the coefficient b is zero. To solve these quadratic equations, do the following:

1. Transform the equation into $x^2 = k$, where k is *nonnegative*.

Tip: Think of this step as "isolating the variable term."

Chapter 3: Review for the General Knowledge Mathematics Subtest

2. Write the solution set: $x = \sqrt{k}$ or $x = -\sqrt{k}$.

Tip: Remember every positive real number has <u>two</u> real square roots: a positive square root and a negative square root, both with the same absolute value.

Here are examples.

Solve: $2x^2 - 50 = 0$

Tip: Start by isolating the x^2 term.

$2x^2 - 50 = 0$
$2x^2 - 50 + 50 = 0 + 50$ Add 50 to both sides of the equation.
$2x^2 = 50$ Simplify.
$\dfrac{2x^2}{2} = \dfrac{50}{2}$ Divide both sides by 2.
$x^2 = 25$ Simplify.
$x = \sqrt{25}$ or $x = -\sqrt{25}$ Write the solution set.
$x = 5$ or $x = -5$ Simplify.

Solve: $81x^2 - 49 = 0$

$81x^2 - 49 = 0$
$81x^2 - 49 + 49 = 0 + 49$ Add 49 to both sides of the equation.
$81x^2 = 49$ Simplify.
$\dfrac{81x^2}{81} = \dfrac{49}{81}$ Divide both sides of the equation by 81.
$x^2 = \dfrac{49}{81}$ Simplify.
$x = \sqrt{\dfrac{49}{81}}$ or $x = -\sqrt{\dfrac{49}{81}}$ Write the solution set.
$x = \dfrac{7}{9}$ or $x = -\dfrac{7}{9}$ Simplify.

Solve: $x^2 = 41$

$x^2 = 41$
$x = \sqrt{41}$ or $x = -\sqrt{41}$ Write the solution set.

Tip: Because $\sqrt{41}$ is irrational, it does not have a terminating or repeating decimal representation. See "What Are Irrational Numbers?" earlier in this chapter (page 76) for a discussion of this topic.

Solve: $12^2 + b^2 = 13^2$

$$12^2 + b^2 = 13^2$$
$$144 + b^2 = 169 \quad \text{Simplify.}$$
$$144 + b^2 - 144 = 169 - 144 \quad \text{Subtract 144 from both sides of the equation.}$$
$$b^2 = 25 \quad \text{Simplify.}$$
$$b = \sqrt{25} \text{ or } b = -\sqrt{25} \quad \text{Write the solution set.}$$
$$b = 5 \text{ or } b = -5 \quad \text{Simplify.}$$

Solve: $x^2 + 16 = 0$

$$x^2 + 16 = 0$$
$$x^2 + 16 - 16 = 0 - 16 \quad \text{Subtract 16 from both sides.}$$
$$x^2 = -16 \quad \text{Simplify.}$$

This equation has no real number solution because no real number multiplies by itself to give –16.

Tip: When you're working with real numbers, k in $x^2 = k$ must be *nonnegative*.

Solving Quadratic Equations When $a = 1$, $b \neq 0$ by Factoring

In many instances, quadratic equations in the form $x^2 + bx + c = 0$, where $a = 1$ and $b \neq 0$, can be solved by factoring. Solving quadratic equations by factoring requires you use the following **zero property of real numbers:** If x and y are real numbers, then $xy = 0$ if and only if $x = 0$ or $y = 0$.

For example, to solve $x^2 + 8x + 15 = 0$, write it as $(x + 3)(x + 5) = 0$. The factors $(x + 3)$ and $(x + 5)$ represent real numbers whose product is 0. Thus, by the zero property of real numbers, the equation will be true if either $(x + 3)$ is zero or $(x + 5)$ is zero. Here are the steps.

$$x^2 + 8x + 15 = 0$$
$$(x + 3)(x + 5) = 0 \quad \text{Factor the left side of the equation.}$$
$$x + 3 = 0 \text{ or } x + 5 = 0 \quad \text{Set each factor equal to zero.}$$
$$x = -3 \text{ or } x = -5 \quad \text{Solve the resulting linear equations to obtain the solution set.}$$

Tip: Check your factoring by multiplying the binomials $(x + 3)$ and $(x + 5)$ using FOIL (First, Outer, Inner, Last).

First—Multiply the first terms in each set of parentheses: $x \cdot x = x^2$
Outer—Multiply the outer terms in each set of parentheses: $x \cdot 5 = 5x$
Inner—Multiply the inner terms in each set of parentheses: $3 \cdot x = 3x$
Last—Multiply the last terms in each set of parentheses: $3 \cdot 5 = 15$

Thus, $(x + 3)(x + 5) = x^2 + 5x + 3x + 15 = x^2 + 8x + 15$

You can use guessing and checking to factor the left side of $x^2 + bx + c = 0$. Here are examples.

Solve: $x^2 - 5x + 6 = 0$

$$x^2 - 5x + 6 = 0$$

Factor the left side of the equation. Put two sets of parentheses side-by-side on the left side to hold places for the two binomial factors of $x^2 - 5x + 6$.

$$(\ )(\ ) = 0$$

Put x as the first term in each parentheses because you need their product to be x^2.

$$(x\ )(x\ ) = 0$$

Because the second (last) terms in the parentheses must multiply to give 6, a positive number, they have the same sign. They must add (algebraically) to give –5, so they are both negative. By guessing and checking, you can determine the pair of integers –2 and –3 satisfies these requirements ($-2 \cdot -3 = 6$ and $-2 + -3 = -5$), so put them in as the second terms in the parentheses.

$$(x - 2)(x - 3) = 0$$

Set each factor equal to zero and solve for x.

$$x - 2 = 0 \text{ or } x - 3 = 0$$
$$x = 2 \text{ or } x = 3$$

> **Tip:** It's a good idea to mentally check your factoring: $(x - 2)(x - 3) = x^2 - 3x - 2x + 6 = x^2 - 5x + 6$. ✓

Solve: $x^2 - 5x - 24 = 0$

$$x^2 - 5x - 24 = 0$$

Factor the left side of the equation. Put two sets of parentheses side-by-side on the left side to hold places for the two binomial factors of $x^2 - 5x - 24$.

$$(\ )(\ ) = 0$$

Put x as the first term in each parentheses because you need their product to be x^2.

$$(x\ )(x\ ) = 0$$

Because the second terms in the parentheses must multiply to give –24, a negative number, they have opposite signs. They must add (algebraically) to give –5, so the one with the greater absolute value is negative. The pair of integers –8 and 3 satisfies these requirements ($-8 \cdot 3 = -24$ and $-8 + 3 = -5$), so put them in as the second terms in the parentheses.

$$(x - 8)(x + 3) = 0$$

Set each factor equal to zero and solve for x.

$$x - 8 = 0 \text{ or } x + 3 = 0$$
$$x = 8 \text{ or } x = -3$$

> **Tip:** Mentally check your factoring: $(x - 8)(x + 3) = x^2 - 8x + 3x - 24 = x^2 - 5x - 24$. ✓

Solving Quadratic Equations When $b \neq 0$, $c = 0$

Quadratic equations that have the standard form $ax^2 + bx = 0$ can be solved by using the distributive property to factor the left side of the equation. Here are examples.

Chapter 3: Review for the General Knowledge Mathematics Subtest

> Solve: $x^2 - 7x = 0$

$$x^2 - 7x = 0$$
$x(x-7) = 0$ Using the distributive property, factor the left side of the equation.
$x = 0$ or $x - 7 = 0$ Set each factor equal to zero.
$x = 0$ or $x = 7$ Solve the resulting linear equation to obtain the full solution set.

Tip: Zero will always be in the solution set of quadratic equations that have the standard form $ax^2 + bx = 0$.

> Solve: $x^2 = -24x$

Tip: Do not make the mistake of dividing both sides by x because you run the risk of unknowingly dividing by zero.

$$x^2 = -24x$$
$x^2 + 24x = -24x + 24x$ Add $24x$ to both sides of the equation to transform it into standard form.
$x^2 + 24x = 0$ Simplify.
$x(x + 24) = 0$ Using the distributive property, factor the left side of the equation.
$x = 0$ or $x + 24 = 0$ Set each factor equal to zero.
$x = 0$ or $x = -24$ Solve the resulting linear equation to obtain the full solution set.

Test Yourself

Solve the given equation.

1. $x^2 - 36 = 0$
2. $3x^2 = 147$
3. $\dfrac{x^2}{4} = 16$
4. $2x^2 - 39 = 11$
5. $x^2 = x + 2$
6. $x^2 - 10x = -25$
7. $2x^2 + 15x = 0$
8. $9x^2 = 27x$

Answers

1. $x = 6$ or $x = -6$

   Solution:
   $$x^2 - 36 = 0$$
   $x^2 - 36 + 36 = 0 + 36$ Add 36 to both sides of the equation.
   $x^2 = 36$ Simplify.
   $x = \sqrt{36}$ or $x = -\sqrt{36}$ Write the solution set.
   $x = 6$ or $x = -6$ Simplify.

2. $x = 7$ or $x = -7$

   Solution:

   $$3x^2 = 147$$
   $$\frac{\cancel{3}x^2}{\cancel{3}} = \frac{147}{3}$$ Divide both sides by 3.
   $$x^2 = 49$$ Simplify.
   $$x = \sqrt{49} \text{ or } x = -\sqrt{49}$$ Write the solution set.
   $$x = 7 \text{ or } x = -7$$ Simplify.

3. $x = 8$ or $x = -8$

   Solution:

   $$\frac{x^2}{4} = 16$$
   $$\cancel{4}\left(\frac{x^2}{\cancel{4}}\right) = 4(16)$$ Multiply both sides of the equation by 4.
   $$x^2 = 64$$ Simplify.
   $$x = \sqrt{64} \text{ or } x = -\sqrt{64}$$ Write the solution set.
   $$x = 8 \text{ or } x = -8$$ Simplify.

4. $x = 5$ or $x = -5$

   Solution:

   $$2x^2 - 39 = 11$$
   $$2x^2 - 39 + 39 = 11 + 39$$ Add 39 to both sides of the equation.
   $$2x^2 = 50$$ Simplify.
   $$\frac{\cancel{2}x^2}{\cancel{2}} = \frac{50}{2}$$ Divide both sides by 2.
   $$x^2 = 25$$ Simplify.
   $$x = \sqrt{25} \text{ or } x = -\sqrt{25}$$ Write the solution set.
   $$x = 5 \text{ or } x = -5$$ Simplify.

5. $x = 2$ or $x = -1$

   Solution:

   $$x^2 = x + 2$$
   $$x^2 - (x+2) = x + 2 - (x+2)$$ Transform into standard form by subtracting $(x+2)$ from both sides of the equation.
   $$x^2 - x - 2 = 0$$ Simplify.

Tip: When a – sign immediately precedes a parentheses, remove the parentheses, but change the sign of every term inside the parentheses.

$$(x-2)(x+1) = 0$$ Factor the left side of the equation.
$$x - 2 = 0 \text{ or } x + 1 = 0$$ Set each factor equal to zero.
$$x = 2 \text{ or } x = -1$$ Solve the resulting linear equations to obtain the solution set.

6. $x = 5$

Solution:

$$x^2 - 10x = -25$$
$$x^2 - 10x + 25 = -25 + 25 \quad \text{Transform into standard form by adding 25 to both sides of the equation.}$$
$$x^2 - 10x + 25 = 0 \quad \text{Simplify.}$$
$$(x-5)(x-5) = 0 \quad \text{Factor the left side of the equation.}$$
$$x - 5 = 0 \text{ or } x - 5 = 0 \quad \text{Set each factor equal to zero.}$$
$$x = 5 \quad \text{Solve the resulting linear equation to obtain the solution set.}$$

Both equations yield 5 as a solution, so write it only once.

7. $x = 0$ or $x = -7.5$

Solution:

$$2x^2 + 15x = 0$$
$$x(2x + 15) = 0 \quad \text{Using the distributive property, factor the left side of the equation.}$$
$$x = 0 \text{ or } 2x + 15 = 0 \quad \text{Set each factor equal to zero.}$$
$$x = 0 \text{ or } x = -7.5 \quad \text{Solve the resulting linear equation to obtain the full solution set.}$$

8. $x = 0$ or $x = 3$

Solution:

$$9x^2 = 27x$$
$$9x^2 - 27x = 27x - 27x \quad \text{Transform into standard form by subtracting } 27x \text{ from both sides of the equation.}$$
$$9x^2 - 27x = 0 \quad \text{Simplify.}$$
$$9x(x - 3) = 0 \quad \text{Using the distributive property, factor the left side of the equation.}$$
$$9x = 0 \text{ or } x - 3 = 0 \quad \text{Set each factor equal to zero.}$$
$$x = 0 \text{ or } x = 3 \quad \text{Solve the resulting linear equations to obtain the solution set.}$$

How Do You Use One-Variable Quadratic Equations to Solve Contextual Problems?

Some real-world contextual problems might require solving a quadratic equation. Here are examples.

> The hypotenuse of a right triangle is 30 centimeters long and one leg is 24 centimeters long. Find the area of the triangle.

Let a = the length of the right triangle's other leg. Make a sketch.

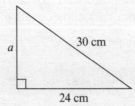

Solve this problem using two steps. First, find a, the length of the right triangle's other leg, using the Pythagorean theorem (from the Mathematics Reference Sheet): $a^2 + b^2 = c^2$, where a and b are the legs and c is the hypotenuse of the right triangle. Next, use the length obtained to find the area of the triangle using $A = \frac{1}{2}bh$ (from the Mathematics Reference Sheet), where b is the base of the triangle and a is its height.

Step 1. Find *a*.

Write an equation to represent the facts. In $a^2 + b^2 = c^2$, substitute $c = 30$ cm and $b = 24$ cm.

$$a^2 + (24 \text{ cm})^2 = (30 \text{ cm})^2$$

Solve the equation for *a* (omitting the units for convenience).

$$a^2 + (24)^2 = (30)^2$$
$$a^2 + 576 = 900$$
$$a^2 + 576 - 576 = 900 - 576$$
$$a^2 = 324$$
$$a = \sqrt{324} \text{ or } a = -\sqrt{324}$$
$$a = 18 \text{ or } a = -18 \text{ (Reject, because measures of length are nonnegative.)}$$

The length of the right triangle's other leg is 18 centimeters.

Step 2. Find the area of the triangle.

Given *a* is perpendicular to *b*, substitute $b = 24$ cm and $h = a = 18$ cm into $A = \frac{1}{2}bh$ to obtain the area.

$$A = \frac{1}{2}(24 \text{ cm})(18 \text{ cm}) = 216 \text{ cm}^2$$

Tip: To do the computation with the calculator, do this: 24 × 18 ÷ 2 =. The display will show 216, the correct value.

The area of the triangle is 216 cm².

> *Did I answer the question?* Yes, I determined the area of the triangle. ✓
>
> *Does my answer make sense?* Yes, the triangle's dimensions are 18 cm, 24 cm, and 30 cm, so an area of 216 cm² seems reasonable. ✓
>
> *Is the answer stated in the correct units?* Yes, the units are cm², which is correct. ✓

The square of a negative number is 72 more than the number. Find the number.

Let x = the number. Write an equation to represent the facts.

$$x^2 = x + 72$$

Solve the equation.

$$x^2 = x + 72$$
$$x^2 - (x + 72) = x + 72 - (x + 72)$$
$$x^2 - x - 72 = 0$$
$$(x - 9)(x + 8) = 0$$
$$x - 9 = 0 \text{ or } x + 8 = 0$$
$$x = 9 \text{ or } x = -8$$

Reject 9, because the question specifies the number is negative. The number is –8.

> *Did I answer the question?* Yes, I found the number. ✓
>
> *Does my answer make sense?* Yes, $(-8)^2$ is 64, which is 72 more than –8. ✓
>
> *Is the answer stated in the correct units?* No units are necessary. ✓

Test Yourself

Solve using a variable and a quadratic equation.

1. Find the length of the diagonal of a rectangle whose length is 12 feet and width is 5 feet.

2. Find the greater of two positive integers whose ratio is 2 to 3 and whose product is 384.

3. The width of a rectangular patio is 4 meters less than its length. The area of the patio is 60 square meters. What is the width of the patio?

4. If the surface area of sphere is 144π in^2, what is its volume in terms of π?

5. The equation for the height in meters above ground, h, of a projectile after t seconds of elapsed time in the air is $t^2 - 4t - 12$. Find t when the projectile returns to ground; that is, when $h = 0$.

Answers

1. 13 feet

    Let d = the length of the rectangle's diagonal. Make a sketch.

    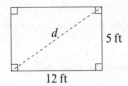

    The diagonal is the hypotenuse of a right triangle with legs 12 feet and 5 feet. Using the Pythagorean theorem, $c^2 = a^2 + b^2$ (from the Mathematics Reference Sheet), write an equation that represents the facts.

    $$d^2 = (12 \text{ ft})^2 + (5 \text{ ft})^2$$

    Solve the equation for d (omitting the units for convenience).

    $$d^2 = (12)^2 + (5)^2$$
    $$d^2 = 144 + 25$$
    $$d^2 = 169$$
    $$d = \sqrt{169} \text{ or } d = -\sqrt{169}$$
    $$d = 13 \text{ or } d = -13 \text{ (Reject, because measures of length are nonnegative.)}$$

    The length of the diagonal is 13 feet.

    Did I answer the question? Yes, I found the length of the diagonal. ✓

    Does my answer make sense? Yes, the rectangle's dimensions are 12 feet by 5 feet, so a diagonal of length 13 feet seems reasonable. ✓

    Is the answer stated in the correct units? Yes, the units are feet, which is correct. ✓

2. 24

    Let $2x$ = the lesser integer and $3x$ = the greater integer. Write an equation that represents the facts.

    $$(2x)(3x) = 384$$

Solve the equation.

$$(2x)(3x) = 384$$
$$6x^2 = 384$$
$$\frac{\cancel{6}x^2}{\cancel{6}} = \frac{384}{6}$$
$$x^2 = 64$$
$$x = \sqrt{64} \text{ or } x = -\sqrt{64}$$
$$x = 8 \text{ or } x = -8 \text{ (Reject, because the integers are positive.)}$$
$$2x = 2(8) = 16 = \text{the lesser integer}$$
$$3x = 3(8) = 24 = \text{the greater integer}$$

The greater integer is 24.

Did I answer the question? Yes, I determined the value of the greater integer. ✓

Does my answer make sense? Yes, 24 is reasonable because 16 times 24 is 384. ✓

Is the answer stated in the correct units? No units are necessary. ✓

3. 6 meters

Let L = the patio's length in meters and $W = L - 4$ = patio's width in meters. A fact from geometry is the area of a rectangle equals its length times its width ($A = lw$, from the Mathematics Reference Sheet). Write an equation that represents the facts.

$$A = LW = L(L - 4 \text{ m}) = 60 \text{ m}^2$$

Solve the equation (omitting the units for convenience).

$$L(L - 4) = 60$$
$$L^2 - 4L - 60 = 0$$
$$(L - 10)(L + 6) = 0$$
$$L - 10 = 0 \text{ or } L + 6 = 0$$
$$L = 10 \text{ or } L = -6 \text{ (Reject, because measures of length are nonnegative.)}$$

L is 10 meters.

$$W = L - 4 \text{ m} = 10 \text{ m} - 4 \text{ m} = 6 \text{ m}$$

The width of the patio is 6 meters.

Did I answer the question? Yes, I determined the width of the patio. ✓

Does my answer make sense? Yes, 6 meters as the width of the patio is consistent with my real-world experiences. ✓

Is the answer stated in the correct units? Yes, the units are meters, which is correct. ✓

4. 288π in^3

To find the volume, use two steps. First, find the sphere's radius, r, using the formula for a sphere's surface area (from the Mathematics Reference Sheet): $S.A. = 4\pi r^2$, where r is the sphere's radius. Next, find the volume, V, using the formula for a sphere's volume (from the Mathematics Reference Sheet): $V = \frac{4}{3}\pi r^3$, where r is the sphere's radius.

Step 1. Find the sphere's radius.

Write an equation that represents the facts.

$$S.A. = 4\pi r^2 = 144\pi \text{ in}^2$$

Solve the equation (omitting the units for convenience).

$$4\pi r^2 = 144\pi$$

$$\frac{\cancel{4\pi} r^2}{\cancel{4\pi}} = \frac{144 \cancel{\pi}}{4 \cancel{\pi}}$$

$$r^2 = 36$$

$$r = \sqrt{36} \text{ or } r = -\sqrt{36}$$

$r = 6$ or $r = -6$ (Reject, because measures of length are nonnegative.)

The sphere's radius is 6 inches.

Step 2. Find the sphere's volume.

$$V = \frac{4}{3}\pi r^3 = \frac{4}{3}\pi(6 \text{ in})^3 = \frac{4}{3}\pi \cdot 216 \text{ in}^3 = 288\pi \text{ in}^3$$

The sphere's volume is 288π in³.

Did I answer the question? Yes, I found the sphere's volume. ✓

Does my answer make sense? Yes, given the sphere's radius is 6 inches, a volume of 288π in³ seems reasonable. ✓

Is the answer stated in the correct units? Yes, the units are in³, which is correct. ✓

5. 6 seconds

Write and solve an equation that represents the facts.

$$t^2 - 4t - 12 = 0$$

$$(t - 6)(t + 2) = 0$$

$t = 6$ or $t = -2$ (Reject, because -2 seconds doesn't make sense in the context of the problem.)

The projectile returns to ground in 6 seconds.

Did I answer the question? Yes, I determined the elapsed time when the projectile returns to ground. ✓

Does my answer make sense? Yes, 6 seconds of elapsed time is consistent with my real-world experiences. ✓

Is the answer stated in the correct units? Yes, the units are seconds, which is correct. ✓

How Do You Locate and Name Points in a Coordinate Plane?

In the Numeration and Operations section (page 59), you learned the real numbers can be represented on a number line. If you take two copies of the number line, one horizontal and one vertical, and position them at right angles so that they intersect at the 0 point on each line, you have a **coordinate plane** (or **coordinate system**).

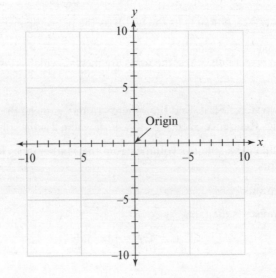

Commonly, the horizontal number line with positive direction to the right is designated the *x*-axis, and the vertical number line with positive direction upward is designated the *y*-axis. The intersection of the two lines is the **origin**. The two intersecting *x*- and *y*-axes divide the coordinate plane into four sections, called **quadrants**. The quadrants are numbered *counterclockwise* using Roman numerals as shown here.

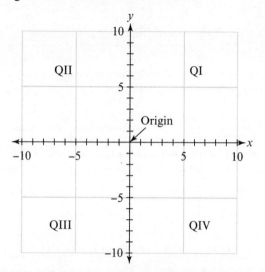

In the coordinate plane, you can match points with an **ordered pair** of numbers, called **coordinates**. An ordered pair of numbers is written in a definite order so that one number is first and the other is second. The first number is the **x-coordinate**, and the second number is the **y-coordinate**. You write ordered pairs in parentheses with the two numbers separated by commas. The ordered pair (0, 0) designates the origin.

Look at these examples.

(3, 5) is the ordered pair with *x*-coordinate = 3, and *y*-coordinate = 5

(–2, 3) is the ordered pair with *x*-coordinate = –2, and *y*-coordinate = 3

An ordered pair gives you directions on how to graph a point in the coordinate plane, starting from the origin (0, 0). The *x*-coordinate tells you how far to go right (for positive numbers) or left (for negative numbers). From that location, the *y*-coordinate tells you how far to go up (for positive numbers) or down (for negative numbers). Then, put a large dot to mark the location of the point.

Here are examples of how to graph a point.

> Graph the ordered pair (3, 5).

Start at (0, 0). Go 3 units right. Then go 5 units up.

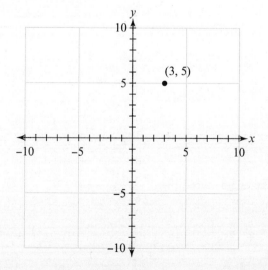

Graph the ordered pair (–2, 3).

Start at (0, 0). Go 2 units left. Then go 3 units up.

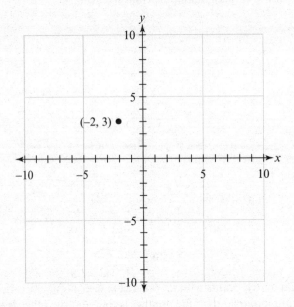

Graph the ordered pair (–4, –5).

Start at (0, 0). Go 4 units left. Then go 5 units down.

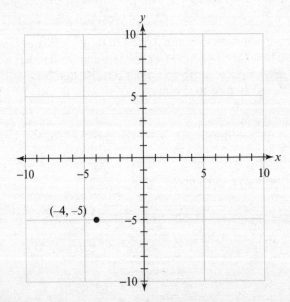

Graph the ordered pair (1, –6).

Start at (0, 0). Go 1 unit right. Then go 6 units down.

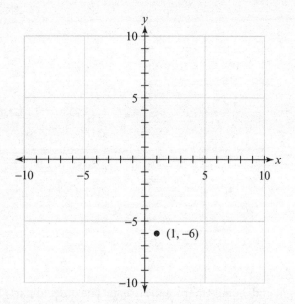

Tip: Note in Quadrant I, both the *x*-coordinate and the *y*-coordinate are positive; in Quadrant II, the *x*-coordinate is negative and the *y*-coordinate is positive; in Quadrant III, both the *x*-coordinate and the *y*-coordinate are negative; and in Quadrant IV, the *x*-coordinate is positive and the *y*-coordinate is negative.

Points that have zero as one or both of the coordinates lie on the axes. If the *x*-coordinate is zero, the point lies on the *y*-axis. If the *y*-coordinate is zero, the point lies on the *x*-axis. If both coordinates of a point are zero, the point is at the origin. For example, as shown in the following, the point (0, 4) lies on the *y*-axis, and the point (–5, 0) lies on the *x*-axis.

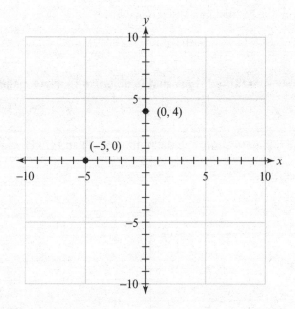

You name a point in a coordinate plane by naming the ordered pair, (*x*, *y*), that specifies the location of the point. The location of every point in the coordinate plane is given by an ordered pair of real numbers. The numbers *x* and *y* are the coordinates of the point. Here is an example.

> What ordered pair of integers represents the point *K*?

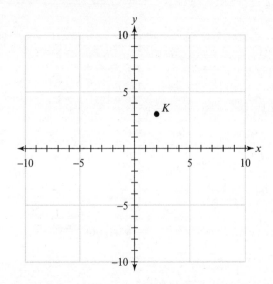

The point K is 2 units to the right and 3 units up from the origin. The ordered pair (2, 3) represents the point K.

How Do You Find the Slope of the Line Between Two Points?

To find the slope of the line that connects the points (x_1, y_1) and (x_2, y_2) in a coordinate plane, do these steps:

1. Sketch a diagram and label it.
2. Specify (x_1, y_1) and (x_2, y_2). This step is *very* important, so don't skip it. Notice the subscript written to the lower right of each variable. The subscripts are used to emphasize the coordinates x_1 and y_1 go together and the coordinates x_2 and y_2 go together. Keep this matching in mind when you do Step 2.
3. Plug into the formula from the Mathematics Reference Sheet.

$$\text{Slope of line} = \frac{y_2 - y_1}{x_2 - x_1}$$

Tip: Enclose in parentheses any substituted value that is negative to avoid making a sign error.

Here are examples.

> Find the slope of the line that passes through the points (5, –7) and (3, 1).

Step 1. Sketch a diagram and label it.

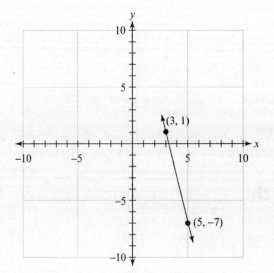

Step 2. Specify (x_1, y_1) and (x_2, y_2).

Let $(x_1, y_1) = (5, -7)$ and $(x_2, y_2) = (3, 1)$. Then $x_1 = 5$, $y_1 = -7$, $x_2 = 3$, and $y_2 = 1$.

Step 3. Plug into the formula.

$$\text{Slope of line} = \frac{y_2 - y_1}{x_2 - x_1} = \frac{1-(-7)}{3-5} = \frac{1+7}{3-5} = \frac{8}{-2} = -4$$

The line through the points (5, –7) and (3, 1) has slope –4.

> Find the slope of the line that connects the points (–4, –5) and (2, 3).

Step 1. Sketch a diagram and label it.

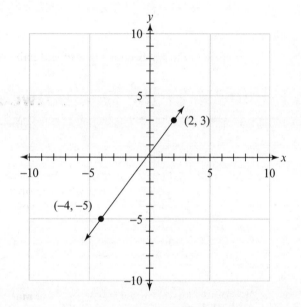

Step 2. Specify (x_1, y_1) and (x_2, y_2).

Let $(x_1, y_1) = (-4, -5)$ and $(x_2, y_2) = (2, 3)$. Then $x_1 = -4$, $y_1 = -5$, $x_2 = 2$, and $y_2 = 3$.

Step 3. Plug into the formula.

$$\text{Slope} = \frac{y_2 - y_1}{x_2 - x_1} = \frac{3-(-5)}{2-(-4)} = \frac{3+5}{2+4} = \frac{8}{6} = \frac{4}{3}$$

The line through the points (–4, –5) and (2, 3) has slope $\frac{4}{3}$.

Lines that slant to the right (that is, slope up from left to right) have positive slope. Lines that slant to the left (that is, slope down from left to right) have negative slope. The slope of a horizontal line is zero. A vertical line has no slope. When you calculate the slope between two points, be sure to note the slant, if any. If your answer has a sign that disagrees with the slant, you made an error.

How Do You Find the Distance Between Two Points?

The steps to find the distance between two points in a coordinate plane are basically the same (except for the last step, where you use a different formula) as the steps for finding the slope of the line between the points:

1. Sketch a diagram and label it.
2. Specify (x_1, y_1) and (x_2, y_2).
3. Plug into the formula from the Mathematics Reference Sheet:

$$\text{Distance between two points} = \sqrt{(x_2 - x_1)^2 + (y_2 - y_1)^2}$$

Here is an example.

> Find the distance between the two points (–4, –5) and (2, 3) in a coordinate plane.

Step 1. Sketch a diagram and label it.

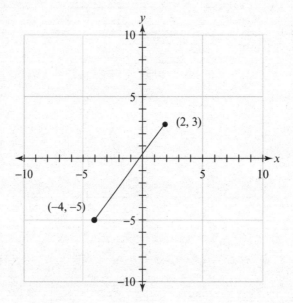

Step 2. Specify (x_1, y_1) and (x_2, y_2).

Let $(x_1, y_1) = (-4, -5)$ and $(x_2, y_2) = (2, 3)$. Then $x_1 = -4$, $y_1 = -5$, $x_2 = 2$, and $y_2 = 3$.

Step 3. Plug into the formula.

$$\text{Distance} = \sqrt{(x_2 - x_1)^2 + (y_2 - y_1)^2} = \sqrt{(2-(-4))^2 + (3-(-5))^2} = \sqrt{(2+4)^2 + (3+5)^2}$$
$$= \sqrt{(6)^2 + (8)^2} = \sqrt{36 + 64} = \sqrt{100} = 10$$

The distance between the two points (–4, –5) and (2, 3) is 10 units.

How Do You Find the Midpoint Between Two Points?

The steps to find the midpoint between two points in a coordinate plane are basically the same (except for the last step, where you use a different formula) as the steps for finding the slope of the line or the distance between the points:

1. Sketch a diagram and label it.
2. Specify (x_1, y_1) and (x_2, y_2).
3. Plug into the formula from the Mathematics Reference Sheet:

$$\text{Midpoint between two points} = \left(\frac{x_1 + x_2}{2}, \frac{y_1 + y_2}{2} \right)$$

Tip: Notice you add, not subtract, the coordinates in the numerator.

Here is an example.

> What is the midpoint of the line segment that connects the points (5, –7) and (3, 1) in a coordinate plane?

Step 1. Sketch a diagram and label it.

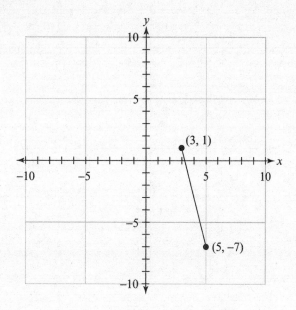

Step 2. Specify (x_1, y_1) and (x_2, y_2).

Let $(x_1, y_1) = (5, -7)$ and $(x_2, y_2) = (3, 1)$. Then $x_1 = 5$, $y_1 = -7$, $x_2 = 3$, and $y_2 = 1$.

Step 3. Plug into the formula.

$$\text{Midpoint} = \left(\frac{x_1 + x_2}{2}, \frac{y_1 + y_2}{2}\right) = \left(\frac{5+3}{2}, \frac{-7+1}{2}\right) = \left(\frac{8}{2}, \frac{-6}{2}\right) = (4, -3)$$

The midpoint of the line segment that connects the points (5, –7) and (3, 1) is the point (4, –3).

Test Yourself

1. The point (0, 0) is the _____ of a coordinate plane.

2. The quadrants of a coordinate plane are numbered _____ (clockwise, counterclockwise) using Roman numerals.

3. In the ordered pair (–5, 8), –5 is the _____ (x-coordinate, y-coordinate), and 8 is the _____ (x-coordinate, y-coordinate).

4. In Quadrant _____, both coordinates are positive.

5. In Quadrant II, the x-coordinate is _____ (positive, negative), and the y-coordinate is _____ (positive, negative).

6. In Quadrant IV, the x-coordinate is _____ (positive, negative), and the y-coordinate is _____ (positive, negative).

7. In Quadrant _____, both coordinates are negative.

8. The point (0, –7) lies on the _____ (x-axis, y-axis).

9. The point (5, 0) lies on the _____ (x-axis, y-axis).

10. The ordered pair of integers that names the point P shown below is _____.

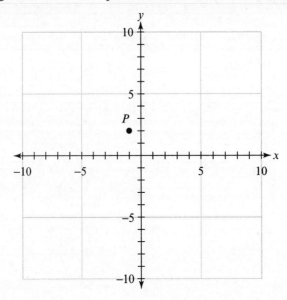

11. The slope of the line that passes through the points (–4, 1) and (0, 5) is _____.

12. If a line slants to the left, its slope is _____ (positive, negative).

13. The slope of a horizontal line is _____.

14. A _____ line has no slope.

15. The x-coordinate of the midpoint of the line segment between two points is the _____ of the x-coordinates of the two points divided by 2, and the y-coordinate is the _____ of the y-coordinates of the two points divided by 2.

Answers

1. origin
2. counterclockwise
3. x-coordinate, y-coordinate
4. I
5. negative, positive
6. positive, negative
7. III
8. y-axis
9. x-axis
10. The point P is 1 unit to the left and 2 units up from the origin. The ordered pair (–1, 2) names the point P.
11. slope = 1

Solution:

Step 1. Sketch a diagram and label it.

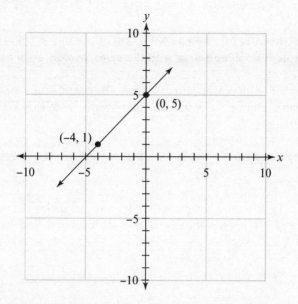

Step 2. Specify (x_1, y_1) and (x_2, y_2).

Let $(x_1, y_1) = (-4, 1)$ and $(x_2, y_2) = (0, 5)$. Then $x_1 = -4$, $y_1 = 1$, $x_2 = 0$, and $y_2 = 5$.

Step 3. Plug into the formula.

$$\text{Slope} = \frac{y_2 - y_1}{x_2 - x_1} = \frac{5 - 1}{0 - (-4)} = \frac{5 - 1}{0 + 4} = \frac{4}{4} = 1$$

The line through the points (–4, 1) and (0, 5) has slope 1.

12. negative

13. zero

14. vertical

15. sum, sum

What Is a Function?

A **relation** is a set of ordered pairs. A **function** is a set of ordered pairs in which each first element (**input value** or *x*-value) is paired with *one and only one* second element (**output value** or *y*-value). Thus, a function is a relation in which no two ordered pairs have the same first element but different second elements.

Note: When discussing functions, the terms *first element, input value*, and *x-value* are interchangeable. Similarly, the terms *second element, output value*, and *y-value* are interchangeable.

Look at the following relations.

$a = \{(-4, -7), (-3, -5), (0, 1), (2, 5), (8, 17)\}$
$b = \{(-5, 0), (-3, -1), (3, 4), (5, 5), (7, 6)\}$
$c = \{(-2, -2), (-3, -3), (0, 0), (2, 2), (3, 3)\}$
$r = \{(1, 1), (2, 1), (3, 1), (4, 1), (5, 1)\}$
$s = \{(4, 2), (9, 3), (9, -3), (16, 4), (25, 5)\}$
$t = \{(-3, -6), (-1, -2), (0, 0), (1, 2), (2, 4)\}$

Only the relation *s* is not a function. Set *s* is not a function because (9, 3) and (9, –3) have the same first element (9), but different second elements (3 and –3). The set *s* can be altered to become a function, call it *s'*, by removing one of the ordered pairs that has first element 9. Thus, *s'* = {(4, 2), (9, 3), (16, 4), (25, 5)} is a function.

Tip: A function CANNOT have two different *y*-values paired with the same *x*-value, such as (9, 3) and (9, –3). But a function CAN have two different *x*-values paired with the same *y*-value, such as (3, 1) and (4, 1).

The **domain** of a function is the set of all possible input values. The **range** is the set of all possible output values. The function *a* shown above has domain {–4, –3, 0, 2, 8} and range {–7, –5, 1, 5, 17}. The function *r* shown above has domain {1, 2, 3, 4, 5} and range {1}.

Tip: On the FTCE GK Test, only functions for which both the domain and the range consist of real numbers are considered.

When the function consists of a finite number of ordered pairs, you can define the function by listing its ordered pairs in a set, in a chart, or as a graph. For instance, here are three ways to define the function *a* shown above.

In a set: *a* = {(–4, –7), (–3, –5), (0, 1), (2, 5), (8, 17)}

In a table:

Input (*x*)	–4	–3	0	2	8
Output (*y*)	–7	–5	1	5	17

As a graph:

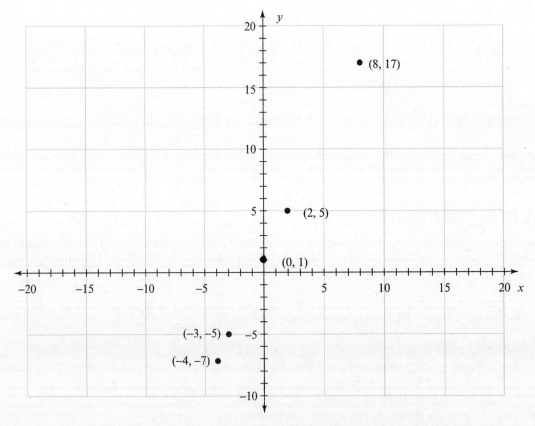

> **Tip:** When a function is defined by a finite set of ordered pairs graphed as points in a coordinate plane, do not connect the points. Only the plotted points are in the function.

You also may be able to define the function a by a rule. You might say a is the function with domain $\{-4, -3, 0, 2, 8\}$ for which the output value is twice the input value plus 1. This rule would generate the set of ordered pairs $\{(-4, -7), (-3, -5), (0, 1), (2, 5), (8, 17)\}$. Notice you have to specify the domain, so that you don't get ordered pairs that do not belong in a.

A function is completely determined when a domain is specified and a rule instructing how to obtain the output value from the input value is given. If no domain is specified, then it's understood that the domain is R, the set of real numbers, except for values that must be excluded. An **excluded value** is a value for the input value (x-value) that would yield an undefined output value (y-value) over the real numbers. Routinely exclude values that lead to division by zero or square roots of negative numbers. Look at these examples.

Rule	Excluded Value(s)
output value = 2 times input value plus 1	none
output value = $\dfrac{1}{\text{input value}}$	zero
output value = $\sqrt{\text{input value}}$	negative numbers
output value = $(\text{input value})^2$	none

When a function has an infinite number of ordered pairs, use a rule or a graph to define it. Commonly, rules for functions are stated in terms of x and y (although other variable names may be used as well). For example, the rule "output value = 2 times input value plus 1" is written $y = 2x + 1$. If f is the function defined by this rule, then f is the set of ordered pairs (x, y) such that $y = 2x + 1$. It has become commonplace to say the rule is the function; that is, to speak of the function $y = 2x + 1$. As long as you understand that what you mean by "the function $y = 2x + 1$" is the set of ordered pairs generated by the equation $y = 2x + 1$, this relaxed way of expressing that idea is acceptable.

The function f defined by the equation $y = 2x + 1$ is a linear function. **Linear functions** are defined by equations of the form $f(x) = mx + b$ or $y = mx + b$. The domain for all linear functions is R, the set of real numbers. When $m \neq 0$, the range is R. But when $m = 0$, the range is the set $\{b\}$, which contains the single value b. The graph of a linear function is always a nonvertical line with slope m. The graph intersects the y-axis at $(0, b)$. One way to graph $y = 2x + 1$ is to make a chart of x and y values that satisfy the equation like this one.

x	0	2
y	1	5

> **Tip:** You need only two points to determine a line.

Plot the points in a coordinate plane and connect them with a line.

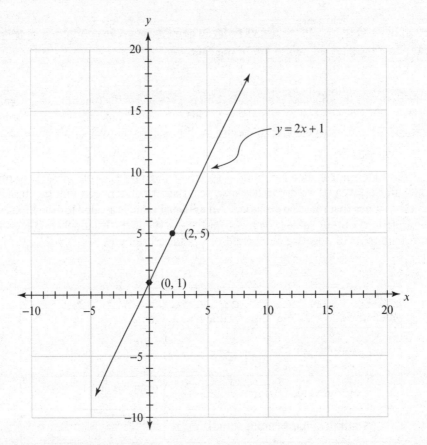

A handy way to express the rule "output value = 2 times input value plus 1" is $f(x) = 2x + 1$. The notation $f(x)$ is another name for y. It denotes the value of the function f at a given x-value. Here are examples.

> Find $f(-4)$ when $f(x) = 2x + 1$.

Tip: The notation $f(x)$ does NOT mean f times x. It is a special notation telling you to do the f rule to the x-value.

$$f(-4) = 2(-4) + 1 = -8 + 1 = -7$$

> Find $f(8)$ when $f(x) = 2x + 1$.

$$f(8) = 2(8) + 1 = 16 + 1 = 17$$

As you can see, changing the x-value changed the y-value. The $f(x)$ notation emphasizes the output value, y, is dependent on the input value, x. The variable x is the **independent variable** and y is the **dependent variable.**

Test Yourself

1. A function is a set of ordered pairs (x, y) in which each x-value is paired with *one and only one* _____.

2. The _____ of a function is the set of all possible input values. The _____ is the set of all possible output values.

3. If no domain is specified, then it's understood the domain is the set of _____ numbers.

4. Any *x*-value that would yield an undefined *y*-value over the real numbers is _____ from the domain of a function.

5. _____ functions are defined by equations of the form $y = mx + b$.

State yes or no whether the relation is a function. Justify your answer.

6. {(–10, 5), (–6, 3), (0, 0), (8, –4), (10, –5)}

7. {(2, 8), (3, 8), (5, 8), (7, 8), (11, 8)}

8. {(0, 0), (2, 2), (2, 3), (3, 3), (4, 2)}

Find *f*(*x*) as indicated.

9. Find $f(-10)$ when $f(x) = 2x + 3$.

10. Find $f\left(\dfrac{1}{2}\right)$ when $f(x) = 6x - 1$.

Answers

1. *y*-value
2. domain, range
3. real
4. excluded
5. linear
6. Yes, because each *x*-value is paired with one and only one *y*-value.
7. Yes, because each *x*-value is paired with one and only one *y*-value.
8. No, because (2, 2) and (2, 3) have the same *x*-value, but different *y*-values.
9. $f(-10) = 2(-10) + 3 = -20 + 3 = -17$
10. $f\left(\dfrac{1}{2}\right) = 6\left(\dfrac{1}{2}\right) - 1 = 3 - 1 = 2$

How Do Recognize Proportional Functions?

If *s*, the length of a side of a regular pentagon, is 1 cm, the pentagon's perimeter, *P*, is 5(1 cm) = 5 cm. If *s* is 2 cm, *P* is 5(2 cm) = 10 cm. If *s* is 3 cm, *P* is 5(3 cm) = 15 cm. Below is a table showing these pairs of values.

s	P
1	5
2	10
3	15

Observe that when you compute the ratios of *P* to *s* for the ordered pairs in the table, the result is the same ratio. The ordered pair (1, 5) yields $\dfrac{5}{1}$ or 5 to 1; (2, 10) yields $\dfrac{10}{2} = \dfrac{5}{1}$ or 5 to 1; and (3, 15) yields $\dfrac{15}{3} = \dfrac{5}{1}$ or 5 to 1. Because the ratio $\dfrac{P}{s}$ is always the same, it is a **constant**, and the set of ordered pairs (*s*, *P*) is said to be a **proportional relationship.** Any set of ordered pairs (*x*, *y*) in which $\dfrac{y}{x} = k$, a constant, is a **proportional function.** You also can write $\dfrac{y}{x} = k$ as $y = kx$. A notable feature of proportional functions is their graphs *always* pass through the origin. Here is an example using the function defined by $y = 5x$.

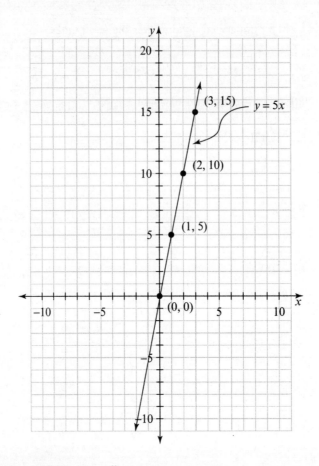

A proportional function is a **direct variation**. If $\frac{y}{x} = k$ (or, equivalently, $y = kx$), y varies **directly** as x. The number k is the **constant of variation** (also called **constant of proportionality**).

Test Yourself

1. For the set of ordered pairs of a proportional function, $\frac{y}{x} = k$, where k is a _____.

2. The graph of a proportional function always passes through the _____.

3. A line contains the pair of points (2, 8) and (4, 20). Is the line the graph of a proportional function? Justify your answer.

4. A line contains the pair of points (3, 0.87) and (15, 4.35). Is the line the graph of a proportional function? Justify your answer.

5. The table below shows c, the number of calories, in x grams of a certain cheese. **(a)** Write an equation that shows the functional relationship between c and x. **(b)** Use the equation from part (a) to find the number of calories in 70 grams of cheese.

Number of Grams x	Number of Calories c
10	45
20	90
30	135

Answers

1. constant

2. origin

3. No, because $\frac{8}{2} = \frac{4}{1}$ or 4 to 1, but $\frac{20}{4} = \frac{5}{1}$ or 5 to 1. The ratios are not the same. Therefore, the line is not the graph of a proportional function.

4. Yes, because $\frac{.87}{3} = \frac{0.29}{1}$ or 0.29 to 1 and $\frac{4.35}{15} = \frac{0.29}{1}$ or 0.29 to 1. The ratios are the same. Therefore, the line is the graph of a proportional function.

5. **(a)** Determine the ratio of c to x: $\frac{45}{10} = \frac{4.5}{1}$, $\frac{90}{20} = \frac{4.5}{1}$, and $\frac{135}{30} = \frac{4.5}{1}$. Thus, $c = 4.5x$.

   (b) When $x = 70$, $c = 4.5(70) = 315$. Therefore, there are 315 calories in 70 grams of the cheese.

How Do You Graph Linear Equations?

The **standard form** of a linear equation is $Ax + By = C$, where A and B are not both zero. For example, $x - 2y = -4$, $x + y = 5$, and $3x - 2y = 14$ are linear equations in standard form. The graph of $Ax + By = C$ is a line with slope $-\frac{A}{B}$ (provided $B \neq 0$). The **slope-intercept form** of a linear equation is $y = mx + b$, where m is the **slope** of the line and b is its **y-intercept**; that is, b is the y-coordinate of the point where the graph intersects the y-axis. There are two common methods for graphing linear equations. Here are examples of each.

> Graph $3x - 2y = 14$.

Method 1:

Step 1. Transform $3x - 2y = 14$ into slope-intercept form by solving for y in terms of x.

$$3x - 2y = 14$$
$$3x - 2y - 3x = 14 - 3x \quad \text{Subtract } 3x \text{ from both sides of the equation.}$$
$$-2y = 14 - 3x \quad \text{Simplify.}$$
$$\frac{-2y}{-2} = \frac{14}{-2} - \frac{3x}{-2} \quad \text{Divide both sides of the equation by } -2.$$
$$y = \frac{3}{2}x - 7 \quad \text{Simplify.}$$

Step 2. Set up an x-y table and determine two ordered pairs that make the equation true.

x	$y = \frac{3}{2}x - 7$
0	-7
2	-4

Step 3. Graph the ordered pairs from Step 2 and connect them with a line extending in both directions.

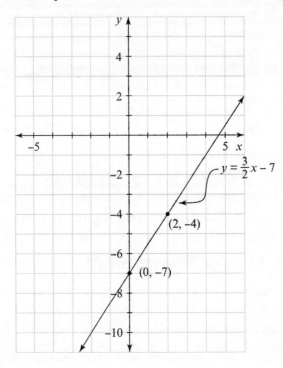

Method 2:

Step 1. Transform $3x - 2y = 14$ into slope-intercept form.

$$y = \frac{3}{2}x - 7 \quad \text{(See Method 1 for details.)}$$

Step 2. Identify the slope m of the line (the coefficient of x) and b, the y-intercept (the constant).

$$\text{slope } m = \frac{3}{2}, \text{ } y\text{-intercept } b = -7$$

Step 3. Graph the point $(0, b)$ and use the slope to find a second point. Then, connect the two points with a line extending in both directions.

$$(0, b) = (0, -7)$$

Given $m = \dfrac{\text{vertical change}}{\text{horizontal change}}$, when x changes 2 units, y changes 3. Start at $(0, -7)$ and move 2 units right and from there move 3 units up to locate a second point. Then connect the two points with a line extending in both directions.

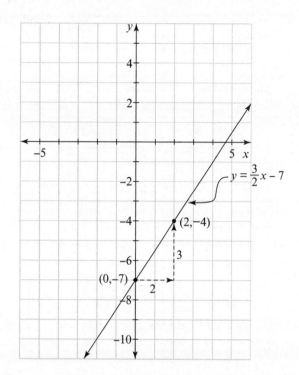

If the slopes of the lines defined by two distinct equations are equal, the lines are parallel. The two lines defined by the equations $3x - 2y = 14$ and $6x - 4y = 30$ are parallel because their slopes are equal: $-\frac{3}{-2} = \frac{3}{2}$ and $-\frac{6}{-4} = \frac{3}{2}$.

If the slopes of the lines defined by two equations are negative reciprocals of each other, the lines are **perpendicular**. The two lines defined by the equations $3x - 2y = 14$ and $4x + 6y = 10$ are perpendicular because their slopes are negative reciprocals of each other: $-\frac{3}{-2} = \frac{3}{2}$ and $-\frac{4}{6} = -\frac{2}{3}$.

Test Yourself

1. The _____ form of a linear equation is $Ax + By = C$, where A and B are not both zero.

2. The graph of $Ax + By = C$ is a _____ with slope _____ (provided $B \neq 0$).

3. If the slopes of the lines defined by two distinct equations are equal, the lines are _____.

4. If the slopes of the lines defined by two equations are negative reciprocals of each other, the lines are _____.

5. (a) Are the lines defined by the equations $x - 2y = -4$ and $6x + 3y = 10$ perpendicular? Justify your answer.
   (b) Graph the two equations in the same coordinate plane.

Answers

1. standard

2. line, $-\frac{A}{B}$

3. parallel

4. perpendicular

5. (a) Yes, because their slopes are negative reciprocals of each other: $-\dfrac{1}{-2} = \dfrac{1}{2}$ and $-\dfrac{6}{3} = -\dfrac{2}{1}$.

   (b) Write $x - 2y = -4$ as $y = \dfrac{1}{2}x + 2$ and $6x + 3y = 10$ as $y = -2x + \dfrac{10}{3}$. Then graph each equation.

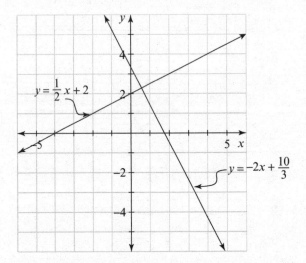

How Do You Determine the Equation of a Line?

To determine the **equation of a line** use one of the following:

The **slope-intercept form:** $y = mx + b$, where the line determined by the equation has slope = m and y-intercept = b; or

The **point-slope form:** $y - y_1 = m(x - x_1)$, where m is the slope of the line and (x_1, y_1) is a point on the line.

When you are given the slope (or can obtain it relatively easily) and the y-intercept, use the slope-intercept form.

Here is an example.

> Write the slope-intercept form of the equation of the line with y-intercept 5 that is perpendicular to the line that has slope $-\dfrac{1}{2}$.

The slope m is 2, the negative reciprocal of $-\dfrac{1}{2}$. The y-intercept b is 5. Substitute into $y = mx + b$.

$$y = 2x + 5$$

The equation of the line in slope-intercept form is $y = 2x + 5$.

When you are given the slope and a point on a line, use the point-slope form.

Here is an example.

> Determine the equation of the line in standard form with slope -3 that passes through the point $(1, 2)$.

Substitute into $y - y_1 = m(x - x_1)$.

$$y - 2 = -3(x - 1)$$
$$y - 2 = -3x + 3$$
$$3x + y = 5$$

The equation of the line in standard form is $3x + y = 5$.

When you are given two points on the line, use the point-slope form.

Here is an example.

> Find the slope-intercept form of the equation of the line that passes through the points $(-3, 4)$ and $(-5, 2)$.

The slope of the line is $m = \dfrac{y_2 - y_1}{x_2 - x_1} = \dfrac{2 - 4}{(-5) - (-3)} = \dfrac{2 - 4}{-5 + 3} = \dfrac{-2}{-5 + 3} = \dfrac{-2}{-2} = 1$. Selecting $(-3, 4)$ from the two points (either point will do), substitute into $y - y_1 = m(x - x_1)$.

$$y - 4 = 1(x - (-3))$$
$$y - 4 = x + 3$$
$$y = x + 7$$

The equation of the line in slope-intercept form is $y = x + 7$.

Tip: Enclose negative values in parentheses when substituting into formulas to avoid making a sign error.

Two special cases of linear equations are the equations for horizontal and vertical lines. **Horizontal lines** have equations of the form $y = k$ ($m = 0$). **Vertical lines** have equations of the form $x = h$ (undefined slope).

The following table summarizes linear equations.

Table 3.15 Linear Equations

Slope-intercept form (functional form)	$y = mx + b$
Point-slope form	$y - y_1 = m(x - x_1)$
Standard form	$Ax + By = C$ (A and B not both zero)
Horizontal line	$y = k$ for any constant k
Vertical line (not a function)	$x = h$ for any constant h

Tip: Not all mathematicians agree on the form of the standard form. Some write the standard form as $Ax + By + C = 0$; others designate $y = mx + b$ as the standard form. We do not anticipate that your correct responses on the FTCE GK Test will be jeopardized by this discrepancy.

Test Yourself

1. Express in slope-intercept form: The line with y-intercept 5 that is perpendicular to the line that has slope $-\dfrac{1}{3}$.

2. Express in slope-intercept form: The line with y-intercept 4 that is parallel to the line that has slope $-\dfrac{1}{3}$.

3. Express in slope-intercept form: The line that has slope 2 and passes through the origin.

4. The equation $y = 10$ defines a _____ (horizontal, vertical) line.

5. The equation $x = -2$ defines a _____ (horizontal, vertical) line.

Answers

1. The slope m is 3, the negative reciprocal of $-\frac{1}{3}$. The y-intercept b is 5. Substitute into $y = mx + b$.

   The equation of the line in slope-intercept form is $y = 3x + 5$.

2. The slope m is $-\frac{1}{3}$. The y-intercept b is 4. Substitute into $y = mx + b$.

   The equation of the line in slope-intercept form is $y = -\frac{1}{3}x + 4$.

3. The slope is 2 and $(x_1, y_1) = (0, 0)$. Substitute into $y - y_1 = m(x - x_1)$.

   $$y - 0 = 2(x - 0)$$
   $$y = 2x$$
   $$-2x + y = 0$$

   The equation of the line in standard form is $-2x + y = 0$ or $2x - y = 0$.

4. horizontal

5. vertical

How Do You Decide Whether an Ordered Pair Satisfies a System of Equations?

A set of two equations, each with the same two variables, is a **system** when the two equations are considered simultaneously; that is, when you are looking for a common solution.

Here is an example of a system of two equations with variables x and y.

$$3x + 4y = 2$$
$$4x - y = 9$$

To solve a system of two equations in two variables, you must find all ordered pairs of values for the two variables that make *both* equations true simultaneously. An ordered pair that makes an equation in two variables true is said to **satisfy** the equation. When an ordered pair makes both equations in a system of two equations true, the ordered pair **satisfies** the system.

To determine whether an ordered pair satisfies a system of two equations, check whether the ordered pair satisfies both equations in the system. Do this by plugging the x and y values of the ordered pair into the two equations, being careful to enclose in parentheses the values that you put in. Here is an example.

> Determine whether the ordered pair $(1, -2)$ satisfies the following system.
>
> $$3x + 4y = 2$$
> $$4x - y = 9$$

First, check whether $(1, -2)$ satisfies $3x + 4y = 2$.

On the left side of the equation, put in 1 for x and -2 for y and simplify: $3x + 4y = 3(1) + 4(-2) = 3 + -8 = -5$. The right side of the equation is 2, since $-5 \neq 2$, $(1, -2)$ does not satisfy $3x + 4y = 2$. Therefore, $(1, -2)$ does *not* satisfy the given system because it fails to satisfy one of the equations in the system.

> Determine whether the ordered pair $(2, -1)$ satisfies the following system.
>
> $$3x + 4y = 2$$
> $$4x - y = 9$$

First, check whether (2, –1) satisfies $3x + 4y = 2$.

On the left side of the equation, put in 2 for x and –1 for y and simplify: $3x + 4y = 3(2) + 4(-1) = 6 + -4 = 2$. The right side of the equation is also 2, so (2, –1) satisfies $3x + 4y = 2$.

Next, check whether (2, –1) satisfies $4x - y = 9$.

On the left side of the equation, put in 2 for x and –1 for y and simplify: $4x - y = 4(2) - (-1) = 8 + 1 = 9$. The right side of the equation is also 9, so (2, –1) satisfies $4x - y = 9$.

Therefore, (2, –1) satisfies the given system because it satisfies both equations in the system.

Test Yourself

1. A set of two equations, each with the same two variables, is a _____ when the two equations are considered simultaneously.

2. To solve a system of equations in two variables, you must find all ordered pairs of values for the two variables that make *both* equations _____ simultaneously.

3. An ordered pair that makes an equation in two variables true is said to _____ the equation.

4. When an ordered pair makes both equations in a system of two equations true, the ordered pair satisfies the _____.

5. Determine whether the ordered pair (1, 2) satisfies the following system.

$$x + 2y = 5$$
$$4x - y = 2$$

Answers

1. system
2. true
3. satisfy
4. system
5. Yes, (1, 2) satisfies the given system.

   Solution:

   First, check whether (1, 2) satisfies $x + 2y = 5$.

   On the left side of the equation, put in 1 for x and 2 for y and simplify: $x + 2y = (1) + 2(2) = 1 + 4 = 5$. The right side of the equation is also 5, so (1, 2) satisfies $x + 2y = 5$.

   Next, check whether (1, 2) satisfies $4x - y = 2$.

   On the left side of the equation, put in 1 for x and 2 for y and simplify: $4x - y = 4(1) - (2) = 4 - 2 = 2$. The right side of the equation is also 2, so (1, 2) satisfies $4x - y = 2$.

   Therefore, (1, 2) satisfies the given system because it satisfies both equations in the system.

How Do You Find Patterns in Sequences?

A **sequence** is a list of numbers, called **terms** of the sequence, written in a particular order. When a problem requires that you find a pattern in a sequence, you use a systematic plan of attack. First, **look for an easily recognizable pattern.** For example, the sequence

$$5, 10, 20, 5, 10, 20, \ldots$$

has an easily recognizable repeating pattern of the block of numbers 5, 10, 20.

If you do not see a pattern right away, check for an **arithmetic sequence.** Do this by subtracting each term from the term that follows it. If the differences are the same, the sequence is arithmetic and you should add the common difference to a term to get the term that follows. Here is an example.

> Find the missing term in the following sequence: 10, 12, ___, 16, 18, ...

Subtract consecutive terms listed from the terms that follow them.

$$12 - 10 = 2$$
$$18 - 16 = 2$$

You get 2 as the difference both times, so the sequence is arithmetic with a common difference of 2. Add 2 (the common difference) to 12 to obtain the missing term: $2 + 12 = 14$.

If the sequence is not arithmetic, check for a **geometric sequence.** Do this by dividing each term by the term that follows it to see if there is a common ratio. If the quotients are the same, the sequence is geometric and you should multiply a term by the common ratio to get the term that follows. Here is an example.

> Find the missing term in the following sequence: 2, ___, 18, 54, 162, ...

Divide consecutive terms listed by the terms that follow them.

$$54 \div 18 = 3$$
$$162 \div 54 = 3$$

You get 3 as the quotient both times, so the sequence is geometric with a common ratio of 3. Multiply 2 by 3 (the common ratio) to obtain the missing term: $2 \cdot 3 = 6$.

If the sequence is not arithmetic or geometric, then list the position numbers under the terms. Look for a relationship between the term and its position number. Here is an example.

> Find the missing term in the following sequence: $1, \frac{1}{2}, \frac{1}{3}, \underline{\quad}, \frac{1}{5}, \ldots$

$$\underset{1}{1}, \underset{2}{\frac{1}{2}}, \underset{3}{\frac{1}{3}}, \underset{4}{\underline{\quad}}, \underset{5}{\frac{1}{5}}, \ldots$$

You can see the nth term is $\frac{1}{n}$, so the 4th term is $\frac{1}{4}$.

If no pattern has been found, then check for a Fibonacci sequence. A **Fibonacci sequence** begins with two repeating terms, and thereafter, each term is the sum of the two preceding terms. Here is an example.

$$1, 1, 2, 3, 5, 8, \ldots$$

The next term would be 13: $5 + 8 = 13$.

With persistence, you should be able to find a pattern that can help you find a missing term of a sequence.

Test Yourself

1. The terms of an arithmetic sequence have a common _____.

2. The terms of a geometric sequence have a common _____.

3. A _____ sequence begins with two repeating terms, and thereafter, each term is the sum of the two preceding terms.

4. Find the missing term in the following sequence: 13, 18, ___, 28, 33, ...

5. Find the missing term in the following sequence: 5, ___, 20, –40, 80, ...

Answers

1. difference

2. ratio

3. Fibonacci

4. 23

    Check for an arithmetic sequence by subtracting consecutive terms listed from the terms that follow them.

    $$18 - 13 = 5$$
    $$33 - 28 = 5$$

    You get 5 as the difference both times, so the sequence is arithmetic with a common difference of 5. Add 5 (the common difference) to 18 to obtain the missing term: $18 + 5 = 23$.

5. –10

    Check for an arithmetic sequence by subtracting consecutive terms listed from the terms that follow them.

    $$-40 - 20 = -60$$
    $$80 - (-40) = 80 + 40 = 120$$

    No common difference is found. Next, check for a geometric sequence by dividing consecutive terms listed by the terms that follow them.

    $$-40 \div 20 = -2$$
    $$80 \div -40 = -2$$

    You get –2 as the quotient both times, so the sequence is geometric with a common ratio of –2. Multiply 5 by –2 (the common ratio) to obtain the missing term: $(5)(-2) = -10$.

Sample Questions

Directions: Read each question and select the best answer choice.

1. The formula for the volume of a cone is $\frac{1}{3}\pi r^2 h$, where h is the height of the cone and r is the radius of the base of the cone. Which of the following is the most accurate interpretation of this formula?

    A. one-third the product of π, the quantity r squared, and h
    B. the quantity one-third π times r times h, all squared
    C. one-third π times one-third r squared times h
    D. one-third the square of the quantity π times r multiplied by h

2. Solve for x in $2(x + 6) = 50$.

   A. 19
   B. 22
   C. 31
   D. 38

3. What is the sum of the roots of $x^2 + x - 20 = 0$?

   A. −9
   B. −1
   C. 1
   D. 9

4. Which relation represents a function?

   A. $\{(4, 5), (2, 1), (2, 10), (-2, 0)\}$
   B. $\{(4, 5), (4, 5^2), (4, 5^3), (4, 5^4)\}$
   C. $\{(2, 3), (4, 3), (8, 3), (16, 3)\}$
   D. $\{(-2, 3), (-4, 3), (5, 5), (5, 10)\}$

5. The table below shows p, the number of grams of protein, in n eggs. Write an equation that shows the functional relationship between p and n.

Number of Eggs n	Number of Grams of Protein p
6	36
12	72
18	108

   A. $p = \dfrac{1}{6}n$
   B. $p = n + 6$
   C. $n = 6p$
   D. $p = 6n$

6. What is the slope of the line perpendicular to the line with equation $4x - 5y = 7$?

   A. $-\dfrac{4}{5}$
   B. $-\dfrac{5}{4}$
   C. $\dfrac{4}{5}$
   D. $\dfrac{5}{4}$

7. Determine which ordered pair satisfies the given system.

   $$x - 2y = -7$$
   $$2x + y = -4$$

   A. (2, −3)
   B. (−2, 3)
   C. (−3, 2)
   D. (3, −2)

8. Find the missing number in the following sequence: 3, ___, 12, −24, 48, ...

   A. −5
   B. 5
   C. −6
   D. 6

Answer Explanations for Sample Questions

1. **A.** This expression is a product of four terms: $\frac{1}{3}, \pi, r^2,$ and h. Notice the exponent ^{2} on r applies only to r. A correct interpretation of the expression is "one-third the product of π, the quantity r squared, and h," Choice **A**. Choices **B** and **D** are incorrect because only r, the radius, is squared in the expression. Choice **C** is incorrect because $\frac{1}{3}$ is a factor only once, not twice, in the expression.

2. **A.**

   $$2(x+6) = 50$$
   $$2x + 12 = 50 \qquad \text{Use the distributive property to remove parentheses.}$$
   $$2x + 12 - 12 = 50 - 12 \qquad \text{Subtract 12 from both sides of the equation.}$$
   $$2x = 38 \qquad \text{Simplify.}$$
   $$\frac{\cancel{2}x}{\cancel{2}} = \frac{38}{2} \qquad \text{Divide both sides of the equation by 2.}$$
   $$x = 19, \text{ Choice A} \qquad \text{Simplify.}$$

   Choice **B** results if you fail to use the distributive property correctly. Choice **C** results if you add 12 to both sides instead of subtracting it. Choice **D** results if you fail to divide by 2.

3. **B.** First, solve the quadratic equation $x^2 + x - 20 = 0$ by factoring.

   $$x^2 + x - 20 = 0$$
   $$(x+5)(x-4) = 0$$
   $$(x+5) = 0 \text{ or } (x-4) = 0$$
   $$x = -5 \text{ or } x = 4$$

   Next, sum the two roots: $-5 + 4 = -1$, Choice **B**.

   Choices **A**, **C**, and **D** occur if you get the signs on the two roots wrong.

4. **C.** A function is a relation in which each first element is paired with *one and only one* second element. Only the relation in Choice **C** satisfies this requirement. In Choice **A**, 2 is a first element paired with two different second elements, namely, 1 and 10. In Choice **B**, 4 is a first element paired with four different second elements. In Choice **D**, 5 is a first element paired with two different second elements, namely, 5 and 10.

5. **D.** Determine the ratio of p to n: $\frac{36}{6} = \frac{6}{1}, \frac{72}{12} = \frac{6}{1},$ and $\frac{108}{18} = \frac{6}{1}$. Thus, $p = 6n$, Choice **D**. Choices **A** and **C** occur if you use the ratio of n to p for the ratio of p to n. Choice **B** occurs if you add instead of multiply by the constant of variation.

6. **B.** Transform $4x - 5y = 7$ into slope-intercept form by solving for y in terms of x.

   $$4x - 5y = 7$$
   $$4x - 5y - 4x = 7 - 4x$$
   $$-5y = -4x + 7$$
   $$\frac{\cancel{-5}y}{\cancel{-5}} = \frac{-4x}{-5} + \frac{7}{-5}$$
   $$y = \frac{4}{5}x - \frac{7}{5}$$

   The slope of the line perpendicular to the line with equation $4x - 5y = 7$ is $-\frac{5}{4}$ (Choice **B**), the negative reciprocal of $\frac{4}{5}$. Choice **A** occurs if you fail to obtain the reciprocal. Choice **C** occurs if you keep the slope unchanged. Choice **D** occurs if you fail to negate the reciprocal.

7. **C.** To determine which ordered pair satisfies the system, find the ordered pair that satisfies *both* equations. Check each ordered pair by plugging the x and y values into the two equations, being careful to enclose in parentheses the values you put in.

Checking **A:** $x - 2y = (2) - 2(-3) = 2 + 6 = 8 \neq -7$. Choice **A** is incorrect because $(2, -3)$ does not satisfy $x - 2y = -7$.

Checking **B:** $x - 2y = (-2) - 2(3) = -2 - 6 = -8 \neq -7$. Choice **B** is incorrect because $(-2, 3)$ does not satisfy $x - 2y = -7$.

Checking **C:** $x - 2y = (-3) - 2(2) = -3 - 4 = -7$ ✓. Since $(-3, 2)$ works in the first equation, try it in the second equation: $2x + y = 2(-3) + (2) = -6 + 2 = -4$ ✓. Choice **C** is the correct response because the ordered pair $(-3, 2)$ satisfies both equations in the system.

You would not have to continue since Choice **C** is the correct response. However, in case you're interested, Choice **D** is incorrect because $x - 2y = (3) - 2(-2) = 3 + 4 = 7 \neq -7$.

8. **C.** Check for an arithmetic sequence by subtracting consecutive terms listed from the terms that follow them.

$$-24 - 12 = -36$$
$$48 - (-24) = 48 + 24 = 72$$

No common difference is found. Next, check for a geometric sequence by dividing consecutive terms listed by the terms that follow them.

$$-24 \div 12 = -2$$
$$48 \div -24 = -2$$

You get -2 as the quotient both times, so the sequence is geometric with a common ratio of -2. Multiply 3 by -2 (the common ratio) to obtain the missing term: $(3)(-2) = -6$, Choice **C**. Choices **A**, **B**, and **D** result if you multiply 3 by -2 incorrectly.

Probability, Statistics, and Data Interpretation

According to the *Competencies and Skills Required for Teacher Certification in Florida*, 20th Edition (see page 59 for the Web address), the competencies/skills you should be able to do for this area of mathematics are the following:

- Analyze data presented in various forms (e.g., histograms, bar graphs, circle graphs, pictographs, line plots, tables) to solve problems.
- Analyze and evaluate how the presentation of data can lead to different or inappropriate interpretations in the context of a real-world situation.
- Calculate range, mean, median, and mode of data sets.
- Interpret the meaning of measures of central tendency (i.e., mean, median, mode) and dispersion (i.e., range, standard deviation) in the context of a real-world situation.
- Solve and interpret real-world problems involving probability using counting procedures, tables, and tree diagrams.
- Infer and analyze conclusions from sample surveys, experiments, and observational studies.

How Do You Organize and Present Data?

There are a number of ways to record, organize, and present data. For the FTCE GK Test, you should be prepared to perform data analysis by reading and interpreting information from **charts** and **tables, pictographs, bar graphs, histograms, circle graphs, line plots, line graphs**, and **stem-and-leaf plots.**

Charts and tables are used to put related information into an organized form. Pictographs, bar graphs, and circle graphs display information that is organized into categories. Histograms summarize data by using totals within intervals. Line graphs show trends, usually over time. Line plots and stem-and-leaf plots show organized visual displays of data.

Charts and Tables

Charts and **tables** organize information in columns and rows. Each column or row is labeled to explain the entries. Look at this example.

> The table that follows shows the number of snow cone sales for each month during the summer. According to the chart shown, in which month were snow cone sales the highest?
>
> | Summer Snow Cone Sales | |
> |---|---|
> | Month | Number of Snow Cones Sold |
> | June | 650 |
> | July | 800 |
> | August | 950 |

Examination of the chart shows the highest number of sales was 950 snow cones, which occurred in the month of August.

A **frequency table** is a tabular representation of data that shows the frequency of each value in the data set. A **relative frequency table** shows the frequency of each value as a proportion or percentage of the whole data set. The total of all relative frequencies should be 1.00 or 100 percent, but instead might be very close to 1.00 or 100 percent, due to round-off error. Here is an example.

> The table that follows shows the grade distribution for a class of 25 students on Test 1. Should the teacher reteach the tested material to the whole class?
>
> | Grade Distribution for Test 1 | | |
> |---|---|---|
> | Grade | Frequency | Relative Frequency |
> | A | 5 | 0.20 |
> | B | 8 | 0.32 |
> | C | 9 | 0.36 |
> | D | 2 | 0.08 |
> | F | 1 | 0.04 |
> | Total | 25 | 1.00 |

According to the table, 0.88 (0.20 + 0.32 + 0.36) or 88% of the students made a C or better on the test. Based on this information, reteaching the tested material to the whole class is not indicated.

Pictographs

In a **pictograph**, pictures or symbols are used to represent numbers. Each symbol represents a given number of a particular item. The symbol, its meaning, and the quantity it represents should be stated on the graph. To read a pictograph, count the number of symbols in a row and multiply this number by the scale indicated on the graph. Sometimes, a fraction of a symbol is shown. In that case, approximate the fraction and use it accordingly. Look at this example.

Chapter 3: Review for the General Knowledge Mathematics Subtest

The graph that follows shows the results of a survey of 30 cat owners to determine whether they also own a dog. According to the graph, how many cat owners responded "Yes" to the survey question, "Do you own a dog?"

Responses of 30 Cat Owners to the Question "Do You Own a Dog?"

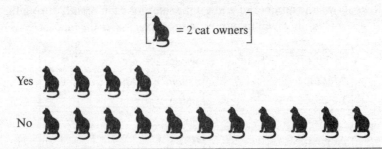

According to the graph, each symbol stands for 2 cat owners. The 4 symbols shown in the graph for "Yes" show that of the 30 cat owners surveyed, the number who also own a dog is 4 · 2 = 8 cat owners.

A **line plot** (or **dot plot**) is a graph that shows the frequency of data values on a number line, and dots (or other similar symbols) are placed above each value to indicate the number of times that particular value occurs in the data set. Here is an example.

The line plot below shows the minutes waited in line by 14 customers at a fast food restaurant. If the restaurant gives a 10 percent discount to customers who wait in line more than 20 minutes, how many customers received the 10 percent discount?

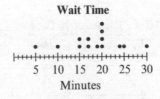

The line plot shows three people waited more than 20 minutes, so three people received the 10 percent discount.

Bar Graphs

A **bar graph** uses rectangular bars to represent frequencies, percentages, or amounts. The bars correspond to different categories that are labeled at the base of the bars. The bars in a bar graph may be arranged vertically or horizontally. The widths of the bars are equal. The length or height of the bar indicates the number, percentage, or amount for the category for that particular bar. A scale (usually beginning with 0), marked with equally spaced intervals, for measuring the height (or length) of the bars is shown on the graph. To read a bar graph, examine the scale to determine the units and the amount corresponding to each interval. Then determine where the heights (or lengths) of the bars fall in relation to the scale. Look at these examples.

The bar graph that follows shows the number of snow cone sales for each month during the summer. According to the graph, how many snow cones were sold in July?

Summer Snow Cone Sales

206

The scale on the horizontal axis shows the number of snow cones sold. The scale is marked in multiples of 200. The bar for July ends at 800, indicating 800 snow cones were sold in July.

> The bar graph that follows shows the grade distribution for the first test in a social studies class. According to the graph, how many students received an A on the first test?
>
>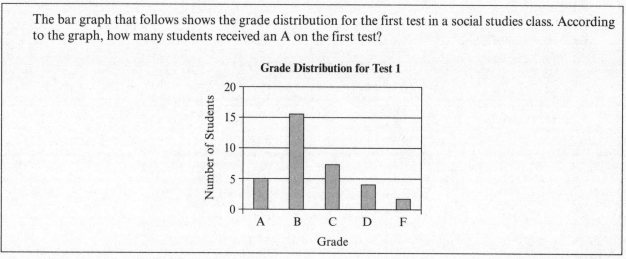

The scale on the vertical axis shows the number of students who achieved the grade. The scale is marked in multiples of 5. The top of the bar for the A category is at 5, indicating 5 students received an A on Test 1.

Bar graphs can show two or more sets of data on the same graph. This allows you to compare how the data sets measure up to each other. Look at this example.

> The bar graph shows the grade distribution for the first test for two different social studies classes. According to the graph, which class appears to have had the poorer performance on the test?
>
>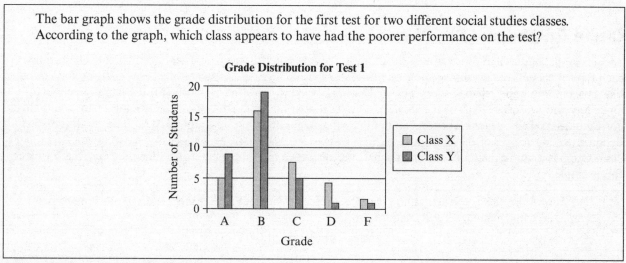

The graph shows Class X had fewer A's and B's and more C's, D's, and F's than Class Y. Therefore, it appears Class X had the poorer performance on the test.

Histograms

A **histogram** is a special type of bar graph that summarizes data by displaying frequencies or relative frequencies of the data within specified intervals, called **class intervals.** Class intervals are of equal length and cover from the lowest to the highest data value. The left and right endpoints for the class intervals are selected so that each data value clearly falls within one and only one class interval. The frequency or relative frequency of occurrence of the data values within a class interval is represented by a rectangular (or vertical) column. The height (or length) of the column is proportional to the frequency or relative frequency of data values within that interval. Unlike the bars in other bar graphs, the bars in a histogram are side-by-side (usually) with no space in between. In a **frequency histogram**, the scale for measuring the height (or length) of the bars is marked with actual frequencies (or counts). In a **relative frequency histogram**, the scale is marked with relative frequencies instead of actual frequencies. The total of the relative frequencies corresponding to the class intervals should be 1.00 or 100 percent, but might instead be very close to 1.00 or 100 percent due to round-off error. Look at this example.

> The histogram that follows shows the grade distribution for the first test in a social studies class. Using the graph, how many students received 90 or above on the first test?
>
>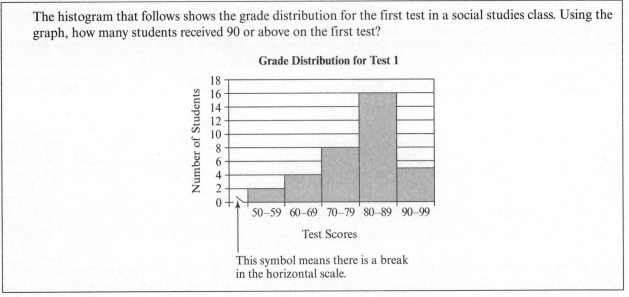

The scale on the vertical axis shows the number of students who achieved the grade. The scale is marked in multiples of 2. The top of the bar for the interval 90–99 is halfway between 4 and 6, indicating that 5 students received 90 or above on Test 1.

Circle Graphs and Pie Charts

A **circle graph**, or **pie chart**, is a graph in the shape of a circle. Circle graphs are used to display the relationship of each type or class of data within a whole set of data in a visual form. It is also called a "pie" chart because it looks like a pie cut into wedge-shaped slices. The wedges are labeled to show the categories for the graph. Each sector angle represents a specific part of the whole. Commonly, percents are used to show the amount of the graph that corresponds to each category. The total amount in percentage shown on the graph is 100%. The graph is made by dividing the 360 degrees of the circle into portions that correspond to the percentages for each category. Reading a circle graph is a simple matter of reading the percents displayed on the graph for the different categories. Look at this example.

> The following circle graph shows how a student plans to budget $2,000 each month. According to the graph, how much money is budgeted for food?
>
>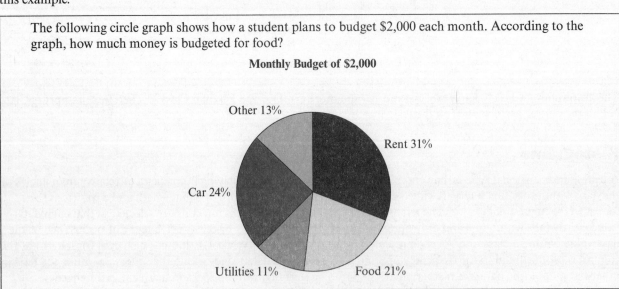

The graph shows 21% of the budget is designated for food. To find how much money is designated for food, find 21% of $2,000: 0.21 · $2,000 = $420.

208

Line Graphs

A **line graph** uses lines or broken lines for representing data. It has both a horizontal and a vertical scale. The data points for the graph are plotted as ordered pairs of numbers, according to the two scales. Line segments are used to connect consecutive points. Sometimes, two or more sets of data are plotted on the same graph. The slant of the line between the points shows whether the data values are increasing, decreasing, or remaining at a constant value. If the line slants upward from left to right, the data values are increasing; if the line slants downward from left to right, the data values are decreasing; and a horizontal line (no slant) means that the data values remain constant. Line graphs are useful for showing change over time. Look at this example.

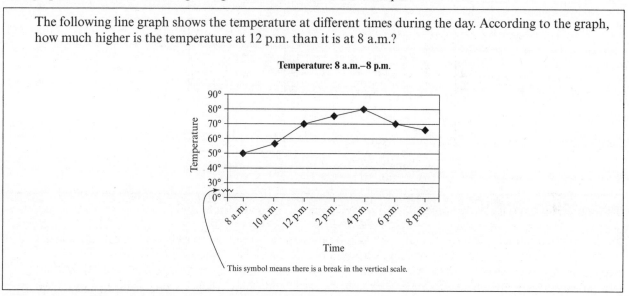

The following line graph shows the temperature at different times during the day. According to the graph, how much higher is the temperature at 12 p.m. than it is at 8 a.m.?

From the graph, you can see that the temperature at 8 a.m. is 50° and the temperature at 12 p.m. is 70°. The difference in temperature at these two times is 70° − 50° = 20°.

Stem-and-Leaf Plots

A **stem-and-leaf plot** is a visual display of data in which each data value is separated into two parts: a stem and a leaf. For a given data value, the leaf is the last digit and the stem is the remaining digits. For example, for the data value 49, 4 is the stem and 9 is the leaf. When you create a stem-and-leaf plot, you should include a **legend** that explains what is represented by the stem and leaf so that the reader can interpret the information in the plot; for example, 4|9 = 49. Note that a feature of a stem-and-leaf plot is that the original data is retained and displayed in the plot. Usually, the stems are listed vertically (from least to greatest), and the corresponding leaves for the data values are listed horizontally (from least to greatest) beside the appropriate stem. Look at this example.

The stem-and-leaf plot that follows shows the ages of 40 people who joined the Over-40 Fitness Health Club in January. What is the age of the oldest person who joined the health club in January?

Ages of 40 People Who Joined the Over-40 Fitness Health Club in January

Stem	Leaf
4	1 2 6 8 9
5	1 1 2 3 3 6 7 7 7 7 8 9
6	0 0 3 3 4 4 5 6 8 8 9
7	0 1 2 3 5 7 8
8	0 1
9	0 3

Legend: 4|9 = 49

According to the graph, the age of the oldest person who joined the health club in January is 93.

Scatterplots

A **scatterplot** is a graph of **bivariate data**, paired values of data from two variables, plotted on a coordinate grid. The data are paired in a way that matches each value from one variable with a corresponding value from the other variable. The pattern of the plot can be useful in determining whether there is a relationship between the two variables; and, if there is, the nature of that relationship. You should be able to examine scatterplots and distinguish between those indicating linear and those indicating nonlinear relationships between two variables. Look at this example.

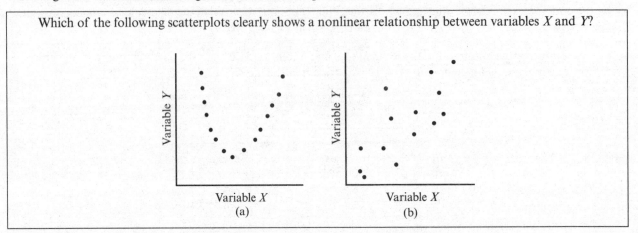

Which of the following scatterplots clearly shows a nonlinear relationship between variables X and Y?

The scatterplot in (a) is clearly nonlinear. The scatterplot in (b) is somewhat linear.

For linear relationships, scatterplots that slant right (that is, upward from left to right) indicate positive linear relationships. In positive linear relationships, whenever one of the variables increases or decreases, the other variable increases or decreases in the same direction. Scatterplots that slant left (that is, downward from right to left) indicate negative linear relationships. In negative linear relationships, whenever one of the two variables increases, the other variable decreases; and conversely. The closer that the data values cluster together in a linear "cigar" shape, the stronger the relationship. Look at this example.

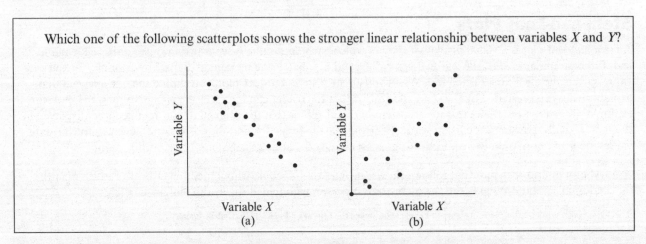

Which one of the following scatterplots shows the stronger linear relationship between variables X and Y?

Both scatterplots show a linear relationship. The plot in (a) indicates a negative relationship between variables X and Y. The plot in (b) shows a positive trend between variables X and Y. The scatterplot in (a) is stronger because the data values are not as spread out as those shown in the plot in (b).

How Can Presentation of Data Lead to Inappropriate Interpretations?

Drawing valid conclusions from graphical representations of data requires you to have read the graph accurately and analyzed the graphical information correctly. Sometimes a graphical representation will distort the data in some way, leading you to draw an invalid conclusion.

Look at these examples.

Responses of 30 Owners of One Pet to the Question "Do You Own a Cat or a Dog?"

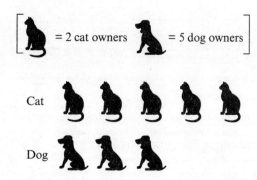

This graph has two major problems. The first problem is that the data are distorted. Visually, it appears that the number of cat owners is greater than the number of dog owners. However, each cat picture represents 2 cats, and each dog picture represents 5 dogs. Thus, the number of dog owners is 15 compared to 10 cat owners, making the number of dog owners greater. The other problem is that the number of pet owners represented in the table is 25, but the number surveyed is 30. The graph should have an additional category for those pet owners surveyed who own neither a cat nor a dog.

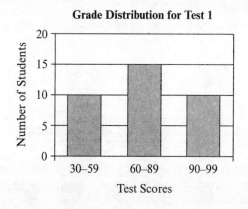

At first glance, the data for this graph look evenly distributed. Upon closer examination, you can see that each of the first two intervals cover a 29-point spread, but the last interval covers only a 9-point spread, making it difficult to draw conclusions from the graph.

When you have to interpret graphical information on the FTCE GK Test, follow these suggestions:

- Make sure that you understand the title of the graph.
- Read the labels on the parts of the graph to understand what is being represented.
- Examine carefully the scale of bar graphs, line graphs, histograms, and scatterplots.
- Make sure you know what each picture in a pictograph represents.
- Look for trends such as increases (rising values), decreases (falling values), and periods of inactivity (constant values, horizontal lines) in line graphs.
- Look for concentrations of data values and note the general shape for line plots, stem-and-leaf plots, bar graphs, histograms, and scatterplots.
- Make sure the numbers add up correctly.
- Be prepared to do some simple arithmetic calculations.
- Use only the information in the graph. Do not answer based on your personal knowledge or opinion.

Test Yourself

1. Pictographs, bar graphs, and circle graphs show information that is organized into _____.

2. In a _____, pictures or symbols are used to represent numbers.

3. The _____ or _____ of a bar graph indicates the number, percentage, or amount for its corresponding category.

4. When reading a bar graph, line graph, or histogram, be sure to examine carefully the _____ to determine the amount between the marked values.

5. A histogram summarizes information using totals within _____.

6. The total percentage in a circle graph is _____.

7. _____ graphs are useful for showing change over time.

8. When interpreting information from a graph, do not draw _____ beyond those represented in the graph.

9. What is a problem with the following pictograph?

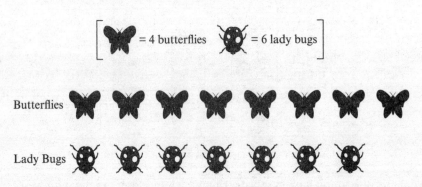

Number of Butterflies and Lady Bugs Observed in a Month

10. According to the bar graph shown here, in which quarter is the number of points scored by each of the two teams closest?

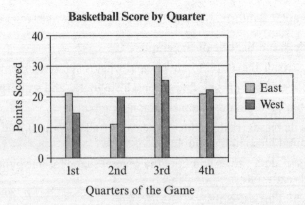

Answers

1. categories
2. pictograph
3. height, length
4. scale
5. intervals
6. 100%
7. Line
8. conclusions
9. The graph is misleading, giving the visual impression that the number of butterflies and lady bugs are roughly the same. However, the butterfly picture represents 4 butterflies, but the lady bug picture represents 6 lady bugs. Thus, more lady bugs than butterflies were observed.
10. The heights of the two bars are closest in the 4th quarter, indicating that the number of points scored by each of the two teams is closest is in that quarter.

What Are Measures of Central Tendency?

A **measure of central tendency** is a numerical value that describes a data set by providing a "central" or "typical" value of the data set. The three most common measures of central tendency are the **mean, median,** and **mode.** Each of these measures represents a different way of describing a typical value of a set of data.

> **Tip:** Measures of central tendency should have the same units as those of the data values. If no units are specified, as in test scores, then the measure of central tendency will not specify units.

Finding the Mean

The **mean** of a set of numbers is another name for the arithmetic average of the numbers. To calculate the mean, first, sum the numbers; then, divide by how many numbers are in the set. Thus, you have the following formula:

$$\text{mean} = \frac{\text{the sum of the numbers}}{\text{how many numbers in the set}}$$

For example, the mean for the set of five scores 50, 87, 50, 95, 78 is

$$\text{mean} = \frac{50 + 87 + 50 + 95 + 78}{5} = \frac{360}{5} = 72$$

On the FTCE GK Test, you may be given a set of numbers and asked to find the missing number that gives the set a certain average (mean). Here is an example.

> A student's grade is based on the average of five exams. The student has four exam scores of 78, 62, 91, and 79. What is the lowest score needed by the student on the fifth exam to achieve an average of at least 80?

Method 1: To obtain an average of 80 on five tests, the student needs a total of $80 \times 5 = 400$ points (because $\frac{400}{5} = 80$). The student has $78 + 62 + 91 + 79 = 310$ points from the first four tests, so $400 - 310 = 90$ additional points are needed.

Method 2: Let $x =$ the score on the fifth exam. Plug into the formula for the mean and solve for x.

$$80 = \frac{78 + 62 + 91 + 79 + x}{5}$$

$$\frac{80}{1} = \frac{310+x}{5}$$ Simplify the numerator on the right. Then write the equation as a proportion.

$(80)(5) = 1(310+x)$ Cross-multiply. *Note*: Enclose quantities in parentheses to avoid errors.

$400 = 310 + x$ Simplify.

$400 - 310 = 310 + x - 310$ Subtract 310 from both sides of the equation.

$90 = x$ Simplify.

The lowest score needed on the fifth exam to achieve an average of 80 for the five exams is 90.

Did I answer the question? Yes, I found the score needed on the fifth exam to achieve an average of 80 for the five exams. ✓

Does my answer make sense? Yes, given that three of the scores are below 80, it seems reasonable that it will take a score of 90 to achieve an average of at least 80. ✓

Is the answer stated in the correct units? No units are required for the answer. ✓

A way to work a multiple-choice question like the preceding problem is to take advantage of the fact that the FTCE GK Test is a multiple-choice test. You are given the answer to the question—you just have to figure out which one of the four answer choices is the correct one. For a problem like the one above, you would plug each answer into the formula for the mean until you found the one that gives you an average of at least 80.

A **weighted mean** is a mean computed by assigning weights to the data values. To find a weighted mean, do the following: First, multiply each data value by its assigned weight, sum the results, and then divide by the sum of the weights. Here is an example.

> A student scores 80, 60, and 50 on three exams. Find the weighted mean of the student's three scores, where the score of 80 counts 20%, the score of 60 counts 20%, and the score of 50 counts 60%.

$$\text{weighted mean} = \frac{20\%(80) + 20\%(60) + 60\%(50)}{20\% + 20\% + 60\%} = \frac{16 + 12 + 30}{100\%} = \frac{58}{1} = 58$$

The student's weighted mean score is 58.

Did I answer the question? Yes, I found the weighted mean for the student's three scores. ✓

Does my answer make sense? Yes, since the grade of 50 counts 60%, it seems reasonable that the weighted mean is 58. ✓

Is the answer stated in the correct units? No units are required for the answer. ✓

Finding the Median

The **median** is the middle number or the average of the two middle numbers in an ordered set of numbers. Determining the median of a set of numbers is a two-step process.

1. Put the numbers in order from least to greatest (or greatest to least).
2. Find the middle number. If there is no single middle number, average the two middle numbers.

Look at these examples.

> Find the median for the set of scores 50, 87, 50, 95, 78.

Step 1. Put the numbers in order from least to greatest.

$$50, 50, 78, 87, 95$$

Step 2. Find the middle number, which is the median. In this example, which contains an odd number of values, there is a middle number. The median is 78.

> **Caution:** When you are asked to find a median, don't make the common mistake of neglecting to put the numbers in order first. In the preceding example, the middle number before the numbers are put in order is 50 (wrong answer).

> Find the median for the set of numbers 100, 10, 10, 36, 30, 36.

Step 1. Put the numbers in order from least to greatest.

$$10, 10, 30, 36, 36, 100$$

Step 2. Find the middle number. This example contains an even number of values, so there is no single middle number. In this case, the median is the average of the two middle numbers, 30 and 36: $\frac{30+36}{2} = \frac{66}{2} = 33$.

In an ordered data set of n values, the median is a value at the $\frac{n+1}{2}$ position. Here is an example.

> Using the stem-leaf plot shown, find the median age of the 40 people who joined the Over-40 Fitness Health Club in January.
>
> **Ages of 40 People Who Joined the Over-40 Fitness Health Club in January**
>
> | Stem | Leaf |
> |---|---|
> | 4 | 1 2 6 8 9 |
> | 5 | 1 1 2 3 3 6 7 7 7 7 7 8 9 |
> | 6 | 0 0 3 3 4 4 5 6 8 8 9 |
> | 7 | 0 1 2 3 5 7 8 |
> | 8 | 0 1 |
> | 9 | 0 3 |
>
> Legend: 4|9 = 49

According to the question, a total of 40 people joined. The median is a value at the $\frac{40+1}{2} = \frac{41}{2} = 20.5$ position, meaning the median is halfway between the 20th and 21st data values. Examination of the plot reveals 60 is the 20th data value and 63 is the 21st data value. Therefore, the median age of the 40 people is $\frac{60+63}{2} = \frac{123}{2} = 61.5$ years.

Finding the Mode

The **mode** is the number or numbers that occur with the greatest frequency in a set of numbers; there can be one mode, more than one mode, or no mode. If two or more numbers occur with the same frequency that is greater than any of the other frequencies, then each will be a mode. When each number in the data set appears the same number of times, there is no mode.

Look at these examples.

- There is one mode in the data set consisting of the numbers 50, 87, 50, 95, 78. The number 50 occurs with the greatest frequency. Therefore, the mode is 50.
- There are two modes in the data set consisting of the numbers 10, 10, 30, 36, 36, 100. The numbers 10 and 36 both occur with the same frequency that is greater than any of the other frequencies. Therefore, the modes are 10 and 36.
- There is no mode for the data set consisting of the numbers 40, 52, 145, 96, 60. Each number in the data set appears the same number of times.

Here is a graphical example.

> Using the stem-leaf plot shown, find the mode age of the 40 people who joined the Over-40 Fitness Health Club in January.
>
> **Ages of 40 People Who Joined the Over-40 Fitness Health Club in January**
>
> | Stem | Leaf |
> |---|---|
> | 4 | 1 2 6 8 9 |
> | 5 | 1 1 2 3 3 6 7 7 7 7 7 8 9 |
> | 6 | 0 0 3 3 4 4 5 6 8 8 9 |
> | 7 | 0 1 2 3 5 7 8 |
> | 8 | 0 1 |
> | 9 | 0 3 |
>
> Legend: 4|9 = 49

The data set in the stem-leaf plot has one mode. The value 57 occurs five times, which is the greatest frequency. Therefore, 57 years is the mode age of the 40 people.

What Are Important Characteristics of the Measures of Central Tendency?

The mean, median, and mode are ways to describe a central or typical value of a data set. To know which of these measures of central tendency you should use to describe a data set, consider their characteristics.

The **mean** has several important characteristics.

- Although the mean represents a central or typical value of a data set, the mean does not necessarily have the same value as one of the numbers in the set. For instance, the mean of 50, 50, 87, 78, and 95 is 72, yet none of the five numbers in this data set equals 72.
- The actual data values are used in the computation of the mean. If any number is changed, the value of the mean will change. For example, the mean of the data set consisting of 50, 50, 87, 78, and 95 is 72. If the 95 in this set is changed to 100, the mean of the new data set is 73.
- A disadvantage of the mean is that it is influenced by outliers, especially in a small data set. An **outlier** is a data value that is extremely high or extremely low in comparison to most of the other data values. If a data set contains extremely high values that are not balanced by corresponding low values, the mean will be misleadingly high. For example, the mean of the data set consisting of 15, 15, 20, 25, and 25 is 20. If the 20 in this set is changed to 100, the mean of the new data set is 36. The value 36 does not represent the data set consisting of 15, 15, 100, 25, and 25 very well, since four of the data values are less than 30. Similarly, if a data set contains extremely low values that are not balanced by corresponding high values, the mean will be misleadingly low. For example, the mean of the data set consisting of 100, 100, 130, and 150 is 120. If the 150 in this set is changed to 10, the mean of the new data set is 85. The value 85 does not represent the data set consisting of 100, 100, 130, and 10 very well, since three of the data values are greater than or equal to 100.

The **median** is the most useful alternative to the mean as a measure of central tendency.

- Like the mean, the median does not necessarily have the same value as one of the numbers in the set. If the data set contains an odd number of data values, the median will be the middle number; however, for an even number of data values, the median is the arithmetic average of the two middle numbers.
- The median is not influenced by outliers. For instance, the median of the data set consisting of 10, 15, 20, 25, and 30 is 20. If the 30 in this set is changed to 100, the median of the new data set remains 20.
- A disadvantage of the median as an indicator of a central value is that it is based on relative size rather than on the actual numbers in the set. For instance, a student who has test scores of 44, 47, and 98 shows improved performance that would not be reflected if the sub median of 47, rather than the mean of 63, was reported as the representative grade.

The **mode** is the least commonly used measure of central tendency.

- The mode is the simplest measure of central tendency to calculate.
- If a data set has a mode, the mode (or modes) is one of the data values.
- The mode is the only appropriate measure of central tendency for data that are strictly nonnumeric like data on ice cream flavor preferences (vanilla, chocolate, strawberry, and so on). Although it makes no sense to determine a mean or median ice cream flavor for the data, the ice cream flavor that was named most frequently would be the modal flavor.
- A disadvantage of the mode as an indicator of a central value is that it is based on relative frequency rather than on all the values in the set. For instance, a student who has test scores of 45, 45, and 99 shows improved performance that would not be reflected if the mode of 45 was reported as the representative grade rather than the mean of 63.

What Are Measures of Dispersion?

A **measure of dispersion** (or **variation**) is a numerical value that describes the spread of a data set. Although measures of central tendency are important for describing data sets, their interpretation is enhanced when the spread or dispersion about the central value is known. Two groups of 10 students, both with means of 70 on a 100-point test, may have very different sets of scores. One set of scores may be extremely consistent, with scores like 60, 62, 65, 68, 70, 70, 72, 75, 78, and 80; while the other set of scores may be very erratic, with scores like 40, 40, 50, 55, 60, 80, 85, 90, 100, and 100. The scores in the first set cluster more closely about the mean of 70 than do the scores in the second set. The scores in the second set are more spread out than are the scores in the first set.

Dispersion (or variation) in data is of foremost interest to users of statistics. Three common measures of dispersion are the **range**, the **mean absolute deviation (MAD)**, and the **standard deviation**.

> **Tip:** Measures of dispersion should have the same units as those of the data values. If no units are specified, then the measure of dispersion will not specify units.

The **range** for a data set is the difference between the greatest (maximum) value and the least (minimum) value in the data set:

$$\text{range} = \text{greatest value} - \text{least value}$$

Here are examples of finding the range of a data set.

What is the range for this data set? 50, 50, 60, 70, 70

$$\text{range} = \text{greatest value} - \text{least value} = 70 - 50 = 20$$

What is the range for this data set? –10, –10, 60, 110, 110

$$\text{range} = \text{greatest value} - \text{least value} = 110 - (-10) = 110 + 10 = 120$$

The range gives some indication of the spread of the values in a data set, but its value is determined by only two of the data values. The extent of the spread of the other numbers is not considered.

A measure of dispersion that takes into account all the data values is the standard deviation. The **standard deviation** is a measure of the dispersion of a set of data values about the mean of the data set. When there is no dispersion in a data set, each data value equals the mean, giving a standard deviation of zero. The more the data values vary from the mean, the greater the standard deviation. You likely will not have to calculate a standard deviation on the FTCE GK Test. Questions about standard deviation might require you to examine two (or more) data sets and decide which data set has the greater (or lesser) standard deviation. Here is an example.

> Both means of the following two data sets are equal to 50.
>
> $$\text{Set 1: } 30, 40, 50, 60, 70$$
> $$\text{Set 2: } 10, 10, 50, 90, 90$$
>
> Which data set has the greater standard deviation?

The data values in Set 1 cluster more closely around the mean of 50 than do the data values in Set 2. Therefore, Set 2 has the greater standard deviation.

The MAD is another measure of dispersion that takes into account all the data values in the data set. It is the average distance between each data value and the mean of the data values. To determine the MAD, use three steps.

1. Find the mean.
2. Find the distance between each data value and the mean by computing the absolute value of the difference between each data value and the mean.
3. Average the distances.

Here is an example.

> Both means of the following two data sets are equal to 50.
>
> $$\text{Set 1: } 30, 40, 50, 60, 70$$
> $$\text{Set 2: } 27, 45, 50, 53, 75$$
>
> Which data set has the greater MAD?

Find the MAD for each set and compare.

Set 1

Step 1. The mean is 50.

Steps 2 and 3. The MAD equals

$$\frac{|30-50|+|40-50|+|50-50|+|60-50|+|70-50|}{5} = \frac{|-20|+|-10|+|0|+|10|+|20|}{5} = \frac{20+10+0+10+20}{5} = \frac{60}{5} = 12$$

Set 2

Step 1. The mean is 50.

Steps 2 and 3. The MAD equals

$$\frac{|27-50|+|45-50|+|50-50|+|53-50|+|75-50|}{5} = \frac{|-23|+|-5|+|0|+|3|+|25|}{5} = \frac{23+5+0+3+25}{5} = \frac{56}{5} = 11.2$$

Set 1 has the greater MAD.

Test Yourself

1. The mean, median, and mode are measures of _____ tendency.

2. The _____ of a set of numbers is another name for the arithmetic average of the numbers.

3. The median is the middle number or the average of the two middle numbers in a(n) _____ set of numbers.

4. The _____ is the data value or values that occur with the greatest frequency.

5. A disadvantage of the mean is that it is influenced by _____.

6. The median _____ (is, is not) influenced by outliers.

7. The _____ is the only appropriate measure of central tendency for data that are strictly nonnumeric.

8. A measure of dispersion is a value that describes the _____ of the data about the central value.

9. The standard deviation and the MAD of a data set are measures of the spread of the data values about the _____ of the data set.

10. The MAD is the _____ distance between each data value and the mean of the data values.

11. Find the mean, median, mode, and range for the following data set: 10, 60, 30, 90, 10, 30, 40, 50.

12. Find the standard deviation for the following data set: 25, 25, 25, 25, 25, 25, 25, 25, 25, 25.

13. Find the MAD for the following data set: 10, 10, 50, 90, 90.

Answers

1. central
2. mean
3. ordered
4. mode
5. outliers
6. is not
7. mode
8. spread
9. mean
10. average
11. mean = 40, median = 35; modes = 10 and 30; range = 80

To find the mean, sum the data values and then divide by 8.

$$\text{mean} = \frac{10+60+30+90+10+30+40+50}{8} = \frac{320}{8} = 40$$

To find the median, do the following:

Step 1. Put the numbers in order from least to greatest.

$$10, 10, 30, 30, 40, 50, 60, 90$$

Step 2. Find the middle number. The median is the average of the two middle numbers, 30 and 40.

$$\text{median} = \frac{30+40}{2} = \frac{70}{2} = 35$$

To find the mode, find the value (or values) that occurs with the greatest frequency in the data set. The numbers 10 and 30 both occur with the same frequency that is greater than any of the other frequencies. Therefore, the modes are 10 and 30.

To find the range, find the difference between the greatest value and the least value in the data set.

$$\text{range} = \text{greatest value} - \text{least value} = 90 - 10 = 80$$

12. standard deviation = 0

There is no dispersion in the data set. Each data value equals the mean of 25, giving a standard deviation of zero.

13. MAD = 32

Step 1. mean = $\dfrac{10+10+50+90+90}{5} = \dfrac{250}{5} = 50$

Steps 2 and 3.

$$\dfrac{|10-50|+|10-50|+|50-50|+|90-50|+|90-50|}{5} = \dfrac{|-40|+|-40|+|0|+|40|+|40|}{5} = \dfrac{40+40+0+40+40}{5} = \dfrac{160}{5} = 32$$

What Is Probability?

Probability is a measure of the chance an event will happen. If all outcomes are equally likely, the probability an event E will occur is determined this way:

$$\text{Probability of event } E = P(E) = \dfrac{\text{number of outcomes favorable to event } E}{\text{number of total outcomes possible}}$$

On the FTCE GK Test, you will be asked to find simple probabilities. Here is an example.

> A bag contains 5 tiles, numbered 1, 2, 3, 4, and 5. The tiles are all identical in size and shape. If a person picks out a single tile from the bag without looking, what is the probability the number on the tile will be even?

The possible outcomes are a 1, 2, 3, 4, or 5 on the tile. There are two favorable outcomes for this event: drawing a 2 or a 4. These are the "favorable" outcomes because these are the outcomes you are looking for.

The probability of drawing an even-numbered tile is

$$P(2 \text{ or } 4) = \dfrac{\text{number of favorable outcomes}}{\text{number of total outcomes possible}} = \dfrac{2}{5}$$

Probabilities can be expressed as fractions, decimals, or percents. In the preceding example, the probability of drawing an even-numbered tile can be expressed as $\dfrac{2}{5}$, 0.4, or 40%.

The probability an event is certain to happen is 1, 1.00, or 100%. The probability of drawing a whole-numbered tile from a bag containing tiles numbered 1, 2, 3, 4, and 5 is 1, since the numbers 1, 2, 3, 4, and 5 are all whole numbers.

If an event cannot occur, then it has a probability of 0. For instance, the probability of drawing a tile with the number 6 on it from a bag containing tiles numbered 1, 2, 3, 4, and 5 is 0, since none of the tiles has a 6 on it.

Thus, the lowest probability you can have is 0, and the highest probability you can have is 1. All other probabilities fall between 0 and 1. You can express this relationship symbolically this way: $0 \leq P(E) \leq 1$, for any event E. Therefore, if you work a probability problem, and your answer is greater than 1 or your answer is negative, you've made a mistake! Go back and check your work.

Tip: In a probability problem, the number of total outcomes possible will always be greater than or equal to the number of outcomes favorable to the event, so check to make sure the denominator is larger than or equal to the numerator when you plug into the formula.

Keep in mind the formula for probability in which the outcomes are equally likely will *not* apply to situations in which the events are not equally likely. For instance, the possible outcomes when you spin a spinner that is one-fourth red, one-fourth yellow, and one-half green are R, Y, and G, where "R" means "the spinner lands on red," "Y" means "the spinner lands on yellow," and "G" means "the spinner lands on green." See the figure shown.

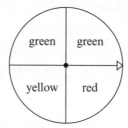

The probabilities for the three different outcomes are the following: $P(R) = \frac{1}{4}$, $P(Y) = \frac{1}{4}$, and $P(G) = \frac{1}{2}$.

The probability of an event B, given that an event A has occurred, is a **conditional probability.** This means that you compute the probability of B by taking into account that A has already occurred. Here is an example.

> Suppose you randomly draw two marbles from a box containing 6 red marbles and 4 blue marbles, all identical except for color. If you draw a red marble on the first draw and do not put it back into the box before you draw the second time, what is the probability you will draw a blue marble on the second draw?

This is a conditional probability problem. After the red marble is drawn and not put back, there are 5 red marbles and 4 blue marbles in the box. Therefore, P(blue on the second draw, given red drawn on first draw and not put back) = $\frac{4}{9}$.

Note: Not putting back the first item drawn is known as drawing "without replacement."

When you want to find the probability that two events A and B will occur, you multiply the probability of A times the conditional probability of B (that is, taking into account that the event A has already occurred). Here is an example.

> Suppose a box contains 10 marbles: 3 red marbles, 5 blue marbles, and 2 green marbles, all identical except for color. If you draw two marbles from the box, what is the probability you will draw two red marbles if your first draw is done without replacement?

This problem involves conditional probability. You use three steps to solve it: First, find P(red on the first draw); next, find P(red on the second draw, given red drawn on first draw without replacement); and then multiply P(red on the first draw) times P(red on the second draw, given red drawn on first draw without replacement).

Step 1. Find P(red on the first draw).

P(red on the first draw) = $\frac{3}{10}$ because initially you have 3 red marbles in a box of 10 marbles.

Step 2. Find P(red on the second draw, given red drawn on first draw without replacement).

P(red on the second draw, given red drawn on first draw without replacement) = $\frac{2}{9}$ because after you draw a red marble without replacement, you have 2 red marbles in a box of 9 marbles.

Step 3. Multiply *P*(red on the first draw) times *P*(red on the second draw, given red drawn on first draw without replacement).

$$P(\text{red on the first draw and red on the second draw}) = \frac{3}{10} \cdot \frac{2}{9} = \frac{\cancel{3}^1}{\cancel{10}_5} \cdot \frac{\cancel{2}^1}{\cancel{9}_3} = \frac{1}{15}$$

Of course, if you are flipping coins or tossing numbered cubes, replacement is not a concern. Each flip of the coin or toss of the numbered cube is independent of the other flips or tosses. Independent events do not affect the probabilities of one another, so you simply multiply the probabilities in these cases. Here is an example.

When flipping a coin three times, the probability of getting three heads is $\frac{1}{2} \cdot \frac{1}{2} \cdot \frac{1}{2} = \frac{1}{8}$ because the probability of getting heads on each flip is $\frac{1}{2}$ (one head out of two possible outcomes).

How Do You Count the Number of Ways to Arrange or Combine Things?

There are different methods to find the number of ways to arrange or combine things. Two ways that are commonly used are to list every possibility in an organized table or in a tree diagram. Another way is to use multiplication to count the total number of possibilities.

Here is an example of using an organized table to count the number of possibilities.

> A woman has a choice of a blue, red, orange, or yellow blouse. She also may select either a brown, white, or black skirt. How many different outfits can she make with one blouse and one skirt?

You should proceed systematically. In the table that follows, first list a blue blouse color with each of the skirt colors that can be chosen. Next, list a red blouse color with each of the skirt colors that can be chosen. Then, list an orange blouse color with each of the skirt colors that can be chosen. Finally, list a yellow blouse color with each of the skirt colors that can be chosen.

Blouse Color	*Skirt Color*
blue	brown
blue	white
blue	black
red	brown
red	white
red	black
orange	brown
orange	white
orange	black
yellow	brown
yellow	white
yellow	black

The table shows the woman can choose 12 possible outfits of one blouse and one skirt.

> **Caution:** When you use an organized table to count possibilities, be sure to proceed in a systematic manner as illustrated in this example. Otherwise, you may overlook a possibility or count one more than once.

You can also use a tree diagram to find the total number of possible outfits.

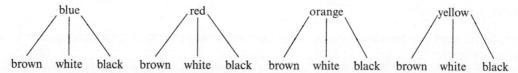

There are 12 endpoints (blue and brown, blue and white, blue and black, ..., yellow and brown, yellow and white, yellow and black) in the tree diagram. This shows the woman can choose a total of 12 possible outfits of one blouse and one skirt.

You can also use multiplication to find the total number of possible outfits.

Total number of possible outfits =

(number of ways to select a blouse color) × (number of ways to select a skirt color) = 4 × 3 = 12

When the order in which you make a selection determines different outcomes, the arrangement is a **permutation.** For instance, if a club is selecting a president, vice-president, and secretary from three possible candidates (A, B, and C), the order in which the selections are made makes a difference in the possible outcomes, as shown in the following table.

President	*Vice-President*	*Secretary*
Candidate A	Candidate B	Candidate C
Candidate A	Candidate C	Candidate B
Candidate B	Candidate A	Candidate C
Candidate B	Candidate C	Candidate A
Candidate C	Candidate A	Candidate B
Candidate C	Candidate B	Candidate A

The table shows there are six different ways that the selection of a president, vice-president, and secretary from the three candidates can be made.

If the order does not determine different outcomes, the arrangement is a **combination.** For instance, if a club is selecting a committee of three people from five members (A, B, C, D, or E), the order in which the selections are made does not determine different outcomes, as shown below.

1st Committee Member	*2nd Committee Member*	*3rd Committee Member*
Member A	Member B	Member C
Member A	Member B	Member D
Member A	Member B	Member E
Member A	Member C	Member D
Member A	Member C	Member E
Member A	Member D	Member E
Member B	Member C	Member D
Member B	Member C	Member E
Member B	Member D	Member E
Member C	Member D	Member E

The table shows there are a total of 10 different possible committees.

How Do You Solve Real-World Problems Involving Counting and Probability?

To solve real-world word problems involving counting and probability, use the problem-solving process that you learned in the "Numeration and Operations" section (page 59).

Here is an example of solving a probability problem.

> A bag contains 15 marbles: 7 green, 5 red, and 3 yellow, all identical except for color. If a person draws a single marble from the bag without looking, what is the probability it will be a red marble?

This is a straightforward probability problem. To solve the problem, find the number of total outcomes possible, find the number of favorable outcomes, and then plug into the probability formula.

There are 15 total possible outcomes. There are 5 favorable outcomes. The probability of drawing a red marble is

$$P(\text{red}) = \frac{\text{number of favorable outcomes}}{\text{number of total outcomes possible}} = \frac{\text{number of red marbles}}{\text{total number of marbles}} = \frac{5}{15} = \frac{1}{3}$$

Did I answer the question? Yes, I found the probability of drawing a red marble from the bag. ✓

Does my answer make sense? Yes, it is consistent with my knowledge of probability. ✓

Is the answer stated in the correct units? No units are required for the answer. ✓

Here is an example of solving a counting problem.

> A man has a choice of a white shirt or a blue shirt. He also may select a striped blue tie, a paisley blue tie, or a solid red tie. How many different outfits can he make of one shirt and one tie?

This is a counting problem. To solve the problem, multiply the number of ways the man can select a shirt by the number of ways he can select a tie.

Total number of possible outfits = (number of ways to select a shirt) × (number of ways to select a tie) = 2 × 3 = 6

Did I answer the question? Yes, I found the number of possible outfits. ✓

Does my answer make sense? Yes, it is consistent with my knowledge of counting. ✓

Is the answer stated in the correct units? No units are required for the answer. ✓

Test Yourself

1. _____ is a measure of the chance an event will happen.

2. The probability an event is certain to happen is _____.

3. The probability an event cannot occur is _____.

4. When a coin is flipped, the probability heads will show on the upface is _____.

5. A die has six faces, numbered 1 through 6. On one toss of the die, the probability the upface will show the number 5 is _____.

6. If you flip a coin five times, what is the probability you will get five heads in a row?

7. The faces of a cube are numbered 5, 10, 15, 20, 30, and 40. If you toss the cube two times, what is the probability the number 40 will show on the upface both times?

8. Suppose Denzel has a bag of 10 colored tiles: 5 blue, 3 red, and 2 yellow, all identical except for color. If Denzel randomly draws a yellow tile from the bag without replacement, what is the probability that, on a second random draw, he will draw a blue tile?

9. Sammy is wrapping a gift. She can choose from six different kinds of wrapping paper, four different colors of ribbon, and five different gift tags. If she selects one kind of wrapping paper, one color of ribbon, and one gift tag, how many different ways can Sammy wrap the gift?

10. To secure his locker, Kush will use a two-character code consisting of a lowercase letter from the English alphabet followed by a digit (0–9). How many such codes are possible if repetition of letters and digits are allowed?

Answers

1. Probability
2. 1
3. 0
4. $\dfrac{1}{2}$
5. $\dfrac{1}{6}$
6. $\dfrac{1}{32}$

    This is an independent events probability problem. For each flip of the coin, the probability of heads on the upface is $\dfrac{1}{2}$, so the probability of five heads in a row is $\dfrac{1}{2} \cdot \dfrac{1}{2} \cdot \dfrac{1}{2} \cdot \dfrac{1}{2} \cdot \dfrac{1}{2} = \dfrac{1}{32}$.

7. $\dfrac{1}{36}$

    This is an independent events probability problem. For each toss of the cube, the probability of 40 on the upface is $\dfrac{1}{6}$, so the probability that 40 will show on the upface on both tosses is $\dfrac{1}{6} \cdot \dfrac{1}{6} = \dfrac{1}{36}$.

8. $\dfrac{5}{9}$

    This is a conditional probability problem. After the yellow tile is drawn and not put back, there are 9 tiles in the bag: 5 blue, 3 red, and 1 yellow. Therefore, P(blue on the second draw, given yellow drawn on first draw without replacement) = $\dfrac{5}{9}$.

    Did I answer the question? Yes, I found the probability Denzel will draw a blue tile on the second draw. ✓

    Does my answer make sense? Yes, it is consistent with my knowledge of probability. ✓

    Is the answer stated in the correct units? No units are required for the answer. ✓

9. 120

    This is a counting problem. To solve the problem, multiply the number of ways Sammy can select a wrapping paper by the number of ways she can select a ribbon color by the number of ways she can select a gift tag.

    Total number of ways to wrap the gift = (number of ways to select a wrapping paper) × (number of ways to select a ribbon color) × (number of ways to select a gift card) = 6 × 4 × 5 = 120

    Did I answer the question? Yes, I found the number of different ways Sammy can wrap the gift. ✓

    Does my answer make sense? Yes, it is consistent with my knowledge of counting. ✓

    Is the answer stated in the correct units? No units are required for the answer. ✓

10. 260

This is a counting problem. To solve the problem, multiply the number of ways to select a lowercase letter from the English alphabet times the number of ways to select a digit.

Total number of 2-character codes = (number of ways to select a lowercase letter from the English alphabet) × (number of ways to select a digit) = 26 × 10 = 260

Did I answer the question? Yes, I found the number of possible two-character codes. ✓

Does my answer make sense? Yes, it is consistent with my knowledge of counting. ✓

Is the answer stated in the correct units? No units are required for the answer. ✓

What Are Differences in Types of Studies?

A **quantitative study** involves the collection and analysis of numerical data. Quantitative studies fall into four broad categories: *survey, correlational, experimental,* or *observational.*

In **survey** studies, the purpose is to gather information from a representative sample in order to generalize to a population of interest. Examples of this type of study include opinion surveys, fact-finding surveys, and questionnaire and interview studies. Results are summarized and reported.

In **correlational** studies, the purpose is to investigate the extent to which variations in one variable correspond with variations in another variable. Examples of such studies include investigating the relationship between performance on a standardized reading test and time spent reading independently, between college grades and high school GPA, and between income and years of education. It is very important to note that correlational studies *cannot* show causation. In other words, if two variables are correlated, it does not mean that one causes the other.

In **experimental** studies, the purpose is to investigate possible cause-and-effect relationships by exposing an **experimental group** to a treatment condition and comparing the results to a **control group** not receiving the treatment. The study is set up in such a way that one group of experimental units gets the treatment (the treatment group) and another group (the control group) does not, and then comparisons are made to see whether the treatment had an influence on the **variable of interest (outcome variable).** The treatment is the **independent variable** and the outcome is the **dependent variable.** Because the researcher controls which group gets the treatment, a defining characteristic of experimental studies is **manipulation** of the independent variable. The investigator does not manipulate the variable of interest, but observes and records the effect of the treatment on it.

Examples of experimental studies include investigating the effectiveness of a new method of teaching reading (the treatment) on reading ability (the variable of interest), the effect of a new drug (the treatment) on blood pressure (the variable of interest), and the effect of a type of fertilizer (the treatment) on plant growth (the variable of interest). In a well-designed experimental study, **experimental units** are randomly assigned to either the treatment or the control group to ensure that groups are similar in all respects *except* for the treatment. Therefore, any difference in the two groups can be attributed to the treatment. For such comparisons to be valid, other sources of variation must be controlled. Only when investigators conduct a well-designed experimental study would a cause-and-effect conclusion be valid.

Observational studies involve collecting and analyzing data without changing existing conditions. Observational studies are conducted when it is not possible (or, perhaps, not appropriate) to randomly assign experimental units to some treatment condition (for example, being a smoker) to investigate a variable of interest (for example, lung capacity). Such studies are conducted in a setting that does not permit the investigator to manipulate the treatment variable. Controlling for other relevant variables (such as medical history) also can be a challenge. The nonrandomness in sampling and the constraint imposed by observing a predetermined condition limit drawing cause-and-effect conclusions from observational studies. There is a possibility that results are due to variables other than the variables being studied. The key question is whether observed changes can be attributed to the "exposure" and not to other possible causes.

Characteristics of Well-Designed Studies

A **sample** is a portion of a population that is examined to gain information about the whole **population**. The **population** is the set of all persons or things (plants, grades, cavities, and so on) of interest to the person conducting the study. **A random sample** is one in which the members of the sample are randomly selected from the population. A **representative sample** is one in which the characteristics of the sample entities mirror the characteristics of the population under investigation. The **sample size** is the number of entities in the sample. Statistical formulas or guidelines are available for determining adequate sample size for various types of studies. In general, increasing the sample size leads to more accurate results. A sample is most likely to be a representative sample when it has been chosen randomly from the population, and it is of adequate size. Generalization of study results to the population is appropriate only when the sample has been randomly chosen from the population and is of adequate size.

> **Tip:** Conclusions from a study should not be based on samples that are far too small (for example, a survey that uses fewer than 10 subjects). For the FTCE GK Test, consider this aspect if you are asked to critique a study's results.

Bias in a study is a type of systematic error that favors particular results by selecting or encouraging one outcome or answer over others. For instance, a campus opinion survey on whether to construct a new athletic facility in which the sample is drawn primarily from physical education majors could bias the results in favor of the new athletic facility.

Extraneous (or confounding) variables are unwanted variables that are not themselves being studied but, nevertheless, influence study outcomes. For instance, a possible extraneous variable in a study investigating the effectiveness of a new method of teaching reading on the reading ability of second-graders is the amount of time students spend reading at home with parents.

To provide results worthy of consideration, a study should be carefully planned and well-designed, investigate issues that are clear and unambiguous, have clearly identified populations, use randomization in selecting representative samples of adequate size, use well-defined variables of interest, avoid bias of various types, and control for outside factors, such as extraneous variables, that could jeopardize the validity of conclusions. Only when investigators use well-designed studies can reliable and valid conclusions be drawn and generalizations to the population made.

Generalizations about a population from a sample are valid only if the sample is representative of that population. Therefore, it's important for researchers to use random sampling techniques (such as using a lottery method of selecting participants). Random sampling tends to produce representative samples and support valid inferences. Randomization is intended to smooth out any differences, other than the treatment, between the treatment and control groups that might affect the variable of interest.

Test Yourself

1. A quantitative study involves the collection and analysis of _____ data.

2. An opinion poll is an example of a(n) _____ study.

3. A study investigating the relationship between college grades and high school GPA is an example of a(n) _____ study.

4. A study investigating the effect of a new drug on cancer patients is an example of a(n) _____ study.

5. A study investigating the relationship between smoking and dental disease is an example of a(n) _____ study.

6. A _____ is a portion of a population that is examined to gain information about the whole population.

7. A random sample is one in which the members of the sample are _____ selected from the population.

8. A _____ sample is one in which the characteristics of the sample entities mirror the characteristics of the population under investigation.

9. _____ in a study is a type of systematic error that favors particular results.

10. If two variables are correlated, it does not mean that one _____ the other.

11. Observational studies limit the investigator's ability to draw cause-and-effect _____.

12. Generalization of study results to the population is appropriate only when the sample has been _____ chosen from the population and is of _____ size.

Answers

1. numerical
2. survey
3. correlational
4. experimental
5. observational
6. sample
7. randomly
8. representative
9. Bias
10. causes
11. conclusions
12. randomly, adequate

Sample Questions

Directions: Read each question and select the best answer choice.

1. The graph that follows represents the monthly average temperature in the city of Townville for 5 months of the year. How much higher is the average temperature in May than in January?

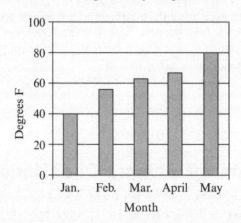

Average Monthly Temperatures

A. 2°
B. 20°
C. 40°
D. 80°

2. Given here are students' scores on a social studies test. What is the median of the set of scores?

Student	Score
A	95
B	42
C	55
D	87
E	68
F	72
G	66
H	87

A. 70
B. 71
C. 77.5
D. 87

3. You have a bag containing 25 colored tiles: 10 blue, 7 red, 5 green, and 3 yellow, all identical except for color. If a person picks out a single tile from the bag without looking, what is the probability it will be a red or green tile?

A. $\dfrac{2}{5}$
B. $\dfrac{3}{25}$
C. $\dfrac{7}{25}$
D. $\dfrac{12}{25}$

4. A boy is making a sandwich for lunch. He has a choice of two kinds of bread (white and whole wheat) and three sandwich fillings (peanut butter, tuna salad, and pimiento cheese). How many different sandwiches can he make if he chooses one type of bread and one kind of sandwich filling?

   A. 5
   B. 6
   C. 8
   D. 9

5. To investigate the effect of drinking green tea on weight loss, a researcher decides to conduct an experimental study with 80 women, between the ages of 25 and 30, all of the same race and ethnicity. The participants are randomly assigned to either the treatment group or control group (40 in each group). The participants in the control group will be asked to

   A. lose weight
   B. not lose weight
   C. drink green tea
   D. not drink green tea

Answer Explanations for Sample Questions

1. **C.** The bar for January goes up to 40°, and the bar for May goes up to 80°. The difference is 80° − 40° = 40°. Choice **A** results if you mistakenly decide that there is 1° between marks on the graph. Choice **B** results if you mistakenly decide that there are 10° between marks on the graph. Choice **D** results if you fail to subtract and use the temperature in May as your answer.

2. **A.** To find the median, do the following:

   Step 1. Put the numbers in order from least to greatest.

   $$42, 55, 66, 68, 72, 87, 87, 95$$

   Step 2. Find the middle number. The median is the average of the two middle numbers, 68 and 72.

   $$\text{median} = \frac{68 + 72}{2} = \frac{140}{2} = 70$$

   Choice **B** results if you fail to order the scores and mistakenly decide to average 55 and 87 to find the median. Choice **C** results if you fail to order the scores and mistakenly decide to average 68 and 87 to find the median. Choice **D** is the mode, not the median.

3. **D.** This is a straightforward probability problem. To solve the problem, find the number of total outcomes possible, find the number of favorable outcomes, and then plug into the probability formula.

   There are 25 total possible outcomes. There are 12 favorable outcomes (7 red and 5 green tiles). The probability of drawing a red or green tile is

   $$P(\text{red or green}) = \frac{\text{number of favorable outcomes}}{\text{number of total outcomes possible}} = \frac{12}{25}$$

   Did I answer the question? Yes, I found the probability of drawing a red or green tile from the bag. ✓

   Does my answer make sense? Yes, it is consistent with my knowledge of probability. ✓

   Is the answer stated in the correct units? No units are required for the answer. ✓

   Choice **A** is the probability of drawing a blue tile. Choice **B** is the probability of drawing a yellow tile. Choice **C** is the probability of drawing a red tile.

4. **B.** This problem is a counting problem. To solve the problem, multiply the number of ways the boy can select a bread by the number of ways he can select a sandwich filling.

   Total number of possible sandwiches =

   (number of ways to select a bread) × (number of ways to select a sandwich filling) = 2 × 3 = 6

   Did I answer the question? Yes, I found the number of possible sandwiches. ✓

   Does my answer make sense? Yes, it is a reasonable answer. ✓

   Is the answer stated in the correct units? No units are required for the answer. ✓

   Choice **A** results if you add, instead of multiply, in the problem. Choices **C** and **D** result if you count or compute incorrectly.

5. **D.** In this study, drinking green tea is the treatment and weight loss is the variable of interest. In an experimental study, the control group does not receive the treatment, so the participants in this group will be asked to not drink green tea. Choices **A** and **B** are incorrect because these choices are related to the variable of interest, which is not manipulated by the researcher. Choices **C** is incorrect because the treatment group, not the control group, will be asked to drink green tea.

Chapter 4
Review for the General Knowledge Reading Subtest

The Reading Subtest of the FTCE GK Test consists of 40 multiple-choice questions, which you must complete in 40 minutes. Each test question consists of four reading comprehension passages followed by multiple-choice questions. Each question requires that you choose from among four answer choices. You must click on the button corresponding to your answer choice on the computer screen. You cannot bring written notes or scratch paper into the testing room.

The Reading Review in This Study Guide

The Reading review in this CliffsNotes study guide is organized around the three reading areas tested on the FTCE GK Test:

1. Knowledge of Key Ideas and Details Based on Text Selections
2. Knowledge of Craft and Structure Based on Text Selections
3. Knowledge of the Integration of Information and Ideas Based on Text Selections

The review sections present reading concepts with examples and explanations for each area. Each area, furthermore, contains a general review. "Test Yourself" exercises, which give you an opportunity to practice what you just learned, are sprinkled throughout the review material. When doing the "Test Yourself" exercises, you should cover up the answers. Then check your answers when you've finished the exercise. There are also sample questions at the end of this chapter for additional practice.

Knowledge of Key Ideas and Details Based on Text Selections

As listed in the *Competencies and Skills Required for Teacher Certification in Florida,* 20th Edition (available at www.fldoe.org/asp/ftce/pdf/ftce20edition.pdf), there are eight main Reading Knowledge of Key Ideas and Details Based on Text Selections competencies/skills in which you should be proficient. They are as follows:

- Identify textual evidence to support conclusions drawn from text.
- Identify explicit meaning and details within text.
- Determine inferences and conclusions based on textual evidence.
- Discriminate among inferences, conclusions, and assumptions based on textual evidence.
- Determine and analyze the development of central ideas or themes from one or more texts.
- Summarize one or more texts using key supporting ideas and details.
- Determine how and why specific individuals, events, and ideas develop based on textual evidence.
- Determine the cause and effect relationship(s) among individuals, events, and ideas based on textual evidence.

Identify Textual Evidence to Support Conclusions Drawn from Text

When you know how to identify textual evidence to support conclusions drawn from text, then you possess the ability to discern logical arguments and conclusions in your reading. Often, readers misinterpret or skip over key words or phrases in their reading and thus fail to identify such textual evidence. This can be corrected by learning to read any given passage with a sharp and discerning eye.

The key to recognizing textual evidence is to identify the *topic sentence* of a passage/paragraph. In the topic sentence, the author states the main idea of the paragraph; it is the sentence upon which all other sentences in the paragraph are dependent. You can identify the topic sentence as the one sentence that explains the paragraph without any further explanation. Some paragraphs and/or passages will not have an explicit topic sentence per se, leaving the reader to infer the writer's intent.

Textual evidence is what supports the topic sentence or main idea of a passage. Textual evidence requires a text reference (such as a word, phrase, sentence, or paragraph). The importance of textual evidence is in the detail and specificity as revealed in the passage under review. Writers often authenticate evidence by citing the source (for example, providing author, title, and page number) and providing the context relevant to their point. For example, one might explain textual evidence by stating "this fact means such and such . . ." or "this quote has relevance because. . . ."

To analyze the ways in which textual evidence supports conclusions drawn from text, ask yourself the following questions:

- What does the text say explicitly?
- What logical inferences can be made from the text?
- What specific textual evidence supports conclusions drawn from the text?

Look at this example passage and see whether you can identify the main idea:

> Staring at my plate, I realized I was now fully awake and ready to face the day. I was groomed and dressed, sitting at my kitchen table while contemplating my next move. I realized, however, that I could not do anything without eating a good breakfast. By midday, my stomach would be growling, and I would be in a lousy mood if I did not have my daily regimen of orange juice, toast, and hot cereal. I definitely needed hot cereal. For without hot cereal, I would certainly feel grumpy. Yes, for me, breakfast is the most important meal of the day.

The main idea of this passage is clearly stated in the last sentence: "Yes, for me, breakfast is the most important meal of the day." All of the accompanying sentences support this main idea and thus, provide for the reader the textual evidence needed to support any conclusions drawn from the text.

Generally, the topic sentence of a paragraph is the first or last sentence. Sometimes, its location may be embedded in the paragraph; but in every instance, the topic sentence of a well-written paragraph can be recognized as the essential or main idea of the passage.

Identify Explicit Meaning and Details Within Text

The word "explicit" refers to what is clearly and directly stated in a passage. If something is explicit, there is no question as to what it means, no hidden connotations, and no room for misunderstanding. When reading a passage, the explicit information is all the details stated in print. For example, if the first sentence of the text is "The sun was shining brightly on the hot summer afternoon," that is explicit information. There is no room for conjecture or argument; the reader cannot be confused and believe that the story is set on a rainy afternoon.

Identifying the explicit meaning and details within a passage is important in mastering reading comprehension questions. The explicit meaning and details are the examples that support and clarify the topic sentence or main idea of a written passage. When you analyze a passage, the explicit meaning and details underscore the writer's main idea by providing clarification of its meaning or evidence to corroborate it.

Explicit facts are fairly simple to identify. Common comprehension identification clues for explicit facts include the basic reporter questions—who, what, when, where, how, and sometimes why.

Look at the following example passage and identify the explicit meaning and details (*The Wonderful Wizard of Oz*, L. Frank Baum, 1900):

> The cyclone had set the house down very gently—for a cyclone—in the midst of a country of marvelous beauty. There were lovely patches of greensward all about, with stately trees bearing rich and luscious fruits. Banks of gorgeous flowers were on every hand, and birds with rare and brilliant plumage sang and fluttered in the trees and bushes. A little way off was a small brook, rushing and sparkling along between green banks, and murmuring in a voice very grateful to a little girl who had lived so long on the dry, gray prairies.

The explicit meaning and details of this passage describe the marvelous beauty of the country surrounding the house, which had been set down after a cyclone. These explicit sentences demonstrate how essential supporting details are to the development of this main idea. They provide substance by making vivid the thesis or main point of the passage.

The key to identifying the explicit meaning and details within a passage is to identify the examples that support and clarify the topic sentence or main idea of a written passage. All writing—whether serious or humorous, objective or personal—depends on support to be effective. The types of support authors use in their writing depends on the answers to the following three questions:

- What is the writing goal?
- Who is the intended audience?
- What is the purpose of the piece of writing?

You need to be aware that authors rely on more than one kind of supporting detail to help their readers understand the explicit meaning of a passage. These are

- **Personal observations:** descriptive remarks and observations about a person, place, or thing
- **Facts:** objective information collected by research or analysis
- **Testimony:** statements, quotations, accounts, observations, and assertions from experts or eyewitnesses
- **Statistics:** hard evidence or facts expressed numerically
- **Examples:** specific illustrations that clarify the thesis statement

Finally, you can reasonably expect that when writing supporting details, authors adhere to the following guidelines:

- Select details that reinforce the thesis statement or main idea.
- Use sources that are reliable, credible, and verifiable.
- Organize supporting details logically and coherently.
- Avoid introducing extraneous or irrelevant information.

Determine Inferences and Conclusions Based on Textual Evidence

Observations occur when we see something happening. In contrast, inferences are what we figure out based on an experience. In real life, we make inferences and draw conclusions based on what we observe with our five senses—seeing, hearing, tasting, touching, and smelling. In reading, inferences are made from information that is either stated directly or implied (not stated directly). Inferences aid readers in drawing conclusions. For example, if we see or read that a house was destroyed by a cyclone, we can easily infer that any survivors will be hurt, or at best, shook up. It is important to recognize that textual evidence in the passage must support inferences or conclusions made.

The key to determining inferences and conclusions based on textual evidence is to identify the examples—stated and implied—that support and clarify the topic sentence or main idea of a written passage. Simply, readers' inferences should logically follow from the text and not be so far-fetched as to be unreasonable.

To determine inferences and conclusions based on textual evidence, ask yourself the following questions:

- What is the context of the passage?
- What is the motive of the passage?

- What are the cause-and-effect relationships of the passage?
- What is the main idea of the passage?
- What is the author's purpose for the passage?
- What is the author's point of view or attitude in the passage?

Look at the example passages that follow and identify the key words or key phrases.

Example 1:

The study of intellectual growth cannot be separated from that of physical growth. During the same years that children are developing physically, their mental concepts and skills are taking form. Research studies have indicated a positive correlation between physical maturity and intellectual ability; although, of course, caution should be exercised in making sweeping generalizations from these findings.

Note that the key phrase or textual evidence in this paragraph is "a positive correlation between physical maturity and intellectual ability." This phrase indicates the author's point of view, and thus means that before any assumptions are made between physical maturity and intellectual ability, the reader should realize that the mentioned research studies might not have taken into account all relevant factors.

Example 2:

The importance of effective motivation is of primary concern in curricular planning. Motivation involves a two-pronged responsibility, which rests both with the teacher and the student. The student must want to learn, and the teacher must provide motivating experiences. Teachers must be constantly sensitive to the various facets of motivation as they contemplate, plan, and revise their curricular offerings. They must be concerned with short-term and long-term motivation, intrinsic and extrinsic motivation, natural and contrived motivation, students' levels of aspiration, and the ultimate goal of self-motivation.

Note that the key phrase or textual evidence in this paragraph is "Teachers must be constantly sensitive to the various facets of motivation." This phrase means that motivation is not determined by one absolute cause, but by a series of causes that directly relate to the developmental needs of the students who are being motivated.

Example 3:

Teachers must be emotionally prepared for children who dislike them and for those whom they have difficulty tolerating. Teachers, like all other human beings, naturally tend to react negatively to anyone who makes life more difficult for them. Responding with loving kindness toward a sixteen-year-old who continually makes irritating remarks in class can be a challenge. A teacher might easily develop a persistent dislike for such a youngster. But the teaching situation is not an ordinary circumstance, and the teacher is not justified in reacting as other, less understanding, people might react in a normal social situation. Teachers have the special responsibility of helping young people grow up in ways best suited to their own growth needs. Dislike is a strong impediment to providing such help. Nevertheless, the students who need the most help are almost always those who are the most trying.

The key phrase or textual evidence is the first sentence: "Teachers must be emotionally prepared for children who dislike them and for those whom they have difficulty tolerating." This sentence is the key to understanding the passage and its implications for what it means to be a professional educator. To the best of their ability, teachers should not look at disruptive students as making trouble for the teacher, but as individuals who, by their misbehavior, make trouble for themselves.

Discriminate Among Inferences, Conclusions, and Assumptions Based on Textual Evidence

Determining the meaning from information that is either explicit or implied is an essential reading comprehension skill. Careful and perceptive readers must be able to find coherent meaning and be able to draw conclusions about the text they are reading. Simply getting the facts in reading is not enough; you must think about what those facts mean.

The key to discriminating among inferences, conclusions, and assumptions based on textual evidence is to identify and classify the examples and details that support and clarify the topic sentence or main idea of a written passage. To accomplish this goal, readers must be able to use two sets of skills:

- Literal reading comprehension skills
- Inferential reading comprehension skills

Literal and inferential reading comprehension skills are used in all reading activities. To become proficient in reading comprehension, you should familiarize yourself with these two distinct skills. They will play a considerable role in helping you to determine the meaning of passages on the FTCE GK Test.

Literal comprehension skills refer to the reader's ability to identify and/or recall information that is explicitly stated in a text. Specifically, the reader should be able to determine and define the following:

- Sequence of events
- Main ideas
- Directly stated facts
- Supporting details, including words, phrases, or sentences
- Directly stated opinions

The word "literal" means "the exact words" or "the most obvious meaning of a term or expression." When writers refer to the literal meaning of a word or a passage, they are referring to the explicitly stated facts without embellishment or exaggeration.

Inferential comprehension skills refer to the reader's ability to use information explicitly stated in a passage to draw conclusions about what is *not* stated. Using these skills, the reader should be able to make predictions and draw conclusions about the following:

- Relationships in the passage, like cause and effect, sequence and time, comparisons and contrasts, and classifications and generalizations
- Events and sequences that could follow logically
- Symbols, patterns, and images that give heightened meaning to the text
- Implicit themes or main ideas embedded in the text
- Unstated reasons for actions and beliefs as implied in the text

Inferring is the process of creating a *personal meaning* from the passage—blending the reader's prior knowledge with what he or she is reading in the text. When readers infer, they create meaning that is not stated explicitly in the passage.

Look at these examples and identify possible meanings of the words in this context:

Sue blew out the candles and got presents.

Is it Sue's birthday? Anniversary? Graduation? Birthday seems most likely, as one does not usually blow out candles for one's graduation. If it were a wedding anniversary, it would likely be Sue and her spouse blowing out the candles, not Sue by herself.

Maria practices her clarinet for three hours a day.

Is Maria a great clarinetist? Does she practice because she "must" or because she "wants to"? We don't know the answers to these questions. All we know is that Maria is faithfully committed to practicing.

When I woke up, there were branches and leaves all over the yard.

Is it the result of a storm? Yard work? Vandalism? A storm seems most likely. Yard work, even done during one's sleep time, shouldn't result in a chaotic mess. Vandalism is a possibility, but ranks second to a storm.

These examples show that the meaning of words or phrases can only be determined when the reader understands the greater context in which the words and phrases appear. Without context, words can mean almost anything.

To discriminate among inferences, conclusions, and assumptions based on textual evidence, it is wise to follow these specific guidelines:

- Determine the purpose of the text.
- Identify the overall organizational pattern of the text.
- Distinguish between fact and opinion as expressed in the text.
- Recognize bias in the text.
- Recognize tone in the text.
- Determine relationships between sentences in the text.
- Analyze the validity of arguments of the text.
- Draw logical inferences and conclusions from the text.

More specifically, skilled inferential readers are able to

- Determine the definition of unknown words from the given context.
- Discern intonation of a character's or narrator's words.
- Understand relationships among characters in a given text.
- Recognize author's bias in a given passage.
- Offer conclusions from facts presented in a specific passage.

Determine and Analyze the Development of Central Ideas or Themes from One or More Texts

The key to determining and analyzing the development of central ideas or themes from one or more texts is to identify and classify the examples that support and clarify the topic sentences or main ideas of the written passages being compared. Follow these specific guidelines:

- Examine the text(s) features—headings, subheadings, italic and bold-type words, and so on—and ask yourself, what hints they provide for the text(s) main ideas.
- Determine the purpose of the text—Entertain? Persuade? Inform? Show cause/effect? Compare/contrast? Express an opinion?
- Analyze organizational structure of the text—Chronological order? Order of importance? Descriptive?
- Select the important points made within or among the text(s). Are they in the first or last sentence(s)?

Look at this example passage and see whether you can identify the main idea:

> The day began as usual. I woke, washed, dressed, and had breakfast. My breakfast was cereal, toast, and orange juice. After breakfast, I took a swift walk around the block, feeling the cool breeze and morning sun greeting me as I welcomed the new day. I felt good. I felt that my good night's rest, light breakfast, and brisk exercise were just the right tonic to prepare me for my first day on my new job.

The main idea of the first passage is clearly stated in the last sentence: "I felt that my good night's rest, light breakfast, and brisk exercise were just the right tonic to prepare me for my first day on my new job." All of the accompanying sentences support this main idea.

Now, look at this next example and see if you can identify the main idea:

> My cold started in the afternoon. I felt chills, followed by terrible aches and finally, fever. I headed to bed, hoping a good rest would knock out whatever had overcome me so suddenly. I tried a pain reliever

and a cold compress. I slept fitfully, and finally, after 2 hours, I called the doctor. She said that she could see me at once if I hurried over now. So, I quickly got dressed, landed behind the wheel of my car, and dashed over to her office. Luckily, the medicine she gave me relieved my ailments. By the next morning, I felt better.

The main idea of the second passage is the first sentence: "My cold started in the afternoon." All the sentences that follow support this main idea.

Summarize One or More Texts Using Key Supporting Ideas and Details

Supporting details are the examples that support and clarify the topic sentence or main idea of a written passage. When you analyze a passage, the supporting details underscore the writer's main idea by providing clarification of its meaning or evidence to corroborate it.

The key to summarizing one or more texts using key supporting ideas and details is to identify the examples that support and clarify the topic sentences or main ideas of the written passages being compared. To summarize one or more texts using key supporting ideas and details, follow these guidelines:

- Determine the central idea of the text(s).
- Extract sentences that support the central idea directly from the text(s).
- Use extracted sentences to write a summary of the text that is clear and concise.
- Write a summary that reflects the structure of the original text(s).
- Leave out minor details found in the text(s).

Look at this example of a passage and identify the supporting details:

The clouds looked threatening. Dark, impending, and voluminous, the once bright lit sunny day was proving to be anything but happy and carefree. Weather forecasters were predicting a storm the likes the county had rarely seen—maybe, tornadoes—and everyone was urged to prepare quickly and take shelter. As windows were boarded and supplies were bought, families gathered together in bathrooms, basements, and shelters hoping that whatever was approaching would do little, if any, damage. Unfortunately, within a few hours, the rain and wind came furiously, leaving widespread and devastating damage in its wake.

The supporting details of this passage describe the weather conditions before and during a terrible storm. These explicit sentences demonstrate how essential supporting details are to the development of a main idea.

Determine How and Why Specific Individuals, Events, and Ideas Develop Based on Textual Evidence

Recognizing relationships among words, phrases, and sentences is a vital reading comprehension skill. This skill requires the reader to go beyond the ideas expressed in a passage and make certain inferences and conclusions about them. Knowing whether sentences are related in context and tone is critical to understanding a passage.

Relationships among words, phrases, and sentences can either be **implicit** or **explicit. Implicit** indicates that the reader understands the *intuitive* meaning of the given passage. The meaning of the passage is implied and not directly stated. **Explicit** indicates that the meaning of the passage is stated directly.

Transitional words and phrases serve to identify the relationship between one sentence and the next and act as links between paragraphs. Understanding the selection of the transitions that link two sentences or paragraphs is critical to perceiving the author's meaning of the text.

To determine how and why specific individuals, events, and ideas are developed based on textual evidence, follow these specific guidelines:

- Explain what the text says by referring to details and examples in the text(s).
- Draw inferences based on details and examples in the text(s).
- Determine the main idea of a text(s).
- Determine the key details of the text(s).
- Explain events, procedures, ideas, or concepts in historical, scientific, and/or technical text(s).
- Explain what happened and examine why based on specific information in the text(s).

For example, take the statements "John is incredibly smart. He does not do well in school."

The explicit meaning of these statements can be simply stated: "John *is* incredibly smart, and he *does not* do well in school."

The implicit relationship is that smart people should do well in school; and, unfortunately, John does not.

Yet, notice that the use of transitional words directly affects the meaning:

> John is incredibly smart, *but* he does not do well in school.

The use of *but* implies that John is very smart, but as a matter of fact, he does not do well in school.

> John is incredibly smart, *and* he does not do well in school.

The use of *and* implies that John is very smart, and unfortunately, he does not do well in school.

> John is incredibly smart, *yet* he does not do well in school.

The use of *yet* implies that although John is very smart, he surprisingly does not do well in school.

In each instance, the distinction is subtle and, of course, open to interpretation by the reader.

Here is a list of transitional words that are effective in indicating the relationships of meanings between parts of sentences, between sentences, and between paragraphs:

- To repeat an idea just started: *in other words, to repeat, that is, again*
- To illustrate an idea: *for example, for instance, in particular, in this manner*
- To announce a contrast or change in direction: *yet, however, still, nevertheless, in contrast, instead of*
- To restate an idea: *to be exact, to be specific, to be precise*
- To mark a new idea: *also, too, besides, furthermore*
- To connect two or more ideas: *and, but, or, nor, because*
- To show cause and effect: *as a result, for this reason, consequently, accordingly*
- To bring to a conclusion: *in short, in brief, to conclude, on the whole*

A related concept is the understanding of the causality and logical sequence of sentence ideas. Causality implies an understanding of the relationship between or among sentence ideas, and that each idea is generated from the idea that preceded it. A logical sequence of sentence ideas occurs when the concepts expressed in the sentence flow together in a coherent fashion.

Here are examples that demonstrate logical causality:

> Professor Wilson is a man. All men are mortal. Therefore, Professor Wilson is mortal.
>
> Julia is a trained athlete. Athletes enjoy being physically fit. Therefore, Julia is a trained athlete who enjoys being physically fit.

In this next example, determine if logical causality exists in the relationships between the sentences:

> Alonzo and Hallie loved the roller coaster. The day began with high excitement. Alonzo and Hallie had planned the perfect outing. On their coaster ride, however, Hallie fell ill. She got a headache and threw up. Sadly, she spent the rest of the day relaxing and nursing a bad stomach. Undaunted, they headed to the roller coaster and waited patiently in a very long line for their ride to begin. They decided to take a trip to the local amusement park. When they arrived, they noticed lots of people heading toward the roller coaster.

Clearly, the sentences in this paragraph are not presented in the correct order. The logical order is as follows:

> The day began with high excitement. Alonzo and Hallie had planned the perfect outing. They decided to take a trip to the local amusement park. Alonzo and Hallie loved the roller coaster. When they arrived, they noticed lots of people heading toward the roller coaster. Undaunted, they headed to the roller coaster and waited patiently in a very long line for their ride to begin. On their coaster ride, however, Hallie fell ill. She got a headache and threw up. Sadly, she spent the rest of the day relaxing and nursing a bad stomach.

The new order makes logical sense and shows the direct relationship between sentences.

Determine the Cause and Effect Relationship(s) Among Individuals, Events, and Ideas Based on Textual Evidence

Causality is the relation between an event (the cause) and a second event (the effect), where the second event is identified as the consequence of the first event. The causes and effects are typically related to changes or events. Individuals, effects, and ideas revealed in textual evidence are the evidence that propel cause and effect relationships within text(s).

To determine the cause and effect relationship(s) among individuals, events, and ideas based on textual evidence, follow these guidelines:

- Focus on the passage's purpose—Is it well-stated? Clearly implied? Justifiable?
- Focus on the passage's key questions—Are they answered? Are the answers objectively stated?
- Focus on the passage's evidence—Is it relevant? Unbiased? Informative?
- Focus on the passage's concepts—Are they clear? Relevant? Justifiable?
- Focus on the passage's assumptions—Are they valid? Reasonable?
- Focus on the passage's conclusions—Are they sound? Logical? Justifiable?
- Focus on the passage's point of view—Is it direct? Indirect? Does it consider alternatives?
- Focus on the passage's implications—Do you understand the consequences?

Knowledge of Craft and Structure Based on Text Selections

As listed in the *Competencies and Skills Required for Teacher Certification in Florida,* 20th Edition (www.fldoe.org/asp/ftce/pdf/ftce20edition.pdf), there are five Reading Knowledge of Craft and Structure Based on Text Selections competencies/skills in which you should be proficient. They are as follows:

- Interpret the meaning of words and phrases as used in text (e.g., figurative language, connotative language, technical meanings).
- Analyze how specific word choices shape meaning or tone.
- Analyze how the author uses organization and text structure(s) to convey meaning.
- Contrast the point of view of two or more authors on the same topic by analyzing their claims, reasoning, and evidence.
- Analyze how point of view and purpose shape the content and style of text.

Interpret the Meaning of Words and Phrases as Used in Text (e.g., figurative language, connotative language, technical meanings)

Authors write for many reasons, and knowing their reasons for writing can help you considerably in determining meaning and purpose in their writing. Some passages explicitly state the author's purpose. Other passages allow you to interpret the purpose. Authors often use various literary devices to present their meaning in words and phrases—e.g., figurative language, connotative language, and technical meanings. As a proficient reader, you should always try to determine the purpose of a passage; doing so enables you to evaluate the passage in terms of whether the author got his or her point across effectively.

Understanding contextual-based evidence is the key to analyzing the author's use of literary devices. Types of literary devices include the following:

- Denotative—the literal meaning of a word
    Example—*A house is a place where one lives.*
- Connotative—the figurative meaning of a word; the ideas associated with the word
    Example—*There is no place like home.*
- Technical—words with a specialized meaning
    Examples—*bandwith, hyperlink.*
- Jargon—a special language belonging to a specialized group
    Examples—*BP (blood pressure), sweat equity (getting a stake in the business instead of pay)*
- Metaphor—comparison of two distinctly different things suggesting a similarity between them
    Example—*You are what you eat.*
- Simile—metaphor using *like* or *as*
    Example—*He ran like the wind.*
- Personification—providing human qualities to non-human objects
    Example—*The wind howled.*
- Hyperbole—exaggeration to make a point
    Example—*Our breakfast cost us a fortune.*
- Idioms—a phrase that means something to speakers of that language
    Example—*He is all thumbs* (meaning he is not a handy person).
- Analogies—compares two sets of things with similar relationships
    Example—*Hot is to sun as cold is to ice.*
- Oxymoron—when two things contradict one another
    Examples—*Bittersweet, speed walking, small crowd, organized chaos*
- Euphemism—using an innocuous expression instead of one that upsets or offends
    Example—*We put our dog to sleep (euthanized); the old man passed away (died)*

To interpret the meaning of words or phrases as used in text(s), ask yourself the following questions:

- Does the passage use literal language? Literal language means exactly what it says.
    Examples: *The sun is hot; the beach sand is white; the tree is tall*
- Does the passage use figurative language? Figurative language uses similes, metaphors, and other methods to describe something, often through comparison, or with something different.
    Examples: *The sun is fiery red hair; the beach sand feels like a hot oven*

Look at these example passages and identify the figurative language in the key words or key phrases.

Example 1:

>The word home has many meanings. For me, though, home is not a place. Home is where my heart is. I have traveled extensively throughout my life. I have lived in many countries—sometimes in urban settings and sometimes in rural. Yet, throughout my travels, I have always felt at home. And why? Good company. I am a loner by nature, and home for me has always been defined by the relationships I made and the relationships I kept. Thus, for me, home has always been where my heart is.

Note that the key phrase in this paragraph is "Home is where my heart is." This phrase means that for this author, home is not a physical space, but an emotional space. Home, for the author, is defined by relationships formed and solidified. Thus, the reader should realize that in this paragraph, the word *home* has a connotative meaning.

Example 2:

>My Frankie has two left feet. Boisterous and demanding, cunning and clever, this 8-year-old is a powerhouse of a child who never knows when to stop and always manages to hurt himself in the process. When he plays, he trips; when he climbs, he falls; and when he eats, he spills. Always on the go, my adorable Frankie is all spunk and heart—he means well, wants to help, and loves to have fun—but always manages to end up with bangs and bruises because his mind races faster than his feet—and somehow, he always ends up landing face down in the mud. He does not, as the saying goes, "trip the light fantastic." Instead, he bungles his way into our hearts.

Note that the key phrase in this paragraph is "My Frankie has two left feet." This phrase means that for this parent, the young son, Frankie, is boisterous, rambunctious, but most importantly, clumsy. Frankie does not literally have two left feet; he is just prone to be careless and thus, trip over himself—whether playing, climbing, or eating. The phrase *two left feet* is being used as idiom—a phrase that means something other than its literal translation. Thus, the reader is asked to infer the meaning of this phrase from the context clues given in the text.

Example 3:

>The day was blistering hot—hot as a car radiator that is overheated. Some people say that there is a difference between a dry and a wet heat. A dry heat is when there is low humidity. A wet heat is when there is high humidity. During a dry heat, you sweat very little. During a wet heat, you will sweat more. For me, though, hot is hot. I am not a big fan of hot weather—and normally, I do not sweat profusely. But regardless if the humidity is high or low, as long as the sun is out, and there is not a cloud in the sky or a breeze in the air, I am going to be hot, irritable, and moody. I don't like hot weather. I am much like the polar bear—I prefer frigid temperatures and a warm jacket to a blistery hot day and swimming trunks. The warmth of a woolen sweater is much preferred to the coolness of nylon trunks.

The figurative phrase is "hot as a car radiator that is overheated." This phrase means that for this individual, the day was extremely warm. The tolerance of different types of weather—warm, cool, wet, dry—is based on personality. For this individual, the hot weather is unbearable. The author simply does not like the heat; it doesn't matter if humidity is high or low. Thus, the key to understanding this passage is to recognize that the author is using an analogy—*hot as a car radiator that is overheated*—an analogy that is both vivid and personal.

Analyze How Specific Word Choices Shape Meaning or Tone

When reading a passage, try to recognize and analyze how specific word choices shape meaning or tone. Knowledge of how specific word choices shape the meaning or tone of a passage increases comprehension and enhances fluency skills. Readers who can discern the general meaning or tone of a passage tend to have a better grasp of the passage's main idea and the purpose for the choices made in the selection. Seeing a larger pattern helps in improving inferential reading comprehension skills and permits a fuller understanding of the author's intent and design in structuring the passage.

Specific language can suggest and shape meaning. The collaborative relationship between author and reader is revealed in the specific language choices that affect the intentions, implications, and direction of the text and shape the message designed for the reader. Readers, thus, should carefully analyze the impact of particular word choices on the meaning and tone of the author's message.

In any given passage, the author's tone is the attitude the author adopts toward the subject of the passage. Recognizing tone is directly related to understanding the author's purpose for writing the passage.

A helpful technique for determining an author's tone is to imagine the sound of the author's voice as if the author were reading the passage aloud. Often, adjectives such as *optimistic, pessimistic, cheerful, cynical, instructive, ominous,* and *informative* are apt descriptions of the tone of a given passage.

To analyze how specific words choices shape meaning or tone, ask yourself the following questions:

- What words did the author use to shape the meaning or tone of the text?
- What is the author's attitude toward the subject, audience, or character?
- What stylistic approach did the author select to present the topic or theme?
- What is the nature of the text—formal or informal?
- How do the choices of adjectives and adverbs, sentence structure, and use of imagery shape meaning or tone?
- What specific phrases—including analogies and illusions—did the author use to shape the meaning or tone?
- How does the author's word choice evoke a sense of time and place?
- Does the author use words or phrases with multilayered meanings?
- What is the cumulative impact of the author's specific word choices on the meaning or tone of the text?
- How does the use and refining of key terms impact the meaning or tone of the text?
- What is the impact of figurative language on shaping the meaning or tone of the text?

Test Yourself

Directions: For the following examples, identify the tone.

1. Attention, ladies and gentlemen! Global warming is destroying our planet—and we are doomed!
2. The beginning of the Civil Rights movement was sparked by the refusal of Rosa Parks to move to the back of a city bus. She quietly told the bus driver that she was not going to move to the rear of the bus where African-Americans, or Negroes as they were called then, were designated to sit.
3. I like lollipops! In fact, lollipops make me smile as soon as I plop one in my mouth.
4. When the skies turn gray, I caution you to be on the alert for an impending thunderstorm.
5. Although Jack was disappointed in his math score, he felt better about his overall understanding of algebra.

Answers

1. Pessimistic. The author is clearly presenting a strong and dire point of view.
2. Informative. The author is describing the results of a factual event.
3. Cheerful. The author is communicating feelings.
4. Ominous. The author is sounding a warning.
5. Optimistic. The author is presenting the positive outlook of a central figure.

Analyze How the Author Uses Organization and Text Structure(s) to Convey Meaning

When reading a passage, try to identify its overall organizational pattern. Knowing the organizational pattern of a passage increases comprehension and enhances fluency skills. Readers who can discern the general structure of a passage tend to have a better grasp of the passage's meaning and the purpose for the choices made in the selection. Seeing a larger pattern clearly helps in improving inferential reading comprehension skills and permits a greater understanding of the author's intent and design in structuring the passage.

There are many types of organizational patterns. Here are types found in most writing:

- **Time-ordered sequence of events:** In this pattern, the events are presented in the order in which they occurred or in a specifically planned order in which they must develop. In either arrangement, the order is important, and changing it would change the meaning of the passage. Signal words/phrases often used to indicate chronological sequence include

first, second, third	later	at last
before, after	until	next
when		

- **Simple listing of events, ideas, and activities:** In this pattern, the items or topics are listed in a series of supporting facts or details. These supporting elements are of equal value, and the order in which they occur in the passage is of no significant importance. Also, changing the order of the topics presented does not alter the meaning of the passage. Signal words/phrases often used for simple listing are

in addition	for example	several
another	also	a number of

- **Definition followed by examples of the definition:** In this pattern, the concept is initially defined and then followed by an explanation with examples or simple restatements of the original concept. This pattern is a familiar organizational technique of most textbook passages. Signal words/phrases often used for defining by example are

is defined as	is called	refers to
is described as	term or concept	means

- **Division or classification of ideas from general to specific:** In this pattern, the organization of ideas is presented from a general concept to a specific detail. The passage discusses a concept or idea and then divides the discussion into its component parts. Signal words/phrases often used for division or classification are

whole	it follows	component
part	category	in conclusion

- **Cause and effect:** In this pattern, one topic or idea is shown as having produced another topic or idea. An event or effect has occurred because of a particular situation or cause. Simply, the cause stimulates the effect or the outcome of the event. Signal words/phrases often used for cause and effect are

hence	for this reason	thus
because	consequently	therefore
made	on that account	

- **Compare and contrast:** In this pattern, topics or ideas are described by their relationship to similar topics or ideas. The author's purpose is to show similarities (comparisons) or differences (contrasts) between or among elements. Signal words/phrases often used for comparing and contrasting relationships are

similar	but	on the other hand
like	however	in contrast
resembles	bigger than	parallels
different	smaller than	

- **Description of place, person, or event:** In this pattern, the topics or ideas that comprise a description are a simple listing of details. In a description, you are writing about what a place, person, or event is like. No specific order is required. Signal words/phrases often used for describing a person, place, or event are

is	in	beside
like	above	near
resembles	below	north, east, south, west

- **Sequence or process of an event:** In this pattern, the listing of processes or events follows a similar arrangement as the time-ordered sequence of events or chronological order. The only difference is that the passage is describing a complex sequence of events, and not single isolated incidents. In the sequence of events, each event is rich in detail and complexity. Signal words/phrases often used for describing a sequence or process of an event are

first, second, third	finally	previously
in the beginning	at last	afterward
before	subsequently	when
then	recently	after
after		

- **Description of spatial or place order:** In this pattern, the topics or ideas are described as they appear in spatial or place order. Attention is paid to classification or grouping things or ideas into specific categories. Signal words/phrases often used in spatial or place order are

is a kind of	belongs to	is related to
can be divided into	is a part of	is associated with
is a type of	fits into	is next to, is adjacent to
falls under	is grouped with	is across from

- **Stating and defining a choice or opinion:** In this pattern, a preference is indicated for a specific idea, object, or action. Attention is paid to stating an opinion or a choice on an action, idea, or event. Signal words/phrases often used in the stating and defining a choice or opinion are

in my opinion	I think that	I prefer
belief	I consider	I hope
idea	I believe	I feel
understanding	it seems to me	

- **Allegorical:** In an allegorical passage, the objects, persons, and actions in a narrative are presented in symbolic meanings that lie outside the narrative itself. The true meaning of an allegory lies in its moral, social, religious, or political significance. In an allegory, the characters are often personifications of abstract ideas—like charity, hope, faith, goodness, evil—and thus represent concepts greater than themselves. An allegory is a story with two meanings: its literal or everyday meaning ("This is the story of two people who…") and its symbolic meaning ("This story is really about the true meaning of…").

- **Narrative:** In a narrative passage, an event or incident is recreated for the central purpose of revealing an insight into the actions of the people or events involved. A narrative has a central focus, is highly descriptive in its presentation, is action-oriented, and is usually based on a personal experience.
- **Inferential:** In an inferential passage, a conclusion is drawn based on available information. For an inference to be considered valid, sufficient evidence supporting the claim and/or supposition must be presented. The result is a thorough examination of the topic in discussion that captures the essence of the text and results in a whole new presentation of the topic.
- **Spontaneous:** In a spontaneous passage, the spoken and uncensored free-flowing of ideas and feelings takes precedence. No particular organizational pattern is employed besides the general whimsical nature of the writer's preferences and predilections.

To analyze how the author uses organization and text structures to convey meaning, ask yourself the following questions:

- **Cause and effect**—Cause is why something happened; effect is what happened.
   Does the author use cause and effect to organize the text?
- **Compare and contrast**—Shows how two or more things are alike and/or how they are different.
   Does the author use compare and contrast to organize the text?
- **Sequence**—Describes items or events in order or tells the steps to follow to do something or to make something.
   Does the author use sequencing to organize the text?
- **Problem and solution**—Tells about a problem (and sometimes says why there is a problem), and then gives one or more possible solutions.
   Does the author use problem and solution to organize the text?
- **Description**— A topic, idea, person, place, or thing is described by listing its features, characteristics, or examples.
   Does the author use description to organize the text?

Look at the examples that follow for identifying overall organizational patterns:

The day was long. The workers arrived at the factory by 7:30 a.m. Upon arrival, they changed into their work clothes and headed directly to the factory's main floor, where they all went to their respective positions and got to work. Each person had an assigned task; and with few interruptions, the workers proceeded to do their jobs until noon. Then, at 12 and 1 p.m., in two previously assigned shifts, they broke and went to lunch, with the second group waiting for all the members of the first group to return before going to lunch themselves. After lunch, the factory was again humming with the sound of workers diligently doing their jobs until around 5 p.m. Then, the whistle blew throughout the factory, and the workers immediately quit their tasks, gathered their belongings, and headed home to rest and prepare for another day.

The overall organizational pattern of this passage is

A. chronological.
B. inferential.
C. allegorical.
D. cause and effect.

The correct answer is **A,** *chronological.* Clearly, the author is providing a timeline description of the exact events in a typical day at this factory. The author chronicles the sequence of events experienced by the workers and no more. Choice **B,** *inferential,* is not correct because the author is not making inferences about the workers' day. Choice **C,** *allegorical,* is not correct because the author has not written a story about life in the factory that is representative of a larger meaning. Choice **D,** *cause and effect,* is not correct because the author is not describing the causes of outcomes.

Thermodynamics is a field of interest studied by a wide array of scientists. They include, among many, physicists, chemists, and engineers. For physicists and chemists, thermodynamics is of interest because they are primarily concerned with basic physical laws, properties of chemical substances, and changes in physical and chemical properties that are caused by the interaction of different kinds of energy. Engineers, however, are interested in these elements as well as in the application of thermodynamic principles to the design and construction of machines. For example, engineers would apply these principles to mechanisms that convert energy from one form or substance into another. And in the field of engineering, specific thermodynamic conversions are the domain of particular engineers. Electrical engineers are primarily interested in the conversion of mechanical energy into electrical energy, whereas mechanical engineers devote their time to the design of systems that will most efficiently convert thermal or heat energy into mechanical energy.

> The overall organizational pattern of this passage is
>
> **A.** chronological.
> **B.** definitional.
> **C.** sequential.
> **D.** allegorical.

The correct answer is **B**, *definitional*. The author constructs this passage by defining terms and distinctions as they appear. Choice **A**, *chronological*, is not the correct choice because the author does not provide a timeline of events. Choice **C**, *sequential*, is not the correct choice because the author is not describing a sequence of events. Choice **D**, *allegorical*, is not the correct choice because the author is not telling a story that is representative of a larger meaning.

After I arrived at college, I realized there were many similarities between my high school and college. First, both schools—my high school and my college—were small in size and number. I attended a small high school with fewer than 1,100 total students, and my college had only about 1,600 students. Second, both were situated in primarily rural communities. My high school was surrounded by farmland that was devoted to growing corn and wheat. My college was situated in a rural homestead that was devoted to raising cattle and hogs. Third, my high school and my college were filled with generations of students whose parents attended the very same institutions. Thus, both student bodies felt a deep and intimate connection to their school, their teachers, and each other.

> The overall organizational pattern of this passage is
>
> **A.** allegorical.
> **B.** narrative.
> **C.** compare and contrast.
> **D.** cause and effect.

The correct answer is **C**, *compare and contrast*. The author constructs this passage by comparing two distinct entities: high school and college. Choice **A**, *allegorical*, is not the correct choice because the author is not telling a story that is representative of a larger meaning. Choice **B**, *narrative*, is not the correct choice because the author is not retelling an incident or an event that has occurred. Choice **D**, *cause and effect*, is not correct because the author does not demonstrate that one incident causes another to occur.

In recent years, modern cities and their surrounding suburbs have grown exponentially in size. There are many reasons for this sudden and significant growth. First, as commerce and business become more prevalent, cities attract more people. People from both rural and urban areas find themselves attracted to urban life because this is where they find jobs and opportunities for a better tomorrow. Second, as individuals settle into the cities and surrounding suburbs, they, in turn, attract other individuals who are seeking the advantages of urban living. Thus, old and young alike gravitate to urban dwellings, seeking affordable housing, strong schools, sophisticated health care, and convenient shopping. Third, as cities and suburbs grow, places of leisure, entertainment, and culture begin to grow as well. Sports stadiums, theaters, and museums soon dot the landscape of these newly defined urban domains. For many people, these facilities and conveniences make life in the city and its surrounding communities much more appealing than life on the farm; and thus, they draw people away from rural communities.

> The overall organizational pattern of this passage is
>
> A. narrative.
> B. cause and effect.
> C. compare and contrast.
> D. allegorical.

The correct answer is **B,** *cause and effect.* The author constructs this passage by showing how a series of events, relating to commerce in cities and their surrounding suburbs, resulted in other events occurring. Choice **A,** *narrative,* is not the correct choice because the author is not retelling an incident or an event that has occurred. Choice **C,** *compare and contrast,* is not the correct choice because the author is not primarily showing the similarities and differences between living in an urban and rural setting. Choice **D,** *allegorical,* is not the correct choice because the author is not telling a story that is representative of a larger meaning.

My hometown is noted for several man-made features. First, it has the largest ice-cream store in America. Serving every flavor imaginable, my hometown ice-cream store occupies an old high school gymnasium. In this large converted building, all that is served is ice cream and assorted desserts. People come from miles around just to sample the delicious treats and to watch how ice cream is actually made. Also, parties and functions are regularly held in this wonderful old building, making it a very special place for all who enjoy its old-fashioned decorations and traditional furnishings. Second, my town boasts itself the home of one of the largest wooden windmills ever constructed. Built originally to celebrate the Dutch who settled in my hometown, this windmill now serves as a tourist attraction throughout the year. Especially during the summer, visitors come to my town just to marvel at the size of the windmill, nearly six stories high, and to walk the winding stairs leading to the top. Finally, my hometown has a genuine castle. Built in the late 1800s when a wealthy landowner came to town to settle and live, this castle resembles something from King Arthur's Camelot. Complete with moat, turret, and drawbridge, this fully staffed and furnished castle serves as both a meeting place and tourist attraction for conventioneers and visitors from far and wide. To be sure, these three man-made landmarks make my hometown a very special place.

> The overall organizational pattern of this passage is
>
> A. descriptive.
> B. conversational.
> C. compare and contrast.
> D. cause and effect.

The correct answer is **A,** *descriptive.* The author constructs this passage by simply listing the characteristics that make his hometown special. Choice **B,** *conversational,* is not the correct choice because the author does not present a dialogue or discussion as the heart of the narrative. Choice **C,** *compare and contrast,* is not the correct choice because the author is not comparing and/or contrasting two different sides or issues. Choice **D,** *cause and effect,* is not the correct choice because the author is not showing how a series of events has resulted in another series of events.

Contrast the Point of View of Two or More Authors on the Same Topic by Analyzing their Claims, Reasoning, and Evidence

Persuasive writing involves the use of argument to motivate the reader to adopt a certain viewpoint, opinion, or attitude. It is up to the reader to decide whether the arguments are valid and convincing. Thus, analyzing the validity of arguments presented in a reading comprehension passage is essential to understanding the passage's meaning. Writers try to inform their readers by writing passages in a logical, coherent progression of ideas that offer a legitimate source of information. Thus, when contrasting points of view of two or more authors, it is important to be able to determine what reasoning skills the authors are using to make their points. Knowing each author's writing style will help considerably in determining the validity of each author's point of view.

Often, controversial topics, such as raising the minimum wage, providing public funds for charter schools, or using student standardized testing performance as a criterion in teacher appraisal, are presented in newspapers and online as contrasting points of view. Their arguments underscore how two different perspectives on any given topic can result in opposing viewpoints.

When analyzing contrasting points of view of two or more authors, scrutinize the claims, reasoning, and evidence presented by the authors.

Generally speaking, there are two basic kinds of arguments or reasoning—**inductive** and **deductive.** Inductive arguments move from specific points to general ideas (conclusions), whereas deductive arguments are considered to be the reverse; they begin with general ideas (conclusions) and move to specific points. Inductive arguments are sometimes based on experience and observation, and deductive arguments are frequently based on widely accepted principles or known truths.

Here are examples of each.

> **Inductive reasoning:** A math student observes that every time she measures the interior angles of a triangle, the sum of the measures of the angles is either 180 degrees or very close to 180 degrees. She concludes that the measures of the interior angles of any triangle sum to 180 degrees.
>
> **Deductive reasoning:** The measures of the interior angles of any triangle sum to 180 degrees. This figure is a triangle. Therefore, the sum of the measures of its interior angles is 180 degrees.

Knowing the difference between these two types of reasoning—inductive and deductive—is essential to analyzing the validity of arguments. When authors use inductive reasoning, previous observations support the argument in question. When they use deductive reasoning, they apply accepted (from their perspective) truths or generalizations to an issue to arrive at a logical conclusion, which, of course, is the focus of the argument in question.

Because inductive arguments are based on observations and examples, you can sometimes be uncertain of the validity of their conclusions. You should, therefore, evaluate an inductive argument in terms of its reasonableness: Does the conclusion make sense, and is it supported by sound assertions?

Deductive arguments use known assertions or premises to logically arrive at their conclusions. You evaluate a deductive argument based on the reasonableness of its assertions and the soundness of the logic used. If the assertions are true and the logic is sound, the conclusion of the argument is valid.

Test Yourself

Directions: For the following examples, ask yourself which type of reasoning is used: inductive or deductive reasoning. Then, more important, ask yourself the following questions: "Does the argument make sense? Are the assertions reasonable? Do they support the conclusions?"

---

1. The city has only fourteen streets. All the streets in the city have tree names. Therefore, the city has fourteen streets named after trees.
2. My friend, Sadie, will win her tennis match because she has won all the county and state tournaments in her division.
3. No sane person would jump off a cliff. Stephano is a sane person. Stephano will not jump off a cliff.
4. Michael is very wealthy. Since Michael is very wealthy, we know that he must be the child of someone famous, as you have to be the child of someone famous to be wealthy.
5. A high school guidance counselor noticed that the most conscientious students were always eager to talk to her about applying to college. And often, she noticed, these same conscientious students would ask about early admission to college. Thus, she concluded that conscientious students were better prepared for college life.

Answers

1. Deductive. The correct choice is *deductive reasoning* because the statement begins with a general statement and then proceeds to a specific point. The first sentence tells us that the city has only fourteen streets. The second sentence tells us that all the streets in the city have tree names. Thus, as stated in the third sentence, all fourteen streets in the aforementioned city are named after trees.

2. Inductive. The correct choice is *inductive reasoning* because the statement relies on specific details to arrive at a general statement. Still, the conclusion is debatable because even though Sadie is a championship player, there is no guarantee that she will win her next tennis match. Please note, though, that the inclusion of the word "probably" would change the meaning of the text and make the argument more acceptable.

3. Deductive. The correct choice is *deductive reasoning* because the statement begins with a general statement and then proceeds to a specific point. The argument makes sense because the assertions are reasonable and the logic is sound.

4. Deductive. The correct choice is *deductive reasoning* because the argument draws a conclusion about a specific case (Michael) from a general assertion (you have to be the child of someone famous to be wealthy). The argument, however, is faulty because the conclusion is drawn from a questionable assertion; obviously, a person can be or can become wealthy without being the child of someone famous.

5. Inductive. The correct choice is *inductive reasoning* because the statement relies on specific details to arrive at a general statement. Still, the conclusion is debatable because even though the guidance counselor noticed that conscientious students applied to college early and often, it does not necessarily mean that they are best prepared for college life. Please note, though, that the inclusion of the word "probably" would change the meaning of the text and make the argument more acceptable. Even with the use of the qualifying word "most," the conclusion does not necessarily follow. Be careful of accepting an argument as valid just because you agree with the conclusion.

To analyze the contrasting points of views of two or more authors on the same topic, follow these specific guidelines:

- Consider the purpose of each of the two or more texts.
- Compare and contrast the tone of the two or more texts.
- Compare and contrast the writing style of the two or more texts.
- Compare and contrast the organizational structure of the two or more texts.
- Generate a list of similarities of the two or more texts.
- Generate a list of differences of the two or more texts.
- Compare and contrast the similarities of the two or more texts.
- Compare and contrast the differences of the two or more texts.
- Compare and contrast the relevancy of the two or more texts.

Following are examples of persuasive writing that try to convince the reader to adopt the author's point of view. See if you can discern how the writers are presenting their arguments and the validity of their work.

Example 1:

Today in the United States, we face considerable unfinished business in public education, for the complexities of modern society have left their impact on current educational issues. Populations are increasing rapidly. The world is shrinking steadily as a result of the rapid progress made in transportation and communication. Many diverse ethnic groups—some unable to speak English, some bilingual, or even multilingual—are appearing in school classrooms. Children are moving frequently, many of them changing schools five or six times in fewer than four years. They lack the security of firmly established roots. Broken homes and juvenile delinquency are not uncommon. Students today can scarcely be expected to remain unaffected by the tensions and upheavals in the modern world.

In this passage, the author lists example after example to prove the point that today's world is filled with inherent challenges that impact schools and thus, children's education. The author is inferring that today's youth face numerous problems—social, emotional, and economical—that impact both the nation's schools and their own academic progress. The author is using *inductive reasoning* to make the argument.

Example 2:

> For the colonists who arrived in New England, a singleness of religious purpose was a determining influence in the development of their early educational programs. They believed in a close unity between the church and state. To them, it was the responsibility of the government to "govern," to support their Calvinistic theology, and to foster the intellectual growth of their children. This was made clear as early as 1642 when the governmental leaders in Massachusetts were empowered to require parents to educate their children. Although this law did not require the establishment of schools, it did require compulsory instruction for youth. It even set up minimum essentials: reading and writing, knowledge of capital laws, study of the catechism, and apprenticeship in a trade. Thus, the early educational developments in New England clearly reflected the study of the values and beliefs of its early colonists and were instrumental in the design and creation of today's public school system.

In this passage, the author cites known assertions to arrive at a logical conclusion. The author is using *deductive reasoning* to make the argument. The author's argument is America's public school system is based on the religious values and beliefs of its earliest settlers, the New England Puritans, who believed in a close unity between church and state.

Both deductive and inductive reasoning are central to understanding persuasive writing and essential to analyzing the validity of arguments as they appear in passages. Deductive and inductive reasoning, though, are not the only techniques for analyzing authors' point of view. Often, authors use the following techniques to demonstrate point of view:

- Inferences
- Contrasting viewpoints
- Tone of voice

Example 3: Inferences

> She was wearing a red dress and waiting at the bar impatiently. She seemed to be a woman in a hurry, not knowing what to do—whether to stay or go. Suddenly, a man appeared and she handed him a package. Quickly, they left the bar in separate directions.

In this passage, the author is using inferences to imply that something mysterious is happening. Without telling us what, the author hints at something dangerous happening before our eyes.

Example 4: Contrasting Points of View

> Do you believe that everyone has the right to own a gun—without restrictions? Should you be a certain age? Be required to register for a license? Have certain restrictions placed on you because of your past history? Many believe that gun ownership should come with little or no restrictions. Others believe that gun ownership comes with rights and responsibilities and that gun use should be restricted to those who pass extensive background checks, and even then, that they be limited in their use of owning and operating a fireman, but more specifically, in the kind of weapon they can own.

In this passage, the author is using contrasting points of view to make his or her points. By presenting both sides of an issue, the author is reflecting a current controversial issue without providing his or her own point of view.

Example 5: Tone of Voice

> Do you know people hate to walk? They do. I see it every day. I live in a big city. And every day, I see thousands of people rushing everywhere to get where they're going—by running. They are clearly not walking. Walking has become an obscure art form. These folks seem to have motorized legs. Which leads me to my point. Why don't we simply outlaw walking, and demand that everyone run to where they are going? That way we can get right to the heart of the matter: making people run so as to impress upon them that nobody walks anymore. Maybe, then, and only then, people will complain when we compel them to run and demand that they be allowed to walk. Wouldn't that be novel?

In this passage, the author is using sarcasm to make his or her point. Naturally, no one would make a law forbidding walking, but the mere mention of the idea might generate enough discussion to make people reconsider the art of walking.

Analyze How Point of View and Purpose Shape the Content and Style of Text

As a proficient reader, you should try to determine the point of view and purpose of a passage, because doing so enables you to evaluate the passage in terms of whether the author got his or her point across effectively. Point of view is the perspective or attitude of the author. Purpose is the author's reason for writing.

Four common purposes for writing are

- Self-expression (often called description)
- Exposition
- Entertainment (often called narration)
- Persuasion

Each writing purpose has its own style and structure. **Self-expressive writing** is free-flowing in its choice of words and ideas and is often the province of journals and diaries. **Expository writing** is designed to inform or convey beliefs and opinions to an outside audience. Generally, this writing is more structured and stylized in content and tone. **Entertaining writing** is meant to amuse or arouse interest in readers so that they find enjoyment in the writer's words. Communicating the writer's interest and enthusiasm for his or her subject is one such method to generate interest. Finally, **persuasive writing** is meant to convince the reader to adopt the writer's point of view. The effectiveness of persuasive writing is dependent on the logic and clarity of the author's argument, the reliability and credibility of the author's evidence, and the attitude of the audience that the author is trying to convince.

Look at this example passage and determine its purpose:

> All day long, wind howled at unheard-of speeds. Houses shook, cars swayed, and water overflowed. The storm, directly off the Atlantic Ocean, was raging with all that violent wind and rain could possibly bring. Still, the tiny hamlet nestled between large cliffs had survived worse in its long and torturous history of enduring violent hurricanes. The angry gods of thunder and wind would not disturb the town's sturdy inhabitants. They had seen much before and were confident they would see more in the future.

The purpose of this passage is to

A. describe a violent storm.
B. explain small-town life.
C. demonstrate resilience.
D. illustrate ocean currents.

The correct answer is Choice **C**, *demonstrate resilience*. Clearly, the author's purpose or intent is to describe the strength and courage with which the citizens of this small ocean town resist its violent storms. By drawing a vivid picture of the storm, the author is showing us how even such raging weather cannot destroy this town's historical precedent for enduring even the most treacherous weather. Choice **A** is not the correct choice because although the passage initially describes a violent storm, the author's purpose is to use the storm as an example or illustration of the passage's larger purpose. Choice **B** is not the correct choice because although the passage does refer to this town as being small in size, the author's purpose is not to explain life in a small town. Finally, Choice **D** is not the correct choice because the passage makes no mention of ocean currents.

Recognizing bias in an author's point of view is a critical task in reading comprehension. **Bias** is a slanted or prejudiced attitude that presents opinion as factual information. The conclusions drawn are based on preconceived beliefs or prejudices and not on the evidence presented. Recognizing bias protects the reader from accepting the personal opinions of others as truths.

Test Yourself

Directions: For the following examples, determine whether the given statement is biased or unbiased.

1. The Civil War was a war instigated by Northerners to make quick money.
2. The Apollo space mission broke new ground in space travel.
3. Our ballet followed the choral presentation.
4. After lunch, the President spoke about his new proposal.
5. Music videos are designed to corrupt today's youth.

Answers

1. Biased. This statement, though presented as fact, is expressing the author's point of view.
2. Not biased. This statement is a self-evident truth. The Apollo space mission did break new ground in space travel.
3. Not biased. This is a statement of literal fact.
4. Not biased. This is a statement of literal fact.
5. Biased. This statement is presented as fact when it is clearly the author's opinion.

Understanding the interconnectedness of point of view and purpose is integral for analyzing a written passage. Readers should strive to determine how an author's point of view and intended purpose in writing affect word choices, selection of information, structures, and formats.

To analyze how point of view and purpose shape the content and style of text, ask yourself the following questions:

- Who wrote the text?
- What is the purpose of this text?
- Is the text written in first person or third person?
- How do point of view and purpose shape the style of the text?
- Does the author show bias?
- Is the author's presentation fair and even-handed?
- Is there other information that should have been included?
- What textual evidence supports the author's point of view?
- What questions does the author leave unanswered?

See the sections "Determine the Purpose of Writing to Task and Audience" and "Maintain a Consistent Point of View" in Chapter 1 for additional discussion of purpose and point of view.

Knowledge of the Integration of Information and Ideas Based on Text Selections

As listed in the *Competencies and Skills Required for Teacher Certification in Florida,* 20th Edition (www.fldoe.org/asp/ftce/pdf/ftce20edition.pdf), there are two Reading Knowledge of the Integration of Information and Ideas Based on Text Selections competencies/skills in which you should be proficient. They are as follows:

- Evaluate and relate content presented in diverse formats.
- Evaluate specific claims in text based on relevancy, sufficiency, and validity of reasoning.

Evaluate and Relate Content Presented in Diverse Formats

Marshall McLuhan coined the phrase "the medium is the message." His point was the format of a message influences the perception of the message. Proficient readers analyze the way main ideas and supporting details are influenced and shaped by the different media or formats in which they are presented. They evaluate the way content presented in diverse formats (for example, in print, in digital print, in photographs, in videos and audiotapes, on the Internet, in multimedia, and so forth) contributes to the presentation of a central thesis. Proficient readers are able to integrate information from multiple sources to deepen their understanding and, thereby, enhance decision making and problem solving. They evaluate the reliability and accuracy of sources and note contradictions or discrepancies in the information.

Photographs are powerful conveyors of information. A passage on meteorology might include a photograph like this one (from the National Oceanic and Atmospheric Administration website) of a weather balloon.

Weather balloon

Source: NOAA

The photograph could be used to enhance the discussion by illustrating the launching of a weather balloon and showing its large size while the text elaborates further on the use of weather balloons in meteorology.

Charts, graphs, and diagrams provide visual depictions of data, presenting complex information in easy-to-understand formats. They can be used to extend or clarify text information. They might also substantiate claims, or, in some cases, dispute them. Video and audio files bring a live dimension to content, connecting to audiences through senses not activated through text-based media. Discerning readers learn to weigh the advantages and disadvantages of using these various formats to package and deliver content for a stated purpose.

Readers should be mindful whether information obtained through diverse formats is from a direct source (original documents, government or professional organization webpages, and the like), a professionally edited source (journal articles, documentaries, and the like), or a freely written source (blogs, wikis, tweets, and so forth). To be sure, there is good information contained within many of these sources, but personal opinion, misinformation, unsubstantiated allegations, and bias abound as well.

To evaluate content presented in diverse formats, ask yourself the following questions:

- Is the source reliable and trustworthy?
- Is the information accurate and valid?
- Does the use of the format contribute to the overall purpose of the presented content?
- Do I detect bias in the information?

Evaluate Specific Claims in Text Based on Relevancy, Sufficiency, and Validity of Reasoning

Evaluating specific claims in a text based on relevancy, sufficiency, and validity of reasoning is a valuable skill in learning to comprehend and analyze textual evidence. To evaluate texts with these three ideas—relevancy, sufficiency, and validity—it is important to know the four basic parts of any argument. They are

- **Claim**—the argument's main idea or thesis statement
- **Evidence**—the argument's textual examples that support the claim
- **Warrant**—the argument's reasoning that connects the evidence to the claim
- **Rebuttal**—the argument's refutation of counterarguments that offer a contrary contention or opinion

Test Yourself

Directions: For the examples below, ask yourself the following questions: Does the author state a claim? Does the author provide evidence to support his or her claim? Does the author's reasoning connect evidence to the claim? Does the author's reasoning support why the claim is valid? Write your reasoning for each of the five statements below.

1. According to scientific evidence, the Sun rises in the east and sets in the west.
2. When we arrived at the accident, the motorcyclist had no pulse.
3. Because we saw no sign of smoke, we concluded that the fire was out and we left the campsite.
4. Some people believe that where there is smoke, there is fire.
5. There are 24 hours in a day.

Answers

1. *According to scientific evidence, the Sun rises in the east and sets in the west.*

    The author states a claim (*the Sun rises in the east and sets in the west*) and provides some evidence (*according to scientific evidence*) to support the claim. The author's evidence (*according to scientific evidence*) supports the claim.

2. *When we arrived at the accident, the motorcyclist had no pulse.*

   The author states a claim (*the motorcyclist had no pulse*), provides context (*the accident*), and evidence (*had no pulse*). The author is simply restating an opinion based on a factual observation.

3. *Because we saw no sign of smoke, we concluded that the fire was out and we left the campsite.*

   The author states a claim (*the fire was out*) and provides some evidence (*we saw no sign of smoke*). The author is stating a conclusion based on a cursory observation of the campsite.

4. *Some people believe that where there is smoke, there is fire.*

   The author states a claim (*where there is smoke, there is fire*) with no evidence or support. The author is stating an opinion without providing additional support for this argument.

5. *There are 24 hours in a day.*

   The author states a claim (*there are 24 hours in a day*) with no evidence or support. The author is stating an accepted fact without providing any additional support for this statement.

To evaluate specific claims in text based on relevancy, sufficiency, and validity of reasoning, ask yourself the following questions:

- What claim is the author making?
- Is the author's claim clear?
- What evidence does the author have to support his or her claim?
- What reasoning does the author present for using the evidence?
- How does the author handle opposing views?
- Does the author's tone lend itself to credibility?
- Is the evidence used to support the author's claim strong enough?
- Does the evidence really prove the author's claim?

Following are examples of persuasive writing that try to convince the reader to adopt the author's point of view. See if you can discern how the writers are presenting their arguments and the validity of their work.

Example 1:

Soccer has quickly become a sport to watch in America. Years ago, soccer enthusiasts were confined to a minority of people who enjoyed the sport as either a hobby or an intramural activity, but did not harbor ambitions of becoming professional, or at best, watching and cheering a professional team. Nowadays, the opposite is nearly true. Americans of every age and background, gender and class, have begun to recognize soccer as the worldwide sport that for many, it already was. They follow soccer stars much as they follow other established athletic professionals, and some even dream of playing for high school, college, and national teams. Indeed, as evidenced by the excitement for the World Cup, soccer has become a force to be reckoned with, bringing this once obscure and esoteric sport into the forefront of American life. The future for soccer in America is truly limitless.

In this passage, the author lists examples to advance the point that soccer has become recognized in America for the truly international sport that it is. The author supports this claim with generalized evidence to validate the thesis that soccer is being recognized by more and more Americans as a sport that is on par with other recognized professional sporting events.

Example 2:

Since the beginning of their existence, human beings have gathered in groups to form communities. Evidence exists that prehistoric individuals lived together in small groups to help each other survive harsh conditions. Human beings—longing to associate for both communal support and strategic survival—have always known that their ultimate survival was most dependent upon what they can do together, rather than individually. The most substantial evidence of such a claim is the existence of marriage as recorded in the Bible and evidenced in ancient Greek and Roman societies. In its earliest historical recordings, marriage was often between one man and multiple women. But as society evolved, the notion of partnerships gradually began to take hold. With this knowledge, it has become incumbent upon all societies to derive rituals around such pairings to ensure continuity of the species and survival of the individuals involved. Thus, as the concept of marriage has evolved, so has society.

In this passage, the author cites known assertions to arrive at a logical conclusion. The author is using specific claims about the nature of the human need to congregate in groups to postulate about the endurance of marriage as a social and economic institution. Thus, the author's reasoning as to why his claims are valid is underlined by his own logical, defined evidence.

Sample Questions

Directions: Read the following passage and answer questions 1–6.

Meteorology: Accuracy Is a Science

(1) Predicting weather patterns is a difficult job, at best. Meteorology is a demanding science; it requires patience, fortitude, and know-how to make careful and accurate forecasts. Most of the time, weather forecasters can be trusted, and their predictions allow others to plan their lives accordingly. Modern forecasting involves technology, science, and advanced math to accurately predict the weather. Relying on time-tested instruments and mathematical models, meteorologists are able to predict weather patterns reasonably, rapidly, and accurately.

(2) The first step in weather forecasting is to get information about the weather. Weather data is collected from the atmosphere by launching balloons twice a day all around the world. These weather balloons gather basic information about the climate conditions around the globe, recording data such as temperature, pressure, humidity, and wind speed. Another successful tool for weather forecasters is satellite technology. Satellites permit meteorologists to see what Earth and its clouds appear like from space. With such knowledge, scientists can see how Earth's atmosphere is behaving. Finally, using sophisticated computers, weather forecasters are able to discern what ordinary people might logically miss. They can predict oncoming storms, ominous weather patterns, and unpredictable hurricanes. They know enough—both intuitively and mathematically—to <u>discern</u> when there is a movement afoot that might predict danger ahead. Thus, their scientific knowledge has implications far beyond simply predicting the weather.

(3) Meteorologists are also instrumental in assisting local and state communities to prepare for future weather patterns. In fact, the largest employers of meteorologists are government agencies. Meteorologists help these agencies predict weather patterns, climatic changes, and environmental problems. Furthermore, sure knowledge of impending storms—in the near future or years to come—helps responsible government agencies and organizations prepare their citizens for possible dangerous and threatening conditions. Such notification is imperative, as emergency and contingency procedures must be set in place long before a real danger actually occurs.

(4) Finally, meteorologists help people live their lives. So much of our daily existence depends upon what we do in the outside world. Our work and play is contingent upon our knowledge of what our day will be like "weather-wise." That situation is one reason that clear, easy-to-understand, and accurate weather forecasts are so much appreciated by the general public. Accuracy and promptness are the hallmarks of good meteorologists. Fortunately, many meteorologists now have sophisticated tools to make predicting the weather easier. Using satellite data, climate theory, and computer models of the world's atmosphere, meteorologists can more effectively interpret the results of these models to make national, regional, and local area forecasts. Their good work informs not only the general public, but also those public, private, and governmental agencies that need accurate weather information for both economic and safety reasons. Indeed, our entire world economy is dependent upon such accuracy.

1. Which sentence best reflects the central idea of the passage?

    A. Weather forecasting is a routine and mundane undertaking.
    B. Weather forecasting is limited in scope and design.
    C. Weather forecasting has far-reaching significance.
    D. Weather forecasting is instrumental in helping people live their daily lives.

2. Closely re-read this sentence from paragraph 3:

   Meteorologists help these agencies predict weather patterns, climatic changes, and environmental problems.

   Which statement does this sentence support?

   A. Meteorologists help local and state communities prepare for future weather conditions.
   B. Government agencies are the largest employers of meteorologists.
   C. Knowledge of impending storms helps government entities prepare citizens for bad weather.
   D. Notification of threatening weather conditions must be set in place before a real danger actually occurs.

3. Closely re-read this sentence from paragraph 4:

   Accuracy and promptness are the hallmarks of good meteorologists.

   This sentence indicates the author most likely would agree with which statement?

   A. Meteorologists are at their best when they base predictions on assumptions and intuitive reasoning.
   B. Meteorologists are at their best when they base their predictions on scientific evidence.
   C. Meteorologists are only accurate when they base their predictions on previous weather patterns and valid assumptions.
   D. Meteorologists should refer to their notes and hunches to predict weather conditions and long-range forecasts.

4. The tone of this passage can best be described as

   A. anxious.
   B. skeptical.
   C. curious.
   D. informative.

5. Identify the relationship between the following two sentences from the fourth paragraph:

   Our work and play is contingent upon our knowledge of what our day will be like "weather-wise." That situation is one reason that clear, easy-to-understand, and accurate weather forecasts are so much appreciated by the general public.

   The second sentence

   A. contradicts the first.
   B. restates the first.
   C. supports the first.
   D. distracts from the first.

6. Which word, when substituted for *discern* in the second paragraph, would maintain the same relationship between the two thoughts in the sentence?

   A. perceive
   B. deceive
   C. illustrate
   D. inform

Directions: Read the following passage and answer questions 7–12.

The Interview: Applying for Your First Job

(1) Remember your first job interview? Remember feeling nervous, unsure, out-of-place? Your hair wasn't right. You thought for sure dirt was on your cheeks, and your clothes were stained with the residue of your hastily eaten breakfast. You were just not sure who you were, what you were doing there, and if the words were coming out of your mouth in coherent sentences—but, you knew, absolutely, that you wanted this job. The thought of a steady paycheck, the chance to do work in a field you love and had studied, and the opportunity to prove all the naysayers wrong (you should have majored in business, not humanities) was just too good to let go. Remember? I bet you do, and if not, this passage will help you prepare for your very first job interview, no matter what your major and/or career goal.

(2) The most important rule for any job interview—even if you are not offered the position or decide you do not want the position—is the ability to make a good impression. First impressions are lasting impressions, and the chance to make a good first impression, naturally, only comes around once. So, take advantage of it. Put your best foot forward. Wear your sharpest clothes. Make yourself look top-notch. And above all, adopt a positive attitude. Yes, this job and/or potential employer might not be your ideal version of what you envisioned your first job and/or career to be, but you never know where this interview might take you. Your potential employer—the person interviewing you for this position—might not think you are right for this position as well, but they might be aware of another position that would fit you well. So no matter who you are talking to—and about what—always put your best foot (and attitude) forward. You never know.

(3) For any job interview, it is always best to be prepared. Visit the company's website. Get to know as much about your prospective employer as possible. Learn about the individuals who work there—their backgrounds, responsibilities, positions inside the company—and try to assess how you would fit in if you were to be hired. Go into an interview with as much knowledge about the company as you can. This strategy will help you make your decision should you be offered a position. The more you know, the better off you will be.

(4) Similarly, when in interview mode, put your good knowledge to work. True, you don't want to come across as a know-it-all, but you do want to display confidence and show that you have researched the company (know the basic organizational structure and how you see yourself as their employee) so you can underscore how they will benefit from your presence and expertise. Adopting a positive, confident, well-rehearsed posture will help you considerably in leaving a favorable first impression.

(5) Above all, be prepared to answer questions about your experiences and abilities. Knowing how you can contribute to this company is just as important as learning how the company can contribute to your professional growth and career. And the trick to underlining how you can contribute to the success of the company at which you are seeking employment is to listen carefully. Listening intently, keenly, and completely is the key to all good interviews. Listen to not only what is said explicitly, but to also what is implied. For it is often what is not said that becomes the key to your own decision-making and eventual questioning about the position itself.

(6) A job interview is the time to demonstrate your strengths. It means highlighting who you are without compromising what you intend to become. It means underlining the very essence of your character without surrendering your self-worth and dignity to a cause that does not define who you are or what you believe. To be sure, job interviews are two-way streets—they are as much about your employer as they are about you. So, when you step up to your next job interview, arm yourself with as much knowledge and self-worth as possible—both will serve you well as you explore the very next step of your life's journey.

7. What is the purpose of the writing style of this passage?

  A. self-expression
  B. exposition
  C. entertainment
  D. argumentative

8. What is the organizational structure of this passage?

    A. time-ordered sequence of events
    B. definition followed by examples of the definition
    C. cause and effect
    D. stating and defining a choice or an opinion

9. As used in paragraph 2, what does the phrase *put your best foot forward* mean?

    A. to make a difficult decision
    B. to take a practical shortcut
    C. to make a good impression
    D. to take longer than needed

10. The author included paragraph 3 most likely to emphasize that

    A. accessing a company's website is important.
    B. making a decision about a job offer is a challenging undertaking.
    C. an applicant should fit into a company.
    D. applicant knowledge of the company is essential.

11. Closely re-read this sentence from paragraph 5.

    For it is often what is not said that becomes the key to your own decision-making and eventual questioning about the position itself.

    This sentence indicates the author most likely would agree with which statement?

    A. In a job interview, the applicant should not volunteer information that is not asked for.
    B. In a job interview, the interviewer should share opinions that should be left unsaid.
    C. In a job interview, the applicant should be mindful of what is left unsaid.
    D. In a job interview, the interviewer should respond only to what the applicant asks.

12. Which choice is NOT given as evidence in this passage?

    A. A job interview is the time to demonstrate your strengths.
    B. For any job interview, it is best to do little preparation so as to seem genuine.
    C. Listening intently, keenly, and completely is the key to all good interviews.
    D. To be prepared, visit the company's website.

Answer Explanations for Sample Questions

1. **C.** The sentence that best reflects the central idea of the passage is *Weather forecasting has far-reaching significance,* Choice **C.** Choices **A** and **B** are contrary to the passage's central idea. Choice **D** is too narrow.

2. **A.** This sentence supports the statement that *Meteorologists help local and state communities prepare for future weather conditions,* Choice **A.**

3. **B.** *Accuracy and promptness are the hallmarks of good meteorologists* indicates the author most likely would agree that *Meteorologists are at their best when they base their predictions on scientific evidence,* Choice **B.**

4. **D.** The tone of this passage can best be described as *informative,* Choice **D.**

5. **C.** The relationship between the two sentences from the fourth paragraph is that the second sentence *supports the first,* Choice **C.**

6. **A.** The word that best substitutes for the word *discern* in the second paragraph and maintains the same relationship between the two thoughts in the sentence is *perceive,* Choice **A.**

7. **B.** The purpose of the writing style of this passage is exposition, Choice **B.** The author is informing the reader of ways to succeed in an interview.

8. **D.** The organizational structure of this passage is stating and defining a choice or an opinion, Choice **D.**

9. **C.** As used in paragraph 2, the phrase *put your best foot forward* means to make a good impression, Choice **C.**

10. **D.** The author included paragraph 3 most likely to emphasize that *applicant knowledge of the company is essential*, Choice **D.**

11. **C.** *For it is often what is not said that becomes the key to your own decision-making and eventual questioning about the position itself* indicates the author most likely would agree that *In a job interview, the applicant should be mindful of what is left unsaid*, Choice **C.**

12. **B.** The choice that is not given as evidence in this passage is *For any job interview, it is best to do little preparation so as to seem genuine*, Choice **B.**

Chapter 5

General Knowledge Practice Test 1

Answer Sheet

(Remove This Sheet and Use It To Mark Your Answers)

Essay

Write your essay on lined paper.

English Language Skills

Mathematics

Reading

Essay

50 Minutes

Directions: This section of the examination involves a written assignment. You are to prepare a written response for *one* of the two topics presented below. Select one of these two topics and prepare a response. Be sure to read both topics very carefully to make sure that you understand the topic for which you are preparing a written response. Use your allotted time to plan, write, review, and edit what you have written for the assignment.

Topic 1

Teaching has become a profession that is considered to be fundamental to the health of our nation. Some people contend teaching certification should be granted only after completion of a university teacher-education program. Others maintain teaching certification via an alternative route through non-university entities such as school districts, education service centers, and private agencies is appropriate. Analyze the advantages and disadvantages of each of these paths to teacher certification.

Topic 2

The sentiment has been expressed that online learning has begun to replace face-to-face instruction. Evaluate whether or not online learning has earned a rightful place as a substitute for face-to-face instruction.

Be sure to read the two topics again before attempting to write your response. Your answer must be on only one of the topics presented, and it must address the topic completely.

Your essay is graded holistically, meaning only one score is assigned for your writing—taking into consideration both mechanics and organization. *You are not scored on the nature of the content or opinions expressed in your work.* Instead, you are graded on your ability to write complete sentences, to express and support your opinions, and to organize your work.

As listed in the *Competencies and Skills Required for Teacher Certification in Florida,* 20th Edition, the Essay competencies/skills you should be able to do are the following:

- Determine the purpose of writing to task and audience.
- Provide a section that effectively introduces the topic.
- Formulate a relevant thesis or claim.
- Organize ideas and details effectively.
- Provide adequate, relevant support by citing ample textual evidence; response may also include anecdotal experience for added support.
- Use a variety of transitional devices effectively throughout and within a written text.
- Demonstrate proficient use of college-level, standard written English (e.g., varied word choice, syntax, language conventions, semantics).
- Provide a concluding statement or section that follows from, or supports, the argument or information presented.
- Use a variety of sentence patterns effectively.
- Maintain consistent point of view.
- Apply the conventions of standard English (e.g., avoid inappropriate use of slang, jargon, clichés).

Before you begin, be sure you plan what you want to say. Organize your thoughts and carefully construct your ideas. This should be your original work, written in your own voice.

As you write your essay, you may revise or add information as necessary.

IF YOU FINISH BEFORE TIME IS CALLED, CHECK YOUR WORK ON THIS SECTION ONLY. DO NOT WORK ON ANY OTHER SECTION IN THE TEST.

English Language Skills

40 Minutes
40 Questions

Directions: For questions 1–4, read the entire passage carefully and then answer the questions. Please note that intentional errors have been included in the passages. The passages are designed to measure both identification of logical order in a written passage and the presence of irrelevant sentences.

Questions 1 and 2 are based on the following passage.

(1) Horses are one of the most useful animals in the world. (2) For centuries, they provided the fastest and most convenient way to travel on land. (3) Horses were used by early settlers in America as they traveled the east coast, looking for land to call their home, later by pioneers as they traversed the rugged plains and mountains of America's West in stagecoaches and covered wagons, and, of course, by the Pony Express. (4) Horses were used by hunters for securing food and by soldiers in battle. (5) Today, horses are used mostly for recreation. (6) Moreover, the automobile has become America's number one transportation problem. (7) Riding horses is one of America's favorite pastimes. (8) And, certainly, horse racing remains a popular spectator sport. (9) Today, horses are seen performing in circuses, parades, rodeos, and, naturally, horse shows. (10) It is in horse shows, though, that the true worth of horses is determined, as wealthy individuals purchase horses for both personal enjoyment and financial gain.

1. Select the arrangement of sentences 3, 4, and 5 that provides the MOST logical sequence of ideas and supporting details in the paragraph. If no change is needed, select Choice A.

A. (3) Horses were used by early settlers in America as they traveled the east coast, looking for land to call their home, later by pioneers as they traversed the rugged plains and mountains of America's West in stagecoaches and covered wagons, and, of course, by the Pony Express. (4) Horses were used by hunters for securing food and by soldiers in battle. (5) Today, horses are used mostly for recreation.

B. (4) Horses were used by hunters for securing food and by soldiers in battle. (3) Horses were used by early settlers in America as they traveled the east coast, looking for land to call their home, later by pioneers as they traversed the rugged plains and mountains of America's West in stagecoaches and covered wagons, and, of course, by the Pony Express. (5) Today, horses are used mostly for recreation.

C. (5) Today, horses are used mostly for recreation. (4) Horses were used by hunters for securing food and by soldiers in battle. (3) Horses were used by early settlers in America as they traveled the east coast, looking for land to call their home, later by pioneers as they traversed the rugged plains and mountains of America's West in stagecoaches and covered wagons, and, of course, by the Pony Express.

D. (5) Today, horses are used mostly for recreation. (3) Horses were used by early settlers in America as they traveled the east coast, looking for land to call their home, later by pioneers as they traversed the rugged plains and mountains of America's West in stagecoaches and covered wagons, and, of course, by the Pony Express. (4) Horses were used by hunters for securing food and by soldiers in battle.

GO ON TO THE NEXT PAGE

2. Which numbered sentence is LEAST relevant to the passage?

   A. Sentence 3
   B. Sentence 4
   C. Sentence 5
   D. Sentence 6

Questions 3 and 4 are based on the following passage.

(1) Diamonds are the hardest naturally occurring material. (2) Diamonds are also one of the world's most valuable natural substances. (3) Because of their hardness, diamonds are the most lasting of all gemstones. (4) Throughout the world, especially in Europe, America, and Japan, diamonds are widely used for engagement and wedding rings. (5) Some people prefer simple wedding bands without precious stones. (6) Diamonds are also widely used for industrial purposes, such as for cutting, grinding, and boring other materials. (7) About half the world's diamonds are used for such purposes, while an even smaller percentage is used for jewelry. (8) When diamonds are cut by hand, the diamond cutter uses another diamond to do the cutting. (9) Furthermore, diamonds cannot be destroyed in acid, although they can be damaged by intense heat. (10) Diamonds are precious stones, and only those with an expert knowledge of diamonds can truly judge the worth of individual stones.

3. Select the arrangement of sentences 2, 3, and 4 that provides the MOST logical sequence of ideas and supporting details in the paragraph. If no change is needed, select Choice A.

   A. (2) Diamonds are also one of the world's most valuable natural substances. (3) Because of their hardness, diamonds are the most lasting of all gemstones. (4) Throughout the world, especially in Europe, America, and Japan, diamonds are widely used for engagement and wedding rings.

   B. (4) Throughout the world, especially in Europe, America, and Japan, diamonds are widely used for engagement and wedding rings. (3) Because of their hardness, diamonds are the most lasting of all gemstones. (2) Diamonds are also one of the world's most valuable natural substances.

   C. (4) Throughout the world, especially in Europe, America, and Japan, diamonds are widely used for engagement and wedding rings. (2) Diamonds are also one of the world's most valuable natural substances. (3) Because of their hardness, diamonds are the most lasting of all gemstones.

   D. (3) Because of their hardness, diamonds are the most lasting of all gemstones. (4) Throughout the world, especially in Europe, America, and Japan, diamonds are widely used for engagement and wedding rings. (2) Diamonds are also one of the world's most valuable natural substances.

4. Which numbered sentence is LEAST relevant to the passage?

   A. Sentence 3
   B. Sentence 4
   C. Sentence 5
   D. Sentence 6

GO ON TO THE NEXT PAGE

Directions: For questions 5–37, select the answer choice that corrects an error in the underlined portion. If there is no error, choose Choice D, indicating "No change is necessary."

5. The passenger <u>who's</u> purse I found in the taxicab
                  A
   <u>came</u> to headquarters to <u>retrieve</u> her belongings.
    B   C
   A. whose
   B. is coming
   C. retreive
   D. No change is necessary.

6. All of the campers <u>at</u> the <u>summer</u> camp, <u>accept</u>
                     A   B   C
   Jamie, will be required to take the swimming test.
   A. in
   B. Summer
   C. except
   D. No change is necessary.

7. I <u>respectively</u> submitted my <u>formal</u> letter of
      A   B
   resignation to the school's <u>principal</u>.
                              C
   A. respectfully
   B. former
   C. principle
   D. No change is necessary.

8. The <u>fourth</u> box of supplies for the party was
         A
   <u>further</u> from my house <u>than</u> I thought.
    B   C
   A. forth
   B. farther
   C. then
   D. No change is necessary.

9. When my <u>aunt</u> came to visit, I <u>could of</u> baked
            A   B
   cookies for <u>dessert</u>.
             C
   A. Aunt
   B. could have
   C. desert
   D. No change is necessary.

10. Juan and Mary went to Tallahassee, the state
    <u>capitol,</u> to <u>receive</u> an award for <u>their</u>
       A   B   C
    outstanding contributions to the local charity.
    A. capital
    B. recieve
    C. they're
    D. No change is necessary.

11. Despite the inclement <u>whether</u>, the musicians
                               A
    performed <u>admirably</u> for the <u>congregants</u>.
                     B   C
    A. weather
    B. admirable
    C. congregents
    D. No change is necessary.

12. After the team was declared <u>ineligible,</u>
                                 A
    <u>everyone</u> <u>preceded</u> to walk off the field.
       B   C
    A. ineligeble
    B. every one
    C. proceeded
    D. No change is necessary.

13. We had <u>certainly</u> won more <u>board</u> games <u>then</u>
             A   B   C
    other players in the class.
    A. for certain
    B. bored
    C. than
    D. No change is necessary.

14. My son's <u>exceptional</u> mechanical abilities
             A
    <u>compliment</u> his wife's <u>considerable</u> analytical
       B   C
    skills.
    A. acceptional
    B. complement
    C. considerate
    D. No change is necessary.

GO ON TO THE NEXT PAGE

15. Between you and me, I don't know whether
                      A   B
you should be first or I.
                      C

- A. I
- B. as to whether
- C. me
- D. No change is necessary.

16. My brothers and sisters may leave after they
                              A
find a sight to eat beside the river.
       B   C

- A. can
- B. site
- C. besides
- D. No change is necessary.

17. The archeologists come up with a list that
                    A   B
included tombs, mummies, pyramids, and
                         C
other Egyptian artifacts.

- A. came
- B. which
- C. pyramids and
- D. No change is necessary.

18. The restaurants location by the beach made it
     A   B
a really romantic place for special dates.
   C

- A. restaurant's
- B. beech
- C. real
- D. No change is necessary.

19. When the tourists visited the lighthouse they
         A   B
were amazed that it looked more like a
skyscraper than a lighthouse.
       C

- A. tourists'
- B. lighthouse, they
- C. then
- D. No change is necessary.

20. The teacher felt badly about giving a failing
               A
grade on the English paper to the daughter of
             B
the school superintendent.
           C

- A. bad
- B. english
- C. Superintendent
- D. No change is necessary.

21. In 1492 Columbus, the explorer, landed on the
        A   B
islands of the west Indies.
           C

- A. Columbus the
- B. Explorer
- C. West
- D. No change is necessary.

22. When they got inside the cabin, the hunters
     A   B
builded a huge fire in the fireplace.
   C

- A. Whenever
- B. cabin the
- C. built
- D. No change is necessary.

23. I am convinced the reason there is animosity
   A
between you and I is that we are so much alike.
        B   C

- A. was
- B. you and me
- C. because
- D. No change is necessary.

24. My daughter, who is a track star, can run
           A
much faster than them other athletes.
     B   C

- A. whom
- B. more faster
- C. those other athletes
- D. No change is necessary.

25. It don't matter how smart you are because you
   A   B   C
still have to work hard to be a success in life.

- A. doesn't
- B. are, because
- C. one
- D. No change is necessary.

GO ON TO THE NEXT PAGE

26. My siblings say they dislike mathmatics, but I always have enjoyed it myself.
    A. siblings'
    B. mathematics
    C. it
    D. No change is necessary.

27. During the recent election, there was much discussion about whether the media is biased.
    A. their
    B. had been
    C. are
    D. No change is necessary.

28. Because the bus trip was going to take several hours, the students should have ate before they left.
    A. should of ate
    B. should have eaten
    C. should of eaten
    D. No change is necessary.

29. As the day ends, the planet Venus appeared in the sky.
    A. had ended
    B. has been ending
    C. ended
    D. No change is necessary.

30. Everyone in my family have enjoyed watching our five new goldfish scurry around the castle in the fish tank.
    A. has enjoyed
    B. goldfishes
    C. castel
    D. No change is necessary.

31. Each of the boys thanked their parents for the support provided prior to the match between the two teams.
    A. his
    B. provided, prior
    C. among
    D. No change is necessary.

32. My students collected books that were still in good condition from various organizations around town, so I gave them to our local library.
    A. books, that
    B. organizations'
    C. the books
    D. No change is necessary.

33. Cory's favorite subject in middle school was English because he enjoyed studying grammar, reading books, and to write papers.
    A. Middle
    B. grammer
    C. writing
    D. No change is necessary.

34. Barbara has become quite annoyed with his meddling in her personal business.
    A. quiet
    B. him
    C. personnel
    D. No change is necessary.

35. One of the forestry professors at the local university was investigating the affect of a new fertilizer on the growth of pine seedlings.
    A. professors'
    B. were
    C. effect
    D. No change is necessary.

36. Michael measured the length, width, and heighth of the box to make sure it would fit in the trunk of his car.
    A. measures
    B. height
    C. box, to
    D. No change is necessary.

GO ON TO THE NEXT PAGE

37. Bess's friends tell her that she has the most unusual hairstyle.
   A. B.   C.

A. Bess'
B. freinds
C. unsualest
D. No change is necessary.

38. Choose the option that is punctuated correctly.

A. Within a year, my new puppy should weigh about 18 pounds, I'm making sure that I feed him a nutritious diet.
B. Within a year, my new puppy should weigh about 18 pounds I'm making sure that I feed him a nutritious diet.
C. Within a year, my new puppy should weigh about 18 pounds. I'm making sure that I feed him a nutritious diet.
D. Within a year my new puppy should weigh about 18 pounds I'm making sure that I feed him a nutritious diet.

39. Choose the option that is punctuated correctly.

A. Preferring to be hand-fed canned tuna, our family's new Siamese cat refuses to eat dry cat food.
B. Preferring to be hand-fed canned tuna, our familys' new Siamese cat refuses to eat dry cat food.
C. Preferring to be hand-fed canned tuna. Our family's new Siamese cat refuses to eat dry cat food.
D. Preferring to be hand-fed canned tuna our family's new Siamese cat refuses to eat dry cat food.

40. Choose the sentence in which the modifiers are placed correctly.

A. Rushing to finish the surprise dinner on time, Melissa borrowed an egg from a neighbor that was rotten.
B. Melissa borrowed an egg from a neighbor that was rotten, rushing to finish the surprise dinner on time.
C. Rushing to finish the surprise dinner on time, Melissa borrowed an egg that was rotten from a neighbor.
D. Melissa borrowed an egg that was rotten from a neighbor, rushing to finish the surprise dinner on time.

IF YOU FINISH BEFORE TIME IS CALLED, CHECK YOUR WORK ON THIS SECTION ONLY. DO NOT WORK ON ANY OTHER SECTION IN THE TEST.

Mathematics

Mathematics Reference Sheet

Area

Triangle		$A = \dfrac{1}{2}bh$	
Rectangle		$A = lw$	
Trapezoid		$A = \dfrac{1}{2}h(b_1 + b_2)$	
Parallelogram		$A = bh$	
Circle		$A = \pi r^2$	$C = \pi d = 2\pi r$

Key	
b = base	d = diameter
h = height	r = radius
l = length	A = area
w = width	C = circumference
$S.A.$ = surface area	V = volume
	B = area of base
Use $\pi = 3.14$ or $\dfrac{22}{7}$.	

Surface Area

1. Surface area of a prism or pyramid = the sum of the areas of all faces of the figure
2. Surface area of a cylinder = the sum of the areas of the two bases + the area of its rectangular wrap

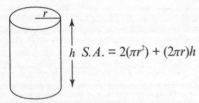

$S.A. = 2(\pi r^2) + (2\pi r)h$

3. Surface area of a sphere: $S.A. = 4\pi r^2$

Volume

4. Volume of a prism or cylinder equals (area of base) times (height): $V = Bh$
5. Volume of a pyramid or cone equals $\dfrac{1}{3}$ times (area of base) times (height): $V = \dfrac{1}{3}Bh$
6. Volume of a sphere: $V = \dfrac{4}{3}\pi r^3$

Mathematics Reference Sheet, continued

Pythagorean Theorem: $a^2 + b^2 = c^2$

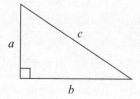

Simple Interest Formula: $I = prt$

I = simple interest, p = principal, r = rate, t = time

Distance Formula: $d = rt$

d = distance, r = rate, t = time

Given a line containing points (x_1, y_1) and (x_2, y_2),

- Slope of line $= \dfrac{y_2 - y_1}{x_2 - x_1}$

- Distance between two points $= \sqrt{(x_2 - x_1)^2 + (y_2 - y_1)^2}$

- Midpoint between two points $= \left(\dfrac{x_2 + x_1}{2}, \dfrac{y_2 + y_1}{2} \right)$

Conversions	
1 yard = 3 feet = 36 inches	1 cup = 8 fluid ounces
1 mile = 1,760 yards = 5,280 feet	1 pint = 2 cups
1 acre = 43,560 square feet	1 quart = 2 pints
1 hour = 60 minutes	1 gallon = 4 quarts
1 minute = 60 seconds	
	1 pound = 16 ounces
1 liter = 1000 milliliters = 1000 cubic centimeters	1 ton = 2,000 pounds
1 meter = 100 centimeters = 1000 millimeters	
1 kilometer = 1000 meters	
1 gram = 1000 milligrams	
1 kilogram = 1000 grams	

Note: Metric numbers with four digits are written without a comma (e.g., 2543 grams). For metric numbers with more than four digits, a space is used instead of a comma (e.g., 24 300 liters).

100 Minutes
45 Questions

Directions: Read each question and select the best answer choice.

1. At an art exhibit at a local gallery, 5 of the 20 paintings displayed were purchased by a well-known art connoisseur. Which number does NOT represent the part of the total number of paintings purchased by the art connoisseur?

   A. $\frac{1}{4}\%$
   B. 0.25
   C. $\frac{5}{20}$
   D. $\frac{25}{100}$

2. How many $\frac{3}{8}$-pound hamburger patties can be made from $4\frac{1}{2}$ pounds of ground beef?

   A. $1\frac{11}{16}$
   B. 12
   C. 8
   D. 6

3. Evaluate: $6 + 2^3 \cdot 3 \div 3 + 7$

   A. 3
   B. 8.4
   C. 17
   D. 21

4. Three grandsons and two granddaughters inherit land from a grandparent's estate. The older granddaughter inherits $\frac{1}{3}$ of the land. The four other grandchildren equally share the remaining land. What fraction of the land does the younger granddaughter inherit?

   A. $\frac{1}{6}$
   B. $\frac{1}{4}$
   C. $\frac{1}{2}$
   D. $\frac{2}{3}$

5. The graph shows the temperature in degrees Fahrenheit at five different locations. How many degrees Fahrenheit is the difference in temperature between Location 2 and Location 4?

   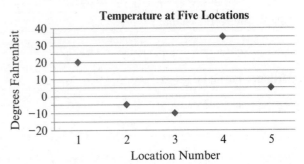

   A. 30°F
   B. 40°F
   C. −40°F
   D. −30°F

6. Which relation does NOT represent a function?

   A. {(4, 5), (3, 1), (3, 10), (−2, 0)}
   B. {(5, 5), (5², 5), (5³, 5³), (5⁴, 5⁴)}
   C. {(2, 3), (4, 3), (8, 3), (16, 3)}
   D. {(0, 0)}

7. In right triangle ABC, what is the approximate length of side $\overline{AB}$, the hypotenuse of the right triangle?

   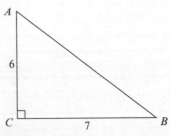

   A. between 6 and 7
   B. between 8 and 9
   C. between 9 and 10
   D. between 81 and 100

GO ON TO THE NEXT PAGE

8. A cellphone company charges $29.99 per month for the first 500 minutes of calls and $0.30 a minute for any calls over the 500-minute limit. Last month Demetria made 615 minutes of calls on her cellphone. Excluding tax, what were the total charges for her cellphone calls last month?

   A. $29.99
   B. $34.50
   C. $64.49
   D. $184.50

9. The numbers shown can all be classified as belonging to which set?

   $-\sqrt{49}, \sqrt{\dfrac{25}{36}}, \sqrt[3]{-27}, \sqrt[4]{16}, \sqrt{64}$

   A. whole numbers
   B. integers
   C. rational numbers
   D. irrational numbers

10. The table shows c, the number of calories, in n raw eggs. Write an equation that shows the functional relationship between c and n.

Number of Eggs n	Number of Calories c
6	432
12	864
18	1296

    A. $c = \dfrac{1}{72}n$
    B. $c = n + 72$
    C. $n = 72c$
    D. $c = 72n$

11. A couple wants to replace their rectangular table that measures 3 feet by 4.5 feet with a circular table that has a diameter of 4 feet. About how much less will the area of the circular table be than the area of the rectangular table? Use $\pi = 3.14$.

    A. 0.94 ft^2
    B. 12.56 ft^2
    C. 26.06 ft^2
    D. 36.74 ft^2

12. A rectangular garden has a perimeter of 50 feet. The width of the garden is 7 feet. What is the area of the garden?

    A. 18 ft^2
    B. 126 ft^2
    C. 50 ft^2
    D. 350 ft^2

13. How many square yards of carpet are needed to cover a rectangular floor that measures 22 feet by 18 feet?

    A. 9 yd^2
    B. 44 yd^2
    C. 396 yd^2
    D. 3,564 yd^2

14. If a crate is packed to capacity with 81 cubes measuring 4 inches on each edge, what is the volume of the crate in cubic inches?

    A. 64 in^3
    B. 81 in^3
    C. 1,296 in^3
    D. 5,184 in^3

15. What is the approximate volume, in cubic feet, of a cylinder that has a diameter of 8 feet and a height of 1.8 feet? Use $\pi = 3.14$.

    A. 45 ft^3
    B. 90 ft^3
    C. 180 ft^3
    D. 362 ft^3

16. How many cubic feet of cement are in a rectangular cement slab that is 4 inches thick and measures 12.5 feet long and 9 feet wide?

    A. 37.5 ft^3
    B. 75 ft^3
    C. 450 ft^3
    D. 375 ft^3

GO ON TO THE NEXT PAGE

17. Use the diagram below to answer the question that follows.

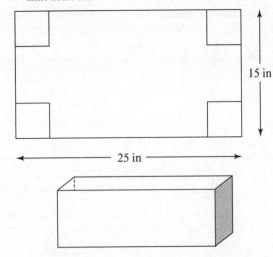

A small, open box is made by cutting out 5-inch squares on each corner from a rectangular piece of tag board, measuring 15 inches by 25 inches. The 5-inch squares are discarded, and the box is formed by folding up the sides of the remaining tag board. What is the volume of the box in cubic inches?

A. 1,125 in³
B. 1,000 in³
C. 625 in³
D. 375 in³

18. A baseball diamond is a square that is 90 feet on a side. What is the approximate distance between consecutive bases in a scale model in which 9 feet = 1 inch?

A. 90 in
B. 9 in
C. 810 in
D. 10 in

19. How many cups of water does a 5-gallon container of water hold?

A. 20 cups
B. 40 cups
C. 60 cups
D. 80 cups

20. A runner ran a cross-country race of 12 500 meters. How many kilometers did the runner run in the race?

A. 1.25 kilometers
B. 12.5 kilometers
C. 125 kilometers
D. 12 500 000 kilometers

21. In triangle ABC, if $\angle A$ measures 25 degrees and $\angle C$ measures 60 degrees, what type of angle is angle B?

A. acute
B. obtuse
C. right
D. straight

22. Which set of angle measures could be the measures of the three interior angles of a triangle?

A. 30°, 50°, 80°
B. 100°, 200°, 60°
C. 120°, 50°, 20°
D. 40°, 50°, 90°

23. What is the approximate diameter of a circle with a circumference of 48 inches? Use $\pi = 3.14$.

A. 301.44 in
B. 150.72 in
C. 30.57 in
D. 15.29 in

24. What are the coordinates of a point located 5 units to the right and 6 units down from point P?

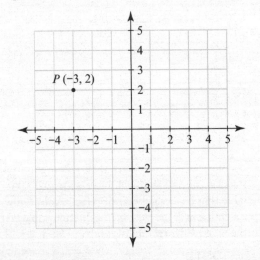

A. (2, 8)
B. (2, −4)
C. (−8, 8)
D. (−8, −4)

GO ON TO THE NEXT PAGE

25. What is the most specific name for the figure below?

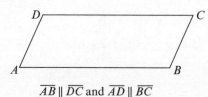

$\overline{AB} \parallel \overline{DC}$ and $\overline{AD} \parallel \overline{BC}$

A. parallelogram
B. rectangle
C. square
D. quadrilateral

26. Cash and Joe join different online clubs. Cash joins a club that charges a one-time enrollment fee of $40 and $20 for each month of membership. Joe joins a club that charges a one-time enrollment fee of $70 and $18 for each month of membership. After how many months of membership will Cash and Joe have paid the same total amount?

A. 15 months
B. 20 months
C. 25 months
D. 30 months

27. A 10-foot ladder is leaning against the side of a building. The bottom of the ladder is 6 feet from the base of the wall. How high up the side of the building does the ladder reach?

A. 4 ft
B. 8 ft
C. 10 ft
D. 16 ft

28. Use the diagram below to answer the question that follows.

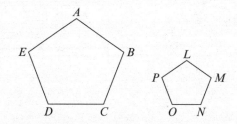

ABCDE and LMNOP are regular pentagons. If AB = 12 units and LM = 6 units, what is the ratio of the area of ABCDE to the area of LMNOP?

A. 1:2
B. 2:1
C. 4:1
D. 24:1

29. The sizes of the screens of television sets are described by the length of the diagonal across the rectangular screen. The rectangular dimensions of the screen of a portable television set measure 12 inches by 16 inches. What is the size of the television screen?

A. 12 in
B. 16 in
C. 20 in
D. 28 in

30. If 108 of the 120 fans who attended a little league baseball game on a particular Saturday were parents of the players, what percent of the fans were players' parents at the game on that Saturday?

A. 90%
B. 89%
C. 10%
D. 0.9%

31. Find $f(-13)$ when $f(x) = -5 - x$.

A. 8
B. −8
C. 18
D. −18

32. What is the distance between the two points R and S?

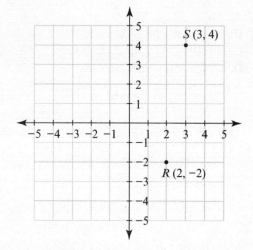

A. $\sqrt{37}$ units
B. $\sqrt{29}$ units
C. 7 units
D. $\sqrt{61}$ units

GO ON TO THE NEXT PAGE

33. Four less than 5 times a number x is 6. What is the number x?

  A. -2
  B. $-\frac{2}{5}$
  C. $\frac{2}{5}$
  D. 2

34. Which graph shows the solution set for the following inequality?

$-2x - 5 < 3x + 15$

  A.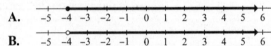
  B.
  C.
  D.

35. For lunch at the end-of-school picnic, students can choose from four types of sandwiches: ham, turkey, tuna, or peanut butter. They can choose from two drinks: milk or juice. They can select from three types of chips: potato chips, corn chips, or tortilla chips. How many possible combinations consisting of one sandwich, one drink, and one bag of chips can the students choose from for lunch?

  A. 8
  B. 9
  C. 11
  D. 24

36. What is the slope of a line parallel to the line through the points T and U?

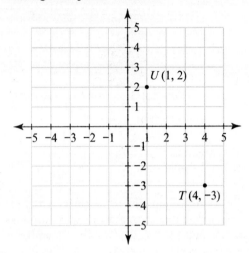

  A. $-\frac{3}{5}$
  B. $-\frac{5}{3}$
  C. -1
  D. $\frac{5}{3}$

37. Find $f(2)$ when $f(x) = 3x^3 - x^2 + 5$.

  A. 225
  B. 217
  C. 33
  D. 25

38. Solve for x: $4(x - 8) = 24$

  A. -2
  B. 4
  C. 8
  D. 14

GO ON TO THE NEXT PAGE

39. The graph shows a budget for a monthly salary after taxes.

Monthly Budget

If the monthly salary is $2,800, how much money is budgeted for food?

A. $105
B. $350
C. $700
D. $1,050

40. A spinner for a board game has 4 red sections, 3 yellow sections, 2 blue sections, and 1 green section. The sections are all of equal size. What is the probability of spinning red on the first spin and green on the second spin?

A. $\frac{1}{4}$
B. $\frac{1}{2}$
C. 4
D. $\frac{1}{25}$

41. The histogram below shows the grade distribution of 35 students on the first test in a social studies class. Using the graph, what is the probability a student randomly selected from the 35 students scored below 70?

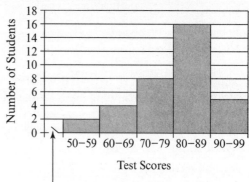

This symbol means there is a break in the horizontal scale.

A. $\frac{2}{35}$

B. $\frac{4}{35}$

C. $\frac{6}{35}$

D. $\frac{14}{35}$

GO ON TO THE NEXT PAGE

42. A student needs an average of at least 80 on four tests to earn a grade of B in chemistry. The student has grades of 78, 91, and 75 on the first three tests. What is the *lowest* grade the student can make on the fourth test and still receive a B in the course?

A. 99
B. 82
C. 80
D. 76

43. Mario has participated in eight track meets so far this season. His running times for the 440-meter race have been 73, 63, 68, 64, 69, 61, 66, and 64 seconds. What is Mario's median running time for the eight meets?

A. 64 seconds
B. 65 seconds
C. 66 seconds
D. 66.5 seconds

44. Yuan has grades of 75, 89, 67, 56, and 92 in her English class and grades of 75, 78, 83, 84, 80, and 77 in her French class. Which statement correctly describes Yuan's grades in the two classes?

A. The grades in the English class have greater variability.
B. The grades in the French class have greater variability.
C. The mean in the English class is higher than the mean in the French class.
D. The means in the two classes are equal.

45. To investigate the effect of Shampoo X on hair loss, a researcher decides to conduct an experimental study with 80 men between the ages of 35 and 45, all of the same race and ethnicity. The participants are randomly assigned to either the treatment group or control group (40 in each group). The participants in the treatment group will be the men who

A. have hair loss.
B. do not have hair loss.
C. use Shampoo X.
D. do not use Shampoo X.

IF YOU FINISH BEFORE TIME IS CALLED, CHECK YOUR WORK ON THIS SECTION ONLY. DO NOT WORK ON ANY OTHER SECTION IN THE TEST.

Reading

40 Minutes

40 Questions

Directions: Please read the following passages carefully. Each passage in this section is followed by questions based on the passage's content. After reading each passage, answer the questions by choosing the best answer from among the four choices given. Be sure to base your answers on what is *implied* or *stated* in the passage.

Passage 1

Encouraging Young People to Read

(1) Young people enjoy escapist entertainment. They watch television, go to the movies, or read books to get away to a world that is often, for many, strange, or at least, unapproachable. They enjoy reading about young protagonists who fall in and out of love, have wild adventures, travel the globe, cope with life's challenges, or experience fantasy worlds. Each journey is marked by a rite of passage, a time-tested travail in which the central character must struggle with some conflict—either external or internal—to become a fully realized human being. By challenging the system or overcoming a long-held fear, the hero of a tale embodies the best of what the watcher or reader hopes for in his or her own life and, thus, symbolizes the hopes and aspirations of many.

(2) To entice young people to become avid readers, teachers and librarians often suggest works that, for some, are difficult to read. Well-intentioned as these informed advocates for young readers are, they often neglect a host of stories and novels that are aimed specifically at youth. Too often, young adults, particularly high school students, are given material that is far beyond their knowledge or age range. Yes, Shakespeare, Dickens, and Hawthorne are representative of a class of longstanding, traditionally revered, classical authors; but they are, to be sure, not the only authors young people should be encouraged to read. Indeed, there are many other authors whose works young people can read with little difficulty, yet that have time-honored themes.

(3) The burgeoning field of literature aimed at young people provides a rich panoply of good books from which they can select to read and enjoy. Hours of escapist fare cloaked in realistic language and stories await eager young readers who find traditional literature too stuffy for their tastes. For younger readers (ages 9–12) there are works by Judy Blume (*Blubber, Are You There God? It's Me, Margaret.*), Paula Danziger (*The Cat Ate My Gymsuit, There's a Bat in Bunk Five*), and E. L. Konigsburg (*From the Mixed up Files of Mrs. Basil E. Frankweiler*). For older readers (ages 13–17), there are S. E. Hinton (*The Outsiders, Rumblefish*) and Robert Cormier (*The Chocolate War*). The books by these authors are but a few of the many books specifically written for young readers. These books appeal to the needs and sensibilities of young people while providing the escape from everyday life that all human beings need when they long for entertainment.

(4) Thus, the task of lovers of good books—librarians, teachers, and parents, to name a few—is simple. They are duty bound to introduce young people to books that not only provide them a chance to explore new universes but edify them and engage their interest as well. Adults who work with young people in an effort to motivate them to become more than they could possibly imagine should become familiar with the world of literature for young readers so that they can, in turn, recommend good books that are relevant to the lives of the young people with whom they work. Otherwise, too often, these young people will never know the pure joy that reading can bring.

1. Which sentence best states the main idea of this passage?

A. Young people should be given literature that speaks to their developmental interests.

B. Young people should read literature that inspires good citizenship.

C. Young people must read books that underline traditional values.

D. Young people must be taught books with universal recognition.

GO ON TO THE NEXT PAGE

2. In the first paragraph, the word *travail* means

   A. annoyance.
   B. parody.
   C. injustice.
   D. tribulation.

3. Which phrase best describes the focus of the second paragraph?

   A. appropriate literature for young readers
   B. young people's choice of entertainment
   C. why young people should read the classics
   D. authors that young people should read

4. What is the relationship between these two sentences from the passage?

   Sentence 1: *To entice young people to become avid readers, teachers and librarians often suggest works that, for some, are difficult to read.* (Paragraph 2)

   Sentence 2: *Well-intentioned as these informed advocates for young readers are, they often neglect a host of stories and novels that are aimed specifically at young readers.* (Paragraph 2)

   A. Sentence 2 expands a point made in Sentence 1.
   B. Sentence 2 contradicts the main idea of Sentence 1.
   C. Sentence 2 clarifies a point made in Sentence 1.
   D. Sentence 2 restates the main idea of Sentence 1.

5. What is the main idea of the third paragraph?

   A. All human beings long to escape from their everyday lives.
   B. Many good books written for young readers are available.
   C. Traditional literature is too stuffy for young readers.
   D. There are only a few books written specifically for young readers.

6. According to the passage, what is one way in which young people can be motivated to read?

   A. Introduce them to classic works of literature.
   B. Explain that reading can be more entertaining than watching television.
   C. Provide literature featuring young protagonists.
   D. Offer works about nonfiction heroes.

7. As used in the third paragraph, the phrase *escapist fare cloaked in realistic language* best describes

   A. fiction books.
   B. nonfiction books.
   C. textbooks.
   D. autobiographies.

8. Based on information in the passage, with which statement would the author most likely agree?

   A. Young people enjoy reading narratives that reflect everyday happenings.
   B. Young people enjoy reading narratives that are highly realistic.
   C. Young people enjoy reading narratives that feature invented settings.
   D. Young people enjoy reading narratives that are grim and serious.

9. The tone of this passage can best be described as

   A. caustic.
   B. optimistic.
   C. objective.
   D. subjective.

10. This passage implies that young people

    A. watch too much television.
    B. enjoy reading Shakespeare.
    C. need to escape from their everyday lives.
    D. prefer going to movies over reading books.

Passage 2

The Quest to Outer Space

(1) Throughout human history, individuals have longed to unlock the eternal mysteries of the universe. They have wanted to know why they are here, what purpose they serve, and what, if anything, is in the vast reaches beyond their world. For the first two questions, the reasons for humankind's existence and its noble purpose, people of all races and creeds have turned to religion. There, amidst ancient myths and modern realities, individuals have found great comfort and joy in the teachings and practices of many of the world's ancient and revered religious traditions. In modern times, for the third question, to unlock the mysteries of the planets and stars, America embarked on a quest to outer space.

GO ON TO THE NEXT PAGE

(2) The quest began in the late 1950s and spawned the creation of the National Aeronautics and Space Administration (NASA). Space was the final frontier, and there was intense interest in exploring it. The efforts of our space program led to the historic walk on the Moon by an American astronaut in July 1969. This giant leap for humankind ignited an age of travel and exploration into the far reaches of space that has yielded untold benefits and information for our modern industrial and technological society. While ancient peoples saw a sky filled with mysterious lights and colors, we now know what we are seeing and why. We can recognize planets and stars with amazing accuracy. Even more, we can send astronauts, secured in spacecraft, hurtling far beyond Earth's boundaries with incredible marksmanship. Ironically, we often can use the heavenly bodies that were once mysteries as guideposts for discovery. Today, more than ever, we witness what at the turn of the previous century was considered unimaginable in the scientific community.

(3) Sadly, Americans have experienced their share of space tragedy. In January 1986, the space shuttle *Challenger*—carrying seven astronauts, including America's first teacher to go into space—exploded immediately after takeoff. Then, space shuttle *Columbia* was lost on re-entry in February 2003. These two space shuttle disasters dramatically curtailed America's exploration into space, but did not dampen the American spirit. Instead, with renewed vigor and intense self-examination, America's space program set a course for exploration within our solar system and beyond. Today, plans for human exploration of the solar system, including landing humans on Mars, are underway.

(4) NASA's missions, programs, and projects have provided invaluable new knowledge and information about Earth, the solar system, and the universe. Indeed, our space program, though marred by tragic setbacks and fatal flaws, continues to move at a steady pace toward unprecedented human progress and scientific growth. Space exploration has helped us understand what lies in the vast reaches of our solar system and, thereby, to some degree, has shed light on the mysteries of the universe. Now, our charge is to use that understanding to improve our lives here on Earth.

11. Which of the following statements is implied in the first paragraph?

   A. Religion is an important part of many people's lives.
   B. Religion plays a limited role in most people's lives.
   C. Religion is the most important aspect of a person's life.
   D. Religion provides answers to all of life's questions.

12. Which statement is an opinion conveyed in this passage?

   A. Today, plans for human exploration of the solar system are underway.
   B. An American astronaut walked on the Moon.
   C. NASA's missions, programs, and projects have provided invaluable new knowledge.
   D. A teacher was on the space shuttle *Challenger* when it exploded.

13. Which word or phrase, when substituted for *Instead* in the third paragraph, would maintain the same relationship between the last two sentences?

   A. Therefore
   B. In addition
   C. Rather
   D. Obviously

14. The most likely reason the author wrote this passage is to

   A. explain humankind's curiosity about the universe.
   B. chronicle the history and impact of America's space program.
   C. challenge whether space exploration is a prudent undertaking.
   D. explain the benefits of space exploration.

GO ON TO THE NEXT PAGE

15. According to information given in this passage,

- A. people seek answers to the reasons for humankind's existence.
- B. astronauts brought back rocks from the Moon.
- C. the Hubble space telescope provides images of planets and stars.
- D. the two shuttle disasters put an end to space exploration.

16. In this passage, the author speaks of

- A. one shuttle disaster.
- B. two shuttle disasters.
- C. three shuttle disasters.
- D. no shuttle disasters.

17. Throughout human history, individuals have been fascinated with exploration because of humankind's

- A. natural inquisitiveness about the universe.
- B. insatiable desire to rule the world.
- C. longing to live in isolation.
- D. fervent need to civilize the world.

18. The author likely would agree that

- A. scientific exploration is a risk-free strategy that is filled with unexpected pleasures.
- B. exploring unfamiliar regions of the Earth is desirable for human development.
- C. only in desperate times do human beings feel the urge to explore.
- D. searching for the unknown is the province of rich entrepreneurs.

19. Which statement is NOT implied in this passage?

- A. Today, because of America's space program, the unimaginable has become reality.
- B. Our exploration of space has had a positive impact on America.
- C. America is a leader in space exploration.
- D. Tragedy has extinguished America's exploratory spirit.

20. In the fourth paragraph, the word *unprecedented* means

- A. unparalleled.
- B. usual.
- C. unremarkable.
- D. unexceptional.

Passage 3

Maria Montessori: A Woman Ahead of her Time

(1) Maria Montessori is considered a woman who was ahead of her time. She is credited with founding a movement that placed children's needs and desires above all other considerations, which—at that time, in the early twentieth century—was considered radical and revolutionary thought, especially in Europe. Nevertheless, Maria, born of humble but progressive parents, learned to take what she had always intuitively felt about the value and dignity of all human beings—regardless of age, status, and ethnicity—and apply her understandings to the everyday world. In so doing, she changed the face of modern education as we know it.

(2) Born in Chiaravalle, Italy, in 1870, Maria moved five years later to Rome. There, under the tutelage of her parents, especially her liberal-minded mother, Maria reveled in her own curiosity. Her natural inclination to explore and learn was encouraged; more important, she recognized that she could do and become anything her heart desired. However in Italy, as elsewhere throughout Europe and the United States at that time, the role of women was primarily subservient to that of men. Asserting their independence—whether at home, at work, or at play—was not something that women in the early twentieth century did. Maria's own learning environment, which had no such restrictions, formed the foundation of her later independent, free-spirited, learning environment for children.

(3) In 1896, Maria Montessori's strong academic record and natural drive to succeed led her to become the first female certified physician in Italy. Graduating at the top of her class, Maria continued her deep and abiding love of the study of psychology, philosophy, and education and gradually began to form the basis of her teaching method known as the "Montessori Method."

GO ON TO THE NEXT PAGE

(4) In 1904, she was appointed professor of anthropology at the University of Rome. Now, having authority and position, Maria was able to apply her theories of child development to work in practical settings. Two years later, in 1906, she wasted no time in founding and establishing the first house for children of the industrial working class in one of Rome's worst slum districts. There, in the house known as the Casa dei Bambini, or "Children's House," Maria, at the age of 36, instructed some 60 children in her care on how to do everyday chores. Her philosophy embraced the idea that by doing ordinary work, children would begin to develop a sense of self and pride that would spur their own growth and independence.

(5) To her delight, the children in her charge prospered. Soon, they were demonstrating self-reliance and maturity to their parents. Left to assert their independence, these young people, who because of position and social class were thought to be useless and unacceptable beyond normal functions, began to demonstrate social usefulness by simply being encouraged. Taking heed to her observations, Maria Montessori began to codify her doctrine of respecting the rights and privileges of young people into a philosophical and practical treatise on how young people learn.

(6) By treating young people with reverence and respect, Maria revolutionized the teaching profession. Young people were no longer regarded as passive, stoic learners, but active, involved, developing human beings who were quite capable of making sound and independent choices about their own learning. Advocating age-appropriate learning activities, Maria documented a teaching philosophy that garnered her worldwide attention and lasting influence in educational circles, most notably in the field of early childhood education.

(7) Nominated three times for the Nobel Peace Prize (1949, 1950, 1951), Maria Montessori continued to work tirelessly, until her death in 1952, training adults in the United States, Europe, and India about her teaching methods for treating young children—indeed, all children—with the respect and dignity they deserve. She was truly an educator ahead of her time.

Maria Montessori

Source: http://childrenstech.com/blog/archives/11454

21. Which statement is implied in the passage?

A. Maria Montessori's parents were old-fashioned.
B. In Maria Montessori's time, women were encouraged to pursue careers that traditionally were considered male careers.
C. Maria Montessori believed that children should be passive learners.
D. Maria Montessori was well-educated.

22. Which statement is an opinion about Maria Montessori expressed in this passage?

A. She revolutionized the teaching profession.
B. She was the first female certified physician in Italy.
C. She founded the Casa dei Bambini.
D. She was nominated three times for the Nobel Peace Prize.

GO ON TO THE NEXT PAGE

23. This passage states that Maria Montessori

    A. advocated age-appropriate learning activities.
    B. believed that doing everyday chores was demeaning to children.
    C. had the greatest influence in the field of secondary education.
    D. won the Nobel Peace Prize in 1951.

24. According to this passage, Maria Montessori's teaching ideas

    A. were rejected by most educators of her time.
    B. gained attention worldwide during her lifetime.
    C. were considered impractical by most educators.
    D. were accepted by only a few educators at the time.

25. Based on information in this passage, which word best describes Maria Montessori?

    A. passive
    B. progressive
    C. cynical
    D. active

26. According to this passage, Maria Montessori revolutionized the education profession because

    A. she understood the importance of subject-matter instruction in the development of young people.
    B. she demonstrated the validity of standardized assessment in classroom instruction.
    C. she respected the emotional experiences that young people brought to their learning.
    D. she emphasized the use of rote-memorization to reinforce classroom instruction.

27. According to this passage, Maria Montessori's philosophy was

    A. learning by doing ordinary work.
    B. learning by memorization.
    C. learning by objectives.
    D. learning by competition.

28. Which activity is most consistent with Maria Montessori's notion of an independent, free-spirited, learning environment for children?

    A. a 4-year-old playing dress-up
    B. a 5-year-old reciting the alphabet
    C. a 6-year-old counting to 120 by ones
    D. a 7-year-old copying definitions from a dictionary

29. As used in the fifth paragraph, *self-reliance* most nearly means

    A. dependence.
    B. persistence.
    C. autonomy.
    D. caution.

30. The author included the photograph after the final paragraph most likely to support that Maria Montessori

    A. was a woman ahead of her time.
    B. had a natural inclination to explore and learn.
    C. had a strong academic record.
    D. revolutionized the teaching profession.

Passage 4

Tropical Rain Forests: Will They Survive?

(1) Around the globe, near the equator, are woodlands flourishing in vegetation and foliage that enrich our planet with beauty and resources. These lush areas of our planet are the renowned *tropical rain forests,* a term purportedly coined by German botanist Andreas F. W. Schimper in 1898 for his book on plant geography. On natural history expeditions, he had seen firsthand the breathtaking beauty and majesty of these complex ecosystems. By all accounts, to capture on film or to convey in words what it is like to stand inside the heart of a tropical rain forest is virtually impossible. Of great concern is that the rain forests' grandeur and richness are in jeopardy as human intervention continues to destroy what nature designed to exist forever.

(2) Tropical rain forests are mostly located in South America, Africa, and southeast Asia. They have the unique distinction of occupying only 6 to 7 percent of Earth's surface, but nourishing more than half of Earth's plant and animal species. In

GO ON TO THE NEXT PAGE

these vast stretches of virtually unexplored territory, literally millions of species of plant and animal life exist. Home to many varieties of amphibians, reptiles, insects, birds, and mammals, the tropical rain forests are a virtual Noah's ark of all creatures great and small.

(3) Scientists believe some riches of the rain forests are yet to be discovered. In addition to finding new animal species, they continue to mine the many exotic plants that can yield untold benefits in developing new medicines for individuals with acute and chronic illnesses. Scientists urge world leaders to take every measure possible to preserve the rain forests because of the many and varied plant species they contain that help to regulate Earth's climate and ensure clean air.

(4) Thus, when the rain forests are threatened by large industrial companies, desiring to clear land for logging, farming, and mining projects, world citizens object and lobby dignitaries and business leaders to use caution in their desires to expand and grow. Both sides of this issue—those advocating for the use of the rain forests for economic growth and gain and those advocating for the preservation of a natural reserve—are locked in a reasonable and vital discussion about the future use of one of (if not *the*) world's greatest natural resources. This debate, though, is never-ending and always exasperating. Each side—the environmentalists and the industrialists—claim that the other side is violating rules that serve to protect the environment from undue harm. Long legal battles ensue, resulting in few if any reasonable compromises.

(5) In some instances, though, the debate is almost futile. In 1950, rain forests covered about 8,700,000 square miles of Earth's surface. Today, in the early twenty-first century, less than half of the original extent of the world's rain forests remains. In an area that once measured in practical terms the equivalent of nearly three-fourths of Africa, today stands vast regions—in places like Madagascar, Sumatra, and the Atlantic coast of Brazil—of arid, dry land.

(6) Scientists estimate that deforestation—the ridding of the rain forests of valuable trees and foliage—eliminates about 7,500 species per year from Earth's surface. Even humankind is threatened. Millions of indigenous people, individuals who know little of the outside world of modern conveniences, make their homes in the rain forests. Explorers have discovered and recorded the comings and goings of such groups as the Yanomami of South Africa, the Dayaks of Southeast Asia, and the Pygmies of Central Africa. These people, the last of Earth's primitive tribes, make their living off this lush and forbidding land; and naturally, they have much to tell about using its natural resources for survival.

(7) Fortunately, a number of governments and conservation organizations like the World Wildlife Fund and the Nature Conservancy are working to preserve the rain forests. Their efforts include establishing protected lands, promoting conservation methods, and increasing public awareness. Specific measures include certifying that timber is harvested in a responsible manner and logging is allowed in only designated areas. To be sure, these are small steps. However, given these efforts to minimize negative impacts and to meet conservation goals, there is reason to hope rain forests will continue to survive as one of Earth's most vital and precious resources.

31. The primary purpose of this passage is to

A. introduce rare rain forest plants and species.
B. inform readers about the plight of the rain forests.
C. argue the benefits of logging in the rain forests.
D. underline the importance of scientific exploration.

32. The tone of this passage is best described as

A. skeptical.
B. humorous.
C. sarcastic.
D. factual.

33. Which statement is a fact about tropical rain forests given in the first paragraph?

A. Tropical rain forests are found near the equator.
B. The breathtaking beauty of a tropical rain forest is indescribable.
C. It is virtually impossible to capture on film or to convey in words what it is like to stand inside the heart of a tropical rain forest.
D. The rain forests' majesty and richness are sadly in jeopardy.

GO ON TO THE NEXT PAGE

34. From this passage, one could infer that the author

  A. likes industrialists, not environmentalists.
  B. thinks industrialists are environmentalists.
  C. believes industrialists are profit-driven.
  D. thinks environmentalists cannot compromise.

35. What is the relationship between these two sentences from the passage?

Sentence 1: *Scientists estimate that deforestation—the ridding of the rain forests of valuable trees and foliage—eliminates about 7,500 species per year from Earth's surface.* (Paragraph 6)

Sentence 2: *Even humankind is threatened.* (Paragraph 6)

  A. Sentence 2 analyzes the main idea in Sentence 1.
  B. Sentence 2 contradicts the main idea of Sentence 1.
  C. Sentence 2 continues the main idea of Sentence 1.
  D. Sentence 2 explains the main idea begun in Sentence 1.

36. In the third paragraph, the author uses the word *mine* in the context of

  A. excavating from Earth's soil.
  B. dissolving with chemicals.
  C. extracting from plants.
  D. supplying with new medicines.

37. Which statement about rain forests is neither stated nor implied in this passage?

  A. They provide safe havens for indigenous people.
  B. They provide natural resources for modern medicines.
  C. They provide unique treasures for materialistic explorers.
  D. They provide a rich laboratory for scientific investigation.

38. According to this passage, all of the following are true EXCEPT

  A. in 1950, rain forests covered about 8,700,000 square miles of Earth's surface.
  B. rain forests nourish more than half of the world's plants and animals.
  C. today, less than half of the world's original rain forests remain.
  D. deforestation is a minor problem in today's rain forest environment.

39. According to this passage, millions of *indigenous* people live in the rain forests. *Indigenous* can best be defined as

  A. people who are transitory migrants on the land in which they live.
  B. people who own property on the land in which they live.
  C. people who are native to the land in which they live.
  D. people who work the land on which they live.

40. The author's claim at the end of the passage that *there is reason to hope rain forests will continue to survive as one of Earth's most vital and precious resources* is a(n)

  A. optimistic assertion not supported by textual evidence in the passage.
  B. inflammatory proclamation based on textual evidence in the passage.
  C. speculative declaration not supported by textual evidence in the passage.
  D. reasonable contention based on textual evidence in the passage.

IF YOU FINISH BEFORE TIME IS CALLED, CHECK YOUR WORK ON THIS SECTION ONLY. DO NOT WORK ON ANY OTHER SECTION IN THE TEST.

Answer Key

English Language Skills

1. B	9. B	17. A	25. A	33. C
2. D	10. A	18. A	26. B	34. D
3. A	11. A	19. B	27. C	35. C
4. C	12. C	20. A	28. B	36. B
5. A	13. C	21. C	29. C	37. D
6. C	14. B	22. C	30. A	38. C
7. A	15. D	23. B	31. A	39. A
8. B	16. B	24. C	32. C	40. C

Mathematics

1. A	10. D	19. D	28. C	37. D
2. B	11. A	20. B	29. C	38. D
3. D	12. B	21. B	30. A	39. C
4. A	13. B	22. D	31. A	40. D
5. B	14. D	23. D	32. A	41. C
6. A	15. B	24. B	33. D	42. D
7. C	16. A	25. A	34. B	43. B
8. C	17. D	26. A	35. D	44. A
9. C	18. D	27. B	36. B	45. C

Reading

1. A	9. D	17. A	25. B	33. A
2. D	10. C	18. B	26. C	34. C
3. A	11. A	19. D	27. A	35. C
4. B	12. C	20. A	28. A	36. C
5. B	13. C	21. D	29. C	37. C
6. C	14. B	22. A	30. B	38. D
7. A	15. A	23. A	31. B	39. C
8. C	16. B	24. B	32. D	40. D

Answer Explanations

Essay

Sample Essays

In this section of the examination, you were to prepare a written assignment on one of two topics.

Topic 1

Teaching has become a profession that is considered to be fundamental to the health of our nation. Some people contend teaching certification should be granted only after completion of a university teacher-education program. Others maintain teaching certification via an alternative route through non-university entities such as school districts, education service centers, and private agencies is appropriate. Analyze the advantages and disadvantages of each of these paths to teacher certification.

Topic 2

The sentiment has been expressed that online learning has begun to replace face-to-face instruction. Evaluate whether or not online learning has earned a rightful place as a substitute for face-to-face instruction.

You were to write a response that would be well written, organized, and defined. You were informed that your writing would be graded holistically, taking into consideration both mechanics and organization.

In your essay, you were to introduce the topic and then either explain the topic you chose or take a position about your topic and support that position.

At least two evaluators will read your essay and assign it a score. Special attention will be paid to whether you observed the following:

- Explain the purpose of your writing
- Introduce your topic effectively
- Develop a relevant thesis or claim
- Organize ideas effectively
- Include relevant details
- Cite ample textual evidence
- Use a variety of sentence patterns
- Provide an effective concluding statement
- Maintain a consistent point of view
- Apply the conventions of standard written English

A strong sample response to each prompt follows.

Topic 1 – Strong Response

Today, teacher certification takes on many pathways. Becoming a teacher can mean enrolling in a traditional college or university program leading to an education degree and/or obtaining licensure by following a non-university-based alternative route either through a private and/or public agency. Each route leading to teacher licensure comes with its own pros and cons. This paper will present an analysis of these paths to teacher certification.

Traditionally, colleges and universities offer a formal route toward becoming a certified public school teacher. Through conventional coursework and training, those wanting to become elementary and secondary teachers, whether in a defined subject matter (English, math, science, social studies, etc.) and/or in one of the many specialized fields (like exceptional education, health education, or foreign language education) can pursue a field of study that will make them eligible to apply for state teacher certification. Customarily, these college and university teacher training programs are approved by nationally-recognized accrediting agencies, which assure the state department of education granting teacher licensure that the individual seeking teacher certification has been trained in a rigorous and reputable program. When the teacher certification is approved and granted, the state department of education can rest assured that it has granted licensure (always subject to renewal requirements) to an individual who has passed a teacher certification program that has been highly recognized by a jury of educators.

Taught by credentialed professionals, most with advanced degrees, university and college programs are carefully designed and regulated. Students are put through a series of required courses in a manner designed to be beneficial to both students pursuing initial certification and the state agencies in charge of certification. Such recognized teacher training programs also come with course requirements that supplement what teachers need to know outside of immediate classroom pedagogy, such as sociology, psychology, and school law. This supplemental training equips potential teacher candidates with information far beyond the tools they need for daily classroom instruction. The intended result is a more rounded teacher candidate for our nation's ever diverse and challenging public and private schools.

The advantages of a university or college training program are certainly considerable. However, obtaining teacher certification through this route is an expensive and time-consuming process. Scheduling time to attend face-to-face classes is an obstacle for potential teacher candidates who have jobs that they cannot give up. Parents with children at home face additional hurdles.

Naturally, with the growing demand for more and more teachers in our nation's schools, non-university-based alternative teacher certification routes have taken a foothold nationwide. These teacher certification programs are usually recognized by state certification agencies and are typically shorter and less expensive than a four-year college program. These programs offer a person already in another career, typically with a college degree in a field other than education, an opportunity to enter the teaching profession. The advantage is that for those already working but contemplating a new career, non-university-based alternative teacher certification programs offer flexibility and convenience that traditional programs (pursuing a degree at a university or college) might not. For example, students who are currently employed but are now wanting to go into teaching as a career can enroll in teacher certification programs that are either held after work or on weekends in face-to-face classrooms or online. These alternative teacher certification programs, typically consisting of only the courses necessary for immediate state certification, are often highly convenient, practical, and accessible.

However, the advantages of non-university-based alternative certification, including flexibility of scheduling and affordability for students, might come at a price. These alternative programs have been criticized as lacking the rigor and quality associated with more traditional programs. For instance, alternative certification programs sometimes lack the thoroughness of preparation of more established college and university teacher-education programs. Some programs provide only superficial discussion of the many ramifications of classroom instruction, particularly, discipline issues. Consequently, alternative programs are considered by some to be quick-fixes rather than scholarly teacher training options. Nevertheless, principals seeking new teachers, especially in the commonly hard to find subject areas of math and science, generally are pleased to acquire teachers who are coming to the profession from alternative pathways.

Still, with the enormous need for more and more teachers every year, the question of who becomes our nation's teachers, and how, is a pressing issue. As the need for teachers continues to grow, more and more nontraditional teacher training programs will populate the teacher certification landscape. More and more agencies, both private and public, will provide would-be teachers the opportunity to enter the profession. At the same time, universities likely will continue to offer teacher preparation programs. With so many public and private agencies involved in teacher certification, what seems most important at the present time is that candidates for teacher certification receive rigorous and quality preparation regardless of the route they choose to take.

Evaluation of Strong Response: This is a well-written exposition. The central thesis—the advantages and disadvantages of traditional versus nontraditional teacher certification pathways—is presented clearly and effectively with relevant textual evidence (such as *Taught by credentialed professionals, most with advanced degrees, university and college programs are carefully designed and regulated.* and *For instance, alternative certification programs sometimes lack the thoroughness of preparation of more established college and university teacher-education programs.*) that clarifies the issue while the writer maintains an objective point of view. Each paragraph has a clearly identified main idea with carefully selected supporting details. Word choice is generally precise and effective (*Some programs provide only superficial discussion of the many ramifications of classroom instruction, particularly, discipline issues.*). The organization is logical and straightforward. Each paragraph transitions smoothly to the next. Point of view is unambiguous and consistent. Word choice and sentence structure vary, and errors in sentence structure, usage, and mechanics are few. Although the writing is not flawless (for instance, the writer overuses the nonstandard *and/or* and there are errors in comma usage), this essay is a strong response.

Topic 2 – Strong Response

Today, more than ever before, the nature and notion of traditional classroom instruction is changing. Increasingly, school districts and institutions of advanced learning (from community college to graduate schools) are offering course instruction in online platforms, either in blended (part online, part face-to-face) or fully online programs. In such programs, both instructors and students are provided the convenience of classroom learning that is flexibly structured and electronically delivered. Indeed, elementary, secondary and college students can take courses from the convenience of their bedroom while, in an ideal scenario, engaging in the same academic rigor required in face-to-face settings. The result, to be sure, is revolutionary, changing the way learning is delivered and consumed by the modern world. The implications, without a doubt, are far-reaching. Nowadays, as more and more individuals take online courses for initial or advanced degrees, for certification or self-improvement, or for course credit or curiosity, educators are forced to consider the pros and cons of an online education. This paper will present an analysis of this innovative approach to delivery of instruction.

Proponents of online education contend that virtual classrooms provide distinct advantages over face-to-face instruction. First, the convenience of online instruction provides a flexibility that few face-to-face classrooms can achieve. Both instructors and students can organize classroom instruction around their own schedules. Teachers can present classroom learning in defined modules, allowing students to complete assignments at their own convenience. Second, online instruction allows time for students of various personalities (aggressive or passive, extroverted or shy) to become fully-immersed in the classroom learning experience. Highly engaged students can shine as they can complete assignments quickly and contribute to online discussion boards, but without the concern that they will not be recognized for their adroitness and expertise. Similarly, less engaged or more reserved students will have the opportunity to participate in the online assignments and discussions but at their own pace and without fear of recrimination from more overpowering and domineering students. Finally, online instruction provides both teachers and students the ability to respond individually to particular needs and desires as they arise during instruction. Feedback, both from teachers and colleagues, often is more detailed and focused than that received in traditional face-to-face classroom instruction.

On the other hand, those who favor face-to-face instruction over online learning call into question the soundness and rigor of virtual instruction. They suggest the preponderance of online classroom instruction, including blended offerings, is the road to mediocrity. Online classroom instruction, especially in fields that are heavily dependent on classroom discussion and sharing diverse viewpoints, often becomes the refuge for students seeking something quick, convenient, and anonymous. Not feeling compelled to contribute in face-to-face classroom settings, some students taking online classes do the minimal work required.

Consequently, many proponents of face-to face instruction favor classroom instruction where students can meet in actual classroom settings to share their personal observations, questions, and concerns with instructors and students in real time. Recognizing and understanding body language is a valuable learning tool that is often talked about theoretically, but not experienced in online instruction. Supporters of face-to-face instruction maintain that online classes lack the spontaneity and unpredictability that live classroom interactions generate. Without the teacher and students physically present for purposeful and clarifying conversations, the spirited and unexpected "give and take" that stimulates deeper learning is absent. Instead, they contend, planned responses and delayed reactions in online classes provide an artificial arena for learning. This situation fails to reflect the reality of the workplace for students entering professions and lines of work where the majority of their time will be in face-to-face interactions. Hence the learning that is required to work cooperatively with people in real space and time is often missing in online environments.

Nevertheless, online learning has certainly earned a place at the table. The advantages of online classroom instruction, either blended or completely online, are too many to ignore. Convenience, flexibility, and self-directed learning are a few of the many advantages that online instruction offers to so many new and current students, from elementary to higher education. Hence, online learning will only increase in popularity in the years to come. Still, educators and other interested stakeholders should pay careful attention to the obvious concerns that must be considered when planning for online instruction so that all individuals involved—teachers, students, and the public at-large—benefit from instruction that is meaningful, rigorous, and sound.

Evaluation of Strong Response: This essay is a well-written, even-minded exposition. The central thesis—the pros and cons of online instruction—is presented clearly and effectively with relevant textual evidence (such as *First, the convenience of online instruction provides a flexibility that few face-to-face classrooms can achieve.* and *Consequently, many proponents of face-to face instruction favor classroom instruction where students can meet in actual classroom settings to share their personal observations, questions, and concerns with instructors and students in real time.*) that clarifies the issue while the writer maintains an objective point of view. Each paragraph has a clearly identified main idea with carefully selected supporting details. Word choice is precise and effective (*Supporters of face-to-face instruction maintain that online classes lack the spontaneity and unpredictability that live classroom interactions generate.*). The organization is logical and straightforward. Each paragraph transitions smoothly to the next. Point of view is unambiguous and consistent. Word choice and sentence structure vary, and errors in sentence structure, usage, and mechanics are few. Although the writing is not flawless (for instance, *a place at the table* is a cliché, and there are errors in comma usage), this essay is a strong response.

English Language Skills

1. **B.** Choice **B** is the correct response. This arrangement provides the most logical sequence of ideas and supporting details in the paragraph. Choices **A, C,** and **D** do not represent a logical arrangement of the possible sentence combinations.

2. **D.** Choice **D** is the correct response. Sentence 6 is the sentence LEAST relevant to this passage. The discussion of the automobile, although important to an overall discussion of transportation, does not belong in a paragraph whose sole discussion is about horses.

3. **A.** Choice **A** is the correct response. This paragraph already reads well. There is no need to rearrange the sentences in a different order.

4. **C.** Choice **C** is the correct response. Sentence 5 is the sentence LEAST relevant to this passage. The discussion of individuals who like engagement and wedding rings without precious stones is interesting but distracting to the paragraph's narrative.

5. **A.** Choice **A** is the correct response. The correct word choice is *whose*. *Who's* is a contraction for the words *who is*. *Whose* is the possessive form of the word *who*. The sentence is in the past tense, so *came* is the correct verb at **B**. The word *retrieve* at **C** is spelled and used correctly.

6. **C.** Choice **C** is the correct response. The correct word choice is *except*. The word *accept* means "to take when offered." The word *except* means "to exclude." The preposition *at* at **A** is used correctly. The word *summer* at **B** is spelled correctly because seasons do not require capitalization.

7. **A.** Choice **A** is the correct response. The correct word choice is *respectfully*. The word *respectively* means "correspondingly." The word *respectfully* means "with respect." The word *formal*, meaning "official," is the correct word choice at **B**. The word *principal*, referring to the person who is the building supervisor of the school, at **C** is the correct word choice.

8. **B.** Choice **B** is the correct response. The correct word choice is *farther*. The word *further* is used to describe abstract ideas. The word *farther* is used to describe concrete distance. The other word choices—*fourth* at **A** and *than* at **C**—are spelled and used correctly.

9. **B.** Choice **B** is the correct response. The correct word choice is *could have*. The phrase *could of* is grammatically incorrect. *Could have* is the grammatically acceptable phrase. (*Should of* is also unacceptable.) The other word choices—*aunt* at **A** and *dessert* at **C**—are spelled and used correctly. Only capitalize the word *aunt* when you are naming a specific aunt, like *Aunt Betty*. The word *dessert* means "a treat you eat after a meal." The word *desert* means "a dry, sandy place with little or no plant life."

10. **A.** Choice **A** is the correct response. The correct word choice is *capital*. The word *capitol* refers to a building. The word *capital* refers to a city. The word *receive* at **B** is spelled and used correctly. The word *their* at **C** is properly used as a possessive pronoun.

11. **A.** Choice **A** is the correct response. The correct word choice is *weather*. The word *whether* refers to a choice between two objects. The word *weather* refers to the climate. The word *admirably* at **B** is an adverb modifying the verb *performed* and is used correctly in this sentence. The word *congregants* at **C** is spelled and used correctly.

12. **C.** Choice **C** is the correct response. The correct word choice is *proceeded*. The word *proceeded* means "to venture forth or go ahead." The word *preceded* means "to come before." The other word choices—*ineligible* at **A** and *everyone* at **B**—are spelled and used correctly.

13. **C.** Choice **C** is the correct response. The correct word choice is *than*. The word *than* is used when making a comparison between two objects. The word *then* implies a time frame. The other word choices—*certainly* at **A** and *board* at **B**—are spelled and used correctly in the sentence.

14. **B.** Choice **B** is the correct response. The correct word choice is *complement*. The word *complement* means "to accompany, to match, or to complete something." The word *compliment* means "to laud praise on someone." The other word choices—*exceptional* at **A** and *considerable* at **C**—are spelled and used correctly.

15. **D.** Choice **D** is the correct response. This sentence is correct as written. The word *me* at **A** is the object of the preposition *Between*, so it should be in the objective case. The word *whether* at **B** refers to a choice between two objects and makes sense in the sentence. The word *I* at **C** is the subject of the verb *should be* (which is understood) and thus, should be in the subjective case.

16. **B.** Choice **B** is the correct response. The correct word choice is *site*. The word *site* refers to a place or setting. The word *sight* refers to one's ability to see. The other word choices—*may* at **A** and *beside* at **C**—are spelled and used correctly.

17. **A.** Choice **A** is the correct response. The sentence should be in the past tense, so *came* is the correct verb. The word *that* at **B** is correct because it introduces a restrictive clause. The comma at **C** is correct. Although you may see the omission of the comma before the coordinating conjunction *and*, the final comma in a series of three or more elements is never incorrect.

18. **A.** Choice **A** is the correct response. The word at **A** shows possession. The location belongs to the restaurant, so *restaurants* should be *restaurant's*. The word *beach* at **B** is spelled correctly. The word *really* at **C** is an adverb modifying the adjective *romantic,* so it is correct.

19. **B.** Choice **B** is the correct response. A comma is needed at **B** to separate the introductory subordinate clause from the rest of the sentence. The word *tourists* at **A** does not show possession, so no apostrophe is needed. The word *than* at **C** is correctly used as a conjunction in a comparison. The word *then* is an adverb indicating time.

20. **A.** Choice **A** is the correct response. In this sentence, the word following the verb *felt* at **A** modifies the subject (a noun). The word *badly* is an adverb. It should not be used to modify a noun. The adjective *bad* should be used instead. The word *English* at **B** is a proper noun, so it should be capitalized. The title *superintendent* at **C** should not be capitalized. Titles are capitalized when they precede proper names, but as a rule are not capitalized when used alone.

21. **C.** Choice **C** is the correct response. The *West Indies* is the name of a specific place. The full name must be capitalized. The comma at **A** is needed to set off the nonrestrictive appositive *the explorer*. The word *explorer* at **B** is not a proper noun, so it should not be capitalized.

22. **C.** Choice **C** is the correct response. The past tense of *build* is *built*, not *builded*. The word *When* at **A** is correct and makes sense in the sentence. The comma at **B** is needed to separate the introductory subordinate clause from the rest of the sentence.

23. **B.** Choice **B** is the correct response. The word *between* is a preposition. The object of a preposition should be in the objective case. Change *I* at **B** to *me* to make the sentence grammatically correct. The sentence is in the present tense, so *am* at **A** is the correct verb. The word *that* at **C** is correct. It would be redundant to use *because* at **C**; the word *because* means "for the reason that."

24. **C.** Choice **C** is the correct response. The underlined portion at **C** is the subject of the verb *can run* (which is understood) and, thus, should be in the subjective case. Change *them other athletes* to *those other athletes* to make the sentence grammatically correct. The pronoun *who* at **A** is correct because it is the subject of the subordinate clause it introduces. The word *faster* at **B** is the correct comparative form of the adverb *fast*.

25. **A.** Choice **A** is the correct response. The singular pronoun *it* is the subject of the verb at **A**, so change *don't* to *doesn't* to make the verb agree with its singular subject. No comma is needed at **B**. The second-person pronoun *you* at **C** is correct. It would be incorrect to switch to the third-person pronoun *one*.

26. **B.** Choice **B** is the correct response. The word at **B** should be spelled *mathematics*. The word *siblings* at **A** does not show possession, so no apostrophe is needed. The reflexive pronoun *myself* at **C** is used correctly to refer to its antecedent *I*.

27. **C.** Choice **C** is the correct response. The plural noun *media* is the subject of the verb at **C**, so change *is* to *are* to make the verb agree with its plural subject. The introductory word *there* at **A** is the correct word choice. The sentence is in the past tense, so *was* is the correct verb at **B**.

28. **B.** Choice **B** is the correct response. The past participle for the verb *to eat* is *eaten*. Note that *should of* in **A** and **C** is an error for *should have*.

29. **C.** Choice **C** is the correct response. The tense of the verb in Choice **C** relates logically to the verb in the main clause. The verb tenses in choices **A** and **B** do not.

30. **A.** Choice **A** is the correct response. The singular pronoun *Everyone* is the subject of the verb at **A**, so change *have enjoyed* to *has enjoyed* to make the verb agree with its singular subject. The plural form of *goldfish* at **B** is written correctly. The word *castle* at **C** is spelled correctly.

31. **A.** Choice **A** is the correct response. The word *Each* is the singular antecedent of the possessive pronoun at **A**. Use *his* instead of the plural pronoun *their* to refer to the singular antecedent *Each*. No comma is needed at **B**. The preposition *between* at **C** is correctly used to indicate a relationship involving two things. The preposition *among* is used when the relationship involves more than two elements.

32. **C.** Choice **C** is the correct response. Without clarification, the reader does not know whether *them* at **C** refers to *students* or *books*. Change *them* to *the books* to avoid ambiguity. No comma is needed at **A**. The word *organizations* at **B** does not show possession, so no apostrophe is needed.

33. **C.** Choice **C** is the correct response. In this sentence the words *studying, reading,* and *to write* should be parallel. You can correct this faulty parallelism by changing *to write* at **C** to *writing*. The word *middle* at **A** is not a proper noun, so it should not be capitalized. The word *grammar* at **B** is spelled correctly.

34. **D.** Choice **D** is the correct response. This sentence is correct as written. The word *quite*, meaning "rather," at **A** is spelled correctly and makes sense in the sentence. The possessive pronoun *his* at **B** is correct because *his* modifies the gerund *meddling*. The verb *personal* at **C** is spelled correctly and makes sense in the sentence.

35. **C.** Choice **C** is the correct response. The word at **C** is a noun, so *affect* should be changed to *effect* to make the sentence grammatically correct. The word *professors* at **A** does not show possession, so no apostrophe is needed. The singular verb *was* at **B** agrees with its singular subject *One*.

36. **B.** Choice **B** is the correct response. The word at **B** should be spelled *height*, not *heighth*. The sentence is in the past tense, so *measured* at **A** is the correct verb. No comma is needed at **C**.

37. **D.** Choice **D** is the correct response. This sentence is correct as written. The possessive word *Bess's* is punctuated correctly. The word *friends* at **B** is spelled correctly. At **C** the superlative form of *unusual* is *most unusual*, not *unusualest*.

38. **C.** Choice **C** is the correct response. All punctuation in sentence **C** is correct. Choice **A** is incorrect because it creates a comma splice with two independent clauses joined by only a comma. Choices **B** and **D** are run-on sentences. Each of these sentences has two independent clauses joined without a word to connect them or a proper punctuation mark to separate them.

39. **A.** Choice **A** is the correct response. All punctuation in Choice **A** is correct. In Choice **B**, the word *familys'* is incorrect. To form the possessive of a noun (either singular or plural) that does not end in *s*, add an apostrophe and *s*. Choice **C** is incorrect because it contains a fragment: *Preferring to be hand-fed canned tuna*. A comma is needed in Choice **D** to separate the introductory participial phrase from the rest of the sentence.

40. **C.** Choice **C** is the correct response. The modifiers in Choice **C** are placed correctly. The participial phrase *Rushing to finish the surprise dinner on time* modifies *Melissa*, the subject of the main clause of the sentence, and should be close to it. In choices **B** and **D,** *Rushing to finish the surprise dinner on time* is separated from the subject *Melissa*, resulting in ambiguity. The subordinate clause *that was rotten* modifies the noun *egg*, and should be close to it. In choices **A** and **B**, *that was rotten* seems to modify the noun *neighbor*, which clearly is not the intent of the writer.

Mathematics

1. **A.** Choice **A** is the correct response. The part of the total number of paintings purchased by the art connoisseur is $\frac{5}{20} = \frac{1}{4} = \frac{25}{100} = 0.25$. Choice **A** is the only choice that is not equivalent to $\frac{5}{20}$.

2. **B.** Choice **B** is the correct response. You need to separate $4\frac{1}{2}$ pounds into equal $\frac{3}{8}$-pound patties. You use division to separate a whole into equal parts. You want the units of your answer to be patties. Carry the units along in your computation, so you can see the units of the answer work out to be patties.

$$4\frac{1}{2} \text{ pounds} \div \frac{3}{8} \frac{\text{pounds}}{\text{patties}} = \frac{9}{2} \text{ pounds} \times \frac{8}{3} \frac{\text{patties}}{\text{pounds}} = \frac{\cancel{9}^3}{\cancel{2}_1} \text{ pounds} \times \frac{\cancel{8}^4}{\cancel{3}_1} \frac{\text{patties}}{\text{pounds}} = \frac{12 \text{ patties}}{1} = 12 \text{ patties}$$

As you can see, the pounds "cancel out" when you multiply.

12 hamburger patties can be made, Choice **B**.

Did I answer the question? Yes, I found how many patties can be made. ✓

Does my answer make sense? Yes, $\frac{3}{8}$ is a little less than $\frac{1}{2}$ pound. Separating $4\frac{1}{2}$ pounds into $\frac{1}{2}$-pound patties would yield 9 patties, so 12 patties seems reasonable. ✓

Is the answer stated in the correct units? Yes, the units are patties, which is correct. ✓

Choice **A** results if you multiply instead of divide. Choices **C** and **D** result if you divide incorrectly.

3. **D.** Choice **D** is the correct response. To evaluate the expression $6 + 2^3 \cdot 3 \div 3 + 7$, follow the order of operations using the mnemonic "Please Excuse My Dear Aunt Sally":

$6 + 2^3 \cdot 3 \div 3 + 7 = 6 + 8 \cdot 3 \div 3 + 7$ No parentheses are involved; so first, perform exponentiation.
$6 + 24 \div 3 + 7 = 6 + 8 + 7$ Next, multiply and divide from left to right.
$= 21$, Choice **D**   Finally, add from left to right.

Choice **A, B,** or **C** results if you fail to follow the order of operations properly.

4. **A.** Choice **A** is the correct response. To solve the problem, do two steps. First, subtract the older granddaughter's part from the whole. Then, divide what remains into four equal parts.

   Step 1. The older granddaughter inherits $\frac{1}{3}$ of the land. Subtract to find the remaining part of the land.
   $$1 - \frac{1}{3} = \frac{2}{3}$$

   Step 2. The younger granddaughter and her three brothers equally share the remaining part of the land. Use division to separate $\frac{2}{3}$ into four equal parts.
   $$\frac{2}{3} \div 4 = \frac{2}{3} \div \frac{4}{1} = \frac{2}{3} \cdot \frac{1}{4} = \frac{\cancel{2}^1}{3} \cdot \frac{1}{\cancel{4}_2} = \frac{1}{6}$$

   The younger granddaughter inherits $\frac{1}{6}$ of the land, Choice **A**.

   Did I answer the question? Yes, I found the fraction of the land the younger granddaughter inherits. ✓

   Does my answer make sense? Yes. The younger granddaughter shares $\frac{2}{3}$ of the land with the three grandsons, so $\frac{1}{6}$ as her share seems reasonable. ✓

   Is the answer stated in the correct units? The answer is a fractional portion, so no units are needed. ✓

   Choice **B** results if you fail to subtract the older granddaughter's part from the whole before dividing. Choice **C** results if you make a computation error in Step 2. Choice **D** results if you fail to do Step 2 after you complete Step 1.

5. **B.** Choice **B** is the correct response. To find the difference in temperature, subtract the temperature shown on the graph for Location 2 (–5°F) from the temperature for Location 4 (35°F): 35°F – (–5°F) = 35°F + 5°F = 40°F. The temperature difference is 40°F, Choice **B**.

   Choice **A** results if you make the mistake of adding the temperatures algebraically, instead of subtracting them. Choice **C** results if you subtract the Location 4 temperature from the Location 2 temperature. Choice **D** results if you mistakenly add the temperatures algebraically and make a sign error.

6. **A.** Choice **A** is the correct response. A function is a relation in which each first element is paired with *one and only one* second element. In other words, no two ordered pairs have the same first element and different second elements. Only the relation in Choice A does not satisfy this requirement because the ordered pairs (3, 1) and (3, 10) have the same first element, but different second elements, namely 1 and 10.

7. **C.** Choice **C** is the correct response.

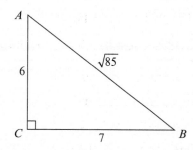

   Using the Pythagorean theorem, where $a = 6$, $b = 7$, and $c = \overline{AB}$, the hypotenuse, you have
   $$\begin{aligned} c^2 &= a^2 + b^2 \\ &= 6^2 + 7^2 \\ &= 36 + 49 \\ &= 85 \end{aligned}$$

   which means $c = \sqrt{85}$, the length of side $\overline{AB}$, the hypotenuse of right triangle ABC.

To approximate the value of $\sqrt{85}$, find two consecutive integers such that the square of the first integer is less than 85 and the square of the second integer is greater than 85. Given 9^2 is $81 < 85$ and 10^2 is $100 > 85$, the approximate value of $\sqrt{85}$ is between 9 and 10, Choice **C**.

8. **C.** Choice **C** is the correct response. To solve the problem, do three steps. First, find the number of over-limit minutes; next, find the cost of the over-limit minutes; and then, find the total charges by adding the cost of the over-limit minutes to the regular monthly charge.

   Step 1. Subtract to find how many minutes of calls are over the 500 limit.

   $$615 \text{ minutes} - 500 \text{ minutes} = 115 \text{ minutes}$$

   Step 2. Find the cost for the over-limit minutes by multiplying by $0.30 per minute.

   $$115 \text{ minutes} \times \$0.30/\text{minute} = \$34.50$$

   Step 3. Add the over-limit charges to the monthly charge.

   $$\$29.99 + \$34.50 = \$64.49$$

   Demetria's total charges for her cellphone calls last month are $64.49, Choice **C**.

   Did I answer the question? Yes, I found Demetria's total charges for her cellphone calls last month. ✓

   Does my answer make sense? Yes, 100 over-limit minutes at $0.30 per minute would add $30 (because 100 × $0.30 = $30) to the regular monthly charge, so $34.50 for 115 over-limit minutes seems reasonable. ✓

   Is the answer stated in the correct units? Yes, the units are dollars, which is correct. ✓

   Choice **A** does not include the over-limit charges. Choice **B** is the over-limit charges only. Choice **D** is the result of treating the 615 minutes as over-limit charges and not adding in the $29.99.

9. **C.** Choice **C** is the correct response. Evaluate the numbers.

   $$-\sqrt{49} = -7, \sqrt{\frac{25}{36}} = \frac{5}{6}, \sqrt[3]{-27} = -3, \sqrt[4]{16} = 2, \sqrt{64} = 8$$

   Each of these numbers is a rational number, Choice **C**. Choice **A** is incorrect because only 2 and 8 are whole numbers. Choice **B** is incorrect because $\frac{5}{6}$ is not an integer. Choice **D** is incorrect because none of the numbers are irrational.

10. **D.** Choice **D** is the correct response. Determine the ratio of c to n:

    $$\frac{432}{6} = \frac{72}{1}, \frac{864}{12} = \frac{72}{1}, \text{ and } \frac{1{,}296}{18} = \frac{72}{1}$$

    Thus, $c = 72n$, Choice **D**.

    Choices **A** and **C** occur if you use the ratio of n to c for the ratio of c to n. Choice **B** occurs if you add instead of multiply by the constant of variation.

11. **A.** Choice **A** is the correct response. Sketch a diagram to illustrate the problem.

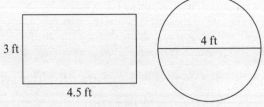

To solve the problem, do three steps. First, find the area of the rectangular table; next, find the area of the circular table; and then find the difference between the two areas.

Step 1. Find the area of the rectangular table.

The Mathematics Reference Sheet shows the formula for the area of a rectangle is $A = lw$.

$$A = lw = 4.5 \text{ ft} \cdot 3 \text{ ft} = 13.5 \text{ ft}^2$$

Step 2. Find the area of the circular table.

The Mathematics Reference Sheet shows the formula for the area of a circle is $A = \pi r^2$. The diameter of the circular table is 4 feet. The radius is half the diameter, or 2 feet.

$$A = \pi r^2 = \pi (2 \text{ ft})^2 \approx 3.14(4 \text{ ft}^2) = 12.56 \text{ ft}^2$$

Step 3. Find the difference between the two areas.

$$13.5 \text{ ft}^2 - 12.56 \text{ ft}^2 = 0.94 \text{ ft}^2$$

The area of the circular table will be 0.94 ft² less than the area of the rectangular table, Choice **A**.

Did I answer the question? Yes, I found how much less the area of the circular table will be than the area of the rectangular table. ✓

Does my answer make sense? Yes. The two tables are close in size, so the difference in area of less than 1 ft² makes sense. ✓

Is the answer stated in the correct units? Yes, the units are square feet, which is correct. ✓

Choice **B** is the area of the circular table, not the difference in the two areas. Choice **C** is the sum of the two areas, not the difference. Choice **D** results if you use 4 feet for the radius in finding the area of the circular table.

12. B. Choice **B** is the correct response. Sketch a diagram to illustrate the problem.

```
        P = 50 ft
     ┌─────────────┐
     │             │
     │   A = ?     │ 7 ft
     │             │
     └─────────────┘
        l = ?
```

The garden has a rectangular shape. The Mathematics Reference Sheet shows the formula for the area of a rectangle is $A = lw$. You are given the width of the garden is 7 feet, but you do not know the length of the garden. You will need to find the length of the garden before you can find its area. To solve the problem, do two steps. First, find the length of the garden using the information given about its perimeter. Then, find the area of the garden using the formula $A = lw$.

Step 1. Find the length of the garden.

The formula for the perimeter of a rectangle is $P = 2l + 2w$. The perimeter, P, is 50 feet. The width, w, is 7 feet. Let l equal the length of the rectangle in feet.

$P = 2l + 2w$

$50 \text{ ft} = 2l + 2(7 \text{ ft})$ Substitute 50 ft for P and 7 ft for w. Solve for l, omitting the units for convenience.

$50 = 2l + 14$ Multiply $2(7) = 14$.

$50 - 14 = 2l + 14 - 14$ Subtract 14 from both sides of the equation.

$36 = 2l$ Simplify.

$\dfrac{36}{2} = \dfrac{2l}{2}$ Divide both sides of the equation by 2.

$18 = l$

The length of the rectangle is 18 feet.

Step 2. Find the area of the rectangular garden.

$$A = lw = (18 \text{ ft})(7 \text{ ft}) = 126 \text{ ft}^2$$

The area of the garden is 126 ft², Choice **B**.

Did I answer the question? Yes, I found the area of the garden. ✓

Does my answer make sense? Yes. The perimeter is 50 feet, so an area of 126 ft² seems reasonable. ✓

Is the answer stated in the correct units? Yes, the units are square feet, which is correct. ✓

Choice **A** results if you stop at Step 1 and incorrectly use your solution to the equation as the area of the garden. Choice **C** results if you mistakenly confuse perimeter with area. Choice **D** results if you incorrectly compute the area of the garden by multiplying 50 feet by 7 feet.

13. **B.** Choice **B** is the correct response. Sketch a diagram to illustrate the problem.

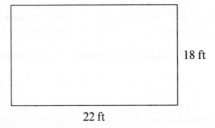

Square yards are units of area, so find the area of the carpet in square yards. To solve the problem, do two steps. First, convert the dimensions of the floor to yards. Next, find the area of the floor in square yards.

Step 1. Convert the dimensions of the floor to yards.

The Mathematics Reference Sheet shows 1 yard = 3 feet. Therefore, the conversion fractions are $\frac{3 \text{ ft}}{1 \text{ yd}}$ or $\frac{1 \text{ yd}}{3 \text{ ft}}$.

Write each dimension of the floor as a fraction with denominator 1 and let unit analysis tell you whether to multiply by $\frac{3 \text{ ft}}{1 \text{ yd}}$ or $\frac{1 \text{ yd}}{3 \text{ ft}}$. Because you want the feet to divide out, multiply by $\frac{1 \text{ yd}}{3 \text{ ft}}$.

$$\frac{22 \text{ ft}}{1} \cdot \frac{1 \text{ yd}}{3 \text{ ft}} = \frac{22 \text{ ft}}{1} \cdot \frac{1 \text{ yd}}{3 \text{ ft}} = \frac{22 \text{ yd}}{3} = 7\frac{1}{3} \text{ yd}$$

$$\frac{18 \text{ ft}}{1} \cdot \frac{1 \text{ yd}}{3 \text{ ft}} = \frac{\cancel{18}^6 \text{ ft}}{1} \cdot \frac{1 \text{ yd}}{\cancel{3}_1 \text{ ft}} = 6 \text{ yd}$$

Step 2. Find the area of the floor.

The Mathematics Reference Sheet shows the formula for the area of a rectangle is $A = lw$.

$$A = lw = \left(7\frac{1}{3} \text{ yd}\right)(6 \text{ yd}) = \left(\frac{22}{3} \text{ yd}\right)\left(\frac{6}{1} \text{ yd}\right) = \left(\frac{22}{\cancel{3}_1} \text{ yd}\right)\left(\frac{\cancel{6}^2}{1} \text{ yd}\right) = 44 \text{ yd}^2$$

At least 44 yd² of carpet are needed to cover the floor, Choice **B**.

Did I answer the question? Yes, I found how many square yards of carpet are needed to cover the floor. ✓

Does my answer make sense? Yes. A 7-yard by 6-yard area is 42 yd², so $7\frac{1}{3}$ yard by 6 yard should be a little more. ✓

Is the answer stated in the correct units? Yes, the units are square yards, which is correct. ✓

Choices **A** and **D** result if you make a computation error. Choice **C** results if you neglect to convert your dimensions to yards.

14. **D.** Choice **D** is the correct response. Sketch a diagram to illustrate the problem.

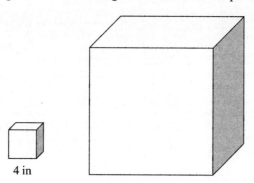

To solve the problem, do two steps. First, find the volume of one 4-inch cube. Then, find the volume of the crate by multiplying the volume of one 4-inch cube by 81.

Step 1. Find the volume of one 4-inch cube.

The Mathematics Reference Sheet shows the formula for the volume of a prism is $V = Bh$, where B is the area of the base of the prism and h is the height. A cube is a prism in which all edges have the same length. A 4-inch cube has a square base that is 4 inches on a side and the height of the cube is 4 inches. The volume of the 4-inch cube is

$$V_{cube} = Bh = s \cdot s \cdot h = 4 \text{ in} \cdot 4 \text{ in} \cdot 4 \text{ in} = 64 \text{ in}^3$$

Tip: It might be easier for you to just memorize the volume of a cube is $V = s^3$, where s is the length of an edge of the cube.

Step 2. Find the volume of the crate.

It takes 81 cubes to fill the crate, so the volume of the crate is

$V_{crate} = 81 \cdot$ (volume of one cube) $= 81 \cdot 64 \text{ in}^3 = 5{,}184 \text{ in}^3$, Choice **D.**

Did I answer the question? Yes, I found the volume of the crate. ✓

Does my answer make sense? Yes. $80 \cdot 60$ is 4,800, so $81 \cdot 64 = 5{,}184$ is reasonable. ✓

Is the answer stated in the correct units? Yes, the units are in³, which is correct. ✓

Choice **A** results if you stop at Step 1 and mistakenly use the volume of one 4-inch cube as the volume of the crate. Choice **B** results if you mistakenly use the number of cubes in the crate as its volume in cubic inches. Choice **C** results if you make a computation error in Step 2.

15. **B.** Choice **B** is the correct response. Sketch a diagram to illustrate the problem.

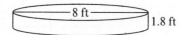

The Mathematics Reference Sheet shows the formula for the volume of a cylinder is $V = Bh$, where B is the area of the base of the cylinder and h is the height. The base of the cylinder is a circle. The Mathematics Reference Sheet shows the area of a circle is πr^2. The diameter of the cylinder is 8 feet. The radius of the circle is half the diameter, or 4 feet. The volume of the cylinder is

$$V = Bh = \pi r^2 h \approx 3.14(4 \text{ ft})^2(1.8 \text{ ft}) = 90.432 \text{ ft}^3$$

The volume of the cube is approximately 90 ft³, Choice **B.**

Choices **A** and **C** result if you use an incorrect formula for the volume of a cylinder. Choice **D** results if you make the error of using 8 feet instead of 4 feet as the radius of the cylinder's base.

16. **A.** Choice **A** is the correct response. Sketch a diagram to illustrate the problem.

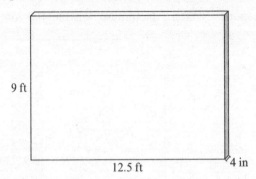

Cubic feet are units of volume. The amount of cement in the slab is equal to the volume of the slab, which has the shape of a rectangular prism. To solve the problem, do two steps. First, convert 4 inches to feet because the question asks for the number of cubic feet of cement. Then, find the volume of the slab in cubic feet.

Step 1. Convert 4 inches to feet.

The Mathematics Reference Sheet shows 3 feet = 36 inches. You can write this fact as $\frac{3 \text{ ft}}{36 \text{ in}}$ and reduce to obtain $\frac{1 \text{ ft}}{12 \text{ in}}$ as one of your conversion fractions and $\frac{12 \text{ in}}{1 \text{ ft}}$ as your other conversion fraction.

Write your measurement as a fraction with denominator 1 and let unit analysis tell you whether to multiply by $\frac{1 \text{ ft}}{12 \text{ in}}$ or $\frac{12 \text{ in}}{1 \text{ ft}}$. Because you want the inches to divide out, multiply by $\frac{1 \text{ ft}}{12 \text{ in}}$.

$$\frac{4 \text{ in}}{1} \cdot \frac{1 \text{ ft}}{12 \text{ in}} = \frac{\cancel{4}^1 \text{ in}}{1} \cdot \frac{1 \text{ ft}}{\cancel{12}_3 \text{ in}} = \frac{1}{3} \text{ ft}$$

Step 2. Find the volume of the slab.

The Mathematics Reference Sheet shows the formula for the volume of a prism is $V = Bh$, where B is the area of the base of the prism and h is the height. The base of the prism is a rectangle. The Mathematics Reference Sheet shows the formula for the area of a rectangle is $A = lw$. The volume of the cement is

$$V = Bh = l \cdot w \cdot h = (12.5 \text{ ft})(9 \text{ ft})\left(\frac{1}{3} \text{ ft}\right) = (12.5 \text{ ft})(\cancel{9}^3 \text{ ft})\left(\frac{1}{\cancel{3}_1} \text{ ft}\right) = 37.5 \text{ ft}^3$$

Tip: It might be easier for you to just memorize the volume of a rectangular prism is $V = lwh$, where l is the length, w is the width, and h is the height of the rectangular prism.

There are 37.5 ft³ of cement in the slab, Choice **A**.

Did I answer the question? Yes, I found how many cubic feet of cement are in the slab. ✓

Does my answer make sense? Yes. The slab is not very thick, so 37.5 ft³ seems reasonable. ✓

Is the answer stated in the correct units? Yes, the units are ft³, which is correct. ✓

Choice **B** results if you use an incorrect formula for the volume of a rectangular prism. Choice **C** results if you fail to change 4 inches to $\frac{1}{3}$ feet. Choice **D** results if you place the decimal point incorrectly when computing the volume.

17. D. Choice **D** is the correct response. Sketch and label the dimensions on the diagram. Show 5-inch squares cut out on each corner.

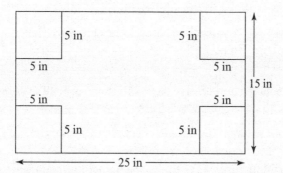

To solve the problem, do two steps. First, use the diagram to find the dimensions of the box in inches. Next, find the volume of the box in cubic inches.

Step 1. Find the dimensions of the box.

From the preceding diagram, you can see the length of the box is 25 in – 2(5 in) = 25 in – 10 in = 15 in. The width of the box is 15 in – 10 in = 5 in. The height of the box is 5 inches.

Step 2. Find the volume of the box.

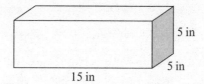

The box is a rectangular prism. The Mathematics Reference Sheet shows the formula for the volume of a prism is $V = Bh$, where B is the area of the base of the prism and h is the height. The base of the prism is a rectangle. The Mathematics Reference Sheet shows the formula for the area of a rectangle is $A = lw$. The volume of the box is

$$V = Bh = lw \cdot h = 15 \text{ in} \cdot 5 \text{ in} \cdot 5 \text{ in} = 375 \text{ in}^3$$

The volume of the box is 375 in³, Choice **D**.

Did I answer the question? Yes, I found the volume of the box. ✓

Does my answer make sense? Yes. The box is small, so 375 in³ for its volume seems reasonable. ✓

Is the answer stated in the correct units? Yes, the units are cubic inches, which is correct. ✓

The other choices result if you determine incorrect measurements for the dimensions of the box.

18. D. Choice **D** is the correct response. Sketch a diagram to illustrate the problem. Of course, you can't draw it exactly to scale, but the sketch will help you "see" the situation.

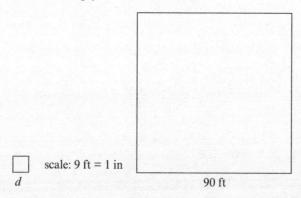

Let d = the distance between consecutive bases in the scale model. The scale model and the baseball diamond can be represented with two squares. The squares are similar figures, so the measurements of their corresponding sides are proportional. Write a proportion and solve it.

The ratio of the distance between consecutive bases in the actual baseball diamond to the distance between consecutive bases in the model is $\frac{9 \text{ ft}}{1 \text{ in}}$:

$$\frac{\text{distance between consecutive bases of actual baseball diamond}}{\text{distance between consecutive bases in model}} = \frac{9 \text{ ft}}{1 \text{ in}}$$

Plug in the values from your diagram. Be sure to check that the units match up correctly.

$$\frac{90 \text{ ft}}{d(\text{in})} = \frac{9 \text{ ft}}{1 \text{ in}}$$ Check: Both ratios have feet in the numerator and inches in the denominator.

For convenience, omit the units while you solve the proportion:

$$\frac{90}{d} = \frac{9}{1}$$

Multiply 90 by 1 and then divide by 9:

$$\frac{90 \cdot 1}{9} = 10$$

The distance between consecutive bases in the scale model is 10 inches, Choice **D**.

Did I answer the question? Yes, I found the distance between bases in the scale model. ✓

Does my answer make sense? Yes. A scale of 10 feet to 1 inch would give 9 inches as the distance between bases, so 10 inches is a reasonable answer for a scale of 9 feet to 1 inch. ✓

Is the answer stated in the correct units? Yes, the units are inches, which is correct. ✓

Choices **A** and **B** result if you make a computation error when solving the proportion. Choice **C** results if you set up the proportion incorrectly.

19. **D.** Choice **D** is the correct response. Three conversion facts from the Mathematics Reference Sheet are needed to solve the problem: 1 pint = 2 cups, 1 quart = 2 pints, and 1 gallon = 4 quarts. From these three facts, you get six conversion fractions:

$$\frac{1 \text{ pt}}{2 \text{ c}} \text{ and } \frac{2 \text{ c}}{1 \text{ pt}}, \frac{1 \text{ qt}}{2 \text{ pt}} \text{ and } \frac{2 \text{ pt}}{1 \text{ qt}}, \text{ and } \frac{1 \text{ gal}}{4 \text{ qt}} \text{ and } \frac{4 \text{ qt}}{1 \text{ gal}}$$

Write your measurement as a fraction with denominator 1 and let unit analysis tell you which conversion fractions to multiply by, keeping in mind you want cups as your final units:

$$\frac{5 \text{ gal}}{1} \cdot ?$$

There are only two conversion fractions that involve gallons: $\frac{1 \text{ gal}}{4 \text{ qt}}$ and $\frac{4 \text{ qt}}{1 \text{ gal}}$. Because you want the gallons to divide out, multiply by $\frac{4 \text{ qt}}{1 \text{ gal}}$.

$$\frac{5 \cancel{\text{gal}}}{1} \cdot \frac{4 \text{ qt}}{1 \cancel{\text{gal}}}$$

This product has quarts as the units. You want to have cups as the units, but there is no conversion fraction that involves quarts and cups, so change quarts to pints by multiplying by $\frac{2 \text{ pt}}{1 \text{ qt}}$:

$$\frac{5 \text{ gal}}{1} \cdot \frac{4 \text{ qt}}{1 \text{ gal}} \cdot \frac{2 \text{ pt}}{1 \text{ qt}}$$

Now the product has pints as the units because both gallons and quarts divide out.

To change the pints to cups, multiply by $\frac{2 \text{ c}}{1 \text{ pt}}$:

$$\frac{5 \text{ gal}}{1} \cdot \frac{4 \text{ qt}}{1 \text{ gal}} \cdot \frac{2 \text{ pt}}{1 \text{ qt}} \cdot \frac{2 \text{ c}}{1 \text{ pt}} = 80 \text{ cups}$$

The final answer is in cups because gallons, quarts, and pints divide out when you do the multiplication.

A 5-gallon container of water holds 80 cups of water, Choice **D**. The other answer choices occur if you use incorrect conversion facts or fractions.

Did I answer the question? Yes, I found the number of cups in a 5-gallon container of water. ✓

Does my answer make sense? Yes. You would expect a gallon to hold a lot of cups. ✓

Is the answer stated in the correct units? Yes, the units are cups, which is correct. ✓

20. B. Choice **B** is the correct response.

Method 1: Use the conversion fact, 1 kilometer = 1000 meters, from the Mathematics Reference Sheet to obtain two conversion fractions: $\frac{1 \text{ km}}{1000 \text{ m}}$ and $\frac{1000 \text{ m}}{1 \text{ km}}$.

Write your measurement as a fraction with denominator 1 and let unit analysis tell you whether to multiply by $\frac{1 \text{ km}}{1000 \text{ m}}$ or $\frac{1000 \text{ m}}{1 \text{ km}}$. Because you want the meters to divide out, multiply by $\frac{1 \text{ km}}{1000 \text{ m}}$.

$$\frac{12\,500 \text{ m}}{1} \cdot \frac{1 \text{ km}}{1000 \text{ m}} = \frac{12\,500 \text{ m}}{1} \cdot \frac{1 \text{ km}}{1000 \text{ m}} = \frac{12\,500 \text{ m}}{1000} = 12.5 \text{ km}$$

Method 2: Use "<u>K</u>ing <u>H</u>enry <u>D</u>oesn't <u>U</u>sually <u>D</u>rink <u>C</u>hocolate <u>M</u>ilk," which is a mnemonic for remembering the following metric prefixes:

kilo-, hecto-, deca-, unit measurement, deci-, centi-, milli-

In this problem, the unit measurement is meters. You are going from meters to kilometers. Because to go from meters to kilometers you move left three times on the list above, you will divide by 10 three times to convert meters to kilometers. Of course, dividing by 10 three times is equivalent to dividing by 1000 one time.

Therefore,

12 500 m = 12 500 ÷ 1000 (3 moves left) = 12.5 km

The runner ran 12.5 kilometers in the race, Choice **B**.

The other choices occur if you make a mistake in where to place the decimal point in your answer.

21. B. Choice **B** is the correct response. The sum of the measures of the interior angles of a triangle is 180°. Thus, the measure of $\angle B$ is 180° − 25° − 60° = 95°. An obtuse angle measures more than 90° but less than 180°. Angle *B* is greater than 90° but less than 180°. It is obtuse, Choice **B**.

An acute angle (Choice **A**) measures more than 0° but less than 90°. A right angle (Choice **C**) measures exactly 90°. A straight angle (Choice **D**) measures exactly 180°.

22. **D.** Choice **D** is the correct response. The sum of the measures of the interior angles of a triangle is 180°. Check the answer choices to find the one that satisfies this requirement.

Checking **A**: 30° + 50° + 80° = 160° ≠ 180°, wrong.

Checking **B**: You should eliminate this choice by sight because 100° + 200° = 300° > 180°.

Checking **C**: 120° + 50° + 20° = 190° ≠ 180°, wrong.

Checking **D**: 40° + 50° + 90° = 180°, correct.

23. **D.** Choice **D** is the correct response. The Mathematics Reference Sheet shows the circumference of a circle is equal to the product of π and the diameter of the circle: $C = \pi d$. To find the diameter, plug in 48 inches for C and 3.14 for π and solve for d:

$$C = \pi d$$
$$48 \text{ in} = 3.14d$$
$$\frac{48 \text{ in}}{3.14} = \frac{3.14d}{3.14} \quad \text{Divide both sides of the equation by 3.14.}$$
$$15.29 \text{ in (approximately)} = d, \text{ Choice } \mathbf{D}.$$

Choices **A** and **B** result if you solve the equation incorrectly. Choice **C** results if you use an incorrect formula for the circumference of a circle.

24. **B.** Choice **B** is the correct response. The coordinates of point P are (–3, 2). The x-coordinate of the new point is 5 units to the right of –3. The number 2 is 5 units to the right of –3. The x-coordinate of the new point is 2. The y-coordinate of point P is 2. The y-coordinate of the new point is 6 units down from point P. The number –4 is 6 units down from 2. The y-coordinate of the new point is –4. The coordinates of the new point are (2, –4), Choice **B**. Choice **A** occurs if you calculate the new y-coordinate incorrectly. Choice **C** occurs if you calculate both new coordinates incorrectly. Choice **D** occurs if you calculate the x-coordinate incorrectly.

25. **A.** Choice **A** is the correct response. Examine the diagram. *Note:* $\overline{AB} \parallel \overline{DC}$ means $\overline{AB}$ is parallel to $\overline{DC}$, and $\overline{AD} \parallel \overline{BC}$ means $\overline{AD}$ is parallel to $\overline{BC}$.

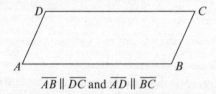

$\overline{AB} \parallel \overline{DC}$ and $\overline{AD} \parallel \overline{BC}$

A parallelogram is a quadrilateral that has opposite sides parallel. The most specific name for the figure shown is parallelogram, Choice **A**. Choices **B** and **C** are incorrect because rectangles and squares are parallelograms that have four right interior angles. The figure does not indicate the angles in the figure are right angles. Choice **D** is incorrect because, although the figure is a quadrilateral, "quadrilateral" is not the most specific name for the figure.

26. **A.** Choice **A** is the correct response. Let n be the number of months of membership at which Cash and Joe will have paid the same total amount. Write an equation to represent the facts.

$$\$40 + \$20n = \$70 + \$18n$$

Solve the equation (omitting the units for convenience).

$$40 + 20n = 70 + 18n$$
$$40 + 20n - 18n = 70 + 18n - 18n \quad \text{Subtract } 18n \text{ from both sides of the equation.}$$
$$40 + 2n = 70 \quad \text{Simplify.}$$
$$40 + 2n - 40 = 70 - 40 \quad \text{Subtract 40 from both sides of the equation.}$$
$$2n = 30 \quad \text{Simplify.}$$
$$\frac{2n}{2} = \frac{30}{2} \quad \text{Divide both sides of the equation by 2.}$$
$$n = 15 \quad \text{Simplify}$$

At the 15th month, Cash and Joe will have paid the same total amount. Choice **A** is the correct response.

Choices **B** and **C** occur if you set up an incorrect equation. Choice **D** occurs if you make an error when solving the equation.

Did I answer the question? Yes, I found the month at which Cash and Joe will have paid the same total amount. ✓

Does my answer make sense? Yes. Cash's enrollment fee was less than Joe's, but she pays more per month, so it will take a while before the total amounts paid are equal. ✓

Is the answer stated in the correct units? Yes, the units are months, which is correct. ✓

27. **B.** Choice **B** is the correct response. Sketch a diagram to illustrate the problem.

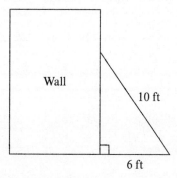

Because the ladder and the wall of the building form a right triangle, use the Pythagorean theorem (from the Mathematics Reference Sheet) to find the length of the missing side. Let b represent the distance from the base of the wall to the top of the ladder. This distance is the length of the missing leg of the right triangle. The length (10 feet) of the ladder is the length of the hypotenuse, c, of the right triangle. The length of the known leg, a, of the triangle is 6 feet. Substitute these values into the Pythagorean theorem, omitting the units for convenience:

$$a^2 + b^2 = c^2$$
$$6^2 + b^2 = 10^2$$
$$36 + b^2 = 100$$
$$36 + b^2 - 36 = 100 - 36 \quad \text{Subtract 36 from both sides.}$$
$$b^2 = 64$$

Because $b^2 = 64$, to find b, you must think of a number that multiplies by itself to give 64. Given $8 \cdot 8 = 64$, $b = 8$ ft.

Note: You will find a list of square roots in the section titled "Are All Square Roots Irrational?" in Chapter 3 (page 77).

The ladder reaches 8 feet up the wall, Choice **B**.

Did I answer the question? Yes, I found how high up the side of the building the ladder reaches. ✓

Does my answer make sense? Yes. The hypotenuse is 10 feet, so the leg must be shorter than 10 feet. ✓

Is the answer stated in the correct units? Yes, the units are feet, which is correct. ✓

Choice **A** results if you mistakenly decide to solve the problem by finding the difference between the lengths of the hypotenuse and the known leg to find the length of the missing leg. Choice **C** results if you mistakenly use the length of the hypotenuse as the length of the unknown leg. Choice **D** results if you mistakenly decide to solve the problem by adding the lengths of the hypotenuse and known leg to find the length of the missing leg.

28. **C.** Choice **C** is the correct response.

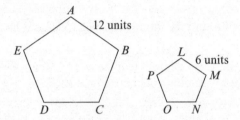

Given *ABCDE* and *LMNOP* are regular pentagons, they are similar figures. In similar figures, corresponding sides are proportional. The ratio of proportionality of the sides of *ABCDE* to *LMNOP* is $\frac{12 \text{ units}}{6 \text{ units}} = \frac{2}{1}$. In other words, the length of each side of *ABCDE* is twice the length of its corresponding side in *LMNOP*. The scale factor is 2. Therefore, the ratio of the area of *ABCDE* to *LMNOP* is $\frac{(2)^2}{(1)^2} = \frac{4}{1}$ or 4:1, Choice **C**.

29. **C.** Choice **C** is the correct response. Sketch a diagram to illustrate the problem.

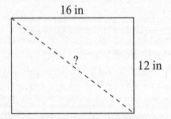

The television screen can be modeled by a 16-inch by 12-inch rectangle. The diagonal divides the rectangle into two right triangles, with legs 16 inches and 12 inches in length. The diagonal is opposite the right angle, so it is the hypotenuse of the right triangle. Use the Pythagorean theorem (from the Mathematics Reference Sheet) to find the length of the diagonal. Let *c* represent the diagonal. Substitute 16 for *a* and 12 for *b* into the formula and solve for *c*, omitting the units for convenience:

$$c^2 = a^2 + b^2$$
$$= (16)^2 + (12)^2$$
$$= 256 + 144$$
$$= 400$$

Because $c^2 = 400$, to find *c*, you must think of a number that multiplies by itself to give 400.

Given $20 \cdot 20 = 400$, $c = 20$.

Note: You will find a list of square roots in the section titled "Are All Square Roots Irrational?" in Chapter 3 (page 77).

The television has a 20-inch screen, Choice **C**.

Did I answer the question? Yes, I found the size of the television screen. ✓

Does my answer make sense? Yes. The diagonal is the longest dimension, so the answer is reasonable. ✓

Is the answer stated in the correct units? Yes, the units are inches, which is correct. ✓

Choice **A** is the incorrect result of using the width of the television as its size. Choice **B** is the incorrect result of using the length of the television as its size. Choice **D** is the incorrect result of using the sum of the length and width of the television as its size.

30. **A.** Choice **A** is the correct response. To solve the problem, you must answer the question: 108 is r% of 120?

Method 1: To solve the problem, identify the elements of the percent proportion, plug the values into the percent proportion, and then solve the proportion:

Step 1. Identify the elements.

$$r = ?$$
$$\text{part} = 108$$
$$\text{whole} = 120$$

Step 2. Plug into the percent proportion.

$$\frac{r}{100} = \frac{108}{120}$$

Step 3. Solve the proportion.

Multiply 108 by 100 (a cross product you can calculate), and then divide by 120 (the numerical term you didn't use):

$$r = \frac{108 \cdot 100}{120} = 90$$

Thus, r% = 90%. Of the 120 fans at the game, 90% were players' parents, Choice **A**.

Did I answer the question? Yes, I found the percent of the fans who were players' parents. ✓

Does my answer make sense? Yes, 108 is close to 120, so the answer should be close to 100%. ✓

Is the answer stated in the correct units? No units are needed for the answer. ✓

Method 2: Write an equation and solve it.

Let $R = r$%

108 = R times 120   Hint: The word "of" is times when it occurs between two numbers.

108 = $R \cdot 120$

For convenience, you should rewrite the expression on the right of the equation as $120R$.

$$108 = 120R$$

You are solving for R, so divide both sides of the equation by 120, the coefficient of R.

$$\frac{108}{120} = \frac{120R}{120}$$
$$0.9 = R$$

Change 0.9 to a percent by moving the decimal point two places to the right and adding a percent sign: $R = 90\%$, Choice **A**.

Choice **B** results if you set up the problem incorrectly. Choice **D** results is if you place a decimal point incorrectly. Choice **C** is the percent of fans who were not players' parents.

31. **A.** Choice **A** is the correct response. Rewrite the function expression, enclosing x on the right side in parentheses:

$$f(x) = -5 - (x)$$

Substitute -13 for x inside the parentheses and evaluate, being sure to follow the rules for computation with signed numbers:

$$f(-13) = -5 - (-13) = -5 + 13 = 8, \text{ Choice } \mathbf{A}$$

Choice **B** occurs if you make a sign error. Choices **C** and **D** result if you deal with the subtraction incorrectly.

32. **A.** Choice **A** is the correct response. Sketch the diagram. Draw a line segment connecting the points $R(2, -2)$ and $S(3, 4)$.

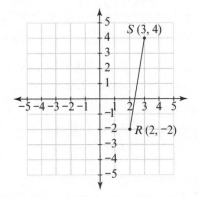

The Mathematics Reference Sheet gives the formula for the distance between two points (x_1, y_1) and (x_2, y_2) as $\sqrt{(x_2 - x_1)^2 + (y_2 - y_1)^2}$. To find the distance between $(3, 4)$ and $(2, -2)$, let $x_1 = 3$, $y_1 = 4$, $x_2 = 2$, and $y_2 = -2$, then plug into the formula:

$$\text{Distance} = \sqrt{(x_2 - x_1)^2 + (y_2 - y_1)^2} = \sqrt{(2-3)^2 + (-2-4)^2} = \sqrt{(-1)^2 + (-6)^2} = \sqrt{1 + 36} = \sqrt{37}$$

The distance between the points R and S is $\sqrt{37}$ units, Choice **A.**

Choices **B, C,** and **D** result if you make a computation error.

33. **D.** Choice **D** is the correct response. Write an equation and solve it.

The statement 4 less than 5 times x is 6 is written symbolically as $5x - 4 = 6$.

$5x - 4 = 6$	
$5x - 4 + 4 = 6 + 4$	Add 4 to both sides of the equation.
$5x = 10$	Simplify.
$\dfrac{5x}{5} = \dfrac{10}{5}$	Divide both sides of the equation by 5.
$x = 2$, Choice **D.**	Simplify.

Check to see whether your answer makes the statement true. Is 4 less than 5 times 2 equal to 6? Yes, because 4 less than 10 is 6.

Choice **A** occurs if you make a sign error. Choice **B** occurs if you write 4 less than 5 times x as $4 - 5x$. Choice **C** occurs if you translate incorrectly and make a simplification error.

34. B. Choice **B** is the correct response.

$$-2x - 5 < 3x + 15$$
$$-2x - 5 - 3x < 3x + 15 - 3x \quad \text{Subtract } 3x \text{ from both sides of the inequality.}$$
$$-5x - 5 < 15 \quad \text{Simplify.}$$
$$-5x - 5 + 5 < 15 + 5 \quad \text{Add 5 to both sides of the inequality.}$$
$$-5x < 20 \quad \text{Simplify.}$$
$$\frac{\cancel{-5}x}{\cancel{-5}} > \frac{20}{-5} \quad \text{Divide both sides by } -5, \text{ and reverse the inequality.}$$
$$x > -4 \quad \text{Simplify.}$$

The solution set includes all numbers to the right of –4. An open circle at –4 indicates it is not included in the solution set. Choice **B** correctly depicts the solution.

Eliminate choices **A** and **C** right off because these graphs have a solid circle at –4. Choice **D** depicts $x < -4$, which occurs if you neglect to reverse the inequality when dividing both sides by –5.

35. D. Choice **D** is the correct response. This problem is a counting problem. First, decide on how many tasks are involved. The students have three tasks to perform. The first task is to choose a sandwich. After that task, the second task is to select a drink. After that, the third task is to make a chip selection. The number of ways each task can occur does not depend on the outcome of the other tasks. To find the possible combinations for the three tasks, multiply the number of ways the first task can occur by the number of ways the second task can occur by the number of ways the third task can occur.

Total number of possible combinations = (number of ways to select a sandwich) × (number of ways to select a drink) × (number of ways to make a chip selection) = 4 × 2 × 3 = 24 ways.

The students can select from 24 different combinations consisting of one sandwich, one drink, and one bag of chips for lunch, Choice **D**.

Did I answer the question? Yes, I found the number of possible combinations the students can choose from for lunch. ✓

Does my answer make sense? Yes. 5 × 2 × 3 would yield 30 ways, so 24 ways for 4 × 2 × 3 is reasonable. ✓

Is the answer stated in the correct units? No units are required for the answer. ✓

Choice **A** is the number of combinations consisting of one sandwich and one drink without including the chip selection. Choice **B** occurs if you add the number of ways each task can occur, instead of multiplying. Choice **C** occurs if you multiply incorrectly.

36. B. Choice **B** is the correct response. Parallel lines have equal slopes. Therefore, the slope of a line parallel to the line through points $T(4, -3)$ and $U(1, 2)$ is the same as the slope of the line through the two points. Find the slope of the line through T and U. Sketch a diagram. Draw a line connecting the points $T(4, -3)$ and $U(1, 2)$.

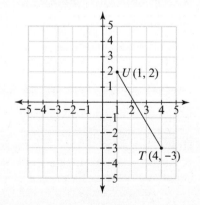

From the diagram, you can see the line slopes downward from left to right, indicating the slope is negative; therefore, you can eliminate Choice **D**.

The Mathematics Reference Sheet gives the formula for the slope of the line between two points (x_1, y_1) and (x_2, y_2) as $\dfrac{y_2 - y_1}{x_2 - x_1}$. To find the slope of the line between (4, –3) and (1, 2), let $x_1 = 4$, $y_1 = -3$, $x_2 = 1$, and $y_2 = 2$. Then plug into the formula:

Tip: Enclose negative values in parentheses.

$$\text{Slope} = \frac{y_2 - y_1}{x_2 - x_1} = \frac{2 - (-3)}{1 - 4} = \frac{2 + 3}{-3} = \frac{5}{-3} = -\frac{5}{3}, \text{ Choice } \mathbf{B}$$

Choice **A** occurs if you make the mistake of putting the difference in the x values in the numerator and the difference in the y values in the denominator. Choice **C** results if you subtract incorrectly. Choice **D** results if you make a sign error.

37. **D.** Choice **D** is the correct response. Rewrite the function expression, enclosing x on the right side in parentheses:

$$f(x) = 3(x)^3 - (x)^2 + 5$$

Substitute 2 for x inside the parentheses and evaluate, being sure to follow PE(MD)(AS):

$f(2) = 3(2)^3 - (2)^2 + 5 = 3 \cdot 8 - 4 + 5$ There are no operations to do in parentheses, so first do the exponentiation.

Tip: The term $3(2)^3$ is not 6^3. Also, do not square the – sign in $-(2)^2$. Remember, an exponent applies only to the number or parenthetical expression immediately to its left.

$= 24 - 4 + 5$ Next, do multiplication and division, from left to right.
$= 25$ Finally, do addition and subtraction, from left to right.

Thus, $f(2) = 3(2)^3 - (2)^2 + 5 = 25$, Choice **D**.

Choice **A** occurs if you incorrectly evaluate by squaring the – sign before $(2)^2$ and multiplying 3 times 2 in $3(2)^3$ before applying the exponent. Choice **B** occurs if you make the mistake of multiplying 3 times 2 in $3(2)^3$ before applying the exponent. Choice **C** occurs if you square the – sign before $(2)^2$.

38. **D.** Choice **D** is the correct response.

$4(x - 8) = 24$
$4x - 32 = 24$ Use the distributive property to remove parentheses. Be sure to multiply the 8 by 4, too.
$4x - 32 + 32 = 24 + 32$ Add 32 to both sides of the equation.
$4x = 56$ Simplify.
$\dfrac{\cancel{4}x}{\cancel{4}} = \dfrac{56}{4}$ Divide both sides of the equation by 4.
$x = 14$, Choice **D**.   Simplify.

Choice **A** results if you subtract 32 from both sides of $4x - 32 = 24$, instead of adding 32. Choice **B** results if you fail to remove the parentheses correctly, and you make a subtraction error. Choice **C** results if you obtain $4x - 8$ when removing the parentheses in $4(x - 8)$, instead of $4x - 32$.

39. C. Choice **C** is the correct response.

From the pie chart, you can see 25% of the monthly salary is budgeted for food. To answer the question, you must find 25% of $2,800.

Method 1: Identify the elements of the percent problem, plug the values into the percent proportion, and solve the proportion:

Step 1. Identify the elements.

$$r = 25$$
$$\text{part} = ?$$
$$\text{whole} = \$2,800$$

Step 2. Plug into the percent proportion (omitting the units for convenience)

$$\frac{25}{100} = \frac{x}{2,800}$$

Step 3. Solve the proportion.

Multiply 25 times 2,800 (a cross product you can calculate), and then divide by 100 (the numerical term you didn't use):

$$x = \frac{25 \cdot 2,800}{100} = 700$$

The amount budgeted for food is $700, Choice **C**.

Did I answer the question? Yes, I found the amount budgeted for food. ✓

Does my answer make sense? Yes. Because 25% equals $\frac{1}{4}$, the answer should be $\frac{1}{4}$ of $2,800, which is $700. ✓

Is the answer stated in the correct units? Yes, the units are dollars, which is correct. ✓

Method 2: Change 25% to a decimal fraction or common fraction and multiply:

$$25\% \text{ of } \$2,800 = 0.25 \times \$2,800 = \$700.00; \text{ or}$$
$$25\% \text{ of } \$2,500 = \frac{1}{4} \cdot \$2,800 = \frac{\$2,800}{4} = \$700, \text{ Choice } \mathbf{C}.$$

Choice **A** results if you make a calculation error. Choice **B** results if you solve the problem incorrectly by finding 12.5% of $2,800. Choice **D** results if you solve the problem incorrectly by finding 37.5% of $2,800.

40. D. Choice **D** is the correct response. You should eliminate Choice **C** immediately because probabilities cannot be greater than 1. Probabilities are always greater than or equal to 0 and less than or equal to 1. This is an independent events probability problem because the outcome of the first spin has no effect on the outcome of the second spin. To find the probability of spinning red on the first spin and green on the second spin, do three steps. First, find the probability of red on the first spin. Next, find the probability of green on the second spin. Then multiply the probabilities of these two events: P(red on first spin) $\cdot$ P(green on second spin).

Step 1. Find the probability of spinning red on the first spin.

There are 4 red sections on the spinner, out of a total of 10 sections: $P(\text{red on first spin}) = \frac{4}{10} = \frac{2}{5}$.

Step 2. Find the probability of spinning green on the second spin.

There is 1 green section on the spinner, out of a total of 10 sections: $P(\text{green on second spin}) = \frac{1}{10}$.

Step 3. Multiply the probabilities from steps 1 and 2.

$$P(\text{red on first spin}) \cdot P(\text{green on second spin}) = \frac{2}{5} \cdot \frac{1}{10} = \frac{2}{50} = \frac{1}{25}$$

The probability of spinning red on the first spin and green on the second spin is $\frac{1}{25}$, Choice **D**.

Did I answer the question? Yes, I found the probability of spinning red on the first spin and green on the second spin. ✓

Does my answer make sense? Yes. The answer is consistent with my knowledge of probability. ✓

Is the answer stated in the correct units? No units are required for the answer. ✓

Choice **A** results if you multiply the two probabilities incorrectly. Choice **B** results if you make the mistake of adding the probabilities together instead of multiplying them.

41. **C.** Choice **C** is the correct response. The scale on the vertical axis shows the number of students who achieved the grade. The scale is marked in multiples of 2. The top of the bars for the intervals 50–59 and 60–69 are 2 and 4, respectively. Thus, 2 + 4 = 6 students scored below 70. The probability a student randomly selected from the 35 students scored below 70 is $\frac{6}{35}$, Choice **C**.

Choices **A** and **B** occur if you do not include all students in the intervals 50–59 and 60–69. Choice **D** occurs if you mistakenly include students in the interval 70–79.

42. **D.** Choice **D** is the correct response. The average of the student's four test grades must be at least 80. This means the sum of the four test grades divided by 4 must be at least 80.

Method 1: You can find the answer by writing and solving an equation.

Let x = the lowest grade the student can make on the fourth test and still have at least an 80 average. Set up an equation and solve for x.

$$\frac{\text{sum of 4 test grades}}{4} = \frac{78+91+75+x}{4}$$

Solve $\frac{78+91+75+x}{4} = 80$.

$\frac{244+x}{4} = 80$ Simplify the numerator.

$\frac{\cancel{4}}{1} \cdot \frac{244+x}{\cancel{4}} = 80 \cdot \frac{4}{1}$ Multiply both sides of the equation by 4 to remove the fraction.

$244 + x = 320$

$244 + x - 244 = 320 - 244$ Subtract 244 from both sides of the equation.

$x = 76$

The lowest grade that will yield an average of at least 80 is 76, Choice **D**.

Did I answer the question? Yes, I found the lowest grade the student can make on the fourth test and still receive a B in the course. ✓

Does my answer make sense? Yes. The score is reasonable considering the student's other scores. ✓

Is the answer stated in the correct units? No units are required for the answer. ✓

Method 2: Another way to work this problem is to check the answer choices—a smart test-taking strategy for multiple-choice math tests. However, be careful with this problem. Because you have to find the *lowest* test score that will work, you must check all the answer choices even if you find an answer choice that gives an average in the 80s.

Checking **A**: $\dfrac{\text{sum of 4 test grades}}{4} = \dfrac{78+91+75+99}{4} = 85.75$

Checking **B**: $\dfrac{\text{sum of 4 test grades}}{4} = \dfrac{78+91+75+82}{4} = 81.5$

Checking **C**: $\dfrac{\text{sum of 4 test grades}}{4} = \dfrac{78+91+75+80}{4} = 81.0$

Checking **D**: $\dfrac{\text{sum of 4 test grades}}{4} = \dfrac{78+91+75+76}{4} = 80.0$, correct because 76 is the lowest grade needed.

The other answer choices are too high.

43. **B.** Choice **B** is the correct response. In an ordered set of numbers, the median is the middle number if there is a middle number; otherwise, the median is the arithmetic average of the two middle numbers. Determining the median of a set of numbers is a two-step process.

Step 1. Put the running times in order from least to greatest (omitting the units for convenience).

$$61, 63, 64, 64, 66, 68, 69, 73$$

Step 2. Find the middle number. If there is no single middle number, average the two middle numbers.

There is no single middle number. Average the two running times, 64 and 66, that are in the middle of the list.

$$\dfrac{64+66}{2} = \dfrac{130}{2} = 65$$

Mario's median running time is 65 seconds, Choice **B**.

Did I answer the question? Yes, I found Mario's median running time. ✓

Does my answer make sense? Yes. Because all but one score is in the 60s, the median should be in the 60s as well. ✓

Is the answer stated in the correct units? Yes, the units are seconds, which is correct. ✓

Choice **A** is the mode running time. Choice **C** is the mean running time. Choice **D** results if you forget to put the running times in order first.

44. **A.** Choice **A** is the correct response. Check each answer choice to determine which statement is true.

Checking **A**: To decide which set of grades has greater variability, you can look at the range of the two sets. The range of a set of data equals the greatest value minus the least value in the set. The range in the English class is 92 – 56 = 36. The range in the French class is 84 – 75 = 9. Because 36 > 9, Choice **A** is a correct statement.

You would not have to continue checking because you know **A** is true.

Checking **B**: This choice is incorrect because 9 is not greater than 36.

Checking **C**: You have to calculate the means in the two classes.

The mean in the English class is

$$\frac{75+89+67+56+92}{5} = \frac{379}{5} = 75.8$$

The mean in the French class is

$$\frac{75+78+83+84+80+77}{6} = \frac{477}{6} = 79.5$$

Choice **C** is incorrect because the mean in the English class is not higher than the mean in the French class.

Checking **D**: This choice is incorrect because the means in the two classes are not equal.

45. **C.** Choice **C** is the correct response. In this study, Shampoo X is the treatment and hair loss is the variable of interest. In an experimental study, the treatment group receives the treatment, so the participants in the treatment group will use Shampoo X, Choice **C**. Choices **A** and **B** are incorrect because these choices are related to the variable of interest, which is not manipulated by the researcher. Choice **D** is incorrect because the control group, not the treatment group, will not use Shampoo X.

Reading

1. **A.** Choice **A** is the correct response. The main idea of the passage is best expressed in the sentence *Young people should be given literature that speaks to their developmental interests.* Clearly, the main idea of this narrative is that young people should be reading books that deal with issues and characters that relate to their age and interests. Choice **B** is incorrect because the author does not imply that the purpose of literature for young people is only to inspire good citizenship. Choice **C** is incorrect because the author does not say that young people should read books that discuss traditional values. Choice **D** is incorrect because the author does not say young people should read only books that are universally recognized as good books.

2. **D.** Choice **D** is the correct response. In the first paragraph, the word *travail* most nearly means *tribulation* (Choice **D**), meaning "a trial of one's ability to overcome adversity." The words in the other answer choices do not have the same meaning as *travail*.

3. **A.** Choice **A** is the correct response. This paragraph focuses on the topic of *appropriate literature for young readers*. Choice **B** is incorrect because this topic is too general to describe the paragraph's focus. Choice **C** is incorrect because it disagrees with the paragraph's intent, which is to point out that young people should be encouraged to read books written specifically for young readers. Choice **D** is incorrect because this topic is too narrow to describe the paragraph's focus.

4. **B.** Choice **B** is the correct response. The relationship between the two sentences is that Sentence 2 *contradicts* the main idea presented in Sentence 1. The gist of the two sentences is that teachers and librarians may suggest difficult reading, BUT they're neglecting reading that could be better-suited. That's why Sentence 2 contradicts Sentence 1. Choice **A** is incorrect because Sentence 2 does not *expand,* or add to, Sentence 1. Choice **C** is incorrect because Sentence 2 does not *clarify,* or explain, Sentence 1. Choice **D** is incorrect because Sentence 2 does not *restate* Sentence 1; it contradicts it.

5. **B.** Choice **B** is the correct response. The main idea of the third paragraph is given by the statement in Choice **B**: *Many good books written for young readers are available.* The information in Choice **A** is given in the last sentence of the third paragraph, but it is not the main idea of the paragraph. The statement in Choice **C** could be inferred from the second sentence of the third paragraph—particularly, when considered in the context of the whole passage—however, it is not the main idea of the third paragraph. The statement in Choice **D** disagrees with the last sentence of paragraph 3, so it is not the main idea of the paragraph.

6. **C.** Choice **C** is the correct response. According to the passage, one way in which teenagers can be motivated to read is to provide them with literature featuring young protagonists. Choice **A** is incorrect because the author emphatically states that introducing nonreaders to only classical literature can be counterproductive. Choice **B** is incorrect because the author does not suggest this strategy in the passage. Choice **D** is incorrect because the author does not discuss the value of providing teenagers with nonfiction.

7. **A.** Choice **A** is the correct response. As used in the third paragraph, the phrase *escapist fare cloaked in realistic language* best describes fiction books. The author of this passage is advocating that young people read books that allow them to escape into both real and imaginary worlds filled with characters and language to which they can relate. Of all the answer choices, Choice **A**, fiction books, is the best choice. Nonfiction books (Choice **B**) are not considered "escapist fare" because nonfiction books are stories about actual persons, places, or events. Textbooks (Choice **C**) are not considered escapist fare, nor are autobiographies (Choice **D**).

8. **C.** Choice **C** is the correct response. According to the passage, young people enjoy narratives set in fantasy worlds. Therefore, most likely the author would agree young people enjoy reading narratives featuring invented settings. The other answer choices are incorrect because they are not supported by textual evidence in the passage.

9. **D.** Choice **D** is the correct response. The tone of this passage can best be described as *subjective*. The author provides a passionate yet practical argument for the use of literature aimed at youth for young people. Choice **A** is incorrect because the author's tone is not *caustic*, meaning "biting and harsh." Choice **B** is incorrect because the author's tone is not *optimistic*, meaning "expectant." Choice **C** is incorrect because the author is not *objective*, meaning "without opinion."

10. **C.** Choice **C** is the correct response. In the third paragraph, the passage states that all humans need to escape from their everyday lives. Thus, by implication, young people need to escape from their everyday lives (Choice **C**). None of the other answer choices are implied in this passage.

11. **A.** Choice **A** is the correct response. A statement that is implied in the first paragraph is the statement given in Choice **A**: *Religion is an important part of many people's lives.* The reader can infer this statement from the third sentence (*For the first two questions, the reasons for humankind's existence and its noble purpose, people of all races and creeds have turned to religion.*) and fourth sentence (*There, amidst ancient myths and modern realities, individuals have found great comfort and joy in the teachings and practices of many of the world's ancient and revered religious traditions.*) of the first paragraph. The other answer choices are not supported by the information given in the first paragraph.

12. **C.** Choice **C** is the correct response. An opinion expressed in this passage is the statement given in Choice **C**: *NASA's missions, programs, and projects have provided invaluable new knowledge.* The word *invaluable* is a judgment word reflecting the author's opinion about NASA's work. The other choices are all statements of fact, not opinions: Choice **A** in the third paragraph, Choice **B** in the second paragraph, and Choice **D** in the third paragraph.

13. **C.** Choice **C** is the correct response. The word or phrase when substituted for *Instead* in the third paragraph that would maintain the same relationship between the last two sentences is *Rather*. *Rather* means the same as *instead* or *besides*. Choice **A** is incorrect because *Therefore* implies a concluding remark to follow the sentence before. Choice **B** is incorrect because *In addition* implies that the sentence that follows is an added thought or conclusion to the preceding sentence. Choice **D** is incorrect because *Obviously* implies something that is understood by many and, in this narrative's section, the logical conclusion to this paragraph is not something generally assumed.

14. **B.** Choice **B** is the correct response. The most likely reason the author wrote this passage is *to chronicle the history and impact of America's space program*. The passage tells about the beginning of the space program, relates some of its benefits and highlights, reports the two shuttle disasters, and speaks of future plans. Choice **A** is incorrect because although America's space program might be tied to humankind's curiosity about the universe, the central focus of the passage is on the history and impact of the space program itself. Choice **C** is incorrect because there is no indication in the passage that the author questions the wisdom of

having a space program. Choice **D** is incorrect because the passage is about America's space program, not space exploration in general. Further, the passage goes beyond explaining the benefits from America's space exploration.

15. A. Choice **A** is the correct response. According to information given in this passage, *people seek answers to the reasons for humankind's existence* (Choice **A**). This information is given in the first paragraph of the passage. Choices **B** and **C** are incorrect because, even though these are true statements, this information is not given in the passage. Choice **D** is incorrect because it disagrees with information given in the last paragraph.

> **Tip: Do not select answer choices based on your personal knowledge that goes beyond the information given in the passage.**

16. B. Choice **B** is the correct response. In this passage, the author speaks of *two shuttle disasters*. They occurred in 1986 and 2003. Choices **A, C,** and **D** are incorrect.

17. A. Choice **A** is the correct response. According to the first paragraph, throughout human history, individuals have been fascinated with exploration because of humankind's *natural inquisitiveness about the universe*. In this paragraph, the author speaks directly about the desire of human beings to explore the vast reaches of the universe—perhaps, simply out of curiosity. Choices **B** and **D** are incorrect because neither is supported by textual evidence in the passage. Choice **C** is incorrect because this passage addresses just the opposite: people's desire to understand and explore what lies beyond their world.

18. B. Choice **B** is the correct response. The author would probably agree that *exploring unfamiliar regions of the Earth is desirable for human development*. The passage explains that space exploration has benefited humankind, so it's likely the author would agree that terrestrial exploration would as well. Choice **A** is incorrect because the author stresses that scientific exploration is not risk-free; instead, it is filled with real and ever-present dangers. Choice **C** is incorrect because the author suggests that individuals feel the urge to explore all the time and not just in times of trouble or despair. Choice **D** is incorrect because the author implies that searching for the unknown is the province of all, regardless of wealth, status, or ambition.

19. D. Choice **D** is the correct response. In this passage, the following statement is NOT implied: *Tragedy has extinguished America's exploratory spirit*. In fact, as the narrative mentions, tragedy, such as the shuttle disasters, has only fueled America's interest to continue on the path of space exploration. Choice **A** is incorrect because the narrative specifically implies that today, for many once undreamed-of inventions and events, the unimaginable has become reality. Choice **B** is incorrect because the narrative does imply that space exploration has had a positive impact in America. Choice **C** is incorrect because the narrative does imply that America is a leader in space exploration.

20. A. Choice **A** is the correct response. In the fourth paragraph, the word *unprecedented* most nearly means *unparalleled* (Choice **A**), meaning "unmatched or never achieved before." The words in the other answer choices have meanings that are opposite that of *unprecedented*.

21. D. Choice **D** is the correct response. A statement that is implied in this passage is the statement given in Choice **D**: *Maria Montessori was well-educated*. Although this statement is not explicitly stated in this passage, from the first sentence of the third paragraph, which states that Montessori had a *strong academic record* and that she became *the first female certified physician in Italy*, the reader can infer that Montessori was well-educated. Choice **A** is incorrect because the statement in this answer choice disagrees with the third sentence of the first paragraph. Choice **B** is incorrect because the statement in this answer choice disagrees with the information given in the second paragraph. Choice **C** is incorrect because it disagrees with Montessori's ideas about teaching children given in this passage.

22. A. Choice **A** is the correct response. An opinion about Maria Montessori expressed in this passage is the statement given in Choice **A**: *She revolutionized the teaching profession*. The word *revolutionized* is a judgment word reflecting the author's opinion about Montessori's impact on the teaching profession. The other three choices are statements of fact, not opinions: Choice **B** in the third paragraph, Choice **C** in the fourth paragraph, and Choice **D** in the last paragraph.

23. **A.** Choice **A** is the correct response. In the sixth paragraph, this passage states that Maria Montessori *advocated age-appropriate learning activities* (Choice **A**). Choices **B** and **C** are incorrect because these answer choices disagree with information given in the passage. Choice **D** is incorrect because in the last paragraph you learn that Montessori was *nominated* for the Nobel Peace Prize in 1951, but the passage does not tell you that she actually *won* the Nobel Peace Prize in that year.

24. **B.** Choice **B** is the correct response. According to the sixth paragraph, Maria Montessori's teaching ideas *gained attention worldwide during her lifetime* (Choice **B**). Choice **A** is incorrect because this statement is neither stated nor implied by the passage. Choice **C** is incorrect because it disagrees with information given in this passage. Choice **D** is incorrect because there is no information in the passage to support it.

25. **B.** Choice **B** is the correct response. According to information in this passage, the word that best describes Maria Montessori is *progressive*. As this passage both implies and states, Maria Montessori was a woman who clearly accomplished goals that were unheard of by a woman in the early twentieth century. She was a true revolutionary leader. Choice **A** is incorrect because Maria Montessori was hardly *passive; passive* implies not reacting to the events or ideas that are happening around you. Choice **C** is incorrect because there is no indication in this passage that Maria Montessori was *cynical,* meaning "sharply negative." Choice **D** is incorrect because although Maria Montessori was *active,* the best word to describe her behavior from the list presented is the word *progressive,* meaning "forward-thinking."

26. **C.** Choice **C** is the correct response. According to this passage, Maria Montessori revolutionized the education profession because *she respected the emotional experiences that young people brought to their learning.* As mentioned, Montessori was a strong advocate for nurturing children's emotional well-being and made it an intimate part of their learning. Choice **A** is incorrect because this passage is more concerned with emotional rather than academic needs. Choices **B** and **D** are incorrect because neither is supported by textual evidence in the passage.

27. **A.** Choice **A** is the correct response. According to this passage, Maria Montessori's philosophy was *learning by doing ordinary work* (Choice **A**). This passage mentions that Montessori was interested in the ordinary, everyday lives of young children and incorporating these activities into their learning. The other three choices are incorrect because the passage does not mention learning by memorization (Choice **B**), learning by objectives (Choice **C**), or learning by competition (Choice **D**).

28. **A.** Choice **A** is the correct response. The activity that is most consistent with Maria Montessori's notion of an independent, free-spirited, learning environment for children is *a 4-year-old playing dress-up.* The situations in choices **B, C,** and **D** are instances of young people performing tasks for which the opportunity to act independently and be free-spirited is limited.

29. **C.** Choice **C** is the correct response. As used in the fifth paragraph, *self-reliance* most nearly means *autonomy* (Choice **C**), which means "independence." *Self-reliance* refers to an ability to rely on no one but yourself to accomplish your goals. Choice **A**, *dependence,* implies just the opposite—to rely on someone else to achieve your objectives. Choice **B**, *persistence,* implies that you are aggressive toward achieving your desires, but not necessarily self-reliant or solely in control. Choice **D**, *caution,* implies that you are hesitant about achieving your goals, which does not mean the same as being actively involved in achieving your objectives independently.

30. **B.** Choice **B** is the correct response. The photograph shows Maria Montessori engaged in study. It supports that she had a natural inclination to explore and learn. Choices **A** and **D** are correct statements about Montessori, but there is nothing in the photograph that points to either of these statements. Choice **C** is too specific. Depicting Montessori engaged in study does not necessary suggest that she had a strong academic record.

31. **B.** Choice **B** is the correct response. The primary purpose of this passage is to *inform readers about the plight of the rain forests* (Choice **B**). In this passage, the author speaks in a concerned voice about the natural beauty of the world's rain forests and how commercial interests threaten to destroy these lush and rich vegetative ecosystems. Choice **A** is incorrect because although this passage does mention that rare plants and species are found in the rain forests, this is not the primary purpose of this passage. Choice **C** is incorrect because the author expresses concern about indiscriminate logging of the rain forests. Choice **D** is

incorrect because although this passage does underline the importance of scientific exploration in the rain forests, it concentrates on how the rain forests can contribute to society in a multitude of ways besides scientific discovery.

32. **D.** Choice **D** is the correct response. The tone of this passage is best described as *factual* (Choice **D**). The author does not use a *skeptical* or disbelieving tone (Choice **A**), a *humorous* or amusing tone (Choice **B**), or a *sarcastic* or mocking tone (Choice **C**).

33. **A.** Choice **A** is the correct response. A statement that is a fact about tropical rain forests that is given in the first paragraph is *Tropical rain forests are found near the equator* (Choice **A**). The other answer choices are statements of opinion by the author.

34. **C.** Choice **C** is the correct response. Based on information in the third paragraph, the reader can infer that the author believes that industrialists are driven by profit, not by environmental concerns. Choices **A** and **D** are incorrect because neither is supported by textual evidence in the passage. Choice **B** implies the author believes industrialists are conscious of their impact on the environment, but nothing in the reading passage supports this inference.

35. **C.** Choice **C** is the correct response. Choice **C** is correct because Sentence 2 continues, or expands upon, the main idea of Sentence 1. Choice **A** is incorrect because Sentence 2 does not *analyze,* or probe the meaning of, Sentence 1. Choice **B** is incorrect because Sentence 2 does not *contradict,* or dispute the meaning of, Sentence 1. Choice **D** is incorrect because Sentence 2 does not *explain* the main idea begun in Sentence 1; it only adds new information. Remember, do not select answer choices based on your personal knowledge that goes beyond the information given in the passage.

36. **C.** Choice **C** is the correct response. In the third paragraph, the author uses the word *mine* to describe the extraction of substances from plants. Choice **A** is incorrect because the word *mine* is not used in the sense of *excavating* or digging in the earth. Choice **B** is incorrect because no mention is made of chemicals in the paragraph. Choice **D** is incorrect because, while mining might help increase the supply of new medicines, the verb *to mine* does not mean *to supply.*

37. **C.** Choice **C** is the correct response. The statement *They provide unique treasures for materialistic explorers* is neither stated nor implied in this passage (Choice **C**). Although this passage mentions the many treasures to be found in the rain forests, this passage does not advocate the use of the rain forests as a place to explore for personal gain. Indeed, this passage advocates the opposite—that any riches to be found in these regions are to be shared under regulation by governments and appropriate organizations. The statements in choices **A, B,** and **D** are stated or implied in the passage. The rain forests do provide a safe haven for indigenous people, serve as a prime source for modern medicines, and act as a rich resource for scientific investigation.

38. **D.** Choice **D** is the correct response. Deforestation is a major, not minor, problem in today's rain forest environments. The statements in the other answer choices are true according to the passage.

39. **C.** Choice **C** is the correct response. According to this passage, the millions of *indigenous* people who live in the rain forests are called by the word *indigenous* because they are native to the land in which they live. *Indigenous* is a term that defines a group of people who inhabit a land long before they are discovered by others; they belong to the land because they were born there and usually are not prepared to live anywhere else. Choice **A** is incorrect because *indigenous* implies permanent residents, not transitory migrants who are known to travel from place to place seeking work and shelter. Choice **B** is incorrect because *indigenous* people do not own, in the economic sense, the property on which they live; instead, they own the land because they were born to the land and have lived there for all their natural lives. Choice **D** is incorrect because although *indigenous* people do work the land on which they live, that alone does not make them an indigenous people.

40. **D.** Choice **D** is the correct response. The author's claim is a *reasonable contention based on textual evidence in the passage.* The author provides a realistic yet hopeful presentation of the facts surrounding the preservation of the rain forests and their chances for continual renewal despite many competing, often self-serving interests. The main reason choices **A** and **C** are incorrect is that the textual evidence in the passage *does* support the author's claim. Choice **B** is incorrect because the author's claim cannot be construed as *inflammatory,* meaning intended to arouse anger.

Chapter 6

General Knowledge Practice Test 2

Answer Sheet

(Remove This Sheet and Use It To Mark Your Answers)

Essay

Write your essay on lined paper.

English Language Skills

Mathematics

Reading

Essay

50 Minutes

Directions: This section of the examination involves a written assignment. You are to prepare a written response for *one* of the two topics presented below. Select one of these two topics and prepare a response. Be sure to read both topics very carefully to make sure that you understand the topic for which you are preparing a written response. Use your allotted time to plan, write, review, and edit what you have written for the assignment.

Topic 1

    Human beings need time to be themselves. They need time to relax, unwind, and just let their mind wander. What do you do to unwind? What hobbies do you pursue? Write an essay in which you identify your favorite hobbies and why you enjoy them.

Topic 2

    It is often said that historical figures change the world. Write an essay about a historical figure who changed the world and explain what significant changes he or she made in the course of world events.

Be sure to read the two topics again before attempting to write your response. Your essay must be on only one of the topics presented, and it must address the topic completely.

Your essay is graded holistically, meaning only one score is assigned for your writing—taking into consideration both mechanics and organization. *You are not scored on the nature of the content or opinions expressed in your work.* Instead, you are graded on your ability to write complete sentences, to express and support your opinions, and to organize your work.

As listed in the *Competencies and Skills Required for Teacher Certification in Florida,* 20th Edition, the Essay competencies/skills you should be able to do are the following:

- Determine the purpose of writing to task and audience.
- Provide a section that effectively introduces the topic.
- Formulate a relevant thesis or claim.
- Organize ideas and details effectively.
- Provide adequate, relevant support by citing ample textual evidence; response may also include anecdotal experience for added support.
- Use a variety of transitional devices effectively throughout and within a written text.
- Demonstrate proficient use of college-level, standard written English (e.g., varied word choice, syntax, language conventions, semantics).
- Provide a concluding statement or section that follows from or supports, the argument or information presented.
- Use a variety of sentence patterns effectively.
- Maintain consistent point of view.
- Apply the conventions of standard English (e.g., avoid inappropriate use of slang, jargon, clichés).

Before you begin, be sure you plan what you want to say. Organize your thoughts and carefully construct your ideas. This should be your original work, written in your own voice.

As you write your essay, you may revise or add information as necessary.

IF YOU FINISH BEFORE TIME IS CALLED, CHECK YOUR WORK ON THIS SECTION ONLY. DO NOT WORK ON ANY OTHER SECTION IN THE TEST.

English Language Skills

40 Minutes

40 Questions

Directions: For questions 1–4, read the entire passage carefully and then answer the questions. Please note that intentional errors have been included in this passage. The passages are designed to measure your identification of logical order and irrelevant sentences in a written passage.

Questions 1 and 2 are based on the following passage.

(1) The outside shell is one of the most important parts of an organism. (2) Shells grow on the outside of living things. (3) Many plants and animals, from tiny nuts to huge turtles, have a shell to protect them at least one time in their life cycles. (4) Some shells are as tiny as a grain of sand. (5) Many people collect shells as a hobby. (6) Shells also vary in color, helping to protect the organism inside from possible predators. (7) They also serve as a necessary protection from the elements. (8) Plants and animals with shells are usually the most vulnerable of living things without their shells. (9) The shell functions as protective outerwear. (10) Shells are nature's way of protecting creatures that otherwise likely would perish.

1. Select the arrangement of sentences 1, 2, and 3 that provides the MOST logical sequence of ideas and supporting details in the paragraph. If no change is needed, select Choice A.

A. (1) The outside shell is one of the most important parts of an organism. (2) Shells grow on the outside of living things. (3) Many plants and animals, from tiny nuts to huge turtles, have a shell to protect them at least one time in their life cycles.

B. (2) Shells grow on the outside of living things. (1) The outside shell is one of the most important parts of an organism. (3) Many plants and animals, from tiny nuts to huge turtles, have a shell to protect them at least one time in their life cycles.

C. (3) Many plants and animals, from tiny nuts to huge turtles, have a shell to protect them at least one time in their life cycles. (2) Shells grow on the outside of living things. (1) The outside shell is one of the most important parts of an organism.

D. (1) The outside shell is one of the most important parts of an organism. (3) Many plants and animals, from tiny nuts to huge turtles, have a shell to protect them at least one time in their life cycles. (2) Shells grow on the outside of living things.

2. Which numbered sentence is LEAST relevant to the passage?

A. Sentence 3
B. Sentence 4
C. Sentence 5
D. Sentence 6

GO ON TO THE NEXT PAGE

Questions 3 and 4 are based on the following passage.

(1) Students whose home language is other than English must learn to function in schools where the main language is English. (2) Today, most urban school districts have an amalgamation of students who speak different languages. (3) Families from all over the world settle in primarily large metropolitan school districts and bring with them their languages, culture, and customs. (4) Learning in a new language is a difficult and serious concern for all involved—teachers, parents, and students. (5) School districts are taking steps to ensure that all eager and eligible learners can participate in classroom lessons. (6) Faced with a diverse population of learners, teachers must learn to adapt their lessons. (7) They must take special courses to learn how to work with students whose first language is not English. (8) Also, administrators must rethink discipline policies for students who are unfamiliar with American lifestyle and traditional norms. (9) These measures should help ensure success for students who are English language learners. (10) With the burgeoning ethnic population in our nation's cities, new specialty foods are being introduced into society.

3. Select the arrangement of sentences 1, 2, and 3 that provides the MOST logical sequence of ideas and supporting details in the paragraph. If no change is needed, select Choice A.

   A. (1) Students whose home language is other than English must learn to function in schools where the main language is English. (2) Today, most urban school districts have an amalgamation of students who speak different languages. (3) Families from all over the world settle in primarily large metropolitan school districts and bring with them their languages, culture, and customs.

   B. (3) Families from all over the world settle in primarily large metropolitan school districts and bring with them their languages, culture, and customs. (1) Students whose home language is other than English must learn to function in schools where the main language is English. (2) Today, most urban school districts have an amalgamation of students who speak different languages.

   C. (2) Today, most urban school districts have an amalgamation of students who speak different languages. (3) Families from all over the world settle in primarily large metropolitan school districts and bring with them their languages, culture, and customs. (1) Students whose home language is other than English must learn to function in schools where the main language is English.

   D. (1) Students whose home language is other than English must learn to function in schools where the main language is English. (3) Families from all over the world settle in primarily large metropolitan school districts and bring with them their languages, culture, and customs. (2) Today, most urban school districts have an amalgamation of students who speak different languages.

4. Which numbered sentence is LEAST relevant to the passage?

   A. Sentence 7
   B. Sentence 8
   C. Sentence 9
   D. Sentence 10

GO ON TO THE NEXT PAGE

Directions: For questions 5–37, select the answer choice that corrects an error in the underlined portion. If there is no error, choose D indicating "No change is necessary."

5. All the actors, <u>accept</u> Martha and John, were
   A
   <u>allowed</u> <u>to eat</u> in the cafeteria.
   B   C
   A. except
   B. aloud
   C. to have eaten
   D. No change is necessary.

6. The children on the school bus <u>are wearing</u>
   A
   brand <u>new</u> t-shirts from <u>Coach Henderson</u>.
   B   C
   A. was wearing
   B. knew
   C. coach Henderson
   D. No change is necessary.

7. We encouraged our visitors <u>too</u> <u>formally</u>
   A   B
   introduce <u>themselves</u> to our neighbors.
   C
   A. to
   B. formerly
   C. theirselves
   D. No change is necessary.

8. After school, I <u>read</u> my <u>french</u> textbook to
   A   B
   prepare for <u>tomorrow's</u> quiz.
   C
   A. red
   B. French
   C. tomorrows
   D. No change is necessary.

9. Repeatedly, the cheerleaders <u>have went</u> to the
   A
   <u>all-American</u> championship to represent <u>their</u>
   B   C
   high school.
   A. have gone
   B. all-american
   C. there
   D. No change is necessary.

10. Police officer Lance Jones <u>sat</u> <u>among</u> Janice
    A   B
    and me at the <u>awards</u> ceremony.
    C
    A. set
    B. between
    C. Awards
    D. No change is necessary.

11. Mark is <u>deep</u> in love with Maria despite <u>their</u>
    A   B
    <u>considerable differences</u> in age and interests.
    C
    A. deeply
    B. there
    C. considerably different
    D. No change is necessary.

12. After the umpire cried <u>fowl</u>, all my teammates
    A
    protested <u>loudly</u> in <u>disbelief</u>.
    B   C
    A. foul
    B. loud
    C. disbelieve
    D. No change is necessary.

13. <u>Unfortunately</u>, the tennis team <u>had</u> lost more
    A   B
    tournaments <u>then</u> they ever had before.
    C
    A. Unfortunate
    B. have
    C. than
    D. No change is necessary.

14. My uncle's <u>surprising</u> musical talents <u>masks</u>
    A   B
    <u>his</u> inability to read.
    C
    A. surprisingly
    B. mask
    C. his own
    D. No change is necessary.

15. Among the three sisters, only me and Nancy
    A   B
    are tall.
        C
    A. Between
    B. Nancy and I
    C. the tallest
    D. No change is necessary.

16. Despite the heavy reign, we found a dry spot
                         A   B
    where we could eat our lunch.
                   C
    A. rain
    B. had found
    C. have eaten
    D. No change is necessary.

17. The students, who seldom were consulted
        A   B
    about issues by the administration, quickly
    seen they must speak up about the injustice
    C
    of the situation.
    A. students'
    B. whom
    C. saw
    D. No change is necessary.

18. The teacher was explaining to the class that
                                              A
    scientists are really careful when they take
                   B   C
    measurements.
    A. how
    B. real
    C. he or she
    D. No change is necessary.

19. When the students performed the experiment
    A   B   C
    they were amazed that the liquid turned a
    dazzling green.
    A. Whenever
    B. students'
    C. experiment, they
    D. No change is necessary.

20. Dustin is happy that his new address is
                 A
    more easier to remember than his previous
    B   C
    one.
    A. happier
    B. easier
    C. remember, than
    D. No change is necessary.

21. The boys' mother asked them whether they felt
    badly about breaking her new Tiffany lamp
    A   B
    when they were playing with the ball in the
                 C
    house.
    A. bad
    B. tiffany
    C. was
    D. No change is necessary.

22. Last November, Ms. Villa's history class went
                                  A   B
    on a field trip to Washington, D.C., the
    nation's capitol.
            C
    A. History
    B. had went
    C. capital
    D. No change is necessary.

23. The girls' mother asked them to water the
        A
    plants and feed the dog after they finished
    B
    there homework.
    C
    A. girl's
    B. plants, and
    C. their
    D. No change is necessary.

24. When they arrived at the mall, the children
    A
    had run into the toy store to find the most
    B
    recent edition of their favorite trading cards.
                     C
    A. Whenever
    B. ran
    C. thier
    D. No change is necessary.

GO ON TO THE NEXT PAGE

Chapter 6: General Knowledge Practice Test 2

25. It is hard for me to believe that we <u>cannot</u> resolve the problems between you and <u>I</u> after all these <u>years</u> of trying.
    A. can not
    B. me
    C. years'
    D. No change is necessary.

26. My daughter and my son <u>are</u> both taller than <u>me</u>, but they still mind what I <u>say when</u> I correct their behavior.
    A. were
    B. I
    C. say, when
    D. No change is necessary.

27. I was anxious during my first semester at the new <u>school because</u> the <u>principal</u> told me she would be strict with <u>whomever</u> broke the rules.
    A. school, because
    B. principle
    C. whoever
    D. No change is necessary.

28. Only one of the contestants <u>who</u> participated in the race <u>want</u> the winner to be disqualified for being <u>too</u> young.
    A. which
    B. wants
    C. to
    D. No change is necessary.

29. Just before Caleb <u>left, he</u> told me he <u>didn't</u> think he did very <u>good</u> on his geometry test.
    A. left he
    B. don't
    C. well
    D. No change is necessary.

30. <u>Me</u> graduating from college <u>has</u> been a dream of my parents, neither of <u>whom</u> ever finished high school.
    A. My
    B. have
    C. who
    D. No change is necessary.

31. The contributors to the fundraiser were pleased to <u>see that</u> every one of the children <u>were</u> wearing a <u>brand new</u> outfit.
    A. see, that
    B. was
    C. brand-new
    D. No change is necessary.

32. The <u>couple's</u> teenage sons had outgrown their board <u>games, so</u> the couple donated <u>them</u> to the local charter school.
    A. couples'
    B. games so
    C. the board games
    D. No change is necessary.

33. Donna, <u>who</u> never seeks recognition, <u>recieved</u> the outstanding teacher <u>award at</u> her school this year.
    A. whom
    B. received
    C. award, at
    D. No change is necessary.

34. Austin, Ricardo's <u>most nicest</u> <u>friend</u>, comes over to Ricardo's house <u>every day</u> after school to play.
    A. nicest
    B. freind
    C. everyday
    D. No change is necessary.

GO ON TO THE NEXT PAGE

35. When you meet the two girls, you will find it difficult to tell which one is <u>oldest</u>.

  A. the oldest
  B. older
  C. more old
  D. No change is necessary.

36. Because the students were going to be gone all day on the field trip to the park, they <u>should have took</u> a lunch.

  A. should of took
  B. should have taken
  C. should of taken
  D. No change is necessary.

37. As the sun <u>sets</u>, the horizon glowed a bright orange.

  A. had set
  B. has been setting
  C. set
  D. No change is necessary.

38. Choose the option that is punctuated correctly.

  A. When you broke your promise, I was extremely upset, I hope that I will be able to trust you in the future.
  B. When you broke your promise I was extremely upset I hope that I will be able to trust you in the future.
  C. When you broke your promise, I was extremely upset. I hope that I will be able to trust you in the future.
  D. When you broke your promise I was extremely upset. I hope that I will be able to trust you in the future.

39. Choose the option that is punctuated correctly.

  A. Having been raised in our household from a puppy, our family's trusted canine is a spoiled pooch.
  B. Having been raised in our household from a puppy, our familys' trusted canine is a spoiled pooch.
  C. Having been raised in our household from a puppy. Our family's trusted canine is a spoiled pooch.
  D. Having been raised in our household from a puppy our family's trusted canine is a spoiled pooch.

40. Choose the sentence in which the modifiers are placed correctly.

  A. Driving through the neighborhood, the woman waved to a child playing with his dog on the sidewalk.
  B. Playing with his dog on the sidewalk, the woman waved to a child driving through the neighborhood.
  C. The woman waved to a child playing with his dog on the sidewalk driving through the neighborhood.
  D. The woman waved to a child driving through the neighborhood playing on the sidewalk with his dog.

IF YOU FINISH BEFORE TIME IS CALLED, CHECK YOUR WORK ON THIS SECTION ONLY. DO NOT WORK ON ANY OTHER SECTION IN THE TEST.

Mathematics

Mathematics Reference Sheet

Area

Shape		Formula		Key	
Triangle		$A = \frac{1}{2}bh$		b = base	d = diameter
				h = height	r = radius
				l = length	A = area
Rectangle		$A = lw$		w = width	C = circumference
				$S.A.$ = surface area	V = volume
Trapezoid		$A = \frac{1}{2}h(b_1 + b_2)$			B = area of base
				Use $\pi = 3.14$ or $\frac{22}{7}$.	
Parallelogram		$A = bh$			
Circle		$A = \pi r^2$	$C = \pi d = 2\pi r$		

Surface Area

1. Surface area of a prism or pyramid = the sum of the areas of all faces of the figure
2. Surface area of a cylinder = the sum of the areas of the two bases + the area of its rectangular wrap

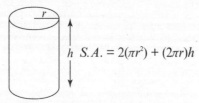

$h \quad S.A. = 2(\pi r^2) + (2\pi r)h$

3. Surface area of a sphere: $S.A. = 4\pi r^2$

Volume

1. Volume of a prism or cylinder equals (area of base) times (height): $V = Bh$
2. Volume of a pyramid or cone equals $\frac{1}{3}$ times (area of base) times (height): $V = \frac{1}{3}Bh$
3. Volume of a sphere: $V = \frac{4}{3}\pi r^3$

Mathematics Reference Sheet, continued

Pythagorean Theorem: $a^2 + b^2 = c^2$

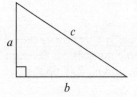

Simple Interest Formula: $I = prt$

I = simple interest, p = principal, r = rate, t = time

Distance Formula: $d = rt$

d = distance, r = rate, t = time

Given a line containing points (x_1, y_1) and (x_2, y_2),

- Slope of line $= \dfrac{y_2 - y_1}{x_2 - x_1}$

- Distance between two points
  $= \sqrt{(x_2 - x_1)^2 + (y_2 - y_1)^2}$

- Midpoint between two points $= \left(\dfrac{x_2 + x_1}{2}, \dfrac{y_2 + y_1}{2} \right)$

Conversions	
1 yard = 3 feet = 36 inches	1 cup = 8 fluid ounces
1 mile = 1,760 yards = 5,280 feet	1 pint = 2 cups
1 acre = 43,560 square feet	1 quart = 2 pints
1 hour = 60 minutes	1 gallon = 4 quarts
1 minute = 60 seconds	
	1 pound = 16 ounces
1 liter = 1000 milliliters = 1000 cubic centimeters	1 ton = 2,000 pounds
1 meter = 100 centimeters = 1000 millimeters	
1 kilometer = 1000 meters	
1 gram = 1000 milligrams	
1 kilogram = 1000 grams	

Note: Metric numbers with four digits are written without a comma (e.g., 2543 grams). For metric numbers with more than four digits, a space is used instead of a comma (e.g., 24 300 liters).

100 Minutes

45 Questions

Directions: Read each question and select the best answer choice.

1. Which statement defines division, assuming $y \neq 0$?

    A. $x \div y = z$ if and only if $z \div x = y$
    B. $x \div y = z$ if and only if $z \cdot y = x$
    C. $x \div y = z$ if and only if $x \cdot y = z$
    D. $x \div y = z$ if and only if $y \div x = z$

2. In the number puzzle shown, if x is the starting number and y represents the final result, which equation is equivalent to the number puzzle?

    > Pick a number.
    > Add 10 to the number.
    > Multiply the result by 5.
    > Subtract 70.
    > Divide by 5.

    A. $y = 5x$
    B. $y = x - 12$
    C. $y = x - 4$
    D. $y = x - 20$

3. In triangle ABC shown, segment $\overline{CE}$ has length 200 meters and segment $\overline{EA}$ has length 100 meters. In triangle ADE, segment $\overline{DE}$ has length 50 meters. What is the area of triangle ABC?

    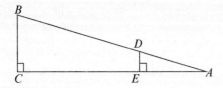

    A. 7500 m²
    B. 15 000 m²
    C. 22 500 m²
    D. 45 000 m²

4. Evaluate $7 + 3(4^2) - 8$.

    A. 23
    B. 32
    C. 47
    D. 152

5. The whole number y is exactly three times the whole number x. The whole number z is the sum of x and y. Which number CANNOT be the value of z?

    A. 314
    B. 416
    C. 524
    D. 1,032

6. Justin bought a souvenir jacket while vacationing in a Texas town where the sales tax rate is 8.25%. He paid $108.25 for the jacket plus tax.

    What was the price of the jacket before sales tax?

    A. $89.31
    B. $99.00
    C. $99.32
    D. $100.00

7. The following Fahrenheit temperatures were the lowest recorded in February for the past 5 years in a particular city.

    2°, 0°, –6°, 4°, –8°

    Which list shows the temperatures in order from coldest to warmest?

    A. 0°, 2°, 4°, –6°, –8°
    B. 4°, 2°, 0°, –6°, –8°
    C. –6°, –8°, 0°, 2°, 4°
    D. –8°, –6°, 0°, 2°, 4°

8. If 30% of a monthly salary of $2,400 is budgeted for rent, how much money is budgeted for rent?

    A. $72
    B. $168
    C. $720
    D. $1,680

GO ON TO THE NEXT PAGE

9. Theo ran a 1500-meter race. How many kilometers did Theo run in the race?

   A. 1.5 km
   B. 15 km
   C. 150 km
   D. 1 500 000 km

10. Sabrina knows she can mow a rectangular lawn that measures 30 yards by 40 yards in 2 hours. She estimates it will take 4 hours to mow a rectangular lawn that measures 60 yards by 80 yards. Is Sabrina's estimate reasonable?

    A. Yes, because doubling the dimensions will double the lawn's area, resulting in twice the mowing time.
    B. Yes, because doubling the dimensions will double the lawn's perimeter, resulting in twice the mowing time.
    C. No, because doubling the lawn's length will reduce the amount of turning by half, resulting in three times the mowing time.
    D. No, because doubling the dimensions will quadruple the lawn's area, resulting in four times the mowing time.

11. If the surface area of a sphere is 144π cm^2, what is the volume of the sphere? Use $\pi = 3.14$.

    A. 36 cm^3
    B. 288 cm^3
    C. 216π cm^3
    D. 288π cm^3

12. If a circular flower garden has a diameter of 3 feet, what is the approximate area of the garden? Use $\pi = 3.14$.

    A. 4.71 ft^2
    B. 7.07 ft^2
    C. 28.26 ft^2
    D. 9.42 ft^2

13. How many cubic feet of cement are in a rectangular cement slab that is 0.5 feet thick and measures 20 feet long and 10 feet wide?

    A. 100 ft^3
    B. 30.5 ft^3
    C. 300 ft^3
    D. 1,000 ft^3

14. A box that has the shape of a cube and measures 10 centimeters on a side is cut open to form the flattened figure shown here.

    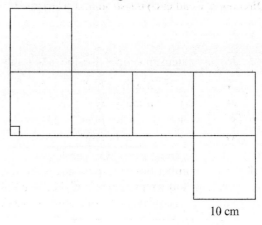

    10 cm

    What is the surface area of the box?

    A. 30 cm^2
    B. 100 cm^2
    C. 600 cm^2
    D. 3 600 cm^2

15. A car travels 221 miles in 3 hours 15 minutes. How many miles per hour did the car travel?

    A. 165.75 mph
    B. 73.7 mph
    C. 70.1 mph
    D. 68 mph

16. A nutrition expert recommends healthy adults drink 64 ounces of water each day. At this rate, how many gallons of water will be consumed in a week by a person who follows the recommendation?

    A. 0.5 gallons
    B. 3.5 gallons
    C. 14 gallons
    D. 16 gallons

17. On a map, the distance between two landmarks is 9.5 inches. If $\frac{1}{2}$ inch represents 10 miles, how far, in miles, is it between the two landmarks (to the nearest mile)?

    A. 0.475 miles
    B. 19 miles
    C. 85 miles
    D. 190 miles

GO ON TO THE NEXT PAGE

18. How much will it cost, without including tax, to carpet a large classroom that measures 18 feet by 15 feet if the cost of the carpet, including installation, is $25.75 per square yard?

    A. $30.00
    B. $772.50
    C. $2,317.50
    D. $6,952.50

19. Which linear equation represents the data in the table shown?

Input x	Output y
−3	−11
0	−5
5	5

    A. $y = x - 8$
    B. $y = x - 5$
    C. $y = x$
    D. $y = 2x - 5$

20. A length of cable is attached to the top of a 16-foot pole. The cable is anchored 12 feet from the base of the pole. What is the length of the cable?

    A. 20 ft
    B. 28 ft
    C. 200 ft
    D. 400 ft

21. A square is NOT which figure?

    A. cube
    B. parallelogram
    C. rectangle
    D. rhombus

22. In the drawings shown, right triangle ABC is similar to right triangle DEF. What is the length of the hypotenuse in triangle ABC?

    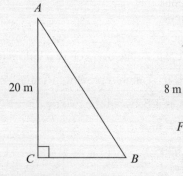

    A. 4 m
    B. 25 m
    C. 28 m
    D. 30 m

23. The figures shown are drawn to scale. Which figure contains an interior obtuse angle?

    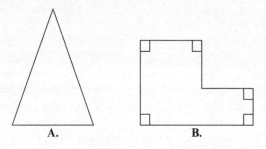

    A. B.

    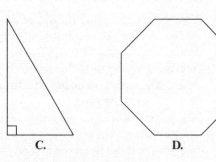

    C. D.

24. Harry, Maria, and Kelly attend a movie together. A ticket for the movie costs $10. Harry has $30. Kelly forgot her purse and needs to borrow the money for her ticket from Harry. Harry owes Maria $9 and will pay her first. Does Harry have enough money for this situation? Which method can be used to arrive at a correct answer for this question?

    A. Subtract $9 from $30, and then subtract three times $10.
    B. Subtract $9 from $30, and then subtract two times $10.
    C. Subtract $10 from $30, and then subtract $9.
    D. Multiply $10 by three, and then subtract the result from $30.

25. Find the slope of the line through the points (−4, 1) and (2, 3).

    A. −3
    B. $-\dfrac{1}{3}$
    C. $\dfrac{1}{3}$
    D. 3

GO ON TO THE NEXT PAGE

26. In the Venn diagram shown, numbers that have a factor of 2 are in the circle labeled "2"; those that have a factor of 5 are in the circle labeled "5"; and those that have a factor of 7 are in the circle labeled "7." In which of the regions A, B, C, or D is the number 50?

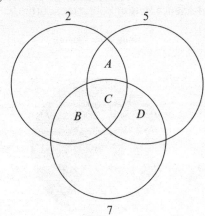

- A. A
- B. B
- C. C
- D. D

27. Simplify $4 + 2(3x + 1)$.

- A. $12x$
- B. $6x + 5$
- C. $6x + 6$
- D. $18x + 6$

28. Find $f(-4)$ when $f(x) = 20 - x$.

- A. -24
- B. -16
- C. 16
- D. 24

29. Solve for x: $3(x - 6) = 21$

- A. 1
- B. 5
- C. 9
- D. 13

30. Determine which ordered pair satisfies the given system.

$2x - y = -7$
$x + 3y = -7$

- A. $(-4, -1)$
- B. $(-4, 1)$
- C. $(4, -1)$
- D. $(4, 1)$

31. If $x = -5$, which statement is true?

- A. $\dfrac{1}{x} > -x$
- B. $3x < 2x$
- C. $-x < 0$
- D. $x - 6 > x + 6$

32. Solve $-2x + 5 < 7$.

- A. $x < -1$
- B. $x < -6$
- C. $x > -1$
- D. $x > -6$

33. A survey of 200 middle school students revealed the 200 students have a median weekly allowance of $10.75, and 35 percent of them receive no allowance at all. Which statement is a definite conclusion from the information provided?

- A. One hundred students receive an allowance of $10.75 or less.
- B. One hundred students receive an allowance of $10.75.
- C. The mean allowance for the 200 students is $10.75.
- D. Thirty-five students receive no allowance at all.

34. The graph shown represents the monthly average low and high temperatures in the city of Townville for 4 months of the year. In which month was the difference in the average low and high temperatures the greatest?

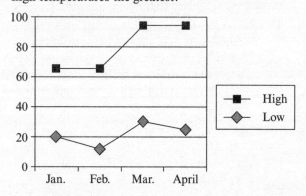

- A. January
- B. February
- C. March
- D. April

GO ON TO THE NEXT PAGE

35. The table shows eight students' scores on a history test. What is the median of the set of scores?

Student	Score
1	96
2	42
3	56
4	88
5	69
6	73
7	67
8	88

A. 71
B. 72
C. 72.375
D. 88

36. Given is a box of 50 marbles, all identical except for color. The box contains 20 blue, 10 red, 14 green, and 6 yellow marbles. If a person picks out a single marble from the box without looking, what is the probability the marble will be yellow or blue?

A. $\frac{6}{125}$
B. $\frac{3}{25}$
C. $\frac{2}{5}$
D. $\frac{13}{25}$

37. Shailene is making a sandwich for lunch. She has a choice of three kinds of bread (white, whole wheat, or rye) and four sandwich fillings (ham, turkey, sliced beef, or pimiento cheese). How many different sandwiches can she make if she chooses one type of bread and one kind of sandwich filling?

A. 7
B. 9
C. 12
D. 16

38. A library surveyed 200 young readers to ask what kind of books they read most often from among adventure, nature, science fiction, and biography or historical books. The results are recorded in the pie graph shown. According to the graph, how many young readers surveyed read science fiction books most often?

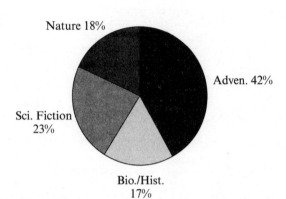

Book Type Survey

A. 34
B. 36
C. 46
D. 84

39. The line plot shown shows the minutes waited in line by 14 customers at a fast food restaurant. What is the range of the data?

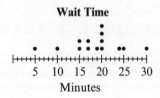

Wait Time

A. 15 minutes
B. 20 minutes
C. 25 minutes
D. 30 minutes

40. Which set of prices has a median of $10.24?

A. $10.29, $9.87, $11.99, $8.45, $10.60, $10.25
B. $7.50, $12.98, $8.25, $10.89, $11.05, $10.67
C. $11.98, $10.50, $9.98, $8.50, $12.95, $9.98
D. $11.05, $12.98, $8.25, $9.55, $7.50, $10.67

GO ON TO THE NEXT PAGE

41. Which set of scores has a mode of 87?

- A. 90, 87, 96, 96, 87, 96
- B. 99, 87, 93, 94, 87, 90
- C. 91, 92, 89, 97, 84, 84
- D. 92, 91, 85, 87, 88, 95

42. A box contains 40 tiles, all of identical shape and size, numbered 1 through 40. If a person picks out a single tile from the box without looking, what is the probability the number on the tile will be a prime number?

- A. $\dfrac{1}{4}$
- B. $\dfrac{3}{10}$
- C. $\dfrac{13}{40}$
- D. $\dfrac{27}{40}$

43. At the beginning of the year, a school district requires administration of a benchmark test in mathematics to all students in grades 6 through 8 in the district's two middle schools. The test results showed 15 percent of the students at Sunshine Middle School, the larger of the two middle schools in the district, were below grade level in mathematics. Based on these data, which conclusion is valid?

- A. 15 percent of all eighth-grade students at Sunshine Middle School are below grade level in mathematics.
- B. 15 percent of all eighth-grade students in the school district are below grade level in mathematics.
- C. 15 percent of all students in grades 6 through 8 at Sunshine Middle School are below grade level in mathematics.
- D. 15 percent of all students in grades 6 through 8 in the school district are below grade level in mathematics.

44. Jolene and Meiko, students in a ninth-grade Algebra I class, are conducting a survey of the opinions of the 600 ninth-grade students in their high school on whether students should be required to wear uniforms. Which method of surveying the students will allow Jolene and Meiko to make valid conclusions about the ninth-grade students' opinions about wearing uniforms?

- A. Ask all the ninth-grade Algebra I students in the school.
- B. Ask 100 students in the high school whose names are chosen at random.
- C. Ask 100 ninth-grade students in the high school whose names are chosen at random.
- D. Ask 100 students randomly selected from those who ride a bus home from school.

45. For a school project, Chad conducted an experiment to determine whether growing roses under artificial red light instead of in ordinary sunlight affects the number of flowers produced. Chad randomly selected 30 rose plants, all of the same variety. The 30 plants were grown under red light and the number of flowers produced was much greater than expected. Based on these data, Chad concluded growing roses under artificial red light produces more flowers than does growing them in ordinary sunlight. Rohan tells Chad his conclusion is not valid. Which critique of Chad's experiment best supports Rohan's statement?

- A. Chad should have grown another group of 30 randomly selected rose plants of the same variety in identical conditions, but under ordinary sunlight.
- B. Chad should have grown another group of 30 randomly selected rose plants of the same variety in identical conditions, but in complete darkness.
- C. Chad should have decreased the number of rose plants in the experimental group to 15.
- D. Chad should have increased the number of rose plants in the experimental group to 100.

IF YOU FINISH BEFORE TIME IS CALLED, CHECK YOUR WORK ON THIS SECTION ONLY. DO NOT WORK ON ANY OTHER SECTION IN THE TEST.

Reading

40 Minutes
40 Questions

Directions: Please read the following passages carefully. Each passage in this section is followed by questions based on the passage's content. After reading each passage, answer the questions by choosing the best answer from among the four choices given. Be sure to base your answers on what is *implied* or *stated* in the passage.

Passage 1

Baseball: America's National Pastime

(1) If you want to know the spirit of America, you need to know the role of baseball in American life. Loved by millions, played by thousands, baseball, since its first introduction into American life, has become to many fans in our country a symbol of all that is good and right about America. Unlike football or basketball, baseball <u>evokes</u> a bygone era of American independence, openness, and simplicity. Perhaps because it is played outside in the fresh air and beneath America's clear blue skies or, perhaps because it is such a civil and simple game, it evokes nostalgia and happiness whenever people, young and old alike, gather to watch this homegrown sport played out on our nation's amateur and professional fields.

(2) Patterned after a game in England, baseball has its roots in America's colonies. Early settlers played "rounders," a game that involved hitting a ball with a bat and advancing around bases. One big difference from the traditional English rounders, though, in this early colonial game is that players were counted out when another threw the ball and hit the man advancing. The practice was known as "plugging" or "soaking" runners. Fortunately, this practice of literally "striking" runners was changed to a simple "tagging" of runners, thereby beginning the game of baseball as we know it today. In fact, by the mid-1800s, baseball was played in America very similar to the way it is played today—a baseball diamond, two teams, three outs, nine innings, and whichever team has the most runs batted in wins.

(3) Although myth has it that Abner Doubleday invented modern baseball, it is most often credited to Alexander Cartwright, a New York City sportsman. In 1845, Cartwright started a club, "The Knickerbocker Base Ball Club of New York," whose sole purpose was to play baseball. Beginning with a dream and a desire, Cartwright wrote many of the rules that baseball follows today. Shortly after Cartwright's New York team was formed, others followed. Ironically enough, the Civil War (1861–1865) helped spread baseball across the United States. For recreation, Union troops played the game to the amusement of onlookers from both sides of America's great conflict. After the war, Northerners and Southerners were playing this popular game, and gradually its popularity grew from state to state.

(4) With popularity came commercialism, and soon baseball became a professional sport. Major American cities—Boston, New York, Philadelphia, Detroit, and others—sported a major league baseball club to rival competing teams. Americans, eager to watch this new sport and cheer their respective home teams, began flocking to makeshift baseball stadiums in the early 1900s, ensuring the success of the country's first professional sports franchise system.

(5) Success meant more competition. Fans followed their favorite teams, hoping for championship seasons. Soon, star players became local and national heroes, and baseball enthusiasts knew the statistics of every player. Baseball became America's national pastime. With each passing game, teams and their players added more to its historical lore and contemporary allure.

(6) Of all of America's obsessions, baseball is one of pure passion. To fans of the game, nothing <u>exemplifies</u> America's spirit, independence, and competitiveness more than an exciting game of baseball. And fans feel that nothing has come along to compete with the feeling of sitting outdoors, soaking in the warm summer sun, and enjoying a favorite team at play in a leisurely and orderly game of baseball. Perhaps, these reasons explain why baseball has so long endured.

GO ON TO THE NEXT PAGE

1. This passage indicates that
   A. baseball should be played outside and on grass.
   B. "plugging" is not a part of modern baseball.
   C. Abner Doubleday invented baseball.
   D. Alexander Cartwright was an American patriot.

2. According to this passage, "rounders" is a game that
   A. was imported from England.
   B. had nine innings.
   C. was played by Civil War soldiers.
   D. was never popular in America.

3. In the first paragraph, third sentence, the word *evokes* means
   A. deters.
   B. entices.
   C. projects.
   D. elicits.

4. The organizational pattern used by the author in paragraphs 2 through 4 can best be described as
   A. order of importance.
   B. spatial order.
   C. comparison and contrast.
   D. chronological order.

5. Which sentence is a statement of opinion?
   A. Early settlers played "rounders."
   B. Alexander Cartwright wrote many of the rules that baseball follows today.
   C. Professional baseball teams were formed by the 1900s.
   D. Baseball is a civil and simple game.

6. According to the passage, why is baseball considered America's favorite pastime?
   A. It provides interested individuals with a casual diversion.
   B. It engages sports enthusiasts in a fast-paced spectator sport.
   C. It is played casually without rules.
   D. It occurs at a leisurely pace in a pastoral setting.

7. As used in the final paragraph, second sentence, the word *exemplifies* means to
   A. define by definition.
   B. illustrate by example.
   C. organize by listing.
   D. delineate by detailing.

8. The tone of this passage can best be described as
   A. derisive.
   B. nostalgic.
   C. subjective.
   D. objective.

9. Which sentence best states the main idea of this passage?
   A. Baseball is a sport that is elitist in tone and style.
   B. Baseball evokes an era of a simpler life and pace.
   C. Baseball reflects the simplicity of all competitive sports.
   D. Baseball inspires youngsters to become competitive athletes.

10. Closely re-read the final paragraph, reproduced below:

    Of all of America's obsessions, baseball is one of pure passion. To fans of the game, nothing exemplifies America's spirit, independence, and competitiveness more than an exciting game of baseball. And fans feel that nothing has come along to compete with the feeling of sitting outdoors, soaking in the warm summer sun, and enjoying a favorite team at play in a leisurely and orderly game of baseball. Perhaps, these reasons explain why baseball has so long endured.

    The second and third sentences
    A. revise the comment in the first sentence.
    B. detract from the comment in the first sentence.
    C. expand the comment in the first sentence.
    D. analyze the comment in the first sentence.

GO ON TO THE NEXT PAGE

Passage 2

Dancing: One Person's Lament

(1) Do you know how to dance? I mean, really dance? Most people know how to "shake, rattle, and roll," and many can do a fairly good imitation of an individual in the "throes of a demonic possession," but very few of us can actually dance well. We might know how to twist and shout, but how many of us can cha-cha, rhumba, or waltz? I know I can't. I have (to repeat a time-honored phrase) two left feet and have tried on numerous occasions to learn to really dance, but have always ended up in the arms of someone desperate enough to be kind, yet not quite assertive enough to say, "Stick to walking."

(2) Dancing, to be sure, is among the oldest of human art forms. Traditionally, it has been a most immediate form of self-expression. Ancient rituals were (and still are to this day) celebrated in dance, as the dance symbolizes a form of prayer. Dancing for rain, good fortune, fertility of crops, and for success in war or hunting was common. Often, elaborate costumes and props were incorporated in these highly ritualistic endeavors as well.

(3) Ritualistic dancing eventually gave rise to social dancing. Instead of being used to strengthen religious connections, dancing became a prime means for social bonding as people gathered for celebrations and used their love for movement and song to unite their heads and hearts. Social dancing became the mechanism through which individuals discovered common bonds and together affirmed their sense of common identity or belonging.

(4) As dance evolved, it naturally took on a life of its own. Soon, formal dancing emerged. In formal dancing, the steps involved are more complicated in design than dancing that is self-willed and free-wheeling. Instead of simple and impulsive movements, the participants learn exact steps that require time, diligence, and a certain nimbleness to master.

(5) I have never had the patience to master formal moves, but I envy all who really know how to dance well—those who have perfected both the art and skill of masterful movement to music and who can cha-cha and tango expertly. Blessed with the gift of mimicry, these strong and able dancers rival professional sports athletes in their dexterity, agility, and nimbleness. Indeed, their expertise lies in making the difficult and strenuous look easy and joyous. In this way, the universal language of dance invites its watchers and participants—even those as seemingly hopeless as I—to engage in an activity that is part seduction, part mystery, and part unifier, and that expresses a range of human emotions.

11. Based on information in this passage, the author likely would agree dancing is

    A. detrimental to one's health and well-being.
    B. always self-willed and free-wheeling.
    C. a waste of time and energy.
    D. a joyous expression of movement to music.

12. The author's claim that "I have ... two left feet" (paragraph 1) is

    A. questionable because of the author's love for dance.
    B. a narrative technique to engage the reader.
    C. full proof that the author dislikes dancing.
    D. an argumentative style to disarm the reader.

13. This passage is an example of a(n)

    A. expository piece about a positive experience.
    B. cynical account on the decline of tradition.
    C. valedictory tribute to a dying art form.
    D. descriptive narrative of an obscure obsession.

14. In the fifth paragraph, the phrase *Blessed with the gift of mimicry* best means being able to

    A. deceive.
    B. reinvent.
    C. imitate.
    D. circumvent.

15. According to this passage, dancing is universally enjoyed because it

    A. is an ancient and mysterious ritual.
    B. speaks to human emotions.
    C. is compelling and consequential.
    D. revels in the known and factual.

16. Which statement is implied in the first paragraph?

    A. Most people know how to shake, rattle, and roll.
    B. The waltz is an easy dance to master.
    C. The cha-cha, rhumba, and waltz are types of dances.
    D. Few people can actually dance well.

GO ON TO THE NEXT PAGE

17. Which sentence is a statement of opinion?

    A. Ancient rituals were celebrated in dance.
    B. Ritualistic dancing gave rise to social dancing.
    C. Dancing has been a human form of self-expression.
    D. In formal dancing, the participants learn exact steps.

18. In the context of the first paragraph, the word *assertive* most nearly means

    A. loud.
    B. skillful.
    C. bold.
    D. anxious.

19. This passage states that

    A. professional sports athletes are good dancers.
    B. ritualistic dancing is no longer practiced.
    C. dancing is an art form.
    D. only expert dancers can learn to cha-cha.

20. According to information given in this passage,

    A. people have an inborn desire to want to learn to dance.
    B. ritualistic dancing is very similar to social dancing.
    C. Native Americans performed ritualistic dances for success in hunting.
    D. formal dancing is difficult and strenuous.

Passage 3

Jean Piaget: The Beginning of Educational Thought

(1)   Jean Piaget's (1896–1980) major contribution to the history of educational thought and the study of cognitive science is that he proposed that children pass through four stages of mental development. Each stage, he believed, lasted for a specified period of time and must be followed in a designated order. He felt that this defined order accounted for why young children perceived the world as they do and why they make their respective choices. Piaget's work is seminal to understanding modern child development and integral to defining his subsequent impact on everything that followed his early findings.

(2)   Piaget's four stages of cognitive development in children are the *sensorimotor period* (birth to 2 years old), the *preoperational period* (2 to 7 years old), the *period of concrete operations* (7 to 11 years old), and the *period of formal operations* (11 to 15 years old). Each stage has its own specific characteristics; and, generally, each is experienced in the chronological order in which it appears. The *sensorimotor period* is the time when infants and toddlers obtain their basic knowledge of the world through their senses. Next, the *preoperational period* is when young children develop such skills as language and drawing ability. In the period of *concrete operations*, older children begin to think logically. Gradually, they begin to take on the ability to organize their knowledge, classify objects, and do thought problems. Finally, during the period of *formal operations,* young people or teenagers begin to think conceptually, applying rational and abstract reasoning to their burgeoning thought processes. Piaget knew, though, that if young children got stuck in a particular stage of mental development, their learning would be, for the most part, defined by that mental stage. Thus, if young people gradually grow into the final developmental stage—the period of *formal operations*—they, more than likely, will have a promising intellectual future. To be stuck in an earlier stage, though, means a life of limited intellectual abilities.

(3)   Piaget had an interesting and full life. Born in 1896 in Neufchatel, Switzerland, Jean Piaget was soon recognized by his family, teachers, and peers as an exceptionally bright and inquisitive child. Not satisfied with simple explanations, Piaget spent hours researching whatever scientific principle or theory caught his interest. Around 10 years of age, his innate curiosity and deep-seated drive led him to publish his first scientific paper on an albino sparrow. This accomplishment was followed by a number of articles on mollusks at the age of 15.

(4)   Naturally, this precocious child excelled in school; and by 1918, at the early age of 22, he received his doctorate in the natural sciences. Not content to know just the physical world, Piaget began studying psychology, hoping to uncover the mysteries of the human mind. Retreating in 1921 to the world-famed Institute J. J. Rousseau in Geneva, Piaget embarked on a career that

GO ON TO THE NEXT PAGE

eventually led to his breakthrough discoveries in human cognition. From 1933 to 1971, Piaget served as the co-director of this famed institute and as the director of the International Bureau of Education (1929–1967). Always busy and engaged, Piaget was also a professor of psychology at the University of Geneva from 1929 until his death in 1980, at age 94.

(5) Piaget's most significant contribution to the world of scientific thought about human cognition is the result of his studies of young children, primarily his own children—Jacqueline, Lucienne, and Laurent. From their infancy, Piaget observed and recorded their cognitive development, crystallizing his observations into his renowned scientific theories. And his lasting contribution, though commonplace today, was radical for its time—that children think differently than adults.

(6) Both a qualitative and a quantitative researcher, Piaget studied human growth and development from a holistic perspective, always trying to integrate disparate elements of information into a cohesive and recognizable human whole. His research on how knowledge grows systematically, that it is a progressive construction of logically embedded structures, each one building on the next, transformed the manner in which psychologists think of young people. No longer are they thought of as miniature adults. Instead, Piaget's seminal work recognized that children's logic and modes of thinking were entirely their own. His theories about child development radically transformed the world of cognitive science; and, to this day, stand as a significant contribution to the field of developmental psychology. Simply by studying his own children, Piaget introduced us to the world of all children.

21. In this passage, the author suggests that Piaget was a(n)

A. curious and prodigious thinker.
B. effete intellectual and disciplinarian.
C. raucous and caustic intellectual.
D. cautious and solitary scientist.

22. As thinking about human cognition has evolved, one principle, according to this passage, has remained constant:

A. Human beings need to reconcile the absurd.
B. Human beings need to understand the misunderstood.
C. Human beings need to develop mentally in defined stages.
D. Human beings need to rediscover ancient truths.

23. The author of this passage would probably agree that

A. developmental psychology has its origins in ritualistic thinking.
B. studying cognitive thinking reveals human behavior patterns.
C. understanding abstract thinking parallels nutritional habits.
D. searching for the unknown is the province of only religious thinkers.

24. Which of the following statements is NOT supported by the passage?

A. Psychology is the study of human developmental growth patterns.
B. Piaget's developmental theories were the result of a small sample size.
C. Developmental thinking can be classified into specified age groups.
D. Cognitive psychology relies on the suspension of disbelief.

25. In the fourth paragraph, the phrase *Not content to know just the physical world* implies that Piaget

A. was a literal scientific researcher.
B. understood only the human body.
C. engaged in quantitative research.
D. intended to explore mental functions.

GO ON TO THE NEXT PAGE

26. What is the relationship between the following two sentences?

    Sentence 1: *No longer are they thought of as miniature adults.* (Paragraph 6)

    Sentence 2: *Instead, Piaget's seminal work recognized that children's logic and modes of thinking were entirely their own.* (Paragraph 6)

    A. Sentence 2 restates the point made in Sentence 1.
    B. Sentence 2 clarifies the point made in Sentence 1.
    C. Sentence 2 questions the point made in Sentence 1.
    D. Sentence 2 disputes the point made in Sentence 1.

27. Which of the following is the topic of the second paragraph?

    A. Piaget's four stages of cognitive development
    B. Piaget's views on teaching and learning
    C. Piaget's ideas about rational thought
    D. Piaget's theories on how infants perceive the world

28. Which of the following is an opinion about Jean Piaget expressed in this passage?

    A. His work is seminal to understanding modern child development.
    B. He received a doctorate degree in natural sciences.
    C. He studied his own children.
    D. He published his first paper before he was 12 years old.

29. This passage states that Jean Piaget

    A. advocated developmentally appropriate learning activities.
    B. made breakthrough discoveries in human cognition.
    C. received a number of honorary degrees in his lifetime.
    D. died before his theories were generally accepted.

30. The tone of this passage is best described as

    A. doubtful.
    B. mocking.
    C. persuasive.
    D. serious.

Passage 4

Whales: Special Mammals Indeed

(1) Many people think whales are a type of fish because whales live in the water. Whales, however, are not fish; they are mammals and have much in common with human beings. It is hard to believe, but it is true. Whales, monkeys, dogs, and people all belong to the same class, and like these other mammals, whales have a highly developed brain and are among the most behaviorally complex of all animals.

(2) Whales differ from fish in multiple ways. For instance, whales have different tails than fish. Fish tails are vertical—they move sideways; whale tails are horizontal—they move up and down. Also, fish breathe through gills, taking in dissolved oxygen from water. Whales, on the other hand, have lungs and must come to the surface to breathe. But, for some whales, the trip to the surface for oxygen can be delayed quite a while; in fact, the sperm whale can hold its breath for up to two hours.

(3) Gestation and birth are other examples of how fish and whales differ. Fish lay eggs and do not feed their offspring. Whales, though, have the "mothering instinct" of mammals. Like apes, dogs, and cats, they give birth to live young and proceed to feed them with milk from the mother's body. Fish are emotionally detached from their offspring, whereas, for a whale, the mothering instinct remains strong throughout a lifetime.

(4) Another major difference between fish and whales is that fish are cold-blooded and whales are warm-blooded. As a cold-blooded creature, a fish's body temperature changes with the water's temperature. When the water is cold, the fish is cold. A whale, on the other hand, remains warm regardless of the temperature of the surrounding water.

(5) Adaptation has played a major role in the evolution of whales. Yes, they are considered mammals, but unlike most mammals, they do not have much hair nor do they have legs or much neck mobility. Through centuries of change and adaptability, whales have developed streamlined, compact, and compressed body frames that allow them to carry enormous weight and still manage to swim through the sea with great ease. In fact, scientists believe their front legs developed into flippers, allowing them to steer and keep their balance.

GO ON TO THE NEXT PAGE

(6) Today, many whales are an endangered species, and some, especially the blue and humpback whales, are in danger of extinction because of unregulated hunting. For years, whalers were permitted to kill whales, like the blue and humpback, for their meat and by-products. The result is that whales of all kinds slowly disappeared from our oceans. Yet, thanks to environmental laws and public awareness, the significance of whales as one of the oldest and most distinct mammals is readily recognized by scientists and citizens alike. Once again, they populate our oceans and add to our knowledge about these unique marine mammals.

Humpback Tails

Credit: National Oceanic and Atmospheric Administration/ Department of Commerce

31. One idea this passage makes clear is that whales have more in common with

   A. mammals than with fish.
   B. reptiles than with mammals.
   C. amphibians than with fish.
   D. fish than with mammals.

32. According to the passage, whales are unique in the animal kingdom because whales

   A. are indigenous only to the northern hemisphere.
   B. can carry enormous weight without much effort.
   C. are nonmaternal and indifferent to their offspring.
   D. rely on protective fish clans for self-preservation.

33. The author of this passage implies that whales are

   A. timid.
   B. aggressive.
   C. intelligent.
   D. unintelligent.

34. Which statement can be inferred from the passage?

   A. Whales are creatures that have experienced successful adaptations.
   B. Whales are ponderous creatures with sluggish metabolisms.
   C. Whales are a species timid in scale and singular in design.
   D. Whales are an anomaly on the scale of biological diversity.

35. At the beginning of the fifth paragraph, the word *Adaptation* can best be defined as

   A. modification.
   B. skillfulness.
   C. awareness.
   D. immutability.

36. Which sentence from this passage is a statement of fact about whales?

   A. Whales are a type of fish.
   B. Whales have lungs.
   C. The blue whale is extinct.
   D. Whales are cold-blooded.

37. Which statement about whales is implied in this passage?

   A. They are known for supplying blubber.
   B. They cannot take in oxygen when underwater.
   C. They have gills.
   D. They have nothing in common with humans.

38. This passage states that the sperm whale can hold its breath for

   A. no more than 30 minutes.
   B. up to 2 hours.
   C. at least 3 hours.
   D. well over 4 hours.

GO ON TO THE NEXT PAGE

39. According to the passage, whales

  A. are the world's largest animal.
  B. nurture their young.
  C. have difficulty swimming.
  D. are of little concern to environmentalists.

40. The author included the photograph after the final paragraph most likely to evoke which emotion?

  A. Concern due to the unregulated hunting of humpback whales.
  B. Awe at the magnificent tails of humpback whales.
  C. Excitement for the opportunity to scrutinize humpback tails.
  D. Impatience to see humpback whales in the ocean firsthand.

IF YOU FINISH BEFORE TIME IS CALLED, CHECK YOUR WORK ON THIS SECTION ONLY. DO NOT WORK ON ANY OTHER SECTION IN THE TEST.

Answer Key

English Language Skills

1. B	9. A	17. C	25. B	33. B
2. C	10. B	18. D	26. B	34. A
3. C	11. A	19. C	27. C	35. B
4. D	12. A	20. B	28. B	36. B
5. A	13. C	21. A	29. C	37. C
6. D	14. B	22. C	30. A	38. C
7. A	15. B	23. C	31. B	39. A
8. B	16. A	24. B	32. C	40. A

Mathematics

1. B	10. D	19. D	28. D	37. C
2. C	11. D	20. A	29. D	38. C
3. C	12. B	21. A	30. A	39. C
4. C	13. A	22. B	31. B	40. C
5. A	14. C	23. D	32. C	41. B
6. D	15. D	24. B	33. A	42. B
7. D	16. B	25. C	34. D	43. C
8. C	17. D	26. A	35. A	44. C
9. A	18. B	27. C	36. D	45. A

Reading

1. B	9. B	17. C	25. D	33. C
2. A	10. C	18. C	26. B	34. A
3. D	11. D	19. C	27. A	35. A
4. D	12. B	20. D	28. A	36. B
5. D	13. A	21. A	29. B	37. B
6. D	14. C	22. C	30. D	38. B
7. B	15. B	23. B	31. A	39. B
8. C	16. C	24. D	32. B	40. B

Answer Explanations

Essay

Sample Essays

In this section of the examination, you were to prepare a written assignment on one of two topics.

Topic 1

> Human beings need time to be themselves. They need time to relax, unwind, and just let their mind wander. What do you do to unwind? What hobbies do you pursue? Write an essay in which you identify your favorite hobbies and why you enjoy them.

Topic 2

> It is often said that historical figures change the world. Write an essay about a historical figure who changed the world and explain in detail what significant changes he or she made in the course of world events.

You were to write a response that would be well written, organized, and defined. You were informed that your writing would be graded holistically, taking into consideration both mechanics and organization.

In your essay, you were to introduce the topic and then either explain the topic you chose or take a position about your topic and support that position.

At least two evaluators will read your essay and assign it a score. Special attention will be paid to whether you observed the following:

- Explain the purpose of your writing
- Introduce your topic effectively
- Develop a relevant thesis or claim
- Organize ideas clearly
- Include relevant details
- Cite ample textual evidence
- Use a variety of sentence patterns
- Provide an effective concluding statement
- Maintain a consistent point of view
- Apply the conventions of standard written English

A strong sample response to each prompt follows.

Topic 1 – Strong Response

Human beings can have many roles. To name a few, we might be parents, friends, lovers, workers, caregivers, cooks, athletes, or students. Yet, despite the responsibilities of our various roles, an activity that we often enjoy the most is one we do just for ourselves. Such an activity is called a hobby. We find a diversion that appeals to us very much and despite bills, problems, and even illness we find time to pursue our enjoyment. I know. I have three hobbies that I enjoy no matter what.

First, I enjoy reading. For me, reading is a luxury that I try to enjoy at every opportunity. When no one is looking or there is a lull at work, I sneak in a few seconds to read just a little bit more of what I am presently enjoying. In truth, wherever I go, I carry something to read. My choices are eclectic. My reading preferences range from mysteries to political biographies. I find each fascinating and intriguing. Each genre—comedy, mystery, romance, thriller, or biography—provides new insights and understandings about life and living it; and, of course, whets my appetite for more.

Second, I enjoy eating. Now, I know eating is not considered a typical hobby, but when you are a conoisseur of fine food as I am, then eating can be considered your hobby. Often, my spouse and I will go miles just to try out a new restaurant, no matter how obscure or famous it might portend to be. We enjoy trying new dishes. Sometimes, we hit a real gem with great dishes, breads, and wines. Other times, well, let's just say, we don't finish our plates. But, despite disappointments, I never tire of eating.

Third, I enjoy laughing. Laughing, you say? Is laughing really a hobby? It is if you laugh like I do. I laugh loud and long and hard. And I constantly look for things to amuse me. I enjoy good jokes (preferably clean and clever), funny books, musical comedies, and silly movies. Each, when done well, tickles my ribs like nothing else possible. Does that mean that I don't like sad things? Sure, I do; but I figure, why cry when laughing is so much more pleasurable? Besides, evoking laughter is harder to execute. Making someone laugh, even a pushover like me, is a skill.

Thus, my hobbies are personal and unique. While many adults enjoy tennis and jogging, I prefer reading, eating, and laughing. I know that likely I won't end up looking as fit as people who have athletic hobbies, but, I will have fun pursuing my passion just like they do. And what more could I ask?

Evaluation of Strong Response: This essay is a well-written exposition. The writer explains the purpose of the writing and introduces the topic effectively (*I have three hobbies that I enjoy no matter what.*). Each paragraph has a clearly identified main idea with carefully selected supporting details. Word choice is generally precise and effective (*Each genre... provides new insights and understandings about life and living it; and, of course, whets my appetite for more.*). The organization is logical and straightforward. Each paragraph transitions smoothly to the next. Point of view is unambiguous and consistent. Word choice and sentence structure vary, and errors in sentence structure, usage, and mechanics are few. Although the writing is not flawless (for instance, in the third paragraph the word *connoisseur* is misspelled as *conoisseur;* in the fourth paragraph, *tickles my ribs* is a cliché; and there are errors in comma usage), this essay is a strong response.

Topic 2 – Strong Response

President Franklin D. Roosevelt is truly a historical figure who changed the world. The only president to be elected to four consecutive terms in office, Roosevelt led the United States through its worst depression and its worst war. In both his personal and political life, he showed courage and great strength of character in meeting and overcoming challenges.

In the prime of his life, Roosevelt became paralyzed from the waist down. Polio left him unable to walk, but not downtrodden. For the rest of his life, he fought desperately to overcome his disability, continuing his political career from a wheelchair. He loved public service and relished the attention that it brought him. He also wanted to prove to himself and the world that any hardship could be overcome with sheer determination. With this in mind, he ran for public office. He was elected governor of New York and then later became president of the United States.

When Roosevelt became president the United States was experiencing an unprecedented social upheaval. A serious economic depression was occurring and millions of people were unemployed. Immediately, Roosevelt and his administration began the difficult work of trying to solve the country's social and economic problems. Quickly, he set up numerous government agencies to provide relief for the jobless and to stabilize the country's economy. He also supplied banks in good financial condition with money so that they would reopen and return the country to a healthy financial position. Finally, he passed laws to protect the investments of those who held stocks and bonds. All these actions were taken to ensure the economic viability of a country and its citizens who were desperate for help.

At the beginning of Roosevelt's third term in office, the United States entered the Second World War. Shortly after the attack by the Japanese on Pearl Harbor, the U.S. Congress declared war on Japan. Three days later, Germany and Italy declared war on the United States. America then declared war on those countries. Under Roosevelt's leadership, the United States together with its allies prevailed over the enemy. America's citizens firmly supported Roosevelt during the difficult war years, but unfortunately, he was never to see the final victory. He died suddenly just before the surrender of the German army.

Truly, Roosevelt was a remarkable historical figure. Despite crippling pain, he managed to achieve political greatness and monumental significance by imposing his own physical and intellectual will onto the American people. Overcoming tremendous odds both at home and abroad, Roosevelt raised the economic conditions of the American people while simultaneously helping to liberate the world from opression and tyranny. In so doing, he was instrumental in changing the course of history and, in the process, demonstrated the power of the human spirit.

Evaluation of Strong Response: This essay is a well-written exposition. The central thesis—a historical figure who changed the world (*President Franklin D. Roosevelt*)—is presented clearly and effectively. The writer explains the purpose of the writing and introduces the topic effectively. Each paragraph has a clearly identified main idea with carefully selected supporting details. Word choice is generally precise and effective (*All these actions were taken to ensure the economic viability of a country and its citizens who were desperate for help.*). The organization is logical and straightforward. Each paragraph transitions smoothly to the next. Point of view is unambiguous and consistent. Word choice and sentence structure vary, and errors in sentence structure, usage, and mechanics are few. Although the writing is not flawless (for instance, in the fifth paragraph the word *oppression* is misspelled as *opression,* and there are errors in comma usage), this essay is a strong response.

English Language Skills

1. **B.** Choice **B** is the correct response. This arrangement provides the most logical sequence of ideas and supporting details in this paragraph. Choices **A, C,** and **D** do not represent a logical arrangement of the possible sentence combinations.

2. **C.** Choice **C** is the correct response. The passage discusses shells as a protective covering, not collecting them.

3. **C.** Choice **C** is the correct response. This arrangement provides the most logical sequence of ideas and supporting details in the paragraph. Choices **A, B,** and **D** do not represent a logical arrangement of the possible sentence combinations.

4. **D.** Choice **D** is the correct response. The passage discusses the challenge of language diversity in schools, not ethnic foods.

5. **A.** Choice **A** is the correct response. The word *accept* is used incorrectly in this sentence. The correction is *except*. The word *accept* means "to receive something." The word *except* means "excluding"; it is an indication that something is not included in the general whole. The word *allowed* at **B** is the correct spelling and used properly. The infinitive *to eat* at **C** is also the proper usage.

6. **D.** Choice **D** is the correct response. No change is necessary. The sentence is correct as written.

7. **A.** Choice **A** is the correct response. The word *too* is used incorrectly in this sentence. The correction is *to*. The word *too* means "also" or "in addition." The word *to* is a preposition used to connect two thoughts together in a sentence. The words *formally* at **B** and *themselves* at **C** are both the correct word choices for this sentence.

8. **B.** Choice **B** is the correct response. The word *french* is presented incorrectly in this sentence. The correction is *French*. A language—English, French, Spanish, German, and so on—is considered a proper noun and, hence, is capitalized. The words *read* at **A** and *tomorrow's* at **C** are spelled and used correctly in this sentence.

9. **A.** Choice **A** is the correct response. *Have went* is incorrect. The correction is *have gone*. The word *all-American* at **B** is properly capitalized. The word *their* at **C** is properly used as a possessive pronoun.

10. **B.** Choice **B** is the correct response. The word *among* is used incorrectly in this sentence. The correction is *between*. *Among* is used when you are referring to three or more objects; *between* is used when you are referring to only two objects. The verb *sat* at **A** is correctly used in this sentence. The word *awards* at **C** does not require capitalization.

11. **A.** Choice A is the correct response. The word *deep* is used incorrectly in this sentence. The correction is *deeply*. The word *deep* is used here as an adverb and, thus, should be replaced with *deeply*. The word *their* at **B** is the correct word choice because it is showing possession. The phrase *considerable differences* at **C** is an appropriate word choice for this sentence.

12. **A.** Choice A is the correct response. The word *fowl* is the wrong word choice in this sentence. The correction is *foul*. The word *fowl* is another word for bird. As used in this sentence, the word *foul* refers to an infringement of the rules in a game of play. The word *loudly* at **B** is an adverb modifying *protested* and is used correctly in this sentence. The word *disbelief* at **C** is used correctly.

13. **C.** Choice C is the correct response. The word *then* is the wrong word choice in this sentence. The correction is *than*. The word *than* is used when making a comparison, as is the case in this sentence. The word *then* refers to time. In this sentence, the word *unfortunately* at **A** is used correctly to modify the action of the tennis team. The auxiliary verb *had* at **B** is used correctly in this sentence.

14. **B.** Choice B is the correct response. The word *masks* is the wrong verb choice in this sentence. The correction is *mask*. The verb *mask* is used because the subject of the sentence is the plural noun *talents*. In this sentence, the adjective *surprising* at **A** is used correctly to modify the noun *talents*. The possessive form *his* at **C** is used correctly in this sentence.

15. **B.** Choice B is the correct response. The phrase *me and Nancy* is the wrong choice for this sentence. The correction is *Nancy and I*. The parts of a compound subject of a sentence are always in the subjective case. The word *among* at **A** is the correct word choice because it refers to more than two sisters. The word *tall* at **C** is correct as used in this sentence.

16. **A.** Choice A is the correct response. The word *reign* is the wrong word choice in this sentence. The word *reign* means "to rule as a monarch." The correction is *rain*. The verbs *found* at **B** and *eat* at **C** are used correctly in this sentence.

17. **C.** Choice C is the correct response. The sentence should be in the past tense, so *saw* is the correct verb at **C**. Keep in mind that the verb *seen* cannot stand alone; it requires an auxiliary verb. The word *students* at **A** does not show possession, so no apostrophe is needed. The word *who* at **B** is correct because it serves as the subject of the nonrestrictive clause it introduces.

18. **D.** Choice D is the correct response. The word *that* at **A** introducing the subordinate clause, which identifies what is being talked about, is correct. The word *really* at **B** is also correct because it is an adverb modifying the adjective *careful*. The plural pronoun *they* at **C** is correct because it agrees with its antecedent *scientists*.

19. **C.** Choice C is the correct response. A comma is needed at **C** to separate the introductory subordinate clause from the rest of the sentence. The word *When* at **A** is correct and makes sense in the sentence. The word *students* at **B** does not show possession, so no apostrophe is needed.

20. **B.** Choice B is the correct response. The phrase *more easier* at **B** is a faulty comparison of two things. The correct comparative form of *easy* is *easier*. The word *happy* at **A** is correct because it is an adjective referring to one thing. Placing a comma between *remember* and *than* at **C** would be incorrect.

21. **A.** Choice A is the correct response. The word following the verb *felt* at **A** modifies its subject, the pronoun *they*. The word *badly* is an adverb, however, and should not be used to modify a pronoun. The adjective *bad* should be used instead. The word *Tiffany* at **B** is a proper noun, so it should be capitalized. The plural verb *were* at **C** agrees with its plural subject *they*.

22. **C.** Choice C is the correct response. The word *capitol* refers to a building, not to a city. Change *capitol* to *capital*, which refers to a seat of government, to make the sentence grammatically correct. The word *history* at **A** is not a proper noun, so it should not be capitalized. The sentence is in the past tense, so *went* is the correct verb at **B**.

23. **C.** Choice C is the correct response. The word *there* at **C** should be changed to the plural third-person pronoun *their* to make the sentence grammatically correct. The possessive form *girls'* of the plural noun *girls* at **A** is correctly formed. To form the possessive of a plural noun that ends in *s*, add an apostrophe

after the *s*. Inserting a comma at **B** would be incorrect. No comma should be placed between two items joined by the word *and*.

24. **B.** Choice **B** is the correct response. The sentence is in the past tense; *ran* is the correct verb instead of *had run*. The word *When* at **A** is correct and makes sense in the sentence. The word *their* at **C** is spelled correctly.

25. **B.** Choice **B** is the correct response. The word *between* is a preposition. The object of a preposition should be in the objective case. Change *I* at **B** to *me* to make the sentence grammatically correct. The word *cannot* at **A** is spelled correctly. The word *years* at **C** is not showing ownership, so it should not be in the possessive case.

26. **B.** Choice **B** is the correct response. The word at **B** is the subject of the verb *am* (which is understood) and thus, should be in the subjective case. Change *me* to *I* to make the sentence grammatically correct. The sentence is in the present tense, so *are* at **A** is correct. Inserting a comma at **C** would be incorrect.

27. **C.** Choice **C** is the correct response. The word at **C** should be in the subjective case because it is the subject of the subordinate clause it introduces. Change *whomever* to *whoever* to make the sentence grammatically correct. Inserting a comma at **A** would be incorrect. The word *principal,* referring to the person who is the building supervisor of the school, at **B** is the correct word choice.

28. **B.** Choice **B** is the correct response. The singular pronoun *one* is the subject of the verb at **B,** so change *want* to *wants* to make the verb agree with its singular subject. The relative pronoun *who* at **A** is correct because it is the subject of the relative clause it introduces. The word *too* at **C** is spelled correctly.

29. **C.** Choice **C** is the correct response. The word *good* at **C** modifies the verb *did,* so it should be an adverb. Change *good* to *well* to make the sentence grammatically correct. The comma at **A** following the introductory clause is correct. The verb *didn't* at **B** agrees with its singular subject *he*.

30. **A.** Choice **A** is the correct response. The pronoun at **A** modifies the gerund noun *graduating,* which is the subject of the main clause; hence you should use the possessive pronoun *My* instead of *Me* to make the sentence grammatically correct. The singular verb *has* at **B** agrees with its singular subject *graduating*. The relative pronoun *whom* at **C** is the object of the preposition *of,* so it should be in the objective case.

31. **B.** Choice **B** is the correct response. The singular pronoun *one* is the subject of the verb at **B,** so change *were* to *was* to make the verb agree with its singular subject. Inserting a comma at **A** would be incorrect. No hyphen is needed at **C**.

32. **C.** Choice **C** is the correct response. As the sentence is written, a reader does not know whether *them* at **C** refers to *sons* or *board games*. Change *them* to *the board games* to avoid ambiguity. The word *couple's* at **A** is the correct possessive form of *couple*. The comma at **B** is needed to separate the two independent clauses.

33. **B.** Choice **B** is the correct response. The word at **B** should be spelled *received*. The relative pronoun *who* at **A** is correct because it is the subject of the clause it introduces. Inserting a comma at **C** would be incorrect.

34. **A.** Choice **A** is the correct response. At **A,** the superlative form of *nice* is *nicest,* not *most nicest*. The word *friend* at **B** is spelled correctly. The noun phrase *every day* at **C** should not be replaced with the adjective *everyday,* which means "common" or "used daily."

35. **B.** Choice **B** is the correct response. The correct comparative form of *old* is *older*. The comparative form is used when two things are compared.

36. **B.** Choice **B** is the correct response. The past participle for the verb *to take* is *taken*. Note that *should of* in **A** and **C** is an error for *should have*.

37. **C.** Choice **C** is the correct response. The tense of the verb in **C** relates logically to the verb in the main clause because both verbs are in the past tense. The verb tenses in **A** and **B** do not relate logically to the verb in the main clause.

38. **C.** Choice **C** is the correct response. All punctuation in Choice **C** is correct. Choice **A** is incorrect because it creates a comma splice, with two independent clauses connected by only a comma. Choice **B** is a run-on sentence. It has two independent clauses joined without a word to connect them or a proper punctuation mark to separate them. The first sentence in Choice **D** needs a comma after the word *promise*.

39. A. Choice **A** is the correct response. All punctuation in Choice **A** is correct. In Choice **B**, the word *familys'* is incorrect. To form the possessive of a noun (either singular or plural) that does not end in *s*, add an apostrophe and *s*. Choice **C** is incorrect because it contains a fragment (*Having been raised in our household from a puppy*). A comma is needed in Choice **D** to separate the introductory participial phrase from the rest of the sentence.

40. A. Choice **A** is the correct response. The modifiers in sentence **A** are placed correctly. The participial phrase *driving through the neighborhood* modifies *woman* and should be close to it. In choices **B** and **C**, *driving through the neighborhood* is separated from the noun *woman*, resulting in ambiguity. Additionally, the participial phrase *playing with his dog* modifies the noun *child* and should be close to it. In Choice **D,** the participial phrase *playing with his dog* is separated from the noun *child*, resulting in ambiguity.

Mathematics

1. B. Choice **B** is the correct response. The answer to $x \div y$ is the number whose product with y is x. Thus, $x \div y = z$ if and only if $z \cdot y = x$ (Choice **B**) is correct.

Eliminate choices **A** and **D** because, commonly, a division problem is defined by a corresponding multiplication problem. The multiplication problem in Choice **C** is incorrect.

2. C. Choice **C** is the correct response. Sequentially perform the indicated operations on x, simplifying as you go along.

Add 10: $x + 10$

Multiply the result by 5: $5(x+10) = 5x + 50$ Tip: Be sure to enclose the quantity $x + 10$ in parentheses.

Subtract 70: $5x + 50 - 70 = 5x - 20$

Divide by 5: $\dfrac{5x-20}{5} = \dfrac{5(x-4)}{5} = \dfrac{\cancel{5}(x-4)}{\cancel{5}} = \dfrac{(x-4)}{1} = x - 4$, Choice **C**

Choices **A, B,** and **D** occur if you simplify incorrectly as you perform the indicated operations.

3. C. Choice **C** is the correct response. From the figure, you can see triangles *ABC* and *ADE* are right triangles. To find the area of right triangle *ABC*, compute $\dfrac{1}{2}$ the product of the lengths of its two perpendicular legs, $\overline{CA}$ and $\overline{BC}$. The length of leg $\overline{CA}$ is the sum of the lengths of the two segments, $\overline{CE}$ and $\overline{EA}$. Because right triangles *ABC* and *ADE* have two congruent right angles and an acute angle in common, namely angle *A*, they are similar triangles. Thus, the length of $\overline{BC}$ can be determined by using properties of similar triangles.

Finding the area of triangle *ABC* will take three steps. First, find the length of leg $\overline{CA}$ by adding the lengths of the two segments, $\overline{CE}$ and $\overline{EA}$. Next, find the length of leg $\overline{BC}$ by using the proportionality of the corresponding sides of the similar triangles *ABC* and *ADE*. Then, find the area of triangle *ABC* by computing $\dfrac{1}{2}bh = \dfrac{1}{2}(\text{length of } \overline{CA})(\text{length of } \overline{BC})$.

Step 1. Find the length of leg $\overline{CA}$.

$CA = 200 \text{ m} + 100 \text{ m} = 300 \text{ m}$

Step 2. Find the length of $\overline{BC}$ and call it *x*.

$\dfrac{x}{300 \text{ m}} = \dfrac{50 \cancel{\text{ m}}}{100 \cancel{\text{ m}}}$

$x = \dfrac{50 \cdot 300 \text{ m}}{100} = 150 \text{ m}$ Find a cross product you can calculate, and then divide by the other number.

Step 3. Find the area of triangle *ABC*.

$$\text{area} = \frac{1}{2}bh = \frac{1}{2}(300 \text{ m})(150 \text{ m}) = 22\,500 \text{ m}^2$$

The area of triangle *ABC* is 22 500 m², Choice **C**.

Did I answer the question? Yes, I found the area of triangle *ABC*. ✓

Does my answer make sense? Yes, the area seems reasonable. ✓

Is the answer stated in the correct units? Yes, the units are m², which is correct. ✓

4. **C.** Choice **C** is the correct response. To evaluate the expression $7 + 3(4^2) - 8$, follow the order of operations using the mnemonic "Please Excuse My Dear Aunt Sally."

$7 + 3(4^2) - 8 = 7 + 3(16) - 8$	First, do the exponentiation inside the parentheses.
$= 7 + 48 - 8$	Next, multiply.
$= 47$, Choice **C**	Finally, add and subtract.

    Choice **A** results if you evaluate 4^2 incorrectly as $4 \times 2 = 8$. Choice **B** results if you add and subtract before multiplying. Choice **D** results if, after you do the exponentiation in the first step, you continue by evaluating from left to right without regard for the order of operations.

5. **A.** Choice **A** is the correct response. Given x and $y = 3x$ are whole numbers and $z = x + y = x + 3x = 4x$, then z is a multiple of 4. Therefore, z represents a whole number that is divisible by 4. A number is divisible by 4 if and only if the last two digits form a number that is divisible by 4. Looking at the answer choices, you can see only Choice **A** fails the test for divisibility by 4—the last two digits of 314 are 14, which is not divisible by 4.

6. **D.** Choice **D** is the correct response. Let x be the price of the jacket before sales tax. Write an equation that represents the facts.

    $$x + 8.25\% = \$108.25$$

    Tip: When sales tax is added to an item, multiply the price of the item times the sales tax rate.

    Solve the equation.

    Note: To change 8.25% to a decimal, move the decimal point two places to the left and drop the percent sign to obtain 0.0825.

    $$x + 0.0825x = \$108.25$$
    $$1.0825x = \$108.25$$
    $$\frac{1.0825x}{1.0825} = \frac{\$108.25}{1.0825}$$
    $$x = \$100.00$$

    The price of the jacket is $100 before sales tax, Choice **D**.

    Did I answer the question? Yes, I found the price of the jacket before sales tax. ✓

    Does my answer make sense? Yes, $100 seems reasonable given the jacket plus tax is $108.25. ✓

    Is the answer stated in the correct units? Yes, the units are dollars, which is correct. ✓

7. **D.** Choice **D** is the correct response. To list the temperatures in order from coldest to warmest, list them in order from lowest to highest. Start with the positive temperatures: 2° < 4°. You know 0° is less than the

positive temperatures and greater than the negative temperatures, so you have this: negative temperatures < 0° < 2° < 4°. To compare –6° and –8°, sketch a number line.

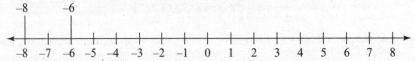

From the number line, you can see –6 is greater than –8 because it lies to the right of –8, so you end up with the following: –8° < –6° < 0° < 2° < 4°, Choice **D**. Choice **A** results if you list the temperatures in order as if all were nonnegative. Choice **B** results if you list the temperatures from warmest to coldest. Choice **C** results if you make the mistake of thinking –6° < –8°.

8. **C.** Choice **C** is the correct response. To find the amount budgeted for rent, answer the question: What is 30% of $2,400?

   Method 1: To solve the problem, identify the elements of the percent proportion, plug the values into the percent proportion, and solve the proportion.

   Step 1. Identify the elements.

   $$r = 30$$
   $$\text{part} = ?$$
   $$\text{whole} = \$2,400$$

   Step 2. Let x = the part. Plug into the percent proportion (omitting the units for convenience).

   $$\frac{r}{100} = \frac{\text{part}}{\text{whole}}$$
   $$\frac{30}{100} = \frac{x}{2,400}$$

   Step 3. Solve the proportion.

   $30 \times 2,400$ Find a cross product you can calculate. You don't know the value of x, so the only cross product you can calculate is 30 times 2,400.

   $x = \dfrac{30 \times 2,400}{100}$ Divide by 100, the numerical term you didn't use.

   $x = 720$

   The amount budgeted for rent is $720, Choice **C**.

   Did I answer the question? Yes, I found the amount budgeted for rent. ✓

   Does my answer make sense? Yes. 10% of $2,400 is $240, so 30% is three times $240, which is $720. ✓

   Is the answer stated in the correct units? Yes, the units are dollars, which is correct. ✓

   Method 2: Change 30% to a decimal fraction or common fraction and then multiply.

   30% of $2,400 = 0.30 × $2,400 = $720.00

   $$\text{Or } 30\% \text{ of } \$2,400 = \frac{3}{\cancel{10}} \times \frac{\$2,40\cancel{0}}{1} = 3 \times \$240 = \$720$$

   Choice **A** results if you place the decimal point incorrectly. Choice **B** results if you solve the problem incorrectly by finding 70% of $2,400, and you place the decimal point incorrectly. Choice **D** results if you solve the problem incorrectly by finding 70% of $2,400.

9. **A.** Choice **A** is the correct response.

   Method 1: The conversion fractions are $\dfrac{1 \text{ km}}{1000 \text{ m}}$ and $\dfrac{1000 \text{ m}}{1 \text{ km}}$.

   Write your measurement as a fraction with denominator 1 and let unit analysis tell you whether to multiply by $\dfrac{1 \text{ km}}{1000 \text{ m}}$ or $\dfrac{1000 \text{ m}}{1 \text{ km}}$. Because you want meters to divide out, multiply by $\dfrac{1 \text{ km}}{1000 \text{ m}}$.

   $$\dfrac{1500 \text{ m}}{1} \cdot \dfrac{1 \text{ km}}{1000 \text{ m}} = \dfrac{1500 \text{ km}}{1000} = 1.5 \text{ km}$$

   Theo ran 1.5 kilometers in the race, Choice **A**.

   Choices **B** and **C** occur if you make a mistake in placing the decimal point in your answer. Choice **D** results if you multiply by 1000 to convert.

   Method 2: Use "King Henry Doesn't Usually Drink Chocolate Milk," which is a mnemonic for remembering the following metric prefixes: kilo-, hecto-, deca-, unit measurement, deci-, centi-, milli-.

   In this problem, the unit measurement is meters. You are going from meters to kilometers. To go from meters to kilometers you move left three times on the list above, so divide by 10 three times to convert meters to kilometers. Of course, dividing by 10 three times is equivalent to dividing by 1000 one time.

   Therefore,

   $$1500 \text{ m} = 1500 \div 1000 \text{ (3 moves left)} = 1.5 \text{ km}$$

   Theo ran 1.5 kilometers in the race, Choice **A**.

10. **D.** Choice **D** is the correct response. Compare the areas of the two lawns. The area of the smaller lawn is $(30 \text{ yd})(40 \text{ yd}) = 1200 \text{ yd}^2$. The area of the larger lawn is $(60 \text{ yd})(80 \text{ yd}) = 4800 \text{ yd}^2$. The ratio of the area of the larger lawn to that of the smaller lawn is $\dfrac{4{,}800 \text{ yd}^2}{1{,}200 \text{ yd}^2} = \dfrac{4{,}800 \text{ yd}^2}{1{,}200 \text{ yd}^2} = \dfrac{4}{1}$ or 4 to 1. Therefore, the larger lawn has four times (quadruple) the area of the smaller lawn, resulting in four times the mowing time, Choice **D**.

11. **D.** Choice **D** is the correct response. From the Mathematics Reference Sheet, the formula for the surface area of a sphere is $S.A. = 4\pi r^2$, and the formula for the volume of a sphere is $V = \dfrac{4}{3}\pi r^3$.

    Finding the volume of the sphere will take two steps. First, find the radius of the sphere by using the formula for the surface area of the sphere. Next, use the radius obtained to find the volume.

    Step 1. Find the radius of the sphere:

    $$\text{Surface area } S.A. = 4\pi r^2 = 144\pi \text{ cm}^2$$

    $$\dfrac{4\pi r^2}{4\pi} = \dfrac{144\pi \text{ cm}^2}{4\pi} \qquad \text{Divide both sides by } 4\pi \text{ to solve for } r^2.$$

    $$r^2 = 36 \text{ cm}^2$$

    Because $r^2 = 36 \text{ cm}^2$, you know that r is the square root of 36 cm^2; that is,

    $$r = \sqrt{36 \text{ cm}^2}$$
    $$r = 6 \text{ cm}$$

    Note: From the list of square roots given in the section titled "Are All Square Roots Irrational?" in Chapter 3 (page 77), you know $\sqrt{36} = 6$.

    Step 2. Find the volume.

    $$\text{Volume } V = \dfrac{4}{3}\pi r^3 = \dfrac{4}{3}\pi (6 \text{ cm})^3 = \dfrac{4}{3}\pi (216 \text{ cm}^3) = 288\pi \text{ cm}^3, \text{ Choice } \mathbf{D}.$$

Did I answer the question? Yes, I found the volume of the sphere. ✓

Does my answer make sense? Yes, the volume seems reasonable for a sphere with radius of 6 centimeters. ✓

Is the answer stated in the correct units? Yes, the units are cm³, which is correct. ✓

12. **B.** Choice **B** is the correct response. Sketch a diagram to illustrate the problem.

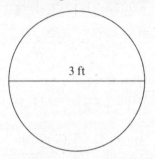

The Mathematics Reference Sheet gives the formula of a circle as $A = \pi r^2$. Finding the area of the circular garden will take two steps. First, find the radius of the circle. Next, plug the radius into the formula.

Step 1. Find the radius.

The radius is half the diameter = 3 ft ÷ 2 = 1.5 ft.

Step 2. Plug into the formula, using $\pi = 3.14$.

$$A = \pi r^2 = 3.14(1.5 \text{ ft})^2 = 3.14(2.25 \text{ ft}^2) \approx 7.07 \text{ ft}^2$$

The area of the circular garden is approximately 7.07 ft², Choice **B**.

Did I answer the question? Yes, I found the approximate area of the circular garden. ✓

Does my answer make sense? Yes. The area seems reasonable for a circle with radius of 1.5 feet. ✓

Is the answer stated in the correct units? Yes, the units are ft², which is correct. ✓

Choice **A** results if you find the radius but do not square it. Choice **C** results if you use the diameter in the area formula instead of the radius. Choice **D** results if you find the circumference instead of the area, and you disregard that the units do not work out to be square feet when you make this mistake.

13. **A.** Choice **A** is the correct response. Sketch a diagram to illustrate the problem.

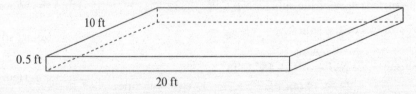

Cubic feet are units of volume. The amount of cement in the slab is equal to the volume of the slab, which is a rectangular prism. The Mathematics Reference Sheet gives the formula for the volume of a rectangular prism as $V = Bh$, where B is the area of the base. Thus, $V = lwh$ for a rectangular prism. To find the amount of cement, plug the dimensions into the formula.

$V = lwh = (20 \text{ ft})(10 \text{ ft})(0.5 \text{ ft}) = 100 \text{ ft}^3$

There are 100 ft³ of cement in the slab, Choice **A**.

Did I answer the question? Yes, I found how many cubic feet of cement are in the slab. ✓

Does my answer make sense? Yes, the slab is only 0.5 feet thick, so a volume of 100 ft³ seems reasonable. ✓

Is the answer stated in the correct units? Yes, the units are ft³, which is correct. ✓

Choice **B** results if you add the dimensions instead of multiplying. Choice **C** results if you multiply the volume by 3. Choice **D** results if you place the decimal point incorrectly when computing the volume.

14. **C.** Choice **C** is the correct response. The surface area of a cube is the sum of the areas of the faces of the cube. The cube in this problem has six congruent faces, each of which is a 10-cm square. To find the surface area of the cube, multiply 6 times the area of one face.

$$\text{Surface area} = 6 \times (10 \text{ cm})^2 = 6 \times 100 \text{ cm}^2 = 600 \text{ cm}^2$$

The surface area of the 10-cm cube is 600 cm^2, Choice **C**.

Did I answer the question? Yes, I found the surface area of the cube. ✓

Does my answer make sense? Yes, it is reasonable. ✓

Is the answer stated in the correct units? Yes, the units are cm^2, which is correct. ✓

Choice **A** results if you add the dimensions instead of multiplying. Choice **B** is the area of only one of the six faces. Choice **D** results if you multiply 6 × 10 before squaring.

15. **D.** Choice **D** is the correct response. To solve this problem, do two steps. First, convert 3 hours 15 minutes to hours. Next, divide 221 miles by the result.

Step 1. Convert 3 hours 15 minutes to hours. The two conversion fractions are $\frac{1 \text{ hour}}{60 \text{ min}}$ and $\frac{60 \text{ min}}{1 \text{ hour}}$. Write 15 minutes as a fraction with denominator 1 and let unit analysis tell you whether to multiply by $\frac{1 \text{ hour}}{60 \text{ min}}$ or $\frac{60 \text{ min}}{1 \text{ hour}}$. Because you want minutes to divide out, multiply by $\frac{1 \text{ hour}}{60 \text{ min}}$.

$$\frac{15 \text{ min}}{1} \times \frac{1 \text{ hour}}{60 \text{ min}} = \frac{\overset{1}{\cancel{15}} \text{ min}}{1} \times \frac{1 \text{ hour}}{\underset{4}{\cancel{60}} \text{ min}} = \frac{1}{4} \text{ hour} = 0.25 \text{ hour}$$

Thus, 3 hours 15 minutes = 3.25 hours.

Step 2. To obtain miles per hour, divide 221 miles by 3.25 hours: $\frac{221 \text{ miles}}{3.25 \text{ hours}} = 68 \frac{\text{miles}}{\text{hour}} = 68 \text{ mph}$

The car traveled at the rate of 68 mph, Choice **D**.

Did I answer the question? Yes, I found the rate of travel in miles per hour. ✓

Does my answer make sense? Yes, at 70 mph, the car would travel 210 miles in 3 hours, so 68 mph for 221 miles in 3 hours 15 minutes is reasonable. ✓

Is the answer stated in the correct units? Yes, the units are miles per hour, which is correct. ✓

Choice **A** results if you divide incorrectly. Choices **B** and **C** result if you convert 3 hours 15 minutes to hours incorrectly.

16. **B.** Choice **B** is the correct response. To determine how many gallons are consumed per week, find how many gallons are consumed per day. Then multiply the result by 7 days per week $\left(\frac{7 \text{ days}}{\text{week}}\right)$.

Step 1. Find how many gallons are consumed per day

The Mathematics Reference Sheet provides the following information:

1 cup = 8 fluid ounces

1 pint = 2 cups

1 quart = 2 pints

1 gallon = 4 quarts

These conversion facts yield 8 conversion fractions: $\frac{1\text{ c}}{8\text{ oz}}$ and $\frac{8\text{ oz}}{1\text{ c}}$, $\frac{1\text{ pt}}{2\text{ c}}$ and $\frac{2\text{ c}}{1\text{ pt}}$, $\frac{1\text{ qt}}{2\text{ pt}}$ and $\frac{2\text{ pt}}{1\text{ qt}}$, $\frac{1\text{ gal}}{4\text{ qt}}$ and $\frac{4\text{ qt}}{1\text{ gal}}$. Write 64 ounces per day as a fraction. Then, using unit analysis, multiply a "chain" of conversion fractions that will result in gallons as the final unit.

$$\frac{64\text{ oz}}{\text{day}} \times \frac{1\text{ c}}{8\text{ oz}} \times \frac{1\text{ pt}}{2\text{ c}} \times \frac{1\text{ qt}}{2\text{ pt}} \times \frac{1\text{ gal}}{4\text{ qt}} = \frac{64\ \cancel{\text{oz}}}{\text{day}} \times \frac{1\ \cancel{\text{c}}}{8\ \cancel{\text{oz}}} \times \frac{1\ \cancel{\text{pt}}}{2\ \cancel{\text{c}}} \times \frac{1\ \cancel{\text{qt}}}{2\ \cancel{\text{pt}}} \times \frac{1\text{ gal}}{4\ \cancel{\text{qt}}} = \frac{64\text{ gal}}{128\text{ days}} = \frac{0.5\text{ gal}}{\text{day}}$$

Step 2. Multiply by 7 days per week $\left(\frac{7\text{ days}}{\text{week}}\right)$.

$$\frac{0.5\text{ gal}}{\text{day}} \times \frac{7\text{ days}}{\text{week}} = \frac{0.5\text{ gal}}{\cancel{\text{day}}} \times \frac{7\ \cancel{\text{days}}}{\text{week}} = \frac{3.5\text{ gal}}{\text{week}}$$

The person will consume 3.5 gallons of water per week, Choice **B**.

Did I answer the question? Yes, I found the number of gallons consumed per week. ✓

Does my answer make sense? Yes. From my knowledge of the real world, I know 64 ounces is half a gallon. So half a gallon a day for 7 days is 3.5 gallons per week. ✓

Is the answer stated in the correct units? Yes, the units are gallons per week, which is correct. ✓

Choice **A** results if you fail to multiply by 7 days per week. Choices **C** and **D** result if you convert 64 ounces to gallons incorrectly by omitting one or more of the conversion fractions.

17. D. Choice **D** is the correct response. This problem is a proportion problem involving a map scale. To solve the problem, do three steps. First, determine the ratios being compared, being sure to compare corresponding quantities in the same order. Next, write a proportion using the two ratios. Then, use cross products to solve the proportion.

Step 1. Determine the ratios being compared.

Let d be the actual distance in miles between the two landmarks. The first sentence gives the first ratio: $\frac{d(\text{in miles})}{9.5\text{ in}}$. The second sentence gives the second ratio: $\frac{10\text{ miles}}{\frac{1}{2}\text{ in}}$. (Notice, you put miles in the numerator in the second ratio because you have miles in the numerator in the first ratio.)

Step 2. Write a proportion using the two ratios.

$$\frac{d(\text{in miles})}{9.5\text{ in}} = \frac{10\text{ miles}}{\frac{1}{2}\text{ in}}$$

For ease of calculation, change $\frac{1}{2}$ to 0.5.

$$\frac{d(\text{in miles})}{9.5\text{ in}} = \frac{10\text{ miles}}{0.5\text{ in}}$$

Step 3. Use cross products to solve the proportion (omitting the units for convenience).

9.5×10 Find a cross product you can calculate. You don't know the value of d, so the only cross product you can calculate is 9.5 times 10.

$d = \frac{9.5 \times 10}{0.5}$ Divide by 0.5, the numerical term you didn't use.

$d = 190$

> **Tip: Key the calculation into the calculator like this: 9.5 × 10 ÷ 0.5 = 190.**

The actual distance in miles between the two landmarks is 190 miles, Choice **D**.

Did I answer the question? Yes, I found the actual distance in miles between the two landmarks. ✓

Does my answer make sense? Yes. On the map, $\frac{1}{2}$ inch represents 10 miles, so 1 inch represents 20 miles. If the distance on the map between the landmarks were 10 inches, this distance would represent 200 miles (10 × 20). Thus, 190 miles is a reasonable answer for 9.5 inches on the map. ✓

Is the answer stated in the correct units? Yes, the units are miles, which is correct. ✓

Choice **A** results if you set up the proportion incorrectly. Choice **B** results if you make a mistake in placing the decimal point in the answer. Choice **C** results if you deal with the $\frac{1}{2}$ in the proportion incorrectly.

18. **B.** Choice **B** is the correct response. Sketch a diagram to illustrate the problem.

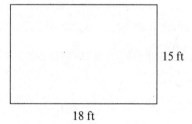

Square yards are units of area. The number of square yards of carpet needed will be the area of the rectangular room. The Mathematics Reference Sheet gives the formula for the area of a rectangle as $A = lw$. The cost of the carpet is $25.75 per square yard. You will need to find the area of the room in square yards. Finding the cost of the carpet will take three steps. First, convert the dimensions of the room to yards. Next, find the area of the room in square yards. Then, multiply the number of square yards by the cost per square yard.

Step 1. Convert the dimensions of the room to yards.

The two conversion fractions are $\frac{1 \text{ yd}}{3 \text{ ft}}$ and $\frac{3 \text{ ft}}{1 \text{ yd}}$. Write each dimension of the room as a fraction with denominator 1, and let unit analysis tell you which conversion fraction to use. Because you want feet to divide out, use $\frac{1 \text{ yd}}{3 \text{ ft}}$.

$$\frac{18 \text{ ft}}{1} \cdot \frac{1 \text{ yd}}{3 \text{ ft}} = \frac{\overset{6}{\cancel{18}} \cancel{\text{ft}}}{1} \cdot \frac{1 \text{ yd}}{\underset{1}{\cancel{3}} \cancel{\text{ft}}} = 6 \text{ yd}$$

$$\frac{15 \text{ ft}}{1} \cdot \frac{1 \text{ yd}}{3 \text{ ft}} = \frac{\overset{5}{\cancel{15}} \cancel{\text{ft}}}{1} \cdot \frac{1 \text{ yd}}{\underset{1}{\cancel{3}} \cancel{\text{ft}}} = 5 \text{ yd}$$

Step 2. Find the area of the room in square yards. Plug into the formula.

$$A = lw = (6 \text{ yd})(5 \text{ yd}) = 30 \text{ yd}^2$$

Step 3. Multiply the number of square yards by the cost per square yard.

$$\frac{30 \text{ yd}^2}{1} \times \frac{\$25.75}{\text{yd}^2} = \frac{30 \cancel{\text{yd}^2}}{1} \times \frac{\$25.75}{\cancel{\text{yd}^2}} = \$772.50$$

Not including tax, it will cost $772.50 to carpet the room, Choice **B**.

Did I answer the question? Yes, I found the cost of carpeting the room. ✓

Does my answer make sense? Yes, 30 yd² at $20 per square yard would be $600, so $772.50 is a reasonable answer given a price of $25.75 per square yard. ✓

Is the answer stated in the correct units? Yes, the units are dollars, which is correct. ✓

Choice **A** results if you fail to multiply by the cost of the carpet, and you disregard that the units do not work out to be dollars when you make this mistake. Choice **C** results if you find the area in square feet and divide this result by 3 to convert to square yards. This approach is incorrect because 1 yd² = 3 ft × 3 ft = 9 ft², not 3 ft². Choice **D** is the result of finding the area in square feet and then multiplying by the cost per square yard.

19. **D.** Choice **D** is the correct response. A simple way to work this problem is to check the *x-y* pairs from the table in the equations given in the answer choices. Only the equation $y = 2x - 5$ (Choice **D**) is true for all three pairs (−3, −11), (0, −5), and (5, 5).

20. **A.** Choice **A** is the correct response. Sketch a diagram to illustrate the problem.

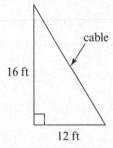

The pole and the cable form a right triangle. From the diagram, you can see the length of the cable is the length of the hypotenuse of a right triangle that has legs of 16 feet and 12 feet. Plug into the Pythagorean theorem (from the Mathematics Reference Sheet), omitting units for convenience.

$$c = \text{hypotenuse} = ?, a = 16, \text{ and } b = 12$$

$$c^2 = a^2 + b^2 = (16)^2 + (12)^2 = 256 + 144 = 400$$

Because $c^2 = 400$, you know $c = \sqrt{400}$.

Note: From the list of square roots given in the section titled "Are All Square Roots Irrational?" in Chapter 3 (page 77), you have $\sqrt{400} = 20$, so $c = 20$. The length of the cable is 20 feet, Choice **A**.

Did I answer the question? Yes, I found the length of the cable. ✓

Does my answer make sense? Yes, a hypotenuse of 20 feet is reasonable for a right triangle with legs 16 feet and 12 feet. ✓

Is the answer stated in the correct units? Yes, the units are feet, which is correct. ✓

Choice **B** results if you mistakenly decide to solve the problem by adding the lengths of the two legs to find the length of the hypotenuse. Choice **C** results if you make the mistake of dividing 400 by 2 to find its square root. Choice **D** results if you fail to find the square root of 400.

21. **A.** Choice **A** is the correct response. A square is not a cube because cubes are three-dimensional figures, but a square is a two-dimensional figure. A square is a parallelogram (Choice **B**) that has exactly four congruent sides and four right angles. A rectangle is a parallelogram that has four right angles. A rhombus is a parallelogram that has exactly four congruent sides. Therefore, a square is a rectangle (Choice **C**) because it is a parallelogram that has four right angles, and it is a rhombus (Choice **D**) because it is a parallelogram that has exactly four congruent sides.

22. **B.** Choice **B** is the correct response. The corresponding sides of similar triangles are proportional. Side $\overline{AB}$ is the hypotenuse of triangle *ABC*. Its corresponding side is $\overline{DE}$, which is the hypotenuse of triangle *DEF*. The corresponding side for side $\overline{AC}$ is $\overline{DF}$. Let *h* = length of $\overline{AB}$. Set up a proportion and solve it.

$$\frac{\text{length of }\overline{AB}}{\text{length of }\overline{DE}} = \frac{\text{length of }\overline{AC}}{\text{length of }\overline{DF}} \quad \text{Tip: Make sure you keep corresponding sides in the same order.}$$

$$\frac{h}{10\text{ m}} = \frac{20\text{ m}}{8\text{ m}}$$

Use cross products to solve the proportion (omitting the units for convenience).

10×20 Find a cross product you can calculate. You don't know the value of *h*, so the only cross product you can calculate is 10 times 20.

$h = \dfrac{10 \times 20}{8}$ Divide by 8, the numerical term you didn't use.

$h = 25$

Tip: Key the calculation into the calculator like this: 10 × 20 ÷ 8 = 25.

The length of the hypotenuse of triangle *ABC* is 25 meters.

Choices **A, C,** and **D** result if you set up the proportion incorrectly.

23. **D.** Choice **D** is the correct response. An obtuse angle measures between 90° and 180°. All of the interior angles of the octagon in Choice **D** are obtuse angles. All of the interior angles in the triangle in Choice **A** are acute angles. All of the interior angles in Choice **B** are either right angles or 270°. The right triangle in Choice **C** contains one interior right angle and two interior acute angles.

24. **B.** Choice **B** is the correct response. Harry has $30. He owes Maria $9, which he will pay first. Then he will have $30 – $9. From this amount, he will pay for two tickets (his and Kelly's) at $10 each. The cost of the tickets will be two times $10. Only Choice **B** correctly summarizes the situation.

25. **C.** Choice **C** is the correct response. Sketch a diagram and label the two points. Draw a line between the two points.

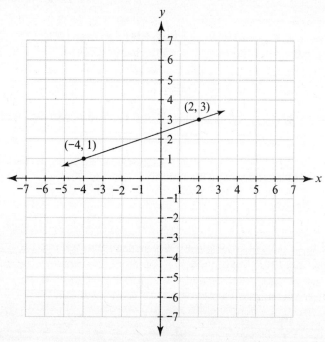

From the sketch, you can see the line slopes upward from left to right, indicating the slope is positive; therefore, you can eliminate choices **A** and **B**. The formula from the Mathematics Reference Sheet for the slope of a line between two points is slope $= \dfrac{y_2 - y_1}{x_2 - x_1}$. To find the slope of the line between (–4, 1) and (2, 3), do two steps.

Step 1. Specify (x_1, y_1) and (x_2, y_2).

Let $(x_1, y_1) = (-4, 1)$ and $(x_2, y_2) = (2, 3)$. Then $x_1 = -4$, $y_1 = 1$, $x_2 = 2$, and $y_2 = 3$.

Step 2. Plug into the formula. (*Tip:* Enclose negative values in parentheses.)

$$\text{slope} = \frac{y_2 - y_1}{x_2 - x_1} = \frac{3-1}{2-(-4)} = \frac{3-1}{2+4} = \frac{2}{6} = \frac{1}{3}$$

The line through the points (–4, 1) and (2, 3) has slope $\dfrac{1}{3}$, Choice **C**.

Choice **A** results if you invert the slope formula and make a sign error. Choice **B** results if you make a sign error. Choice **D** results if you invert the slope formula.

26. **A.** Choice **A** is the correct response. The numbers 2 and 5 are factors of 50 because $2 \cdot 5 \cdot 5 = 50$. The number 7 is not a factor of 50. The number 50 is in the 2 and 5 circles, but not in the 7 circle. Thus, the number 50 is in region *A* only.

27. **C.** Choice **C** is the correct response.

$4 + 2(3x + 1) = 4 + 2 \cdot 3x + 2 \cdot 1 = 4 + 6x + 2$ Using the distributive property, multiply each term in the parentheses by 2.

$= 6x + 4 + 2 = 6x + 6$, Choice **C**   Simplify, using the commutative and associative properties.

Choice **A** results if you make the mistake of combining the coefficients after you obtain $6x + 6$. Choice **B** results if you fail to use the distributive property correctly. Choice **D** results if you make the mistake of adding 4 and 2 before applying the distributive property.

28. **D.** Choice **D** is the correct response. Rewrite the function expression, enclosing x on the right side in parentheses.

$$f(x) = 20 - (x)$$

Substitute –4 for x inside the parentheses and evaluate, being sure to follows the rules for computation with signed numbers.

$$f(-4) = 20 - (-4) = 20 + 4 = 24, \text{ Choice } \mathbf{D}$$

Choice **A** occurs if you make a sign error. Choices **B** and **C** result if you deal with the subtraction incorrectly.

29. **D.** Choice **D** is the correct response.

Method 1: Solve using the steps for solving an equation.

Solve $3(x - 6) = 21$

$3x - 18 = 21$ Use the distributive property to remove parentheses.

$3x - 18 + 18 = 21 + 18$ Add 18 to both sides of the equation.

$3x = 39$ Simplify.

$\dfrac{\cancel{3}x}{\cancel{3}} = \dfrac{39}{3}$ Divide both sides of the equation by 3.

$x = 13$

Choice **A** results if you subtract 18 from both sides instead of adding 18. Choices **B** and **C** result if you fail to use the distributive property correctly.

Method 2: Check each answer choice by plugging the value into the equation.

Checking **A:** $3(x-6) = 3(1-6) = 3(-5) = -15 \neq 21$. Choice **A** is incorrect because $x = 1$ does not satisfy $3(x-6) = 21$.

Checking **B:** $3(x-6) = 3(5-6) = 3(-1) = -3 \neq 21$. Choice **B** is incorrect because $x = 5$ does not satisfy $3(x-6) = 21$.

Checking **C:** $3(x-6) = 3(9-6) = 3(3) = 9 \neq 21$. Choice **C** is incorrect because $x = 9$ does not satisfy $3(x-6) = 21$.

Checking **D:** $3(x-6) = 3(13-6) = 3(7) = 21$ ✓. Choice **D** is correct because $x = 13$ makes $3(x-6) = 21$ a true statement.

30. **A.** Choice **A** is the correct response: To determine which ordered pair satisfies the system, find the ordered pair that satisfies *both* equations. Check each ordered pair by plugging the x and y values into the two equations, being careful to enclose in parentheses the values you put in.

$$\text{Checking } \mathbf{A}: 2x - y = 2(-4) - (-1) = -8 + 1 = -7 \checkmark.$$

Since $(-4, -1)$ works in the first equation, try it in the second equation: $x + 3y = (-4) + 3(-1) = -4 + -3 = -7$ ✓. Choice **A** is correct because the ordered pair $(-4, -1)$ satisfies both equations in the system.

In a test situation, you should go on to the next question since you have obtained the correct answer. Here are the other checks.

Checking **B:** $2x - y = 2(-4) - (1) = -8 - 1 = -9 \neq -7$. Choice **B** is incorrect because $(-4, 1)$ does not satisfy $2x - y = -7$.

Checking **C:** $2x - y = 2(4) - (-1) = 8 + 1 = 9 \neq -7$. Choice **C** is incorrect because $(4, -1)$ does not satisfy $2x - y = -7$.

Checking **D:** $2x - y = 2(4) - (1) = 8 - 1 = 7 \neq -7$. Choice **D** is incorrect because $(4, 1)$ does not satisfy $2x - y = -7$.

31. **B.** Choice **B** is the correct response. Check each response by replacing x with -5 in the statement.

Checking **A:** When $x = -5$, $\frac{1}{x} > -x$ becomes $\frac{1}{-5} > -(-5)$. When you evaluate both sides, this statement becomes $-\frac{1}{5} > 5$, which is false because 5 is to the right of $-\frac{1}{5}$ on the number line.

Checking **B:** When $x = -5$, $3x < 2x$ becomes $3(-5) < 2(-5)$. When you evaluate both sides, this statement becomes $-15 < -10$, which is true because -10 is to the right of -15 on the number line.

In a test situation, you should go on to the next question since you have obtained the correct answer. Checking the remaining choices, you would find:

Checking **C:** When $x = -5$, $-x < 0$ becomes $-(-5) < 0$. When you evaluate both sides, this statement becomes $5 < 0$, which is false because 5 is to the right of 0 on the number line.

Checking **D:** When $x = -5$, $x - 6 > x + 6$ becomes $(-5) - 6 > (-5) + 6$. When you evaluate both sides, this statement becomes $-11 > 1$, which is false because 1 is to the right of -11 on the number line.

32. **C.** Choice **C** is the correct response.

$-2x + 5 < 7$	
$-2x + 5 - 5 < 7 - 5$	Subtract 5 from both sides of the inequality.
$-2x < 2$	Simplify.
$\frac{-2x}{-2} > \frac{2}{-2}$	Divide both sides of the inequality by -2 and reverse the inequality because you divided both sides by a negative number.
$x > -1$	Simplify.

$x > -1$, Choice **C.**

363

Choice **A** results if you fail to reverse the inequality. Choice **B** results if you add 5 to both sides of the inequality instead of subtracting 5. Choice **D** results if you add 5 to both sides of the inequality instead of subtracting 5, and you fail to reverse the inequality.

33. **A.** Choice **A** is the correct response. The median is the "middlemost" value in a set of data values that have been put in order (from smallest to largest or largest to smallest). For an odd number of data values, the median is the middle value of the data set. For an even number of data values, the median is the average of the two middle values. The data values in this question are the 200 allowance amounts the students receive. These amounts are put in order, and because 200 is an even number, the average of the two middle values is determined to be $10.75. Therefore, you know definitely half (100) of the allowance amounts are $10.75 or less, Choice **A**.

    Choices **B** and **C** are possibilities that could describe the data, but you are not given sufficient information to say definitely the statement is correct. Choice **D** is a false statement because 35% of 200 students is 70 students who receive no allowance at all.

34. **D.** Choice **D** is the correct response. From the graph, you can see the greatest gap between the average low and high temperature lines occurs in April, Choice **D**. The gaps for choices **A, B,** and **C** are not as great.

35. **A.** Choice **A** is the correct response. To find the median, do two steps.

    Step 1. Put the scores in order from least to greatest.

    $$42, 56, 67, 69, 73, 88, 88, 96$$

    Step 2. Find the middle score. The median is the average of the two middle scores, 69 and 73.

    $$\text{median} = \frac{69 + 73}{2} = 71$$

    Choice **B** results if you fail to order the scores and mistakenly decide to average 56 and 88 to find the median. Choice **C** is the mean, not the median. Choice **D** is the mode, not the median.

36. **D.** Choice **D** is the correct response. This problem is a straightforward probability problem, meaning you will find the probability by using the formula: $\text{probability} = \frac{\text{number of favorable outcomes}}{\text{number of possible outcomes}}$. To find the probability the marble will be yellow or blue, do three steps. First, determine the number of total outcomes possible. Next, determine the number of favorable outcomes. Then, plug into the probability formula.

    Step 1. Determine the number of total outcomes possible.

    There are 50 total possible outcomes.

    Step 2. Determine the number of favorable outcomes.

    There are 26 favorable outcomes—6 yellow marbles and 20 blue marbles.

    Step 3. Plug into the probability formula.

    The probability of drawing a yellow or a blue marble is $\frac{\text{number of favorable outcomes}}{\text{number of possible outcomes}} = \frac{26}{50} = \frac{13}{25}$, Choice **D**.

    Did I answer the question? Yes, I found the probability of drawing a yellow or blue marble from the box. ✓

    Does my answer make sense? Yes, about half of the marbles are yellow or blue, so $\frac{13}{25}$ is a reasonable answer. ✓

    Is the answer stated in the correct units? No units are required for the answer. ✓

    Choice **A** results if you multiply the probability of drawing a yellow marble times the probability of drawing a blue marble. Choice **B** is the probability of drawing a yellow marble. Choice **C** is the probability of drawing a blue marble.

37. **C.** Choice **C** is the correct response. This problem is a counting problem. To solve the problem, multiply the number of ways Shailene can select a bread by the number of ways she can select a sandwich filling.

Total number of possible different sandwiches =
(number of ways to select a bread type) × (number of ways to select a sandwich filling) =
$3 \times 4 = 12$ possible different sandwiches

Did I answer the question? Yes, I found the number of possible different sandwiches. ✓

Does my answer make sense? Yes, it is consistent with my knowledge of counting. ✓

Is the answer stated in the correct units? No units are required for the answer. ✓

Choice **A** results if you add instead of multiply in the problem. Choices **B** and **D** result if you count or compute incorrectly.

38. **C.** Choice **C** is the correct response. From the pie chart, you can see 23% of the young readers surveyed responded they read science fiction books most often. To answer the question, find 23% of 200.

Method 1: To solve the problem, identify the elements of the percent proportion, plug the values into the percent proportion, and then solve the proportion.

Step 1. Identify the elements.

$$r = 23$$
$$\text{part} = ?$$
$$\text{whole} = 200$$

Step 2. Let x = the part. Plug into the percent proportion (omitting the units for convenience).

$$\frac{r}{100} = \frac{\text{part}}{\text{whole}}$$

$$\frac{23}{100} = \frac{x}{200}$$

Step 3. Solve the proportion.

23×200 Find a cross product you can calculate. You don't know the value of x, so the only cross product you can calculate is 23 times 200.

$x = \dfrac{23 \times 200}{100}$ Divide by 100, the numerical term you didn't use.

$x = 46$

The number of young readers surveyed who responded they read science fiction books most often is 46, Choice **C**.

Did I answer the question? Yes, I found the number of young readers surveyed who responded they read science fiction books most often. ✓

Does my answer make sense? Yes, 23% is about one-fourth. One-fourth of 200 is 50, so 46 is a reasonable answer. ✓

Is the answer stated in the correct units? No units are required for the answer. ✓

Method 2: Change 23% to a decimal fraction or common fraction and then multiply.

$$23\% \text{ of } 200 = 0.23 \times 200 = 46. \text{ Or } 23\% \text{ of } 200 = \frac{23}{100} \cdot \frac{200}{1} = \frac{23}{1\cancel{00}} \cdot \frac{2\cancel{00}}{1} = 46.$$

Choice **A** is the number of young readers surveyed who responded they read biography or historical books most often. Choice **B** is the number of young readers surveyed who responded they read nature books most often. Choice **D** is the number of young readers surveyed who responded they read adventure books most often.

39. **C.** Choice **C** is the correct response. The range is the difference between the greatest and the least times waited.

range = greatest time − least time = 30 minutes − 5 minutes = 25 minutes, Choice **C**

40. **C.** Choice **C** is the correct response. To answer the question, find the median for each answer choice.
Checking **A**: $10.29, $9.87, $11.99, $8.45, $10.60, $10.25

Step 1. Put the prices in order from least to greatest.

$8.45, $9.87, $10.25, $10.29, $10.60, $11.99

Step 2. Since there are six values, the median is the average of the two middle values, $10.25 and $10.29.

You can eliminate Choice **A** at this point because you can see the average of these two prices is greater than $10.24. Just so you know, the median $= \frac{\$10.25 + \$10.29}{2} = \$10.27$.

Checking **B**: $7.50, $12.98, $8.25, $10.89, $11.05, $10.67

Step 1. Put the prices in order from least to greatest.

$7.50, $8.25, $10.67, $10.89, $11.05, $12.98

Step 2. Since there are six values, the median is the average of the two middle values, $10.67 and $10.89.

You can eliminate Choice **B** at this point because you can see the average of these two prices is greater than $10.24. Just so you know, the median $= \frac{\$10.67 + \$10.89}{2} = \$10.78$.

Checking **C**: $11.98, $10.50, $9.98, $8.50, $12.95, $9.98

Step 1. Put the prices in order from least to greatest.

$8.50, $9.98, $9.98, $10.50, $11.98, $12.95

Step 2. Since there are six values, the median is the average of the two middle values, $9.98 and $10.50.

$\frac{\$9.98 + \$10.50}{2} = \$10.24$. Choice **C** is the correct response.

In a test situation, you should go on to the next question since you have obtained the correct answer. Just so you know, the median for Choice **D** is $10.11.

41. **B.** Choice **B** is the correct response. To answer the question, find the mode for each answer choice.

Choice **A** is incorrect. The mode is 96 because it occurs three times.

Choice **B** is correct. The mode is 87 because it occurs two times.

In a test situation, you should go on to the next question since you have obtained the correct answer. However, here are the checks for the remaining choices.

Choice **C** is incorrect; the mode is 84 because it occurs two times.

Choice **D** is incorrect; there is no mode because each score occurs the same number of times.

42. **B.** Choice **B** is the correct response. This is a straightforward probability problem, meaning you will find the probability by using the formula: probability $= \frac{\text{number of favorable outcomes}}{\text{number of possible outcomes}}$. To find the probability the number on the tile will be a prime number, do three steps. First, determine the number of total outcomes possible. Next, determine the number of favorable outcomes. Then, plug into the probability formula.

Step 1. Determine the number of total outcomes possible.

There are 40 total possible outcomes.

Step 2. Determine the number of favorable outcomes.

The primes between 1 and 40 are 2, 3, 5, 7, 11, 13, 17, 19, 23, 29, 31, and 37. Thus, there are 12 favorable outcomes.

Step 3. Plug into the probability formula.

The probability of drawing a prime-numbered tile is $\frac{\text{number of favorable outcomes}}{\text{number of possible outcomes}} = \frac{12}{40} = \frac{3}{10}$, Choice **B**.

Did I answer the question? Yes, I found the probability of drawing a prime-numbered tile. ✓

Does my answer make sense? Yes, it is consistent with my knowledge of probability. ✓

Is the answer stated in the correct units? No units are required for the answer. ✓

Choice **A** is the result of mistakenly determining there are 10 favorable outcomes. Choice **C** is the result of including 1 as a prime number. The number 1 is neither prime nor composite. Choice **D** is the probability of drawing a composite-numbered tile.

43. **C.** Choice **C** is the correct response. All students in grades 6 through 8 at Sunshine Middle School were tested, so you can make the valid conclusion that 15 percent of all students in grades 6 through 8 at Sunshine Middle School are below grade level in mathematics.

    You don't know the results for the other middle school, nor do you know specific results for eighth-grade students at Sunshine Middle School or in the district, so you cannot draw conclusions about those populations. Thus, choices **A, B,** and **D** are incorrect.

44. **C.** Choice **C** is the correct response. Asking 100 randomly selected ninth-graders will allow Jolene and Meiko to make valid conclusions about ninth-grade students' opinions about wearing uniforms. The sample is random and of sufficient size. Eliminate Choice **A** because the opinions of Algebra I students might be different from those of ninth-grade students in general. Jolene and Meiko are interested in the opinions of ninth-graders only, so eliminate choices **B** and **D** because some of the students selected might not be ninth-graders.

45. **A.** Choice **A** is the correct response. Chad's conclusion is not valid because the experiment lacks a control group of rose plants. In experimental studies, the purpose is to investigate possible cause-and-effect relationships by exposing an experimental group to a treatment condition (in Chad's experiment, artificial red light) and comparing the results to a control group not receiving the treatment. An experimental study is set up in such a way that one group of experimental units gets the treatment (the experimental group) and another group (the control group) does not, and then comparisons are made to see whether the treatment had an influence on the variable of interest (in Chad's experiment, the number of flowers produced). Chad should have grown another group of 30 randomly selected rose plants of the same variety in identical conditions, but under ordinary sunlight (Choice **A**). This group of plants would have served as the control group for the experiment.

Reading

1. **B.** Choice **B** is the correct response. This passage indicates that *"plugging" is not a part of modern baseball.* This information is given in the second paragraph. None of the other answer choices are indicated in this passage.

2. **A.** Choice **A** is the correct response. According to this passage, rounders is a game that *was imported from England.* Although this information is not stated explicitly in this passage, it can be inferred from the information given in the second paragraph. The other answer choices are not supported by the passage.

3. **D.** Choice **D** is the correct response. In the first paragraph, the word *evokes* most nearly means *elicits,* "to draw forth." The words in the other answer choices do not mean the same as the word *evokes.*

4. **D.** Choice **D** is the correct response. In this reading passage, paragraphs 2 through 4 are in chronological order. The organization patterns in choices **A, B,** and **D** do not accurately describe the organizational pattern of the three paragraphs.

5. **D.** Choice **D** is the correct response. *Baseball is a civil and simple game* (Choice **D**) is an opinion. This description of baseball is a view, not a fact, expressed by the author, reflecting the author's opinion about baseball. The other choices are all statements of fact, not opinions: Choice **A** in the second paragraph, Choice **B** in the third paragraph, and Choice **C** is in the fourth paragraph.

6. **D.** Choice **D** is the correct response. According to the passage, baseball is considered America's pastime because *it occurs at a leisurely pace in a pastoral setting*. Remember, the question reads "according to this passage," and this reference to baseball and its natural allure to wide open spaces is exactly the description the reader needs to select Choice **D**. Choice **A** is incorrect because as the passage implies, baseball provides interested individuals with more than a "casual diversion." It provides a dramatic confrontation of a competitive sport in which fans can cheer for their respective teams and watch the game leisurely unfold before them. Choice **B** is incorrect because it is not supported by the passage. Choice **C** is incorrect because the passage indicates baseball has rules.

7. **B.** Choice **B** is the correct response. As used in the final paragraph, the word *exemplifies* best means *to illustrate by example*. Choices **A**, **C**, and **D** are incorrect meanings of the word *exemplifies* and, thus, are incorrect choices.

8. **C.** Choice **C** is the correct response. The tone of this passage can best be described as *subjective*. The author provides a passionate yet practical analysis of the reasons that baseball is regarded as America's favorite pastime. Choice **A** is incorrect because the author is not *derisive,* meaning "mocking or sarcastic." Choice **B** is incorrect because the author is not *nostalgic,* meaning "remembering the past longingly." Choice **D** is incorrect because the author is not *objective,* meaning "without bias or opinion."

9. **B.** Choice **B** is the correct response. The sentence that best states the main idea of this passage is *Baseball evokes an era of a simpler life and pace*. The author expresses this view in the first paragraph with the statement: "[B]aseball evokes a bygone era of American independence, openness, and simplicity." Choice **A** is incorrect because the passage does not indicate that baseball is a sport that is elitist in tone and style. Choice **C** is incorrect because the passage describes baseball, not all competitive sports, as simple in design and pace. Choice **D** is incorrect because although watching professional baseball might inspire youngsters to become competitive athletes, this thought is not expressed in the passage.

10. **C.** Choice **C** is the correct response. In the final paragraph, the second and third sentences *expand the comment in the first sentence.* The two sentences that follow the first sentence expand by illustration what the author means by *Of all of America's obsessions, baseball is one of pure passion.* Choice **A** is incorrect because the second and third sentences do not *revise,* or change the meaning of, the comment in the first sentence. Choice **B** is incorrect because the second and third sentences support the comment in the first sentence, not *detract,* or undermine, the comment in the first sentence. Choice **D** is incorrect because while the second and third sentences relate to the comment in the first sentence, they do not *analyze,* or scrutinize, the comment.

11. **D.** Choice **D** is the correct response. The author of this passage likely would agree that dancing *is a joyous expression of movement to music.* The passage demonstrates the author's fondness for dancing as a form of self-expression. Choice **A** is incorrect because the passage does not portray dancing as detrimental to one's health and well-being. Choice **B** is incorrect because the author says that formal dancing is not self-willed and free-wheeling. Choice **C** is incorrect because nowhere in the passage does the author imply that dancing is a waste of time and energy.

12. **B.** Choice **B** is the correct response. The author's claim that "I have … two left feet," meaning that the author is a poor dancer, is clearly *a narrative technique to engage the reader.* The author uses the technique of self-deprecating humor to lure the reader into a discussion of dance and the many forms it has taken throughout human history. Choice **A** is incorrect because even though the author is writing positively about dancing, the author might truly be a poor dancer. Choice **C** is incorrect because the self-deprecating humor is no indication that the author dislikes dancing; indeed, it is an indication of the contrary. Choice **D** is incorrect because the author does not engage in an argumentative style; instead, the author uses a self-deprecating style to entice and tease the reader into the discussion about dance.

13. **A.** Choice **A** is the correct response. This passage is an example of an *expository piece of a positive experience*. The author writes in a clear and optimistic voice about the power of dance to transform the lives of all who participate in it or observe it. Choice **B** is incorrect because the author's tone is upbeat, not

cynical. Choice **C** is incorrect because, based on textual evidence, the author does not view dance as a dying art form. For instance, in the fourth paragraph, the author states, *As dance evolved, it naturally took on a life of its own.* Choice **D** is incorrect because the author points out that dancing is universally enjoyed and, thus, is not an obscure obsession.

14. **C.** Choice **C** is the correct response. In the fifth paragraph, the phrase *Blessed with the gift of mimicry* best means *being able to imitate.* Choices **A, B,** and **D** are incorrect meanings of the word *mimicry* and, thus, are incorrect choices.

15. **B.** Choice **B** is the correct response. According to information given in the fifth paragraph, dancing is universally enjoyed because *it speaks to human emotions.* Choices **A, C,** and **D** are not supported by the passage.

16. **C.** Choice **C** is the correct response. A statement that is implied in the first paragraph is *The cha-cha, rhumba, and waltz are types of dances* (Choice **C**). The author does not state explicitly that these are types of dances, but the reader can draw this conclusion based on the topic of the paragraph. Even though you may disagree with the statements in choices **A** and **D,** these statements are explicit in the first paragraph. The statement given in Choice **B** is neither stated nor implied in the first paragraph.

17. **C.** Choice **C** is the correct response. An opinion expressed in this passage is *Dancing has been a human form of self-expression* (Choice **C**). The description of dancing as *a human form of self-expression* is a view, not a fact, expressed by the author, reflecting the author's opinion about dancing. The other answer choices are statements of fact, not opinions: Choice **A** in the second paragraph, Choice **B** in the third paragraph, and Choice **D** in the fourth paragraph.

18. **C.** Choice **C** is the correct response. The word *assertive,* meaning "aggressively self-confident," most nearly means *bold.* Choice **A** is incorrect because one can be assertive without being *loud.* Choice **B** is incorrect because assertive does not mean *skillful,* or "adept." Choice **D** is incorrect because an assertive person is confident, not *anxious.*

19. **C.** Choice **C** is the correct response. This passage states that *dancing is an art form.* This information is given in the second paragraph. The statement in Choice **A** is neither stated nor implied in the passage. Choice **B** disagrees with information given in the second paragraph. Choice **D** is implied, but not stated, in the first paragraph.

20. **D.** Choice **D** is the correct response. According to information given in this passage, *formal dancing is difficult and strenuous.* This determination can be inferred from the third sentence in the last paragraph, "their [referring to those who do formal dancing] expertise lies in making the difficult and strenuous look easy and joyous." Choices **A** and **B** are not supported by the passage. Neither is Choice **C**; even though **C** is a true statement, this information is not given in the passage.

Tip: Do not select answer choices based on your personal knowledge that goes beyond the information given in the passage.

21. **A.** Choice **A** is the correct response. The author's description of Piaget and his work suggests that Piaget was *a curious and prodigious thinker.* As the passage indicates, from a very early age, Piaget showed signs of the intense intellectual curiosity that served him well all his life. Choices **B, C,** and **D** are not supported by the passage.

22. **C.** Choice **C** is the correct response. As thinking about human cognition has evolved, one principle, according to the passage, has remained constant—*Human beings need to develop mentally in defined stages.* Piaget defined human cognitive development as a series of well-defined stages of growth and maturity. Each stage defined a different thinking process and learning perspective. Choices **A, B,** and **D** are not supported by the passage.

23. **B.** Choice **B** is the correct response. The author would probably agree that *studying cognitive thinking reveals human behavior patterns.* The thrust of this piece is how Piaget's investigations of cognitive thinking led him to define human behavior into recognizable patterns of development. None of the other answer choices are supported by the passage.

24. D. Choice **D** is the correct response. In this passage, the following statement is NOT supported: *Cognitive psychology relies on the suspension of disbelief.* In fact, as the passage mentions, cognitive psychology relies on validated truths based on scientific observation. Choice **A** is incorrect because the passage specifically implies that psychology is the study of the mind and its mental and emotional processes. Choice **B** is incorrect because Piaget's developmental theories were the result of a small sample size. Choice **C** is incorrect because developmental thinking can be classified into specified age groups.

25. D. Choice **D** is the correct response. In the fourth paragraph, the phrase "Not content to know just the physical world" implies that Piaget *intended to explore mental functions.* The paragraph goes on to discuss Piaget's pursuit of psychology. Choice **A** is incorrect because Piaget was much more than a literal or "just the facts" scientific researcher. Choice **B** is incorrect because Piaget understood more than the human body when he explained his theories. Choice **C** is incorrect because Piaget engaged in more than quantitative or "numbers only" research; he relied on qualitative or observed characteristics as well.

26. B. Choice **B** is the correct response. Sentence 2 *clarifies,* or explains, the point (*that children are no longer thought of as miniature adults*) made in Sentence 1. Sentence 2 explains Piaget *recognized that children's logic and modes of thinking were entirely their own.* Choice **A** is incorrect because Sentence 2 does not *restate* the point made in Sentence 1, but clarifies or explains the point. Choices **C** and **D** are incorrect because Sentence 2 does not *question* or *dispute* the point made in Sentence 1, but rather supports it.

27. A. Choice **A** is the correct response. The topic of the second paragraph is *Piaget's four stages of cognitive development.* The topic in Choice **B** is too broad to describe the information in the second paragraph. The topics in choices **C** and **D** are too narrow to describe the information in the second paragraph.

28. A. Choice **A** is the correct response. An opinion about Jean Piaget expressed in this passage is the statement given in Choice **A**: *His work is seminal to understanding modern child development.* The word *seminal* is a judgmental word reflecting the author's opinion about Piaget's impact on the field of child development. The other choices are all statements of fact, not opinions: Choice **B** in the fourth paragraph, Choice **C** in the fifth paragraph, and Choice **D** in the third paragraph.

29. B. Choice **B** is the correct response. In the fourth paragraph, this passage states that Jean Piaget embarked on a career that led to *breakthrough discoveries in human cognition.* Choices **A** and **C** are incorrect because, although these are well-known assertions, this information is not given in this passage. Remember, you must not select answer choices based on your personal knowledge that goes beyond the information given in the passage. Choice **D** is not supported by the passage.

30. D. Choice **D** is the correct response. The tone of this passage is best described as *serious.* The author does not show a *doubtful* (disbelieving) tone (Choice **A**), a *mocking* (sarcastic) tone (Choice **B**), or a *persuasive* (convincing) tone (Choice **C**).

31. A. Choice **A** is the correct response. One idea this passage makes clear is that whales have more in common with *mammals than with fish.* A key point in the first paragraph is that whales belong to the class of mammals, although most people think of them as fish. Choices **B**, **C**, and **D** are not supported by the passage.

32. B. Choice **B** is the correct response. According to this passage, whales are a unique creature in the animal kingdom because *whales can carry enormous weight without much effort.* They are the largest sea creatures, yet their bodies are structured so that they can glide through the ocean without much difficulty or effort. Choice **A** is incorrect because the passage makes no mention of their being indigenous to the northern hemisphere. Choice **C** is incorrect because whales are very maternal and, like all mammals, nurture their offspring. Choice **D** is incorrect because the passage makes no mention of their reliance on protective fish clans for self-preservation.

33. C. Choice **C** is the correct response. The author of this passage implies that whales are intelligent by stating whales have a *highly developed brain* (Paragraph 1). From this statement, the reader can infer that they are intelligent. Choices **A**, **B**, and **D** are not supported by the passage.

34. A. Choice **A** is the correct response. After reading this passage, the following statement can be inferred: *Whales are creatures that have experienced successful adaptations.* Clearly, this passage implies that the adaptations whales have experienced have helped them survive. Choices **B**, **C**, and **D** are not supported by the passage.

35. A. Choice **A** is the correct response. In the fifth paragraph, the word *Adaptation* can best be defined as *modification*. As the passage states, whales have developed into the successful creatures they are because their bodies have adapted to life in the ocean. Choices **B, C,** and **D** are not accurate definitions for *adaptation*.

36. B. Choice **B** is the correct response. A statement of fact about whales that is given in the second paragraph is *Whales have lungs* (Choice **B**). The statements in choices **A, C,** and **D** disagree with information given in the passage.

37. B. Choice **B** is the correct response. A statement about whales that is implied in this passage is given in Choice **B**: *They cannot take in oxygen when underwater*. This statement can be inferred from information given in the second paragraph. The statements about whales given in choices **A, C,** and **D** are not supported by textual evidence in this passage.

38. B. Choice **B** is the correct response. In the second paragraph, this passage states that *the sperm whale can hold its breath for up to two hours*. The timeframes given in choices **A, C,** and **D** disagree with information in this passage.

39. B. Choice **B** is the correct response. According to information given in the third paragraph of this passage, whales *nurture their young*. Choice **A** is a true statement, but this information is not given in this passage. *Remember:* Do not select answer choices based on your personal knowledge that goes beyond the information given in the passage. Choice **C** is incorrect because it disagrees with information given in the fifth paragraph. Choice **D** is incorrect because it disagrees with information given in the sixth paragraph.

40. B. Choice **B** is the correct response. The photograph contributes additional information to the passage by showing the large, impressive tails of two humpbacks. From the title and text of the passage, the reader can surmise that the author has great admiration for whales. The author's most likely purpose for including the photograph was to evoke in the reader *Awe at the magnificent tails of humpback whales*. This purpose is most consistent with the underlying theme of the passage—that whales are special creatures. Upon reviewing the photograph, the reader might experience, to some degree, one or more of the emotions described in choices **A, C,** and **D**; however, none of these answers is the best response to the question.